Katharina Möller 10c

World Energy Resources

1:160,000,000

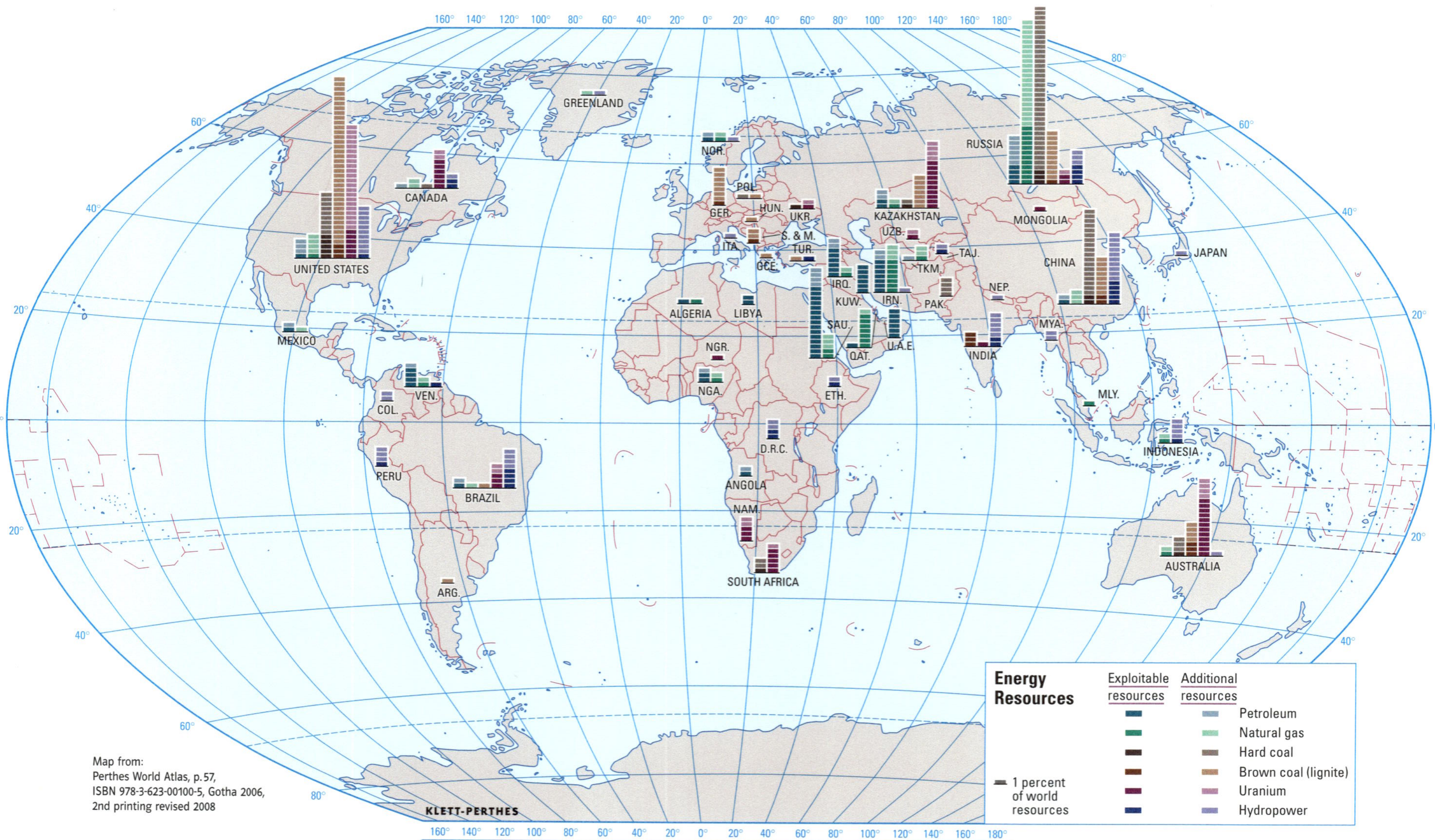

Map from:
Perthes World Atlas, p.57,
ISBN 978-3-623-00100-5, Gotha 2006,
2nd printing revised 2008

World Energy Consumption

1:160,000,000

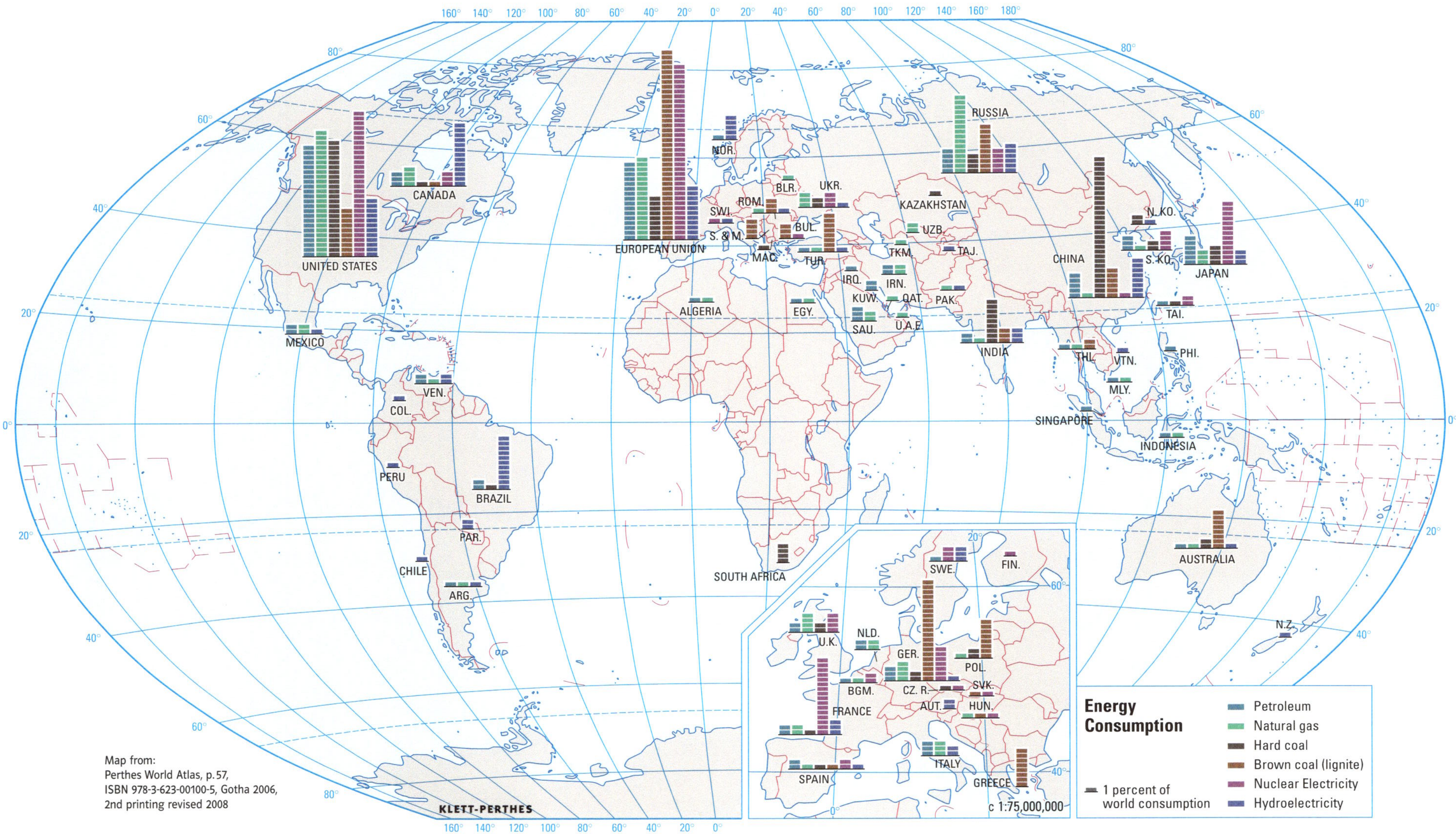

Map from:
Perthes World Atlas, p.57,
ISBN 978-3-623-00100-5, Gotha 2006,
2nd printing revised 2008

Green **Line**
6
Transition

von
Marion Horner
Louise Carleton-Gertsch
Elizabeth Daymond
Peter Lampater
Hartmut Klose

herausgegeben von
Harald Weisshaar

Ernst Klett Verlag
Stuttgart · Leipzig

Green Line 6 Transition für Klasse 10 an Gymnasien
und für den Bildungsstandard Klasse 10 in Baden-Württemberg

Herausgeber: Harald Weisshaar, Bisingen
unter besonderer Mitwirkung von Frank Haß, Kirchberg

Autorinnen und Autoren: Marion Horner M.A., Cambridge; Louise Carleton-Gertsch, M.A., München; Elizabeth Daymond M.A., Kiel; Peter Lampater, Ehingen; Hartmut Klose, Seevetal
unter Mitwirkung von Rosemary Hellyer-Jones M.A., Ehingen

Beratung: Paul Dennis M.A., Lahnstein; Hartmut Klose, Seevetal; Antje Körber, Merseburg; Axel Plitsch, Wülfrath; Elisabeth Renner, Freiburg

1. Auflage 1 8 7 | 14

Alle Drucke dieser Auflage sind unverändert und können im Unterricht nebeneinander verwendet werden.
Die letzte Zahl bezeichnet das Jahr des Druckes.

Redaktion: Dr. Gregory Fuller, Michael Mattison, Manuela Brumme
Herstellung: Anita Bauch

Gestaltung: Anita Bauch
Umschlaggestaltung: Koma Amok, Stuttgart
Illustrationen: David Norman, Meerbusch; Dorothee Wolters, Köln sowie Kognito, Berlin
Satz: Satzkiste GmbH, Stuttgart; Wiebke Hengst, Ostfildern
Reproduktion: Meyle + Müller, Medien-Management, Pforzheim
Druck: Stürtz GmbH, Würzburg

Printed in Germany
ISBN 978-3-12-547170-2 (fester Einband)
ISBN 978-3-12-547171-9 (flexibler Einband)

Welcome to Green Line 6 Transition

Green Line 6 Transition is a textbook that provides a successful transition from *Sekundarstufe I* to *Sekundarstufe II*. It will help you to develop the skills and knowledge you have gained over the past five years, and prepare you for the *Oberstufe*.

This is how the book is designed:

- *Green Line 6 Transition* contains four **Topics**, each dealing with a specific theme, with many authentic texts.
- Within the four Topics there are frequent references to the **Skills section**. This section presents all the important skills that you will need when doing the tasks in each Topic.
- After the Skills section you will find the **Grammar section**. It summarizes all the important grammar of the last five years, as well as any grammar which may be new to you this year. Each chapter ends with one or more exercises. They are there to help you with your own self-evaluation: Can you do the exercises without any help? Where do you need to read up on grammar and try again? To check your answers look at the solutions at the back of the book.
- **Revision A** and **B**, both optional, contain the types of texts and exercises you might get in examinations inside or outside school.
- There are three optional Project units in *Green Line 6 Transition*. **Project: Short story**, after Topic 2, is an unabridged short story by a South African author. **Project: Drama** and **Project: Ethics** both deal – in completely different ways – with the question of how to act in an ethically correct way.
- After the Grammar section you will find the usual **Vocabulary** and **Dictionary**.

This is how each Topic is structured:

1. ***Introduction:*** These two pages are designed to get you thinking about the Topic. They also present some useful phrases and vocabulary for this Topic.
2. ***Texts:*** This is the main section of each Topic, with lots of authentic texts (some of them optional) and related exercises. Various skills are practised, with a particular focus on the central skill of each Topic, the CORE SKILL. Example in Topic 1: Reading skills / narrative techniques. Each section also has a film page suggesting films linked to the Topic.
3. ***Language:*** The four Language pages deal with grammar (mainly revision) and communicative situations. One of the pages is devoted to intercultural awareness to help you avoid social misunderstandings in the UK and the US.
4. ***Conclusion:*** These two pages round off the Topic by asking you to look back and think about the material you have been working with. Here you have the opportunity to show that you can speak and write about the theme of the Topic.

[two people]	Do this task with another person.
[group]	Do this task in a (small) group.
[CD-ROM]	This listening text is on the CD-ROM in the Language and Skills Trainer *and* on the Teacher's CDs.
[CD]	This listening text/song is only on the Teacher's CDs.
[film]	This film clip is on the CD-ROM in the Language and Skills Trainer and on the Teacher's CDs.
[pencil]	A writing exercise/exercise part.
CORE SKILL	This is the central skill in this Topic.
→S13	This is a reference to the Skills section.
→G4	This is a reference to the Grammar section.
[folder]	Exercise/exercise part for your personal folder.
⟨ ⟩	Optional text or exercise/exercise part.
[difficult]	A difficult exercise/exercise part.
[easy]	An easy exercise/exercise part.

Online-Links to a variety of online resources are featured at the top of many pages. To access those resources, enter the code (e.g. Online-Link: 547170-1001) in the search box at www.klett.de.

Topic 1 Growing up

WORD BANK

Legal language
age limit • legal • age of consent • to ban • compulsory • to take sb to court • law • to pass/ break a law • rights • privileges • independence • to sentence sb to life imprisonment • to take responsibility for sth

Minimum legal age limits

	USA	UK	Germany	Peru	Pakistan
Leaving school	16–18*	16	16–18*	18	at any time***
Employment	14	13	13	12	14
Age of consent (AOC)	14–18*	16	14	14	only in marriage
Marriage	18	16 (with parental consent)	18	14 females 16 males	16 females 18 males
Driving a car	14–17*	17	17–18*	18	18
Buying alcohol (MPA)	21	18	16, 18**	18	illegal for all
Smoking	18–19*	18	18	12	18
Voting in an election	18	18	18	18	18
Criminal responsibility	6–10*	10	14	12	7

*varies from state to state **18 for spirits ***no compulsory education

FACT FILE

- The **age of consent (AOC)** refers to when people can legally have sex. In Germany it is 14 if the older partner is younger than 18.
- The **age of criminal responsibility** is when children can be taken to court, depending on the type of crime.
- The **minimum purchasing age (MPA)** refers to the purchase of alcohol. This may not be the same as the **minimum drinking age (MDA)** for drinking alcohol in bars. China, for example, has an MPA of 18 but no MDA.

1 *What kind of photos would you choose to illustrate 'growing up'? Why?*

2 *Look at the figures and the Fact file. Comment on the age limits in different countries.*

3 *Explain whether you feel adults act more responsibly than under-18s. Give examples.*

4 [ ] ***Your country:*** *Which age limits do you think should be changed in your country? What should the new age limits be? Explain your reasons.*

5 [ ] ***Mediation:*** *Tracy, an American exchange student in Germany, is looking at this English book and sees the chart on p. 8. She can't believe Germany lets kids drink alcohol when they're so young. "Every dummy knows 16-year-olds can't handle alcohol," she says. The little brother in her host family wants to know why US laws are so weird. "Häh…? Drüben darfst du mit 14 Auto fahren, aber wählen erst mit 18 und Alkohol kaufen erst mit 21! Wer kommt denn auf so einen Schwachsinn?" The mediator translates for him, and he and Tracy start to argue.*
Role play: *There are three roles: Tracy, the brother and a mediator. The mediator not only translates, but also helps the other two to see both sides of the argument. Discuss what those sides are before acting out the situation.* →S34

6 [ ] *Thinking back to your discussion from exercise 1, bring a photo to class that you feel best illustrates the topic 'Growing up'. Present the photo with your interpretation of it.*

WORD BANK

Reacting and commenting
I was surprised to see that … • I never knew that … • It depends on … • In my opinion … • On the one hand …, but on the other hand … • I think the reason for this is… • I think/don't think 18 is an appropriate age to … • I think it should be up to … to decide the age limit for … • I respect your opinion, but … • You make it sound like … • Correct me if I'm wrong, but … • … could be dangerous • … should be protected

Paranoid Park

1 *Pre-reading: Have you ever done anything risky for fun? Take five minutes to write a short letter to yourself (real or fictional) in which you describe your experience – and any regrets you might have had later. Put your letter in an envelope and give it to your teacher. Your teacher will give you back your letter, unopened, after you have read and discussed the following text.*

This is the story of Alex, a 16-year-old from Portland, Oregon. Alex is from one of the city's better neighborhoods, but feels attracted to the rough downtown skater scene.

Dear ________,

I'm here at my uncle Tommy's beach house. It's about nine o'clock at night. I'm upstairs, by myself. I've got my pen, my spiral notebook … I don't know how to start. I don't even know if I can do this. But I will try. It can't make anything worse … Outside it's raining and dark. I can hear the surf crashing in the distance like little bombs going off. All right. Just went downstairs and made some hot chocolate. Dude, chill out and write something. That's me talking to myself. I just have to start at the beginning, take it easy, take it slow …

Paranoid Park. That's where it started. Paranoid Park is a skatepark in downtown Portland. It's under the Eastside Bridge, down by the old warehouses. It's an underground 'street' park, which means there are no rules, nobody owns it, and you don't have to pay to skate. A lot of the best skaters come there, from California and the East Coast and all over. It's also kind of a street-kid hangout. There's all these stories, like how a skinhead got stabbed there once. That's why they call it Paranoid Park. It has that dangerous, sketchy vibe to it.

My first connection to Paranoid was through Jared Fitch. He's a senior at my school. He's pretty insane, but cool, though, and one of the best skaters at our school. Last summer we skated every day. We'd go downtown to different places, like this old parking garage that was condemned that everyone snuck into and partied in. I wasn't on Jared's level yet, but I was learning. He liked being the teacher and showing me stuff.

During the last week of summer, Jared said we should check out Paranoid Park. I had heard of it, but I had assumed it was out of my league. But when I said I didn't think I was ready, Jared laughed and said something like: "Nobody's ever *ready* for Paranoid Park."

So we went. I was nervous, but I was also kinda psyched. Skating Paranoid. That was an accomplishment. That was something you could tell people about.

We drove over the Eastside Bridge and circled around underneath it. I remember seeing the train tracks in the street. They were shiny, like they were still in use. As it turned out, they were.

The park itself was above us, tucked right under the bridge. You could hear the cars and trucks rattling by overhead. The area around there was mostly industrial buildings.

We carried our boards up the dirt hill and ducked through a hole in the chain-link fence. We crawled onto the platform and found ourselves looking out over the whole layout. It was actually smaller than I expected, and also kind of trashed. There were old beer cans around, and garbage, and Cholo graffiti. But there was something about it, a kind of aura.

[10] **dude** Mann
[18] **sketchy vibe** odd, strange, unpredictable feeling
[19] **Jared** ['dʒærəd]
[19] **senior** a student in his / her last year at an American high school
[22] **condemned** closed (so it can later be destroyed)
[29] **psyched** [saɪkt] AE slang for 'excited'
[40] **trashed** *in sehr schlechtem Zustand*
[40] **Cholo graffiti** ['tʃəʊləʊ] a type of graffiti typical of Latino neighbourhoods

There weren't many people – a couple of guys were skating, a dozen or so more stood along the wall to our right. We watched a scrawny guy in the bowl across from us nail a lip-grind. He had two huge tattoos on his arms and a big scar across his stomach. His deck was some weird old thing, totally beat to hell, but he killed. He was great.

The other guys there were the same. I had seen hard-core skater guys here and there downtown. But I had never seen them all in one place. The center of the true skate universe. Jared dropped in and rode up the bowl across from us. Like I said, he was one of the best skaters I knew, but that was nothing compared to those guys. I dropped in, too, and went around a couple of times and managed not to make an ass of myself. It was sweet, though – the adrenaline rush of it. You were in the big leagues at Paranoid.

A few weeks later: Alex is already tired of the new school year, tired of his parents' constant fighting, and tired of Jennifer, a girl who likes him. To get away from it all, he wants to go back to Paranoid Park with Jared. But Jared cancels to spend the night with a girl. Angry, Alex decides to go alone. At Paranoid Park that night, he runs into a rough-looking skater clique and hangs out with them for a while. Then one of them, Scratch, has an idea …

"Hey," Scratch said to me. "Wanna hop a train?"

I looked up at him. I kinda did. "What sort of train?"

"The ten-twenty. It comes right through here every night. We can ride it all the way to Safeway."

They talked me into it. Or I agreed. I don't remember, exactly.

The other guy and the girl offered to watch my board, but I said I would take it with me. Scratch said it would get in the way, but I insisted.

We left Paranoid through the hole in the chain link fence. I followed Scratch and hoped I wasn't doing something stupid. He wouldn't rob me, would he? Or take my board? But whatever. I sort of didn't care at that point.

I heard the train horn blare. I could feel the rumble of it under my feet.

"That's it!" shouted Scratch, and he broke into an excited run. I couldn't believe I was doing this. I was going to hop a train! Jared would be so jealous. It served him right!

We ran through the old buildings, until we came to the train tracks. The train was really there, it was really coming. The single front headlight shone directly at us. "Get back," said Scratch when we reached the gravel track bed. "You can't let them see you."

The locomotive came even with us. I couldn't believe how big and powerful it looked. After it passed, Scratch leaned forward. He studied the different cars, watching them pass. Then he picked one and started to jog alongside it.

"Come on, run!" he shouted over the noise.

The train didn't seem to be going very fast – until you tried to run alongside it. We had to sprint to keep up. Scratch ran after a metal ladder on the side of a grain car. He jumped for it, caught it, and pulled himself up until he stood on the lowest rung. He pointed for me to do the same.

I still had my skateboard, which was in the way. But I switched it to my left hand and grabbed the ladder on the next car. Still holding my board, I crawled up enough to swing my feet into the bottom rung.

Scratch gave me a thumbs-up when he saw that. I had proved myself to not be a total idiot. Now we were on the train. We were riding it. Scratch yelled stuff

[43] **scrawny** thin
[44] **nail a lip grind** successfully do a skateboarding trick
[45] **deck** skateboard
[46] **he killed** (slang) AE he was fantastic
[52] **ass** idiot
[52] **sweet** (slang) AE great
[63] **Safeway** name of a supermarket company
[72] **It served him right!** *Das geschah ihm recht!*
[76] **gravel** a mix of small rocks
[86] **switched it** *here Ich nahm es …*

to me over the noise. He said the train went another quarter mile or so to a train yard. We'd jump off there.

I was so psyched. I couldn't believe I was riding a train. I imagined telling all my friends, even telling Jennifer. I secured my skateboard in the rungs of the ladder and hung out as far as I could. Scratch was doing the same. The whole thing was so awesome. I wondered if we could ride it the other direction, too. Maybe you could ride it all the way across town.

Unfortunately, after a couple of minutes, the train started to slow down. Scratch shouted that we should hop off, the train yard was coming up.

I regretted that my little ride had come to an end. But I had done it. I had hopped a train! I lingered there for a moment, hanging out as far as I could.Then Scratch began waving frantically at me. I didn't understand. Then I saw the car.

There was a private security car parked on the gravel up ahead. It faced the train, its headlights shining directly onto the freight cars as they passed. Standing beside it was a man in a security uniform. He had black gloves on and a black nightstick in his hands.

The security guard spotted us immediately. He was big, not fat exactly, but he kind of waddled in his uniform. Scratch climbed farther up the metal ladder. When the security guard reached us, I thought he would yell at us or tell us to get down. I figured we'd hop off and walk away. What could he do to us. Yell at us? Call our parents? There was nothing he could do.

I was wrong. The security guard went for me first. I was high up, so he could only reach my knees. But he took a vicious swing with his nightstick and I swear, if he had connected, he would have broken every bone in my leg. By pure luck and reflexes, I jerked my feet up and he missed. I tried to climb higher, to get away from him. The train was still moving, thank God. The security guy had to jog beside it to keep up with us. He took another swing at me, hitting the metal ladder so hard the vibrations nearly shook me loose. I dropped down a rung, almost falling. He wound up to swing again. Now I was vulnerable. I wasn't high enough to avoid the nightstick.

I jumped. I had no choice. I threw myself as far out as I could. I landed hard and tumbled on the gravel. Scratch jumped, too. The security guard must have tripped or fallen somehow, because when I came out of my roll, he and Scratch were both on the ground.

96 **awesome** (slang) cool
104 **freight car** the train cars which carry industrial materials / products
108 **to waddle** *watscheln*
113 **vicious** ['vɪʃəs] violent
113 **swing** a quick movement of the arm

I scrambled to my feet. I ran for my skateboard. I was going to grab it and run like hell. Obviously, this security guard was out of his mind.

As I snatched up my board, I saw the guard chase down Scratch and hit him in the back with his nightstick. It dropped Scratch like a gunshot. I swear to God, I thought it killed him. And it was so brutal. Why was some rent-a-cop doing this? For riding on a train? It didn't make sense.

Scratch tried to crawl away. The security guard, breathing hard, stood over him. The guard was big and out of shape, but he knew how to swing that stick. He wound up to hit Scratch again.

I couldn't let that happen. Without thinking, I ran at the security guard and rammed the front of my board into his ribs. He barely noticed. He was very big. But he did turn and swing the club at me, this time just missing my head.

Scratch, meanwhile, scrambled to his feet and ran toward the train. The guard caught the back of his shirt for a moment and swung again with his nightstick. By now I was so scared I didn't know what was happening. I honestly thought he was going to kill us both.

So I charged him again. I reared back with my skateboard and slammed it into the back of his fleshy head. I put all my weight into it this time and I could feel the thock of my board hitting his skull. He definitely felt it this time. He froze for a moment, then stumbled, then fell forward onto the gravel beside the train.

Scratch and I both ran back a few feet, watching to see if he would get up. He started to – he lifted his head and felt around for his nightstick. When he found it he struggled to stand.

Then something strange happened. It was hard to see exactly, in the dark, but it looked like his coat got caught on something under one of the moving cars. It lifted him up and dragged him sideways. Scratch and I were still backing away, but we couldn't resist the bizarre sight of the guard getting pulled along by the train. We watched him try to reach around and unhook himself, all the while skipping sideways, like a crab, trying to keep his feet under him.

Then he got turned around. He got twisted into an awkward position under the train. You could see him start to panic and try to tear himself loose. But he couldn't. The train had him. He got folded up. It was like a rag doll getting folded up and stuffed inside a narrow container. The security guard got rolled up and kind of … *crushed* … and ground into a ball.

It must have broken his back. Or his neck. He probably died right then.

Scratch bolted. I never saw anyone move so fast in my life. He looked like a rat, clawing his way up the hill and vanishing into the weeds.

I did not run. I stood. I saw my skateboard a few feet away and picked it up. I stared at the dark spot on the ground where the security guard lay. I took a few steps forward. I felt like I should do something, like I should try to help. A terrible sense of dread flooded into my chest.

The last car of the train passed by. I followed that last car forward to where the body was.

I tripped over something and fell. That broke the spell. I looked around. Where was I? What had just happened? Suddenly the air all around me seemed to crackle with bad energy. I felt like every molecule on earth had turned against me. My lungs wouldn't work. I couldn't breathe. I had to call the police. I had to call someone. Should I yell for help? But I couldn't get any air. I started walking. I came to the security guard's car. It was still idling by the side of the tracks. The driver's side door was open, and the inside light was on. A copy of *Guns & Ammo* magazine hung off the dash.

[126] **out of his mind** completely crazy
[129] **rent-a-cop** (slang) negative expression for a security guard
[141] **to charge sb** *here* to run towards sb to attack him / her
[143] **thock** *Geräusch*
[149] **to get caught** *sich verfangen*
[160] **to bolt** to run away suddenly
[161] **to vanish** to disappear
[168] **to break the spell** *den Bann brechen*
[174] ***Guns & Ammo*** name of a gun magazine
[175] **dash** = dashboard *(Armaturenbrett)*

VIP FILE

Blake Nelson
- born in 1965; grew up in Portland, Oregon
- best-selling author of young adult novels, two of which have been filmed (*Girl* [*see p. 23*] and *Paranoid Park*)

There must be a radio inside, I thought. I would call the police. I would explain to them what happened. There had been a terrible accident. They needed to come right away. I leaned inside the car to find the radio, but then I found I didn't want to touch anything. No, I shouldn't touch things. I should be careful about that. Just in case … just in case I needed … to *what*?

I stepped back from the car. I had to think about this. What if I got accused of something? It was an accident, but what if the cops didn't see it that way? Or what if it wasn't an accident? I did hit him with my skateboard. Was that against the law? Maybe it was self-defense. I didn't know. I had to think. I had to process in my brain just exactly what had happened. We were on the train … The security guard saw us …

My brain wouldn't work. My whole body shook violently. Tears were pouring down my face. I backed away from the car. I had to go someplace where I could calm down for a minute and stop freaking out. I walked in one direction, then another. My brain was in chaos, and my body was in total panic. There was a big parking lot across from the tracks. I went toward it. I walked at first, then walked faster, then I started to run …

[182] **cop** (slang) policeman / woman

Abridged extract from *Paranoid Park*, by Blake Nelson

WORD BANK
… was more to blame than … • It was right / wrong to … • In my opinion it was (not) understandable that … • It was (un)acceptable to … • It was completely right / wrong to … • feelings of freedom / helplessness / guilt / shock • He was / wasn't acting in self-defense • responsibility • to face the consequences (of one's actions) • dilemma • to deny • prison • to trespass

FACT FILE
Juvenile crime in the US
- 35% of all crimes committed by juveniles in the US fall under the category of **personal assault** (e.g. sexual assault, murder, injury). **Property damage** (e.g. arson, theft) accounts for 29% of all under-18 crimes.
- **Girls** are responsible for just 15% of all juvenile crimes in the US.

2 ***Your reaction:*** *What do you think of the story? How did it make you feel?*

3 ***Comprehension:***
1. *Describe the setting of the story.*
2. *What motivated Alex to go to Paranoid Park each time?*
3. *When did Alex's troubles begin?*
4. *Identify the turning point in the text.*

4 ***Discussion:***
a) *Who could Alex blame for what went wrong? Explain.*
b) *What – if anything – did Alex do that was actually illegal?*
c) *Weigh the pros and cons of Alex's options. What would you do?*
d) *Look at your letter from exercise 1. Have your ideas about regrets changed after reading Paranoid Park?*

5 CORE SKILL *Narrative technique – Perspective:*
a) *The story is told from Alex's point of view. What effect does this have on how the story is told?*
b) *With a partner, discuss whether a **third**-person narrator could have told the story just as effectively as Alex. Give examples to make your point.* → S6, S7

6 CORE SKILL *Narrative technique – Character archetypes:*
a) *Most writers feature character archetypes in their stories – 'the good guy', 'the bad influence', 'the worry-wart'. Why do you think they do this? Make a list of as many character archetypes as you can think of.*
b) *Can you identify character archetypes in this text? (Look at line…)* → S5, S7

7 CORE SKILL *Narrative technique – Vocabulary for atmosphere:*
a) *Describe the atmosphere in Paranoid Park. Can your class agree on one word or expression to describe it?* → S7
b) *In groups, make mind maps around the central theme from 7a) using words from the text. (You can use this vocabulary in exercise 8.)*

⟨8⟩ ***Creative writing:*** *Continue the story as you think it could go on.* → S23

The genre of the teen film

1 ***Thinking about the film genre:*** *What do you think of when you see the phrase 'teen film'? List elements you feel are typical of the genre.* →S10, S12

2 [👥] ***Talking about popular teen films:*** *Work with a partner. Take five minutes and write down your favourite teen films; share your results with the class. Have some groups listed the same films? Discuss why that might be.*

3 ***Analyzing a film classic*** – **Rebel without a cause:**

a) *Read the following synopsis of* Rebel without a cause *(1955) which film historians consider to be one of the first – if not* **the** *first – 'teen film'.*

Jim Stark (James Dean) is a troubled 17-year-old. He feels alienated from his parents – a cold, pushy mother and a weak father who are always fighting. Jim, neglected and misunderstood, is always getting into trouble, one of the reasons his family has moved with Jim to L.A. to start a new life.

As the outsider at his new school, he has to deal with bullies, gangs and fights. But he also finds friends like Plato (Sal Mineo), a sensitive and troubled 15-year-old who looks up to him, and Judy (Natalie Wood), a girl he is attracted to. The bullies won't leave Jim alone, though. One of them, Buzz (Corey Allen), challenges Jim to a 'chicken race'. The two of them are to race in stolen cars to the edge of a cliff. The first one who jumps out before the car goes over the edge is the chicken – and the winner is the real man.

The chicken race ends in tragedy for Buzz, but the trouble does not end there, as the action leads up to a finale full of drama and emotion, not just for Jim but for the entire cast of characters.

b) *From the information you have, what aspects of the film make it a 'teen film'? Make a list to show your results for the following points:*
characters • storyline • action • clichés

⟨4⟩ [👥👥] ***Project – Analyzing and presenting a film:*** *Divide into four groups. Each group is responsible for one of the films you see here.*

Grease
(1978)

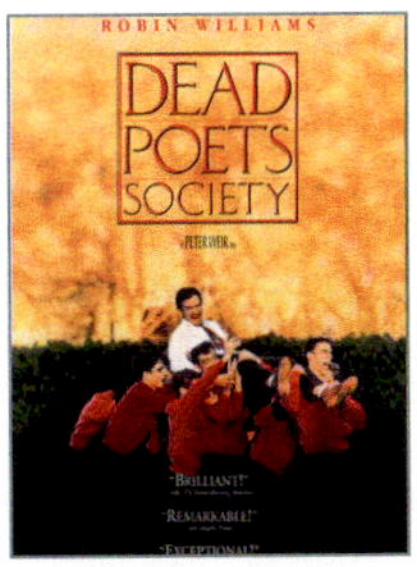

Dead Poets Society
(1989)

Bring it on
(2000)

Paranoid Park
(2007)

Your tasks:

1. *Get a copy of the film in English and watch it together as a group.*
2. *Directly afterwards, analyze the film as you analyzed the synopsis for* Rebel without a cause *in exercise 3b).*
3. *In a short presentation to the class, explain why you feel the film you watched was or was not worth watching.* →S10, S11

VIP FILE

James Dean
- born 1931 in Marion, Indiana; died 1955 in Cholame, California
- made only two other films, both of which have also achieved cult status: *East of Eden* (1953) and *Giant* (1956)
- loved race cars; died in a car accident with his Porsche Spyder which helped to establish him as a symbol of the 'rebel' and 'free spirit'

⟨Friendship⟩

1 *Pre-reading:*

a) 1. *Explain the ideas behind these famous proverbs:*
Books and friends should be few but good. • A hedge between friends keeps friendship green. • To have a friend, be a friend. • The best mirror is an old friend. • A friend in need is a friend indeed.

2. *Do you agree with the message in each proverb? Explain why/why not.*

b) *Discuss what friendship means to you.*

How to test true friendship

While it is not wise to intentionally wreck a friendship, it may become necessary to test the loyalty of those people you call your friends. Testing true friendship requires you to be honest while determining the intentions and real basis of your friendship. Read on to learn how to test true friendship.

Step One: Attempt to discuss controversial issues with your friend. Topics like politics and religion can serve as a reliable gauge in determining whether a friendship is true. A true friend will not harass you to change your mind. True friendship is not ruined by differences of philosophies or ideals.

Step Two: Entrust your friend with a dark or juicy secret. Trust is an important component of true friendship. A true friend should be able to keep your secret to herself/himself no matter how much it aches to spill the news. If word gets back to you that your friend has divulged your secret, you know that you need to watch what you do and say around them.

Step Three: Ask your friend for a huge favor. Make sure the favor you ask for will inconvenience your friend in a significant way. This will test just how far your friend is willing to go to help you out of a rough situation.

Step Four: Tell your friend the truth about their horrible singing. Although your declarations may sting your friend's ego, it shouldn't damage your friendship. True friendship is able to survive the honest truth. The ability to be honest with your friend will also test your commitment to a genuine friendship.

Step Five: Allow your friend to borrow money from you. Because money often brings out people's true intentions and motivations, the lending of it can test a true friendship. A true friend will respect your right to be repaid as soon as they are able to do so; you shouldn't have to send them reminders.

by K.T. Logan, www.ehow.com

[1] **intentionally** as part of a plan
[6] **gauge** [geɪdʒ] *Maßstab*
[7] **to harass sb** to put pressure on sb to do sth
[9] **to entrust** *jdm. etw. anvertrauen*
[11] **to ache** *here* to really want to do sth
[11] **If word gets back to you** If you hear about it from sb else
[12] **to divulge** to tell
[14] **favor** sth you do to help sb or to be nice to sb
[15] **to inconvenience** *Umstände bereiten*

TIP
There are lots of websites with lists of English proverbs on many topics. Try adding some to your active vocabulary to give your English extra colour.

2 *Reactions:*
Say how you feel about the idea of testing a friend to see if he/she is a ***true*** *friend. Can you imagine testing a friend?*

3 [ ] *Comprehension:*
In your own words, say what the idea behind each of the five steps/tests is.

4 [ ] *Ranking:*
Rank the five situations discussed in the article from 1 to 5.
1 is for the situation in which you would be the least disappointed if a friend let you down. 5 is for the situation in which you would be most disappointed. Count the votes in class to reveal the most disappointing situation collectively.

[◎] A song: *Umbrella* by Rihanna

You have my heart
And we'll never be worlds apart
Maybe in magazines
But you'll still be my star
Baby 'cause in the dark
You can't see shiny cars
And that's when you need me there
With you I'll always share
Because …

[CHORUS]
When the sun shines, we'll shine together
Told you I'll be here forever
Said I'll always be a friend
Took an oath, I'm a stick it out till the end
Now that it's raining more than ever
Know that we'll still have each other
You can stand under my umbrella
You can stand under my umbrella
(Ella ella eh eh eh)
Under my umbrella …

These fancy things will never come in between
You're part of my entity, here for infinity
When the war has took its part
When the world has dealt its cards
If the hand is hard, together we'll mend your heart
Because …

Words and music: Carter, Shawn C./Harrell, Thaddis Laphonia Jr./Nash, Terius Youngdell/Steward, Christopher A.

umbrella *Regenschirm*
Rihanna [rɪ'hænə]
[2] **to be worlds apart** to feel far away from each other
[13] **to take an oath** to promise sth
[13] **to stick it out** *durchhalten*
[20] **in between** *dazwischen*
[21] **my entity** *here* me
[21] **infinity** *Unendlichkeit*
[23] **to deal cards** *Spielkarten geben*
[24] **hand** *Blatt*

VIP FILE

Rihanna
- born 1988 on the Caribbean island of Barbados
- has had several number one hits including 'S.O.S.' (2006), 'Umbrella' (2007) and 'Take a bow' (2008)
- won a Grammy Award for 'Umbrella'

5 *Comprehension:*
Explain what is meant in these key lines:
1. *"You can stand under my umbrella".*
2. *"Baby 'cause in the dark/You can't see shiny cars."*

6 *Discussion:*
a) *Whether you like the song or not, say what you feel about the message.*
b) *This song was a worldwide hit in 2007. Name the factors you think played the biggest role in making it such a success:*
the lyrics • the music • singer's voice • singer's looks • all of these factors
c) *How big a role does friendship play in partnership?* →S9

7 [⏍] ***Vocabulary:*** *Are there any words or phrases in the song you feel are typical of or important for a friendship song? Which ones, and why?*

Slam

slam bad accident / bad fall in skateboarding
[5]**Alicia** [əˈlɪsiə]
[5]**urgent** extremely important
[34]**to get choked up** to feel as if you are going to start crying
[35]**to reckon** to think / to be of the opinion

Read how a London teenager, Sam, experiences his 16th birthday.

The day began with cards and presents and doughnuts – Mum had already been to the baker's by the time I woke up. My dad was supposed to be coming over for tea and cake in the afternoon, and in the evening, believe it or not, Mum and I were going to go to Pizza Express and the cinema. I got the first text from Alicia straight after breakfast – it just said, 'I NEED 2 CU URGENT Axx'.

"Who was that?" said Mum.

"Oh, no one."

"Is that a Miss No One?" said Mum. She was probably thinking of Nikki, because she knew we'd been out the previous evening.

"Not really," I said. I knew it didn't make any sense, because either someone was a girl or they weren't, unless you're talking about men who dress up as girls, but I didn't care. Part of me was panicking. It wasn't my head so much as my guts – I think my guts knew what it was about, even if my head didn't. Or pretended it didn't. I'd never forgotten that time when something half-happened when I hadn't put anything on. The part of me that was panicking because of the text had never really stopped panicking since the half-happening day.

I went and locked myself in the bathroom and texted her back. I said, 'NOT 2DAY MY BIRTHDAY Sxx'. If I got something back from that, then I knew I was in trouble. I flushed the loo and washed my hands, just to make Mum think I'd actually been doing something, and even before I'd opened the door my phone beeped again. The text just said, 'URGENT, OUR STARBUCKS 11 am'. And then all of me knew – guts, head, heart, fingernails.

I texted back 'OK'. I didn't see how I could do anything else, even though I wanted to do anything else.

When I went back into the kitchen, I wanted to sit on my mum's lap. I know that sounds stupid and babyish, but I couldn't help it. On my sixteenth birthday, I didn't want to be sixteen, or fifteen, or any teen. I wanted to be three or four, and too young to make any kind of mess, apart from the mess you make when you scribble on walls or tip your food bowl upside down.

"I love you, Mum," I said when I sat down at the table.

She looked at me as if I'd gone mad. I mean, she was pleased, but she was pretty surprised.

"I love you too, sweetheart," she said. I tried not to get choked up. If Alicia was going to tell me what I thought she was going to tell me, I reckoned it would be a long time before Mum said that again. It might be a long time before she even felt it.

All the way there, I was doing all kinds of deals, or trying to. You know the sort of thing: 'If it's OK, I'll never skate again.' As if it had anything to do with skating. I offered never to watch TV again, and never to go out again, and never to eat at McDonald's again. Sex never came up, because I already knew I was never going to have sex again, so that didn't seem like a deal God would be interested in. I might as well have promised Him that I wouldn't fly to the moon, or run down Essex Road naked. Sex was over for me, forever, no doubt.

Alicia was sitting at the long counter in the window with her back to everyone. I saw her face as I was walking in, without her seeing me, and she looked pale and frightened. I tried to think of some other things that could

VIP FILE

Nick Hornby
- born 1957 in Surrey, England
- popular novelist throughout the world
- best-known novel (and film): *About a boy*

make her that way. Maybe her brother was in trouble. Maybe her ex-boyfriend had threatened her, or threatened me. I wouldn't mind taking a beating, I thought. Even if it was a serious beating, I'd be better in a few months, probably. Say he broke both my arms and both my legs … I'd be walking around again by Christmas.

I didn't go over and say hello straight away. I got in the queue to buy myself a drink. If my life was about to change, then I wanted the old life to last for as long as possible. There were two people in front of me, and I hoped they had the longest and most complicated orders Starbucks had ever heard of. I wanted someone to order a cappuccino with all the bubbles taken out by hand, one by one. I felt sick, of course, but it was better to feel sick without knowing for sure. In the queue I could still imagine that it was only going to be a beating, but once I'd spoken to her, that would be that.

The woman in front of me wanted a cloth to wipe up some orange juice her kid had spilled on the table. It took no time at all. And I couldn't think of a difficult drink. I asked for a frappuccino. At least the ice takes a long time. And then when I'd got my drink there was nothing else to do except go and sit next to Alicia at the counter.

"Hello," I said.

"Happy birthday," she said. And then, "I'm late."

Abridged extract from *Slam*, by Nick Hornby

TIP
See p. 28 for more of *Slam*.

1 *Comprehension:*
1. *"I'm late." (line 67). Explain what Alicia means.*
2. *"All the way there, I was doing all kinds of deals, or trying to." What does Sam mean when he refers to deals in lines 38–44?*

2 CORE SKILL *Narrative technique – Characterization:*
With a partner, discuss whether or not Sam is acting his age. Give examples from the text that tell the reader about his maturity level. → S5, S7

3 CORE SKILL *Narrative technique – Humour in serious situations:*
a) *It is typical of tragicomedies to show humour in situations that are not funny. Give examples of the humour in this extract.* → S7
b) *Is it appropriate to show humour in serious situations? Explain.*

4 CORE SKILL *Narrative technique – Suspense:*
The author could have just told the reader what Alicia's news was right away – but then there would have been no suspense. Give examples from the text that show how the author builds up suspense for the episode's climax. → S7

⟨5⟩ *Discussion:*
Imagine Alicia and Sam talking about their problem.
Discuss the pros and cons of the following options:
- *"Let's keep the baby. We'll take responsibility and learn to be good parents."*
- *"Let's have the baby, but give it up for adoption. There are lots of childless couples who would love the chance to give the baby a good family life."*
- *"Get an abortion. We're only 16 – we're too young to be parents!"*

6 *Watching and understanding a television interview:*
1. *What comparison does Hornby make between skateboarding and football?*
2. *What advantages does Hornby see for his storyline by making Sam a skater?*
3. *What does Hornby say about teenage pregnancy?*

WORD BANK
to dread sth (e.g. bad news) • to regret sth • to face the truth • to put sth off for as long as possible • (im)mature • maturity • to be ready to … • to take responsibility for one's actions • promiscuous behaviour • teen pregnancy • to keep her baby • to have an abortion • to give a baby up for adoption • You have to look at it from both perspectives … • There are two sides to every story • to act your age • condom

FACT FILE
Teenage pregnancies
- US: 5.2% of all teenage girls become pregnant
- UK: 3.1% (the highest teenage pregnancy rate in Europe)
- Germany: 1.6%

⟨Infinity⟩

This American short story takes place directly before and after the female narrator's 16th birthday.

1 *Pre-reading: Think about the title of the story. What does the word 'infinity' mean? What associations / feelings does it give you?*

[1] **Anthony** [ˈæntəni]
[2] **implication** a close connection
[9] **to negotiate sth** to handle sth successfully
[10] **to digress** not to talk about the main topic
[13] **to yield** to let other cars pass before you join the traffic
[14] **to poke off of sth** *here* to lead out of sth
[15] **to merge in** to drive smoothly into moving traffic
[17] **to poke** *here* to push
[24] **to ease into** to go into sth slowly and carefully
[27] **to jerk sth** to suddenly move sth in a different direction

Lately I don't dream about Anthony. I dream about the rotary.

Now, Mr. Haskell, my psychology teacher, would say this has implications. That somehow my fear of the rotary is linked to my issues with Anthony. The truth is, I was scared of the rotary before I even met Anthony.

Most people don't even know what rotaries are. That's because most towns have those most modern of inventions, stoplights, to deal with traffic. Not here. Instead, some genius decided however many years ago to put in this big circle, with all the main roads feeding into it, then sat back to watch people crash to their deaths as they attempted to negotiate it.

But I digress.

My first experience with the rotary was when I was about seven. We'd just moved to town. My mother and I were on our way to the grocery store when we suddenly came up on this big sign that said YIELD with an arrow pointing to the right. Cars were going around a big circle, off of which poked several different exits to different roads. The trick, apparently, was to kind of merge in, follow around until your exit, then merge out. Simple as that.

"Oh my God," my mother said, poking her glasses up the bridge of her nose, which she always does when she's really nervous. "What is this?"

The answer came in the form of a loud, impatient beep from behind us. My mother looked nervously to her left, then tentatively poked at the gas pedal, sending us inching out into oncoming traffic. Another beep.

"Mom," I said.

"I'm merging!" she shrieked, as if this were on the level of splitting atoms. And we were merging, pretty well, slowly easing into traffic. In fact, we were almost relaxed when we had to try to get back out; no easy trick, as there were many cars merging in. We got stuck on the inside track for two more turns, watching our exit go by, before my mother panicked and just sort of jerked the wheel, sending us in its general direction. And that was when the station wagon hit us. The entire episode ended with a ticket, our insurance rates rising, and my mother swearing to never do the rotary ever again, which seemed somewhat overdramatic, until we realized that she meant it.

What this means, essentially, is that she has spent nine years taking the longest possible route everywhere. Because the rotary is the hub of our town, avoiding it takes work. And maps. And no end of secret shortcuts and long detours.

My boyfriend, Anthony, is a year older than me. He's good at the rotary, but he understands my hesitation. In fact, since I got my permit, we've spent a lot of time going in circles together, practicing. We started late at night, when it was pretty much deserted.

"Okay, now the first thing you're gonna do is stop and look to the left here," he instructed me one night. "There's someone coming, so unless they merge off before they get here, we'll wait for them to pass."

We waited. It was a Cadillac, moving slowly. It had the whole rotary to itself.

"Okay now," Anthony said. "Just ease out."

I did. Just as my mother had, all those years earlier. But this time there was no one coming; it was dark. No problem.

"See?" Anthony said, reaching over to squeeze my leg. He left his hand there, warm on my skin, as we eased around the circle. "Piece of cake, right?"

"Right," I said. We passed all the exits once, then started through again. Of course this was okay, I thought. Like a merry-go-round, only faster. But it was a trial run. And trial runs are always easier.

After a few more turns Anthony pointed toward the beach route exit, and I took it, before finally hitting the turnoff to the shore parking lot. I slowed down, pulling up into a space right behind the lifeguard stand. Then I cut the engine.

"You did good tonight," Anthony said. And then he leaned over and kissed me. I knew he would. I knew it just like I knew that after a few minutes he'd reach up and undo my shirt, then slide off my bra straps, easing me back against the seat behind me. He'd tell me he loved me, kiss my neck, run his hand down my back and into the waistband of my jeans, pressing his fingers there. I knew because we'd been practicing this, too, trial run after trial run. As with the rotary, what came next was obvious. And scary. And, it seemed, inevitable.

He wanted to sleep with me. He was a senior; we'd been together six months. Us having sex would be a natural progression, after kissing to letting him go up my shirt, then down my pants: And so I have this choice. To either merge in or take the long way home.

A few weeks later. At the beach parking lot.

His urging was gentler, but no less insistent. "I love you, I love you," he'd whisper, and I'd feel that same hot flush, travelling up from my feet, the adrenaline rush that was a mix of fear and longing. We'd gotten very close, but again, I pulled back. Scared.

"I just don't understand why you don't want to," he asked me one night as we sat looking at the water, him now leaning against his door, as far away from me as possible, as if the fact that I didn't want him made it necessary to put the maximum amount of distance between us.

"I want it to be right," I told him.

"How can this not be right?" He sat up straighter, jutting a finger up at the windshield. "Moonlight? Check. Crashing waves? Check. I love you? Check. You love me? ..."

It took me a second, just a second, to realize it was my turn to say something.

"Check," I said quickly, but he glared at me and let his finger drop, as if this explained everything.

[33]**hub** centre
[37]**permit** a driving student needs this to be allowed to practice driving on the road
[38]**to go in circles** *sich im Kreis drehen*
[48]**Piece of cake, right?** Easy, right?
[50]**merry-go-round** *Karussell*
[51]**trial run** test of how sth works
[54]**to cut the engine** to turn the engine off
[61]**inevitable** impossible to stop
[67]**urging** putting pressure on
[69]**longing** a feeling of wanting something very much
[76]**to jut** to point

As the days passed, and I found myself consistently taking the long way everywhere, I got frustrated with all these decisions. A part of me wanted to barrel into the rotary blindfolded, pushing the gas pedal hard, and let whatever was going to happen just happen, anything for it to be over. The same part sometimes was so close to giving in to Anthony's pleadings, wanting to finally just relax against the seat and let him do what he wanted. Scenario number one, of course, was stupid: I'd cause a multicar pileup and kill myself. As far as number two, well, it was harder to say. What would change? Just because you don't see it doesn't mean something isn't there. Or gone.

The fall carnival appeared in one afternoon, with the huge Ferris wheel cropping up in a field by the shopping mall as if dropped from the sky itself. In daylight, as I took my shortcut to school, everything looked tired and rusted. But by that night, with the lights blazing, it was like a whole new world.

Anthony bought some cotton candy, and proceeded to lose twenty bucks in about five minutes playing a game that involved shooting water pistols at stuffed frogs. I just stood and watched him, silent after my first three tries to point out he was never, ever going to win.

"How badly do you really need a frog, anyway?" I asked him.

"It's not about the frog," Anthony snapped at me, bending down to better line up his shot. "It's about winning."

We got on the Ferris wheel. As we started moving, Anthony wrapped both his hands around mine and kissed my neck. I closed my eyes as we moved up, higher and higher. We were at the very top when I looked down and felt dizzy. Anthony was pressing against me, his fingers digging, hardly caring that this was not the place, not the time. All those nights at the beach, when I'd pushed him away, I hadn't known exactly why, just that it hadn't felt right. But as my view from high up narrowed, I realized that my relationship with Anthony had done the same, going from a wide endless horizon of possibilities to one pinpoint of a destination. I wanted to have choices, to know that I could, at any moment, still take the long way home. Sure, there was a quick way to anywhere. But sometimes, when you took the shortcut, you missed the view.

"I love you," he whispered in my ear. "I want you."

But it wasn't enough, this time. Maybe later it would have been, but as I pushed him away, I knew that time would never come. Winning might not have been everything, but Anthony was tired of losing at this game.

The ride hadn't even come to a full stop when he pushed the safety bar away from us. It rattled loudly and sent a ripple of force through my metal seat, an echo I felt in my bones. Then he stomped down the stairs. I climbed out slowly, taking my time, telling myself to pay attention to how the earth felt beneath me and not take it for granted anymore.

A few minutes later. Alone in the car.

When I finally made it to the light, I hit my blinker, signalling the left turn that would lead me around the shopping mall and through two neighborhoods before depositing me onto my own road. It was the way I'd always gone, up until now, but this time I didn't feel that burning burst of shame in it, knowing I was taking the easy way out. I just remembered the view from up high, the way all the roads led to one another eventually. It didn't matter which route you took, as long as you got home.

I was thinking this as I moved up to the solid green of the light. There was that burst of freedom in realizing that my choice was okay. But even so, at the

82 **consistently** regularly; systematically
84 **to barrel into sth** to move into sth very quickly
84 **blindfolded** *here blindlings*
91 **carnival** *Kirmes, Jahrmarkt* (AE)
94 **blazing** shining brightly
95 **proceeded to lose** … went on to lose …
95 **bucks** (coll) dollars
100 **to snap at sb** to speak angrily and impatiently
104 **dizzy** *schwindelig*
121 **to take sb / sth for granted** to expect sb / sth always to be there
125 **to deposit sb somewhere** to bring sb somewhere and leave them there
126 **burst** *here Aufwallen, Auflodern*

last minute, I turned my wheel to the right, surprising even myself, and shifted into second as the rotary came up into my sight. It was crowded with carnival traffic, cars whizzing past: I could see it, as if I was still up high, the absolute of that perfect circle. This was normally the moment I was dumb scared, hands shaking, but this time I only moved closer, pressing my shoulders back against the seat as if taking the scariest and most exhilarating of rides.

As I got closer, I glanced in my rearview and saw the Ferris wheel. Another circle, representing the kind of infinity that I was only beginning to understand. So as I looked back at the road, easing myself closer to the rotary traffic, I sealed that image in my mind as I eased in, holding my breath, and felt myself fall into the rhythm of the cars around me. I turned the wheel, leaning into the first curve, feeling that rush of accomplishment and speed as we all moved away from the center, further and further out. It was happening so fast, but I was there, right there, alive, wanting this moment to be like Ferris wheels and all the circulars of this life and others, never ending.

Infinity (abridged), by Sarah Dessen, from the short story collection *Sixteen*

[134] **to whiz past** to go by very fast
[137] **exhilarating** [ɪgˈzɪlrˌeɪtɪŋ] very exciting
[143] **accomplishment** what one has achieved
[146] **circular** sth with the qualities of a circle (Note: The word is usually used as an adjective.)

WORD BANK
to put sb under pressure • symbol • symbolic language • to see sth / sb as a symbol of… • relationship • (to be in) love • (to have) sex • natural progression from … to … • one-track mind • to go round and round • to go in circles • to take the long way / route • to take a shortcut • to realize sth won't work / is over • to (over)analyze a situation

2 *Reactions:*
Who can you sympathize with more: the narrator or Anthony?

3 *Comprehension:*
a) *The turning point: "It's about winning." (line 101) Explain the original context of Anthony's statement. What significance does it take on for the narrator and for her relationship with Anthony?*
b) *Explain what the story means by 'choice'. (Perhaps lines 109–111, starting with 'endless horizons …', can help you.)*

4 [ ] CORE SKILL *Narrative technique – Symbols:*
a) *Find the circular symbols in the story. What do they represent? Comment on the relationship between these symbols and the title of the story.* →S7
b) *Compare your answers to a) with your ideas from exercise 1.*

5 [ ] [ ] *Creative writing:*
Rewrite the beach scene or the carnival scene from Anthony's point of view. →S23, S24

6 *Your own difficult choices:*
Have you ever felt pulled in different directions by a difficult choice you had to make? How did you deal with the situation?

7 [ ] *Listening* – **Girl:**
a) *Look at the cartoon on the right. Define the term "in-crowd".*
b) *Now listen to Andrea, the 16-year-old narrator of the novel* Girl. *What are the issues in her life?* →S29
c) *Compare Andrea's life with the narrator of* Infinity. *What similarities and differences are there between the two girls?*

Improve your style: More emphasis, more colour

1 *Present progressive for emphasis:*

a) *Look at the photo. Explain what is odd about one of the verb forms the girl uses. Look at* → G1d) *to see if you were right.*

b) *Now think of an appropriate example for each of the following situations.*
Example: 1. "I have problems with my parents.
→ **They're always complaining** about my friends."

2. "Dan doesn't act like a good friend any more. …"
3. "Gwyneth has got the best boyfriend in the world. …"
4. "Tara is really bothering us with her stupid new diet. …"
5. "One of our neighbours is really strange. …"
6. "My girlfriend doesn't take our relationship seriously. …"
7. "I hate this girl at school. …"
8. "Cody embarrasses himself every weekend at the disco. …"

count the calories in our food at lunch • trying to steal my boyfriend • try to make me do things I don't want to do • say embarrassing things to all the girls • smile at other guys • complain about my friends ✔ • look out of the window at me • surprise her with great presents • …

2 *Revision – Emphatic forms:*

a) *Think of one example for each of the forms listed here:*
- *emphatic 'do'*
- *adverbs of degree*
- *emphasis with 'what'*
- *emphasis with 'it was/it is'*
- *emphasis with **self**-pronouns*

b) *Decide which emphatic forms are missing.*

TIP
Emphatic forms are typical of **spoken** English, but they do appear in written form, too.

Tia: Ray, you just fell asleep about five times in class! You need some sleep. You [1] remember what that is, right?
Ray: [2] I need is for you to get out of my ear.
Tia: Hey, what's wrong? You've been [3] rude to everyone all week. What do you do at night that makes you so tired and edgy the next day?
Ray: Oh come on. *Everyone* falls asleep in Business.
Tia: But you [4] were always so crazy about becoming a big success in the business world.
Ray: There's time for that when I'm 30. But I can't hang out late at the skatepark with Ian when I'm 30. That would be [5] pathetic!
Tia: So that's where you've been going at night. Do you [6] think that's the right crowd to be hanging out with? It's a super scary place and I'm [7] hearing lots of drug and alcohol stories about it. I mean, they [8] have a reason for calling it 'Candyland'! And we're *not* talking about chocolate.
Ray: Tia, you [9] said I should stop being so driven about getting into a good college and enjoy life a little before everything gets so serious. Anyway, gotta go now. I'm helping Ian to organize a skater event over at Candyland.
Tia: Ian can organize it [10]. *You've* got History now.
Ray: Sorry, 'Mom', no time for History today. I'd just fall asleep anyway, remember?

c) [⏍] *Think of ways you could you use emphatic forms in these situations. (There is more than one possibility.)*
Example: 1. Ray always thought the skater crowd was so stupid. Now you see him with skaters every day. Talk to him about it. → But you **yourself** always said how stupid skaters were!

2. You want to make it clear to your best friend that you didn't spread those rumours about her.
3. Your brother tells you how stupid your new look is. But you don't care about his opinion.
4. You're worried your boyfriend won't remember it's your anniversary tomorrow. Remind him.
5. You think it's awful that Derek wants to break up with Zoe in a text message. Tell him what you would do.
6. Your parents crashed your birthday party – and danced with all your friends! You can't believe how they embarrassed you like that. Tell them.

3 ***More emphasis with adverbs:***

a) *What does the adverb in the following sentence refer to?*
*"**Unfortunately**, I can't make it to your party." Look at* →G3b) *to see if you were right.*

b) *Marcus and his careers adviser Mrs Lee are discussing a letter of application he has written for a summer job.*
Where do these adverbs fit best into their conversation?
basically • frankly • honestly • hopefully • luckily • obviously • unfortunately

Marcus: Was the letter really that bad?
Mrs Lee: Well … you didn't spend more than a few minutes on it – anyone can see that. I mean, look at all the typing errors alone! But … there are people like me who stop bad applications from being sent out in the first place, right?
Marcus: Oh, sorry about that. But … the letter is OK in general, isn't it?
Mrs Lee: Well … I have some bad news.
Marcus: You mean I'll have to change a few things?
Mrs Lee: A few touch-ups? …, you should be able to see yourself that this version is just not going to work! You can't just write, "It doesn't matter to me what tasks I am given, as it will only be for a few weeks anyway, unlike a real job." …, Marcus, the employer would think you didn't care.
Marcus: So …, Mrs Lee, you're saying this is going to be a rewrite for me?

4 ***Revision – Word order with adverbs and adverbials:***
Put the sentence parts in a suitable order. (Refer to →G3a) and 3b) *for an adverb overview.)*

1. Many adults assume … without thinking • usually • their money • spend • that teenagers
2. show • carefully • that most American teens • quite • but new studies • watch their money
3. less than ever before • readers learn • spending • actually • in the new *Money Talk* • that teens are
4. just last year • teens • spent • such as clothing • on things • *more* than ever before
5. basically • in spending habits • high gasoline prices • are the main reason • for the change • this year
6. and staying trendy • having to choose between • as never before • teens are • mobility
7. One student said: the money • I don't have • unfortunately • for new clothes • I realized
8. He continued: looking like a model • simply • getting to • more important than • my part-time job is

5 ***More colour with adjectives and adverbs:***
*Damian Lord is the new star in Hollywood and has just received an important Cinema Society nomination. He has prepared a speech to make if he wins, but his manager is disappointed: "Show more feeling! This isn't just **ANY** award, Damian. This is the **CINEMA SOCIETY**!" Improve the speech using new / different adverbs and adjectives.* →G3a)

"Thank you for this award. This is a nice day in my life. Getting the nomination had already changed my life. But now, the Society has decided I'm good enough to win. I'm in shock. I'm 18, how could I have expected to win? Now, as I look out into the audience and see the actors who were also nominated for 'Best Actor', I have to think to myself: even if I were half as good as these colleagues of mine, I could be satisfied with myself. So I am happy that the Society has chosen me for this award. But let me thank a group of people out there: my fans! You've always supported me, and I'll never forget the love and support you have shown me the last two years. Thank you."

Online-Link 547170-1003

Preparing for an exchange program

Before you actually take part in an exchange program, it can be helpful to give some thought to some general aspects of exchanges.

1 [group] [write] ***An intercultural gallery walk:***

a) *Divide up into four groups. Each group creates a profile of one of these people:*
a typical American woman • a typical German woman • a typical American man • a typical German man
For each profile, illustrate your ideas with a drawing and written notes.

b) *When all four groups have finished, hang your profiles up in the classroom. Then the whole class takes a walk through the 'gallery'. Each group explains its profile. No questions during this step, though!*

c) *Class discussion:*
1. *Where do you feel stereotypes are involved in the drawings of the American man and woman?*
2. *Do you think the portraits of the German man and woman would have been any different if Americans (or anybody from outside Germany) had drawn them? Explain.*
3. *Discuss why stereotypes can be a problem – and how they can be avoided.*

2 ***Thinking about a stay in the US:***

a) [write] *Imagine you will be staying with an American host family and going to an American high school for a year. What do you think it will be like?*
Take three minutes to write down your ideas (in keywords) on these aspects of American life:
location (city / state / region) for exchange year • family lifestyle • friends • free time

b) *Share your ideas with the rest of class. What ideas are mentioned most often?*

c) *Read the interview questions below, any of which could be asked by an exchange program placement officer. What answers would show that you have the intercultural competence to do well in an exchange program with a foreign family?*

1. "Imagine that your host family is *much* different than you had expected. (much more religious, completely different financial situation, completely different lifestyle etc.).
Would that be a problem for you? Explain why or why not."
2. "How would you react if a classmate at your new American high school asked you why you aren't wearing your little leather shorts and feathered cap / your 'dirndl' dress?"
3. "You may have expectations of your host family. But what do you think they might expect of *you*?"

3 [listen] ***Preparing for exchange program interviews:***

a) *Listen to what an exchange program interviewer says about deciding who is well-suited – or not – to an exchange program in the US.*

b) 1. *What does the man say about teenagers' expectations?*
2. *What does he say about the actual application process?*

c) [pair] ***Role play – 'Hot seat':***
Act out exchange program interviews. Write down questions you think an interviewer might ask, each question on a separate slip of paper. Take turns as the interviewer and as the student on the 'hot seat'. Each student draws a question and has to answer it on the spot.

Free-time activities

1 [◎] *Listening – Planning a picnic:* →S29, S30
First listen to the dialogue, then read the questions below and listen again, taking notes about the arrangements made.

1. *Which of these things are Tony and Sharon not going to take?*
   Tony: something to drink, plates, sandwiches, a football
   Sharon: peanuts[1], bananas, knives and forks, sandwiches
2. *Say what the others are supposed to bring, and where and when they are meeting.*

2 [✎] *Interpreting a cartoon – The picnic: Write a dialogue to go with the cartoon on the right.*

It was a perfect day until a squirrel[2] stole his sandwich and ruined everything.

3 [👥] *Making arrangements:*
Work with a partner and make arrangements for something you can do together one day next week.

a) *First make a plan of all your commitments[3]. (Look at your diary if you keep one.)*
b) *Then decide what you want to do together and discuss details (looking up times, booking tickets, reserving a tennis court, where to meet, how to travel, what to take/wear etc.)*

WORD BANK

Some useful phrases for making plans:
Shall I pick you up? Let's arrange to meet at …
Sorry, I can't manage Friday. I'm meeting … then.
I've got an appointment[4] with … at …
Thursday would suit me better/best.
That's no good, I'm afraid. What about …?
I've got a date[5] with … on … I'm seeing … then.
Shall we book seats/tickets/a court?
When does the performance start? It starts at …
If there's a problem, give me a ring[6].

4 ***Saying the right thing:*** *Jens is staying with the Hamiltons, an English family. His responses to some of their suggestions are a little unfortunate. Explain why and think of more appropriate ones.*

Mrs H:	Would you like to go sailing on Sunday, Jens? The weather forecast for the weekend's great.
Jens:	Sailing? I don't know if I'd like it or not. I've never done any sailing before.
Paul H:	Would you be interested in visiting Windsor Castle?
Jens:	No, I wouldn't, because I've been there before.
Mrs H:	Are you sure you won't have another sandwich, Jens?
Jens:	Thank you. I said before that I was full.
Mr H:	I'm going into town, Jens. Do you want to come? Or is there anything I can get for you?
Jens:	No. Take me with you. I need some things which are indescribable.
Paul H:	How about going to see 'Pirates of the Caribbean' at the cinema this afternoon?
Jens:	Good. I don't mind seeing a film.
Mr H:	Is there anything you'd like to do today, Jens?
Jens:	Yes. Going to the swimming pool would suit me fine.

[1]Erdnüsse • [2]Eichhörnchen • [3]Verpflichtung • [4]Termin • [5]Verabredung (privat) • [6]ruf mich an

Acting responsibly

1 *A look back: Think about the subjects, situations and characters in this Topic. What actions and attitudes would you say are examples of being responsible or irresponsible? Explain.*

2 [group icon] ***Group activity:***

a) *In groups, discuss the different materials (texts, films) you have worked on in terms of these criteria:*

characterization	gender roles	lessons for life
How likeable or unlikeable do the writers make their characters? What narrative techniques help them to achieve this?	How are boys and girls portrayed? What clichés are confirmed and/or broken down in your opinion?	Assuming the writers were trying to make a point, what was the point in each text / situation, how was it made, and how well?

b) *Compare the different groups' results. What similarities / differences are there?*

3 CORE SKILL ***A further extract from*** **Slam*:***

a) *Sam has run away from home and is now in Hastings. Read how the story continues.*

"I need a room," I said.

"For yourself?"

"Yes."

"Where is she?"

"Who?"

"How old would you say I was?"

I looked at her. I'd played this game before, with one of my mum's friends from work. For some reason mum's friend asked me to guess how old she was and I said fifty-six and she was thirty-one and she started crying. It never ends well. And this woman – she definitely wasn't, I don't know, under forty. I don't think. But she could have been sixty-five. How was I supposed to know? So I stood there, probably with my mouth open.

"I'll help you out," said the woman. "Would you say I'm more than one day old?"

"Yes," I said. "Course. You're much older than a day." And even then she sort of frowned a bit at the way I said it, as if I was telling her she was a horrible ancient old witch, whereas all I actually meant was that she wasn't a new-born baby. I mean, what are you supposed to say to these people? 'Oh you look so young you could even be a new-born baby not even a day old?' Is that what they want?

"Right," she said. "So I wasn't born yesterday."

"No." Ah. I got it now.

"And that's how I know you have a girl waiting outside."

A girl! That was too funny. She thought I wanted a room so that I could sleep with a girl in her hotel, when the truth was that I was never going to sleep with anyone for the rest of my life, in case I made her pregnant.

"Come out and look."

"Oh, I know she won't be standing out on the street. You may be naive, but I'm sure you're not actually daft."

"I don't know anyone in Hastings and I don't like girls."

That was a mistake, obviously.

"Or boys. I don't like girls or boys."

And that didn't sound right.

"I like them as friends. But I'm not interested in sharing a room in a B&B with anyone."

"So what are you doing here?" she said.

"It's a long story."

b) *Why has Sam run away from home? Discuss whether he is acting responsibly.*

c) *Is this the way you would have expected the story to develop? Explain your answer.*

4 CORE SKILL ***Narrative techniques:*** *In the extract above, identify and analyze examples of these techniques, all of which are familiar to you:*
character archetypes • narrative perspective • humour →S6, S7

Are you a responsible person?

Start / Yes / No

5 *Think – pair – share:*

a) *Take a few minutes to think of what it means to you to be a responsible person.*

b) [👥] *Discuss your thoughts from a) with a partner. Agree on a definition for 'acting responsibly' and write it down in 1–2 lines.*

c) *Share your ideas with another pair and then report back to the class.*

6 ***Analyzing your actions:*** *Now take this short test to find out how responsible you are.*

Do you get up on time every day?

Do you always get to school on time?

Although you get up late, do you still manage to get to school on time?

Do you always do your homework?

Do you always try to do your best in your school subjects, whether you like them or not?

Do you want to work harder at being on time?

Do you always prepare well for tests?

Would you lie to your teacher about why you don't have your homework ("dog ate it") instead of telling the truth?

Do you feel that since it isn't always possible to be perfect in everything, why even try?

You normally don't believe in cheating in tests, but would you cheat if you felt it was important enough e.g. in an exam situation?

At a party, one of the most popular kids at school offers you drugs. Although you don't take drugs, would you take what he/she offers you?

Do you believe that it doesn't really matter how long it takes you to pay a friend back after borrowing money from him/her?

Your best friend has told you something very private, in confidence. Do you tell your other best friend about it even if you promised you wouldn't?

Your cousins, aged 6 and 8, are at your house. You get a phone call and use a four-letter word. Your cousins giggle. Do you continue using bad language in front of them?

Instead of Periods 1-3 tomorrow morning, there is a special 'Careers Day' assembly. If you don't go, you could sleep longer and arrive at school later. Do you go to the assembly?

Consider yourself a responsible person. You set a good example, and you think about how your actions affect yourself and others.

You know how to be responsible and set a good example – when you feel like it. Try to be more *consistently* responsible.

You don't seem like a responsible person – yet. Work harder at setting a good example and setting better priorities.

7 *Test results:*

a) *Do you agree with your test results? Explain why/why not.*

b) *What is your opinion of tests like these? Are they valid, useful, fun? Are they quickly read and just as quickly forgotten? Explain.*

⟨Revision for tests⟩

TIP
Dictonary work:
Look up the new words of Revision A in a dictionary.

What's your ambition?

Marathon kids: Too young to run?

Two weeks ago Nicholas Burke completed his second marathon in just under three and a half hours. There's nothing sensational about this story – except that Nicholas is only 17.

Nicholas is among a small but growing number of teenagers reported to be completing marathons and 21-kilometer half marathons at important races all over Canada. Their participation highlights one of the most controversial questions in the running world: How young is too young to run 42.2 kilometers? Many adults are worried about these young competitors, fearing that some are being forced to dangerous extremes by over-ambitious parents. Marathons can cause permanent injury to growing bodies, say some sports doctors, who warn that the road race may be the newest sports arena where children's bodies are being pushed too hard. On the other hand, so many organizations are worried about overweight kids and their sedentary lifestyle of computers, TV and cars that running programs for the young are now promoted at marathon events all over North America – and they are becoming very popular. One doctors' organization sees nothing wrong in letting children run marathons, as long as they train properly.

But does it have to be the full 42.2-kilometer marathon? "Yes," Nicholas says. He caught the marathon bug at 10, when he saw athletes on TV running over the finish line at the Boston Marathon. By 12, he was running two kilometers a night after dinner. At 15, he completed his first five-kilometer competitive race. Not being able to find a running coach in the small Canadian village where he lives, Nicholas followed a 6-month marathon training program online. "My doctor gave me the green light, too," he said, "so my mom quit worrying about my health."

Nicholas's goal is to qualify for the race that first inspired him: the Boston Marathon. By the time he has to qualify in May, Nicholas will be 18 and thus able to meet Boston's age requirement. "When I run, I get this fantastic feeling," he says. "That it's my own time and everything, just for me. – And nobody can stop me."

1 ***Understanding the text:** Which answer is correct?*

1. Nicholas Burke is in the news
   a) because he has won a marathon.
   b) because of his age.
   c) because he is a fast runner.
2. There is often a danger that
   a) parents worry too much.
   b) kids like to go to extremes.
   c) parents expect too much.
3. Some doctors say that
   a) marathons should be run in arenas.
   b) some children already train more than is good for them.
   c) marathons help young people's bodies to grow.
4. Others see marathons as a way of getting
   a) children to eat less.
   b) more children to train properly.
   c) children to exercise more.
5. When Nicholas was 15
   a) he ran in his first running race.
   b) he won his first race.
   c) he started training regularly.
6. Nicholas trained with the help of a website because
   a) his doctor recommended it.
   b) he didn't have any help locally.
   c) he didn't have to train outside all the time.
7. Next May Nicholas hopes to
   a) be fast enough for the New York Marathon.
   b) win the Boston Marathon.
   c) qualify for the Boston Marathon.

2 [◎] ***Listening – The life of a 'wunderkind':***

a) *Listen to this radio interview with Wendy Long and find the right answers.*

1. Wendy took part in her first competition when
   a) she was 3.
   b) she was 5.
   c) she was 12.
2. The teachers at Wendy's school
   a) liked having a famous pupil.
   b) gave her extra lessons before exams.
   c) bought Wendy's CDs.
3. Wendy is sad that she missed
   a) some parts of her school education
   b) normal life among schoolfriends
   c) the chance to take up other hobbies.
4. Most of Wendy's recordings are of
   a) jazz.
   b) classical music.
   c) jazz and world music.
5. People say that some parents of a wunderkind
   a) try to influence their child.
   b) think normal schools aren't good enough.
   c) are jealous of their child's success.

b) [✎] *Listen again. Make notes in two lists about the positive and negative aspects of Wendy's life as a wunderkind. (You can use some of your notes for exercise 3.)*

3 [👥] ***Speaking – Should Max take his chance?***

Tom and Jess are talking about Max, the star actor of the school drama group and the local theatre. He has just been offered a leading role in a TV soap. Tom thinks Max should see school as more important and not accept the offer. But Jess feels the opportunity is too good for Max to miss.
Prepare a dialogue between Tom and Jess. Start with your notes from exercise 2b) and add more ideas.

4 [✎] ***Writing – Being ambitious:***

Read these two posts on a forum for teenagers, then write your own post in which you give your opinion.

Are there no normal kids left? Everyone seems crazy with ambition. *Nikki*	If you don't want to win, there's no point in taking part in anything. *BeeJay*

5 ***Mediation – A holiday in Germany:***

Your visitor Malcolm from Ireland would like to know more about the course below. Read the text and summarize the information in English, telling Malcolm what the course offers and what rules there are.

Dieser 3-wöchige Jugendkurs im Januar im Wintersportort Grainau ist die beste Gelegenheit für Jungen und Mädchen zwischen 14 und 17 Jahren Deutsch lernen mit Ski fahren und anderen Wintersportarten zu verbinden.

Die Unterbringung erfolgt in einem gut ausgestatteten Tagungshaus. Die Jugendlichen werden entsprechend ihren Vorkenntnissen in Klassen mit maximal 16 Teilnehmern eingestuft. Sie lernen im Unterricht, sich im deutschen Alltag angemessen zu äußern und grammatische Strukturen richtig anzuwenden.

- 4 bis 6 Unterrichtseinheiten täglich
- insgesamt 12 Stunden Ski- oder Snowboard-Kurs
- Freizeitprogramm
- Unterkunft, Vollpension, Kranken- und Unfallversicherung im Kurspreis enthalten
- Rundumbetreuung

Die Hausordnung wird den Teilnehmerinnen und Teilnehmern am Beginn des Kurses mitgeteilt und ist für alle verbindlich. Sie regelt z.B. Nachtruhe sowie Rauchen und Alkoholkonsum für die entsprechenden Altersgruppen während des Kurses. Bei Verstößen gegen die Hausordnung behält sich unser Team die Benachrichtigung der Eltern vor. Konsequenzen können nötigenfalls bis zum Verweis und dem Ausschluss aus dem Kurs reichen.

Topic 2 Multi-ethnic Britain

In the classroom

On the Underground

WORD BANK
multi-ethnic society • race • minority • the majority of • cultural influence • to belong to • to have the right to do sth • mass immigration • for economic reasons • to judge sb by • physical appearance • statistics • pie chart • compared to • to predict

1 [✎] *In class, collect ideas about the percentage of Black and Asian people there are in the UK and where they live. Can you imagine how they changed the UK (food, film, fashion …)? At the end of the Topic you can look at your ideas again.*

2 a) [✎] *What do you know about the development of a multi-ethnic population in the UK? Use the Fact file and also any other knowledge you may have to help you and note down your ideas.*
b) [✎] [👥] *Think about minority groups in Germany. Why did they come to Germany? Collect and note down information.*

3 ***Looking at statistics:*** →S35
Look at the table, the pie chart and the map, and study the statistics they show. Comment on what you think is important, interesting, or surprising.

4 *What does the cartoon on page 33 say about how people see each other?* →S15

Round the corner

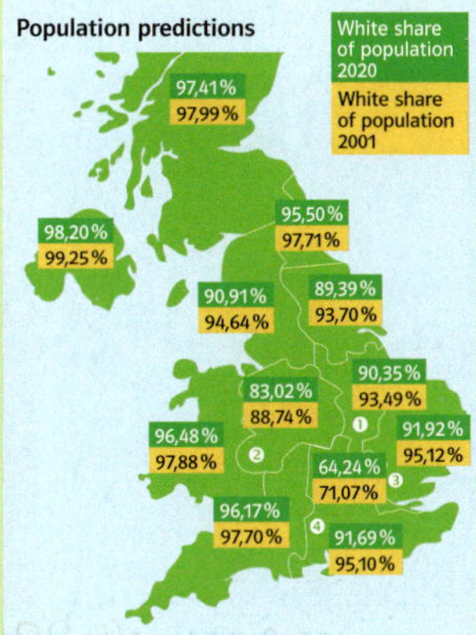

Proportion of ethnic minorities over 50%

Town	Date	Town	Date
❶ Leicester	2019	❸ Luton	2030
❷ Birmingham	2024	❹ Slough	2030

In the family

UK National Statistics Online

Total population: 60 million

Ethnic origin	%		%
White	92.0	Black	2.0
Mixed	1.2	Black Caribbean	1.0
Asian	4.0	Black African	0.8
Indian	1.8	Black Other	0.2
Pakistani	1.3	Chinese	0.4
Bangladeshi	0.5	Other	0.4
Other Asian	0.4		

Britishness perceptions

Do you agree or disagree that 'To be truly British you have to be white'?

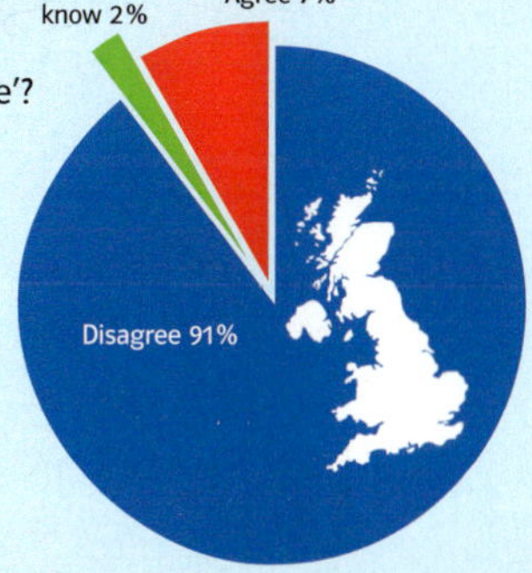

Ipsos MORI interviewed 1001 adults aged 18+ by telephone. Data is weighted to match the profile of the population.

Source: Ipsos MORI

FACT FILE

- Most **ethnic minority British citizens** have their origins in countries belonging to the Commonwealth, a group of nations that were once British colonies. Black people came mainly from the Caribbean while the large majority of Asians were immigrants from India, Pakistan and Bangladesh.
- **Afro-Caribbean people** are descended from slaves from Africa, many of whom were transported to the Caribbean by British ships and sold to British plantation owners until Britain stopped the slave trade there in 1807.
- **Until the middle of the 20th century** the British population was mainly white. The mass immigration of Blacks and Asians after the Second World War, during which men from across the Empire had fought for Britain, was started by the need for more workers in the British economy.
  Although at first all **Empire and Commonwealth citizens** had the right to enter Britain because they carried a British passport, by the 1970s new and stricter rules had started to control immigration.
- Most immigrants arriving in the UK now come from countries in **eastern Europe**.
- The fastest-growing ethnic group in the UK today is **'mixed race'**.

"This is Singh. He wants to join our gang."

Caribbean London

1 ***Brainstorming:*** *What ideas do all of you have about the Caribbean?*

2 a) *Read the text and identify the Caribbean influences found in London.*
b) *Which of your ideas in exercise 1 were right or wrong?*

FACT FILE
These Caribbean islands, which were once British colonies, are independent nations, each with their own identity and culture.

[1]**Jamaica** [dʒəˈmeɪkə]
[1]**Trinidad** [ˈtrɪnɪdæd]
[1]**Barbados** [bɑːˈbeɪdɒs]
[1]**St. Lucia** [snt ˈluːʃə]
[7]**to contribute** [kənˈtrɪbjuːt] to help achieve sth
[13]**encounter** *Begegnung*
[16]**abuse** [əˈbjuːs] *here Übergriff*
[28]**Black History Month** programme of entertainment and education organised by local communities to celebrate Afro-Caribbean culture and achievement

Jamaica, Trinidad, Barbados and St Lucia are just a few of the Caribbean islands represented in London. The strength of Caribbean culture can be felt across the capital – from arts to food to language.

London would be quite different if Caribbean people had not come here. The relationship between the Caribbean and Britain has been long and sometimes troubled. The slave trade, and later the colonisation of the Caribbean by the British Empire has contributed greatly to the prosperity of Britain today.

The distance between Britain and the Caribbean soon closed when Caribbean people answered the calls from British industries to help rebuild a post-war nation. When people started to arrive in larger numbers from the Caribbean in the late 1940s, they left the ships with a passion and excitement for the place they considered to be the "Motherland".

First encounters with London were often less than welcoming. Finding a home or a room to rent was a difficult task for Caribbeans. Rooms were often in bad condition and they were charged extortionate rents. Caribbean people could experience physical and racial abuse and found it hard to get work. Some had to accept jobs with low wages that no one else wanted to do. When British industries did start to employ Caribbeans in larger numbers, they often came into conflict with trade unionists who objected to working with Caribbean people.

Police protection was not adequate and some black people experienced harassment from the police themselves. Caribbean children had to deal with verbal and physical abuse in the education system.

Such harsh treatment may have been the spur that urged London's Caribbeans to develop self-help organisations. The failure to achieve recognition in the mainstream press led to the launch of The Voice newspaper – one of the first aimed at a black audience in Britain. And frustration at the lack of information about their history and origins led some Caribbeans to press for Black History Month, which has now become part of the education calendar for many schools and institutions every October.

Over half a century later, many people from the Caribbean consider London to be their home, and later generations are well-established in the capital. Brixton and Notting Hill were the first areas to house Caribbeans. To this day,

Brixton is often considered to be the Caribbean Capital of Britain, though the Caribbean influence is not confined to just a few areas but spreads right across our city.

Many of today's Caribbean Londoners have become business people, running their own restaurants, barbers, nightclubs, bookshops and grocers. Others have achieved high positions in big business and public life. The strength of the black pound is so great that it can no longer be ignored and Caribbean Londoners find themselves singled out for attention by advertisers.

Over half a century since people from the Caribbean started to arrive in London in large numbers their influence is widespread throughout London's social and cultural life. A host of actors, musicians, presenters, sportspeople and politicians who are second and third generation Caribbeans, are dynamic role models for future generations.

On the *BBC* website

41 **the black pound** all the money that black people have available to spend on products and services

Caribbeans now

3 *Text analysis:*

a) ***Examining the structure:***

1. *Divide the text into parts and say whether each part deals with the present or the past. How does this help to structure the text?* → S1, S3
2. *Note down the keywords or facts in each part.*

b) ***Looking at the language:*** *Describe the style in which the text is written. Think about: the length and complexity of the sentences; the forms and structures used; the choice of vocabulary.* → S3

WORD BANK
the present • historical background • (in)formal language • subordinate clauses • of French / Latin origin • shocked and disappointed • homesick • second-class citizen • racial / verbal abuse • low wages • (to) rent • fear • prejudice

4 *Discussing the content:*

1. *How did the first immigrants feel when they first arrived in Britain?*
2. *How were people from the Caribbean treated in Britain in the early years?*
3. *What information does the text give about the influence people of Caribbean origin have had on London over the past fifty years?*

5 CORE SKILL ***Writing a summary:*** *Use your notes from exercise 3a) and summarize the text. First make sure that you know how to plan and write a summary of a factual text.* → S20, S24

6 ***Listening:*** *Teacher and community social worker Mary Douglas, whose father was an immigrant from Jamaica, was born and still lives in Birmingham. Listen to part of a radio interview and find out what she says. Make notes and use them to give a short summary of the interview.*

7 ***Watching a video clip:*** *Watch the video clip on Caribbeans in the UK and describe the following: the function of the 'front room' in a West Indian home • childhood memories – good or bad? • the atmosphere of a typical front room as seen in this clip*

8 CORE SKILL ***Collaborative writing – A factual text:*** *Working with a partner or in small groups, write a website text about one of the minority groups in Germany. Include information about the origins of the people in that group and how they contribute to German society today. Work like this:*
If necessary, do more research. → *Decide what information you want to include and collect the vocabulary you need.* → *Using the structure of the BBC text to help you, make a plan.* → *Each of you writes a part of the text (example: a section about the present / past, the conclusion …).*
→ *Having put the parts together, check and improve the complete text.* → S23, S24

TIP
- Use formal style in a factual text: long forms, complete sentences, participle constructions etc.
- Do not include your own opinions in a factual text.

⟨Family differences⟩

The Buddha of Suburbia

The following two texts are both by Hanif Kureishi. The first text is an extract from 'The Buddha of Suburbia', Kureishi's funny and satirical novel about a British Asian teenage boy growing up in the suburbs of South London in the early 1980s. This teenager, Karim, is the narrator of the story, and the other characters mentioned are Anwar, a close friend of Karim's father, Anwar's wife Jeeta and their daughter Jamila.

Jamila had started exercising every day, learning karate and judo, getting up early to run. She was preparing for the guerilla war she knew would be necessary when the whites finally turned on the blacks and Asians.

This wasn't as ludicrous as it sounded. The area in which Jamila lived was closer to London than our suburbs, and poorer. It was full of neo-fascist groups. At night they roamed the streets, beating Asians. Many of Jamila's attitudes were inspired by the possibility that a white group might kill one of us one day.

Anwar didn't like these training sessions of hers. He thought she was meeting boys at these karate classes and long runs through the city.

Soon Anwar got a phone installed and started to lock himself in the living room with it for hours. The rest of the time the phone was locked. Anwar had secretly decided it was time Jamila got married.

Through these calls Anwar's brother in Bombay had fixed up Jamila with a boy eager to come and live in London as Jamila's husband. Except that this boy wasn't a boy. He was thirty. As a dowry the ageing boy had demanded a warm winter overcoat, a colour television and the complete works of Conan Doyle.

Anwar had told Jamila what he'd decided: she was to marry the Indian and he would come over, slip on his overcoat and wife and live happily ever after.

Then Anwar would rent a flat nearby for the newly-weds. "Big enough for two children," he said to Jamila. He took her hand and added, "Soon you'll be very happy." Her mother said, "We're both very glad for you, Jamila."

Not surprisingly for someone with Jamila's beliefs, Jamila wasn't too pleased.

"What did you say to him?" I asked, as we walked.

"Creamy, I'd have walked out there and then. I'd have got the Council to take me into care. Anything. I'd have lived with friends, done a runner. Except for my mother. He abuses her."

"Hits her? Really?"

"He used to, yes, until I told him I'd cut off his hair with a knife if he did it again. But he knows how to make her life terrible without physical violence. He's had many years of practice."

"Well," I said, "in the end he can't make you do anything you don't want to."

She turned on me. "But he can! You know my father well, but not that well. There's something I haven't told you. Come with me. Come on, Karim."

We went back to their shop, where she quickly made me a kebab and chapati with onions and green chillis.

"Bring it upstairs, will you, Karim?" she said.

Her mother called through to us from the till. "No, Jamila, don't take him up there!" And she banged down a bottle of milk and frightened a customer.

"What's wrong, Auntie Jeeta?" I asked. She was going to cry.

"Come on." Jamila pulled me upstairs, her mother shouting after her, "Jamila, Jamila!"

VIP FILE

Hanif Kureishi
- born 1954
- mother English, father Pakistani
- many plays, films and novels about multi-ethnic Britain

13 **to fix up** (coll) *here* to bring together two people to make them marry
15 **dowry** *Mitgift*
16 **Conan Doyle** British author (1859–1930) who invented the character Sherlock Holmes
24 **Creamy** Jamila's nickname for Karim
24 **the Council** *here* social workers employed by the local government
25 **to do a runner** (coll) *abhauen*

By now I wanted to go home; I'd had enough of family dramas.

Half-way up the stairs I smelled something rotten. Their flat was always a junk shop, but it never stank, except of Jeeta's wonderful cooking, which went on permanently in big burnt pans.

Anwar was sitting on a bed in the living room, which wasn't his normal bed in its normal place. He was wearing a mouldy-looking pyjama jacket, and I noticed that his toenails resembled cashew nuts. For some reason his mouth was hanging open. He was unshaven, and thinner than I'd ever seen him. His skin looked yellow and his eyes were sunken. Next to the bed was a dirty pot with piss in it. I'd never seen anyone dying before, but I was sure Anwar qualified. Anwar was staring at my kebab as though it were a torture instrument. I chewed speedily to get rid of it.

"Why didn't you tell me he's sick?" I whispered to Jamila.

But I wasn't convinced that he was simply sick. She was glaring at her old man, but he wouldn't meet her eyes. He stared straight in front of him as he always did at the television screen, except that it wasn't on.

"He's not ill," she said.

"No?" I said, and then, to him, "Hallo, Uncle Anwar. How are you, boss?"

His voice was changed: it was weak now. "Take that damn kebab out of my nose," he said. "And take that damn girl with you."

Jamila touched my arm. "Watch." She sat down on the bed and leaned towards him. "Please, please stop all this."

"Get lost!" he croaked. "You're not my daughter. I don't know who you are."

"Please stop it! Here, Karim who loves you –"

"Yes, yes!" I said.

"He's brought you a tasty kebab!"

"Why is he eating it himself, then?" Anwar said. She snatched the kebab from me and waved it in front of her father, bits of meat and chilli and onion scattering over the bed. Anwar ignored it.

"What's going on here?" I asked her.

"Look at him, Karim, he hasn't eaten or drunk anything for eight days! He'll die, Karim, won't he, if he doesn't eat anything!"

"Yes. You'll cop it, boss, if you don't eat."

"I won't eat. I will die. If Gandhi could shove out the English from India by not eating, I can get my family to obey me by exactly the same."

"What do you want her to do?"

"To marry the boy I have selected with my brother."

"But it's old-fashioned, Uncle," I explained. "No one does that kind of thing now. They just marry the person they're into, if they bother to get married at all."

"That is not our way, boy. She must do what I say or I will die. She will kill me."

Jamila started to punch the bed.

"It's so stupid! What a waste of time and life!"

Anwar was unmoved. I'd always liked him because he was so casual about everything; he wasn't like my parents. Now he was making a big fuss about a marriage and I couldn't understand it. I know it made me sad to see him do this to himself. I couldn't believe the things people did to themselves. It wasn't as if circumstances forced them; it was illusion in the head.

Anwar's irrationality was making me tremble, I can tell you. I know I kept shaking my head. Even happiness was irrelevant here – Jamila's happiness, I mean. Like her I wanted to express myself physically in some way. It seemed to be all that was left to us.

74 **to cop it** (slang) to die
80 **to be into sb** (coll) to like or love sb
85 **to make a fuss** *einen Aufstand machen*

VIP FILE

Mahatma Gandhi (1869–1948)
helped to end British rule in India through non-violent protest, including hunger strike

I kicked Uncle Anwar's piss-pot so that a small wave of urine splashed against the bed-sheets. He ignored me. Jamila and I stood there, about to walk out. But now I was making my uncle sleep in his own piss. Hadn't he always been kind to me? Hadn't he always accepted me exactly as I was? I fetched a wet cloth. It was irrational of me to hate his irrationality so much that I sprayed piss over his bed. But as I scrubbed his sheet I realized he had no idea what I was doing on my knees beside him.

Jamila came outside while I unlocked my bike.

"What are you going to do, Jammie?"

"I don't know. What do you suggest?"

"I don't know either."

"No."

"But I'll think about it," I said. "I promise I'll come up with something."

"Thanks."

She started to cry, not covering her face or trying to stop. Usually I get embarrassed when girls cry. Sometimes I feel like clouting them for making a fuss. But Jamila really was in the shit. We must have stood there outside Paradise Stores for at least half an hour, just holding each other and thinking about our futures.

[108] **to clout** (coll) to hit
[109] **in the shit** (vulg) in trouble
[109] **Paradise Stores** the name of Anwar and Jeeta's shop

WORD BANK
strong-willed • attitude • independent • to convey • tension • oppressive • frustration • to identify with • arranged marriage • conflicting viewpoints • to put pressure on • to feel responsible for • a sense of guilt • to tear sb / sth apart

1 ***Looking at the characters:***
a) *In two sentences each: What could the futures of Jamila and Anwar be?*
b) [✎] *What impression do you get of Jamila? Scan the extract for actions, behaviour and opinions that tell you what kind of person she is. Make notes, and then use your notes to write a character outline.* →S5, S23
c) *If you were in Jamila's situation, what would you do?*

2 ***Thinking about the atmosphere:*** *Describe the atmosphere created in the text.* →S7

3 ***Summarizing the content:*** *How do lines 79–81 (from: "But it's old-fashioned, Uncle …" to "… she will kill me.") present the conflict in a nutshell? What exactly is the problem?*

My son the fanatic

This second text by Kureishi is an extract from the story 'My son the fanatic'. Parvez, a London taxi driver originally from Punjab, is telling a friend named Bettina about his son Ali.

"What's happened?"

"I've just had the worst experience of my life."

As Bettina rubbed his head Parvez told her that the previous evening he and Ali had gone to a restaurant. As they studied the menu, the waiter, whom Parvez knew, brought him his usual whisky and water. Parvez had been so nervous he had even prepared a question. He was going to ask Ali if he was worried about his exams. But first, wanting to relax, he loosened his tie, crunched a popadom, and took a long drink.

Before Parvez could speak, Ali made a face.

"Don't you know it's wrong to drink alcohol?" he said.

"He spoke to me very harshly," Parvez told Bettina. "I was about to castigate the boy for being insolent, but managed to control myself."

Parvez ['pɑ:vez]
Punjab [pʌn'dʒɑ:b] region in north-west India and Pakistan
[7] **popadom** ['pɒpədəm] thin piece of Indian bread cooked in oil

He had explained patiently to Ali that for years he had worked more than ten hours a day, that he had few enjoyments or hobbies and never went on holiday. Surely it wasn't a crime to have a drink when he wanted one?

"But it is forbidden," the boy said.

Parvez shrugged. "I know."

"And so is gambling, isn't it?"

"Yes. But surely we are only human?"

Each time Parvez took a drink, the boy winced or made a face. This made Parvez drink more quickly. The waiter, wanting to please his friend, brought another glass of whisky. Parvez knew he was getting drunk, but he couldn't stop himself. Ali had a horrible look on his face, full of disgust. It was as if he hated his father.

Halfway through the meal, Parvez suddenly lost his temper and threw a plate on the floor. He had felt like ripping the cloth from the table, but the waiters and other customers were staring at him. Yet he wouldn't stand for his own son telling him the difference between right and wrong. He knew he wasn't a bad man. He had a conscience. There were a few things of which he was ashamed, but on the whole he had lived a decent life.

"When have I had time to be wicked?" he asked Ali.

In a low monotonous voice the boy explained that Parvez had not, in fact, lived a good life. He had broken countless rules of the Koran.

"For instance?" Parvez demanded.

Ali hadn't needed time to think. As if he had been waiting for this moment, he asked his father if he didn't relish pork?

"Well …"

Parvez couldn't deny that he loved bacon sandwiched between slices of fried bread. In fact he ate this for breakfast every morning.

Ali then reminded Parvez that he had ordered his own wife to cook pork sausages, saying to her, "You're not in the village now, this is England. We have to fit in!" Parvez was so annoyed and perplexed by this attack that he called for more drink.

"The problem is this," the boy said. He leaned across the table. For the first time that night his eyes were alive. "You are too implicated in Western civilization."

Parvez burped; he thought he was going to choke. "Implicated!" he said. "But we live here!"

"The Western materialists hate us," Ali said. "Papa, how can you love something which hates you?"

"What is the answer then?" Parvez said miserably. "According to you."

Ali addressed his father fluently as if Parvez were a rowdy crowd that had to be convinced. The Law of Islam would rule the world; the skin of the infidel would burn off again and again. The West was a sink of hypocrites, homosexuals, drug takers and prostitutes.

As Ali talked, Parvez looked out of the window as if to check that they were still in London.

"My people have taken enough. If the persecution doesn't stop there will be jihad. I, and millions of others, will gladly give our lives for the cause."

"But why, why?" Parvez said.

"For us, the reward will be in Paradise."

"Paradise!"

Finally, as Parvez's eyes filled with tears, the boy urged him to mend his ways.

23 **disgust** *Abscheu*
25 **to lose one's temper** to get very angry
33 **Koran** main religious book of Islam
42 **attack** *Angriff*
45 **implicated** *Teil von sein*
58 **persecution** *Verfolgung*
59 **jihad** Arabic word which for militant Islamists has become a synonym for violent action

"How is that possible?" Parvez asked.

"Pray," Ali said. "Pray beside me."

Parvez called for the bill and ushered his boy out of the restaurant as soon as he was able. He couldn't take any more. Ali sounded as if he'd swallowed someone else's voice.

On the way home the boy sat in the back of the taxi, as if he were a customer.

"What has made you like this?" Parvez asked him, afraid that somehow he was to blame for all this. "Is there a particular event which has influenced you?"

"Living in this country."

"But I love England," Parvez said, watching his boy in the mirror. "They let you do almost anything here."

"That is the problem," he replied.

For the first time in years, Parvez couldn't see straight. He knocked the side of the car against a lorry, ripping off the wing mirror. They were lucky not to have been stopped by the police: Parvez would have lost his licence and therefore his job.

[71] **to blame for** *verantwortlich sein für*

WORD BANK

confrontation • miserable • perplexed • fanatical • extremist views • Islamist • liberal • according to • generation conflict • to reverse (roles) • similar • to lose one's temper • to have a (guilty) conscience • (in)tolerant • to fit in

4 ***Working with the text:***

a) *In two or three sentences, summarize the "worst experience" of Parvez's life. Why is it so bad for him?*

b) [✎] [👥] *One of you picks out words and phrases that show what Ali thinks, while the other looks for words and phrases that show what Parvez thinks. You each make a list for your character and then you tell your partner about him.*

5 [◻] ***Interpretation:***

a) *Check the context and say what is meant by these statements: "But it is forbidden." (line 16); "We have to fit in!" (line 41); "You are too implicated in Western civilization." (line 45); "For us, the reward will be in Paradise." (line 61); "They let you do almost anything here." (line 73)*

b) *Look at the way Parvez and Ali communicate. Explain why their communication doesn't work.*

Exercises for both texts:

6 ***Comparing the texts:*** *Compare and contrast the situations and characters in the two Kureishi texts. Use these questions to help you think and make comments:*

1. *What is the problem in each extract?*
2. *Who is the conflict between?*
3. *What roles do the different generations play?*
4. *What views do they have?* →S3

TIP

"Sympathizing" doesn't always mean you agree with someone. It can also mean you understand the reason for someone's feelings although you don't share their opinion.

7 [◻] ***Discussion:***

a) *Say whether you sympathize with the characters in both texts or not. (You can include Karim, too, if you like.) Give your reasons.*

b) *Discuss which of the two texts you preferred reading and why.*

8 [✎] ***Creative writing:*** *Choose one of the following tasks:* →S23

Either: *A blog of Jamila's in which she writes about her problem and asks for other people's comments.*

Or: *A letter from Parvez to Ali (instead of another argument) suggesting compromises on both sides to help their relationship.*

Ethnic minority characters

Eastenders (TV soap)

Holby City (TV drama)

Bhaji on the beach (feature film)

1 *Look at the title and genre of the British televison and cinema films above. Guess what they might be about.*

2 *Read part of a speech given by Lenny Henry to the Royal Television Society in 2008. Explain the problem he wants his audience to think about.*

"The British public is now becoming used to seeing the occasional black, brown or yellow face in mainstream drama. There's a black actor playing an assistant in Waking the Dead, there's a black actor playing an assistant in Spooks and until recently there was a black actress playing an assistant in Dr Who. Who knows, one day we might actually see a black actor playing someone in charge ... There is still work to do. And while we're about it – let's cut the stereotyping right now: when you can cast a Somalian girl in your piece simply because she is the best actor for the job, when you can cast an Asian actress and she's not the victim of an arranged marriage, when you can cast a Jamaican man with dreadlocks and he's not a drug dealer ... then we will have achieved something. When you can see past their foreignness – and just live with their talent and make a decision based on that, and that alone, then we'll have made a change and I can't wait for that day."

VIP FILE

Lenny Henry
- writer, comedian, actor
- born 1958 in Dudley, England, son of Jamaican immigrants
- campaigns for equal opportunities for ethnic minorities in the media
- also involved in charity work for developing countries

⟨3⟩ [group] ***Project:*** *Get one of these films in English and watch it. In your group, discuss the roles of the Black or Asian person / people in the film. Relate this role / these roles to the speech by Lenny Henry.* →S12

This is England

My beautiful laundrette

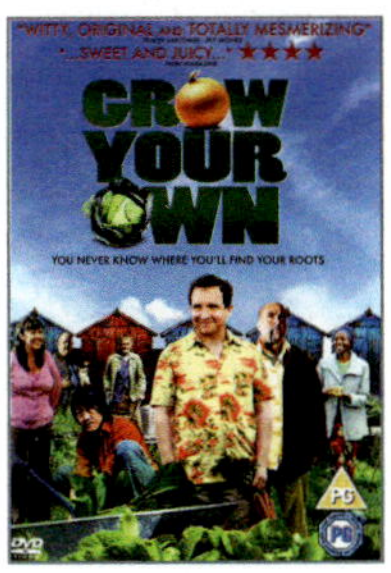

Grow your own

Bhaji on the beach

⟨4⟩ [group] ***Your country:*** *Talk about the situation in Germany. Think of films or television programmes you know that include actors from minority groups or which deal with minority group topics in your society, and discuss how the characters played by these actors are presented. Say what kind of role they play in the film and whether you think this presents a cliché or not.* →S26

Bhaji Indian vegetable dish
[3] **Waking the Dead** TV detective series
[4] **Spooks** TV drama
[5] **Dr Who** TV science fiction series

[ ] ⟨Dub poetry⟩

VIP FILE

Benjamin Zephaniah

- poet and novelist
- born in Birmingham, England in 1958
- grew up in Jamaica and Birmingham, leaving school at 14.
- campaigner for racial equality

FACT FILE

Caribbean English is a dialect which developed during colonial times. Although British English was the main language, it was influenced by the African languages of the slaves brought to work on the plantations.

1 *Dub poetry is written to be performed. Because it is closely linked to reggae music, which started in Jamaica, the language is influenced by Caribbean English. Close your eyes and listen to the following poem by Benjamin Zephaniah. Then say what your first impressions and feelings are.*

Dis poetry

"Dis poetry" is from a collection of poems called "City Psalms".

Dis poetry is like a riddim dat drops
De tongue fires a riddim dat shoots like shots
Dis poetry is designed fe rantin
Dance hall style, big mouth chanting
Dis poetry nar put yu to sleep
Preaching follow me
Like yu is blind sheep,
Dis poetry is not Party Political
Not designed fe dose who are critical
Dis poetry is wid me when I gu to me bed
It gets into me dreadlocks
It lingers around me head
Dis poetry goes wid me as I pedal me bike
I've tried Shakespeare, respect due dere
But did is de stuff I like.

Dis poetry is not afraid of going in a book
Still dis poetry need ears fe hear an eyes fe hav a look
Dis poetry is Verbal Riddim, no big words involved
An if I hav a problem de riddim gets it solved,
I've tried to be more romantic, it does nu good for me
So I tek a Reggae Riddim an build me poetry,
I could try be more personal
But you've heard it all before,
Pages of written words not needed
Brain has many words in store,
Yu could call dis poetry Dub ranting
De tongue plays a beat
De body starts skanking,
Dis poetry is quick an childish
Dis poetry is fe de wise and foolish,
Anybody can do it fe free,
Dis poetry is fe yu and me,
Don't stretch yu imagination
Dis poetry is fe de good of de Nation,
Chant,
In de morning
I chant
In de night
I chant
In de darkness

[2] **to fire** to shoot (with a gun)
[3] **to rant** to shout wildly
[4] **dance hall style** fast reggae music over which a DJ speaks improvised lyrics
[4] **to chant** to speak with a strong rhythm
[6] **to preach** *here* to convince sb with words
[11] **dreadlocks** the style of Zephaniah's hair
[12] **to linger** to stay in one place for a long time
[14] **due** *schuldig; fällig*
[25] **in store** kept in order to use in the future
[28] **to skank** to dance in reggae style

An under de spotlight
I pass thru University
I pass thru Sociology
An den I got a dread degree
In Dreadfull Ghettology.
Dis poetry stays wid me when I run or walk
An when I am talking to meself in poetry I talk,
Dis poetry is wid me,
Below me an above,
Dis poetry's from inside me
It goes to yu
WID LUV.

[41] **spotlight** light shining directly on place or person
[44] **dread** invented adjective
[44] **degree** university qualification
[45] **dreadful** terrible
[45] **Ghettology** invented noun meaning to study ghettos as a subject

2 ***Looking at the style:*** → S8

a) *What kind of poetry does 'Dis poetry' describe? Find examples that show what it is like and what effect it has.*

b) *Why is it different from traditional poetry?*

3 ***'No problem':***

Like most dub poets, Zephaniah often deals with social or political issues. Listen to and then read a poem which deals with his experiences as a child in the British education system. Then summarize in one sentence the message that he wants to give.

No problem

I am not de problem
But I bare de brunt
Of silly playground taunts
An racist stunts,
I am not de problem
I am a born academic
But dey got me on de run
Now I am branded athletic,
I am not de problem
If yu give I a chance
I can teach yu of Timbuktu
I can do more dan dance,
I am not de problem
I greet yu wid a smile
Yu put me in a pigeon hole
But I a versatile.

These conditions may affect me
As I get older,
An I am positively sure
I have no chips on me shoulders,
Black is not de problem
Mother country get it right,
An just for de record
Sum of me best friends are white.

[2] **(to bear) the brunt** (to suffer) the worst part of sth
[3] **taunt** comment to make sb feel angry or hurt
[4] **stunt** action to attract attention
[7] **on the run** trying to get away
[8] **branded** *gebrandmarkt*
[15] **to put in a pigeon hole** to see as a stereotype
[16] **versatile** able to do lots of different things
[20] **to have a chip on one's shoulder** to feel one suffers from disadvantage or prejudice
[23] **for the record** so that the facts are known

4 [⌂] ***Analyzing the poem 'No problem':*** → S8

1. *Who is the speaker in the poem talking to when he says 'yu'?*
2. *What two examples are given of how black people are stereotyped?*
3. *Which phrase is repeated again and again? What effect does this have?*

5 [👥] ***Comparing the two poems:***

a) *In what ways are 'Dis poetry' and 'No problem' similar or different?*

b) *Even when dub poetry has a serious theme, the language is often playful. Find examples in the two poems of how Zephaniah plays with words.*

WORD BANK

a play on words • funny images • words / phrases with two meanings • to play with a familiar phrase • pairs of opposites • to invent new / funny words • irony • to repeat similar sounds

English for everyone

1 ***Pre-reading:*** *What can happen when minority groups arrive in a new country? Think of positive developments and also possible problems.*

Hope of escape lost in translation

"Providing interpreters instead of encouraging immigrants to speak English keeps them in their ghettos", says **Zia Haider Rahman**

It's a shocking figure: more than £100m was spent in the past year on translating and interpreting for British residents who don't speak English. The financial cost is bad enough, but there is a wider problem about the confused signals we are sending to immigrant communities. We are telling them they don't have to learn English, let alone integrate.

The evidence is plain to anyone who visits Brick Lane in the East End of London. In the Bangladeshi community from which I come, English is a foreign language. Even the street signs are in Bengali. Every year Bangladeshis sit at the bottom of rankings of educational achievement. Their society persists in economic stagnation. Drug abuse and crime are on the rise in the East End. Illiterate young Bangladeshi males, with no hope of employment, can choose between extremists in the mosques or the gangs in the streets.

I didn't speak a word of English when I arrived in Britain, but I learnt quickly. I was lucky. My parents were determined not to be absorbed into the East End, which represented a recreation of the country they had left. My parents wanted to learn English and wanted me to do so, too.

My parents' aspirations were reinforced by my primary school head. It was the mid-1970s and I was a rarity as a Bangladeshi pupil, although my teachers made no acknowledgement of my racial difference. By contrast, schools today seem intent on celebrating difference. I'm not convinced this helps.

"Awareness-raising programmes" are all the rage – we have to celebrate our diversity. But you don't learn to stand on your own two feet if someone is holding you up. Indulging differences can be harmful if it prevents communities from integrating.

I believe we should curb the translation and interpreting services, and think about making English compulsory for all citizens. Public figures are understandably fearful of being labelled racist. But the greater danger lies in not speaking up. There is much to be gained in getting us all to speak English.

The Sunday Times

2 ***Thinking about the issue:*** *What is the main point that the writer of the article wants to make? What reasons does he give for his opinion? How do you think someone with the opposite point of view might react?*

3 ***Collecting arguments for and against:***

a) *Starting with the ideas expressed in exercise 2, collect arguments for and against encouraging immigrants to learn the language of their new country. Make two lists with as many arguments as you can think of.*

b) *Compare your ideas with another pair's.*

4 CORE SKILL ***Writing an argumentative essay:*** *Write an essay discussing the statement: 'All immigrants should attend language classes in their new country.' The arguments you collected in exercise 3 can help you.* →S19

5 ***Mediation – Summarizing a text:*** →S34

a) *A British friend told you that students at her school in London speak lots of different languages. You thought that she might be interested in this article you found on the Internet. Read the article and pick out the main points.*

b) *Give a short summary in English in your own words.*

c) *Write a summary in English for your friend.* →S20

TIP

In argumentative or comment essays:

- divide your text into clear parts and paragraphs.
- write in formal style.
- use connecting words to link arguments.
- include your own opinions if you like.

OHNE SPRACHE, KEIN WISSEN

Gute Deutschkenntnisse sind an einer Lehranstalt, deren Schüler zu 90 Prozent aus Zuwandererfamilien stammen, keine Selbstverständlichkeit. Auch nicht an der Herbert-Hoover-Schule. Die Berliner Schule hatte sich deshalb entschlossen, den Deutschkenntnissen mit einer besonderen Maßnahme auf die Sprünge zu helfen: Deutsch ist nicht nur im Unterricht die Pflichtsprache, sondern auch in den Pausen und auf Klassenfahrten.

Was für die Schüler der Herbert-Hoover-Schule Alltag ist, sorgt bundesweit für Diskussionen. Befürworter träumen schon vom Ende aller Integrationsprobleme, wenn Deutsch als Schulhofsprache gesetzlich vorgeschrieben würde. Kritiker sehen darin die Verletzung der Persönlichkeitsrechte und warnen vor einer staatlich betriebenen Diskriminierung.

Einen anderen Weg hat die Heinrich-Wolgast-Schule in Hamburg gewählt. Auf der deutsch-türkischen Grundschule wird in beiden Sprachen unterrichtet. „Die Erfahrungen sind sehr gut," sagt Schulleiterin Petra Demmin. In der Pause wechselten die türkischen Kinder unbewußt ins Deutsche, sobald ein deutsches Kind dazustoße. „Die Gefahr der Ausgrenzung der einen oder anderen Gruppe besteht daher nicht." Das Deutschgebot der Berliner Schule sieht die Pädagogin dagegen kritisch: „Für die Integration ist es wichtig, die Muttersprache und damit die Identität wertzuschätzen."

Andererseits sind es auch an der Berliner Herbert-Hoover-Schule vor allem nichtdeutsche Eltern, die das Konzept der Schule unterstützen. Sie sehen darin die Voraussetzung für einen guten Schulabschluß ihrer Kinder und für mehr Chancengleichheit im deutschen Ausbildungssystem.

„Unser Deutsch ist wirklich besser geworden," versichert Schülersprecher Asad Suleiman, 17 – auch wenn er zugibt, daß viele sich nicht immer an die Deutschpflicht halten. Und was passiert in einem solchen Fall? „Sanktionen oder Kontrollen gibt es bei uns nicht," sagt der stellvertretende Schulleiter Hans-Joachim Schriefer. Denn natürlich gehe es an seiner Schule nicht darum, die Muttersprache zu unterdrücken, vielmehr sollten die Voraussetzungen für eine gemeinsame Sprache geschaffen werden.

Welt online

Developing fluent and concise written style

1 *Revision: Participle constructions:* →G5

a) *Study all the participles (marked like* this *) in the article. Name the form (present, past, perfect) and say how they are used: as adjectives, in place of relative clauses, to express reason or time, to link two main clauses, after a verb of perception and an object.*

b) *Comment on how the participles help to improve the style of the article.*

Although the sun did not appear at the weekend, this did not put off the crowds filling the streets for the Notting Hill Carnival. Having come to join the party, everyone just wanted to have fun.

As every year, the parade of colourful costumes was the highlight, providing a fantastic contrast with the grey sky above. Visitors were also able to choose from hundreds of stalls selling all kinds of food and drink and to listen to bands playing world music. Having started in 1964 as a small local festival organized by immigrants from Trinidad, the Notting Hill Carnival is now the biggest street event in Europe, and while Caribbean traditions are still at its heart, it has developed and grown, bringing many different cultures together.

Reporting their view of the Carnival, the police said it had been a great success. Hoping to prevent the usual problem of pick-pocketing, they had put up warning signs, and this seemed to have worked. As a result, they also had time to enjoy themselves. Johannes Schulz from Germany told our reporter: "It was a surprise to see a police officer playing in a steel drum band!"

2 *Participles after verbs expressing rest or movement:* →G5

a) *Look at the following sentences and comment on the position of the participle after verbs expressing rest or movement. How would you translate these sentences into German?*

The gang *went* running down the street. People *stood* watching at their windows.

b) *The text below is a true story told by Peterborough teenager Ricki Elliot.*
Find the correct pairs of verbs and put in the right tenses and forms.
come / march • stay / live • go / look • hang around / wait • sit / talk • stand / shout • lie / bleed

"I used to be the leader of the local white gang. In the evenings we always 1 in the street until the enemy arrived. Shaahid, a British Pakistani, and his Asian gang were always looking for trouble, too. They 2 towards us aggressively, stopping before they got to us. Then both gangs 3 racist names at each other. Sometimes this developed into fights. At the end of one fight I 4 on the ground after I had been hit with a hammer.

Finally the Youth Service got involved. Shaahid and I were told we couldn't 5 in our world of prejudice and hate and were sent away together to learn how to get on. Although at first we did not like this idea, in the end we 6 all night and discovered that we liked the same music, the same football team, and also each other!

Now when Shaahid and I 7 for each other, it is not to fight the enemy – it is to meet a friend."

3 ***Present, past, perfect participles:*** *Complete the article with the correct participle forms.* →G5

A young businessman (live) in Birmingham is starting a new community magazine for black youths in the city. (feel) little hope himself in the past, Andrew Lindo understands that black teenagers often have low expectations. So (want) to show them positive role models, he is featuring successful black people in his magazine.

"I left school (think) I had no chance of an (interest) career," he says. "But now I am a (qualify) graphic designer. If young black people (read) my magazine see a black doctor or a black lawyer (achieve) success, it will help them to be more ambitious themselves."

(have) the idea of the magazine over two years ago, Andrew has finally almost completed the first edition. He explains that the name (choose) for it, Wispa, has its origins in black history. "(live) as slaves, black people had to whisper because they couldn't be seen (talk) to each other. The title means that you can give an important message (speak) quietly."

He plans to print 5,000 copies of Wispa, (hope) to attract lots of readers and also the advertisers (need) to help with costs. It is a (challenge) project, but Andrew feels strongly about the problems (affect) young black people. (manage) to create his own magazine, he himself is a role model, (show) how talent and energy can be used to improve people's lives.

4 ***Improving the style:*** →G5

a) *Rewrite the text using participles in place of clauses or to link ideas.*

b) [👥] *Compare texts with a partner. Where they are different, discuss whose version is better.*

Madhur Jaffrey was born in India in 1933. She came to Britain at the age of 19 because she wanted to study drama. It was actually in Britain that she learned to cook Indian food. After she had arrived in London, she missed her favourite dishes from home. Although she had sometimes watched while her mother cooked them, she had never made them herself. So she wrote home. She asked for the recipes.

When she left drama school in 1957 Jaffrey became an actress. In her free time, however, she cooked for her friends, and because they had never tasted such delicious food, they got her to write an Indian cookery book. Because she knew that the people who would use the book would not be familiar with "real" Indian food, she kept it simple. It was a huge success. It led to more books and also television programmes.

After they had seen Jaffrey on television, more and more people wanted to cook her dishes themselves, and you can say that the choice of Indian ingredients that are sold in shops now is a direct result of her programmes. If you listen to British people when they talk about their favourite food today, it is clear that the Indian influence is greater then ever. Words like popadom, naan and chicken tikka masala have now become everyday words in English.

5 [📄] [✍] ***Writing your own text:*** *Think of someone from a minority group in Germany who has achieved success or had influence in some way (singer, actor, politician, …). Research, plan and write a text about the person, using participle constructions to help improve your style.* →S23

Avoiding social gaffes in the UK

The activities on this page show three different aspects of social interaction in the UK. Knowing how to deal with situations can save you from making embarrassing social gaffes.

1

2

3

1 ***Everyday life in the UK (I):***
a) *What social rule is the subject of cartoon number 1?*
b) *What other aspects of life in Britain might show up on a 'Britishness test'? Explain why, and how you know about these aspects.*

2 ***Everyday life in the UK (II):***
1. *Look at cartoon number 2. Why doesn't the woman just say she wants coffee after being asked the first time?*
2. [group] *What is the 'social rule' at the heart of the cartoon? In groups, formulate that rule as a tip to anyone travelling to the UK, and then compare your results with the other groups.*
3. *Your country: Discuss whether this social rule applies in your own country.*

3 ***Everyday life in the UK (III):***
1. *Look at cartoon number 3. Explain what social rule the man has not followed.*
2. [pair] *With a partner, rewrite what the man says and turn it into an appropriate conversation starter. Give the woman an appropriate reply.*
3. *Your country: Discuss whether this gaffe could just as easily have happened in your country.*

⟨4⟩ [writing] ***Writing a survival guide of dos and don'ts:*** *Write survival guides with tips for avoiding social gaffes in everyday situations. Divide the class into two groups, each group writing one of these guides:*
- *'Survival guide for Britons visiting Germany'*
- *'Survival guide for Germans visiting the UK'*

Here are some subjects you might want to include:
in public • at home • food / drink • school • conversation • …

TIP
Make your survival guides come to life with **illustrations**, **photos** and **cartoons** about the subjects you are covering.

Looking at food in the UK

The English breakfast

... is still a classic in most hotels. It usually consists of orange juice with any combination of eggs, sausages, bacon, tomatoes and mushrooms, followed by toast and jam, tea or coffee. Porridge and kippers are often served in Scotland, Northern Ireland and the north of England. If you eat all this, you won't need any lunch. Most places offer a buffet breakfast. A continental breakfast consisting of toast or croissants, jam and coffee or tea is, however, becoming more and more popular.

Lunch in a British restaurant ...

Of course you can get a sandwich from a sandwich bar, or eat in a typical café like The Old Greasy Spoon and get your sausages with chips and baked beans. Or you can go to a restaurant and get something which is better, but more expensive.
British food isn't as bad as some people say! If you're lucky, you will still find a traditional fish 'n' chips shop, or 'chippie', where you can get traditional deep-fried fish and chips. You must put vinegar on both – it's the thing to do. Alternatively, there are more and more restaurants and supermarkets offering organic food – even 'organic' meat – that tastes good and is said to be healthy. Organic food is the big trend in the UK.

WORD BANK

- I'd like to try your traditional English breakfast. Could you please explain what ... consists of?
- I think I'll go for the roast beef with Yorkshire pudding, and a mineral water, please.
- I'd like a steak with vegetables and chips, please.
- How would you like your steak done?
- Rare / Medium / Well-done, please!
- Could I have the bill, please? Do you take credit cards?

... and dinner in an Indian • Thai • ... restaurant

Indian restaurants are extremely popular in the UK and most are very good. You can choose a Balti dish or chicken tikka masala or butter chicken with basmati rice or naan bread, have a mango lassi and finish your spicy meal with an Indian chai (spiced tea). Or, if you don't fancy Indian cuisine, there are lots of others you can try. The UK is a multicultural society, so wherever you are, you will probably have a great choice of foods from different countries.

1 [👥] [✎] ***What would you like?***

a) *Read the texts and start three lists for UK food: one for breakfast, one for lunch and one for dinner. Add more ideas of your own.*

b) *Imagine you are in a restaurant in the UK with a friend. You order a meal and something to drink. Write a dialogue and act it out.*

⟨c)⟩ *Design a leaflet or a poster to promote British food. Vote for the best one in class.*

Presenting information about ethnic minorities

1 *Thinking about Topic 2:*

a) *Look back at the ideas you collected in exercise 1 on page 32. Say how they have changed or developed after what you have learned in Topic 2.*

b) [👥] *Design a large mind map around the idea of 'Multi-ethnic Britain' showing as many aspects of the topic as possible: general information, different minority groups, positive influence, problems etc. Perhaps you can use the phrases for the next tasks.*

2 [✎] CORE SKILL ***Writing a short factual text:***
First study the chart about the exam results of ethnic groups in the UK, identifying the comparisons it shows and making notes. Then decide how you want to organize the information. Don't forget to write in a suitable style of language and also to check and improve your work when you have finished. →S23, S24

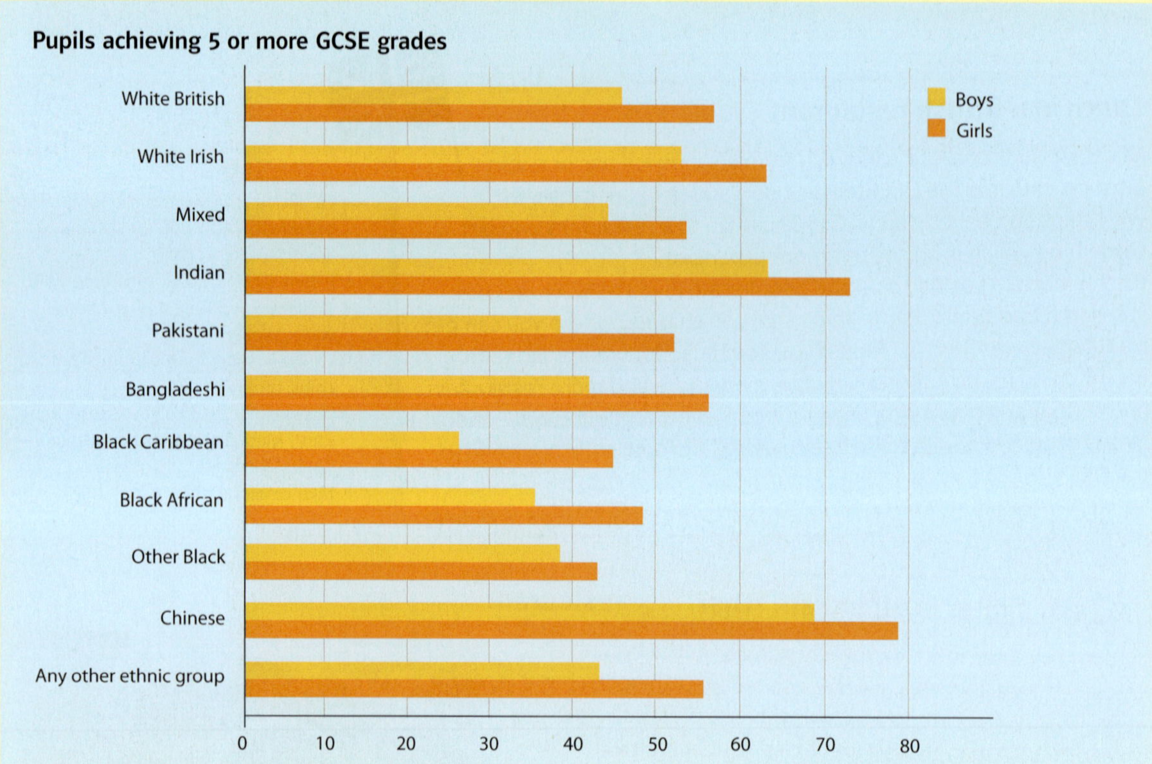

3 [👥] [✎] *What can help people from ethnic minorities to feel that they are accepted as equal citizens by the majority? Discuss this question in your group and write down three things you think are important. Then join with another group and compare your ideas.*

4 [🎬] ***Watching a TV news report – The Notting Hill Carnival:***

a) ***Atmosphere:*** *Watch the short news report and say what adjectives you could use to describe the atmosphere at the carnival, based on what you see in the pictures.*

b) ***Details:*** *1. What anniversary did this particular carnival mark? 2. What information was given in numbers? 3. Is the carnival still as popular as when it first started in 1964? How do you know?*

c) ***Discussion:*** *Judging from what you have seen and heard about the carnival, do you feel it is an example of multi-ethnic Britain being a success story – or not? Give your reasons.*

5 ***Interpreting photos:***
[👥] *"These pictures show that multi-ethnic Britain works." Choose one or two of the photos on this page and do research on the person or topic shown. Then give a presentation, saying whether you think the statement above is correct, and giving your reasons. You can choose how to present the information you want to give.* →S14, S36

Hindus celebrating *Diwali* in London

Lewis Hamilton

Zadie Smith

Caribbean food at a restaurant in Notting Hill

Bradford Mela

Dev Patel

⟨Project⟩ Short story

She doesn't speak *by Marita van der Vyver*

BEFORE YOU READ:

a) *What do the words in the Word bank have in common?*

b) *Brainstorming: What reasons might someone have for not speaking?*

This short story takes place in Britain and South Africa in the present. While you are reading it, think about which elements of a short story (see TIP) it contains. Short stories are supposed to be read in one sitting. So when you read the story for the first time, concentrate on the gist and not on understanding every word.

VIP FILE

Marita van der Vyver
- born 1958 in Cape Town
- studied in South Africa and became a journalist and writer
- has written many novels and short stories
- now lives in southern France

WORD BANK

mute • dumb • silent • chatterbox • talkative • chatty • communicative • talker

TIP

Short story
Short stories often start in an unexpected way ('medias in res' – right in the middle of the action). There is often a turning point in the action and a surprise ending. The action is usually closely packed. Symbols often play an important role.

"Her name is *Anouk* and she doesn't speak."

That is how my mother always introduces me to other people.

My name is *Noekie*, I always say without moving my lips or making a sound. I speak all the time in my head, to myself.

If anybody wants to know more about it she would say: "No, she isn't dumb." Almost casually, as if there was nothing strange about a fourteen-year-old who doesn't speak. "She stopped speaking after experiencing a traumatic incident."

Usually people don't ask any more questions after that. At least not immediately. Usually they would be scared off by the words *traumatic incident*. But later, if they wanted to know more, she would tell them everything. Like a tap that had been opened, the words would just pour from her – how the robbers burst into our lounge one evening and shot my father dead and how she was seriously wounded and how I saw it all while I was hiding behind the kitchen door with the maid, Rebecca. How Rebecca had pushed me behind the door and had held her hand over my mouth while Dad's blood stained the Persian carpet. How she had tried to crawl to her handbag to get to her cell phone while the robbers were searching the bedroom for money or jewels or whatever they were looking for. How she pretended to be dead when they came back into the lounge.

Do you see what I mean? I don't need to speak. My mother speaks enough for both of us.

The robbers had hardly looked at her. They had run out through the verandah door when they saw a car with a blue light patrolling the street. It was a security company's car, a routine patrol, like there was every evening. But the robbers probably didn't know about this. They had probably thought that one of the neighbours had heard suspicious sounds. Usually when my mother gets to this part of the story she gives a dejected little laugh: "Even if someone had suspected something," she would add, "they wouldn't have been able to see anything from the street. A few months before, my husband had built a high wall around the property to protect us."

My mother believes that the more you talk about a difficult thing the easier it will be to bear – my mother and all the psychologists I have already seen. But as yet, no one has been able to tell me about what you should do when something is so difficult that you simply can't talk about it. In the beginning I really tried. Forcing the sounds out of my throat like dry vomit. They said that if I forced myself to speak about it I would stop dreaming about it. But after a few awful sessions with a psychologist the nightmares just got worse.

"It was Rebecca who dialled the emergency number and got the ambulance to come. Saved my life. And Anouk's. If the child had made a single sound ..."

7 **incident** *here* event that causes a crisis
11 **robber** thief
14 **Rebecca** [rɪ'bekə]
23 **security company** *Sicherheitsdienst*
26 **dejected** sad
31 **psychologist** *Psychologe, Psychologin*
34 **vomit** *Erbrochenes*
36 **nightmare** very bad dream

The 'veld'

What my mother doesn't say is that maybe we could have saved my father's life, too. Maybe if I had slipped out the back door and called the neighbours, if I had stayed calm and done something. If I had just acted like Buffy against the vampires or someone like that. But I went rigid, scared stiff. Mute.

"And that is why we are living in England now."

That is how my mother always ends her story. As if the attack was the only reason why we had left. She doesn't say that she had wanted to go and live in England long before the attack. Her father was British and she had the right passport. She had always stood with one foot in the sea, ready to emigrate, every time she read a newspaper heading that scared her. It was my father who didn't want to go. He loved his country. So did I.

"I'm not going anywhere," Dad had said in his quiet way. "Over my dead body."

Then he died. And then we left.

It's almost three years since we moved. We live in a quiet village east of London where everything is so green that after a while you start longing for something pale and dry to look at. Brown soil that has been baked dry, this is what I miss. Soil that burns your feet, like on my father's family farm in the Free State. Pale veld and a cloudless sky and the taste of dust.

My mother doesn't miss anything. At least that is what she says. She didn't even want to come back on a holiday. I think she is scared to see all the things she misses. But now we are here on holiday – because she thinks it will be good for me. She wants to see me laugh again. But we have been back for a week already and I still haven't seen anything that makes me want to laugh.

"Doesn't she want to talk?" asks one of my mother's friends. She wears far too much make-up. All my mother's old friends from Pretoria wear far too much make-up. But this one's neck almost snaps from all the mascara. "Or is it that she can't talk?"

I am sitting on the other side of the same room, reading. People seem to think that if you can't speak you also can't hear. After a while they don't see you any more. I have become used to being treated like a piece of furniture. At school too, the kids talk right over my head, look right past me as if I am not there.

"It's probably a combination of factors," my mother replies, giving her what-did-I-do-to-deserve-such-a-daughter sigh. "At first she couldn't speak and then she didn't want to any more, and now … who knows?"

"Doesn't she know how lucky she is to be living in England!" Lashes heavy with mascara flutter and she utters a forced little laugh. "I wish I could leave this country!"

"Anouk won't be happy anywhere," my mother says after another long drawn-out sigh. "Not until she has worked through the past."

Work through the past. A combination of factors. A traumatic experience.

41 **Buffy** *Buffy the Vampire Slayer* US cult TV series also shown in Germany
42 **to go rigid** *gelähmt vor Angst sein*
42 **mute** not able to speak
44 **attack** *here Überfall*
53 **to long for** to want sth very much
54 **pale** with little colour
54 **soil** *Erde*
55 **Free State** one of South Africa's nine provinces
56 **veld** *Steppe*
56 **dust** *Staub*
71 **to deserve sth** *etw verdienen*
71 **sigh** a loud breath expressing emotion
77 **to work through** to deal with

[83]**bare** *here ohne Schminke*
[84]**barefoot** with nothing on one's feet
[85]**I can't help it** *Ich kann nichts dafür*
[88]**to refuse to do sth** to be unwilling to do sth
[91]**frequent** often
[92]**unbearable** terrible
[96]**rattling** *ratternd*
[97]**to sob** to cry
[102]**terribly** *here* very
[106]**to iron** *bügeln*
[111]**Granny** short for grandmother
[112]**support** help
[113]**Highveld** area of South Africa that includes Johannesburg
[123]**to clutch** to hold tightly
[123]**steering wheel** *Lenkrad*
[124]**burglar bars** *Gitter*

My mother uses words like bricks to build walls around her, to protect herself. As if she doesn't know that walls cannot protect one.

Anouk is another one of her bricks. Anouk isn't me, Anouk is someone exotic, worldly, my mother's dream daughter with long dark hair. I am not exotic. I am small and ordinary. My hair is short and my face bare. I wear boy's clothes and like to walk barefoot even in England where no one does that. People generally think that I am two years younger than my real age. I can't help it, I don't look like someone called Anouk, and I don't feel like someone called Anouk.

"And the psychologists?" asks my mother's friend. "Couldn't they help?"

No, Mrs Mascara, the psychologists couldn't help. After a while I refused to go, refused to try and vomit out words. And once everybody started to leave me alone I had fewer nightmares.

They weren't less terrible, just less frequent. When they do come at night it is still as unbearable as ever. Blood on the carpet, a carpet that stains darker and darker, blood that flows over everything, furniture and walls, like brown-red paint, blood that streams out of the front door and runs down the street. Streets of blood, rivers of blood, a country full of blood. Then I also make strange noises in my sleep, my mother says, gargling, rattling noises like words in a language that doesn't exist. Sometimes I sob loudly and then my mother shakes me softly, waking me up and holding me. Sometimes she cries with me.

I loved my father. My mother probably too. I don't know. Nowadays she is going out with another man. Dad was tall and thin with a soft voice. My mother's new friend is short and stocky (well, actually he is quite fat, but my mother describes him as short and stocky). He likes to laugh loudly. He tries terribly hard to be nice to me. It's probably quite difficult to be nice to someone like me.

I wish I were someone else. No, I wish I was myself, three years ago when Dad was still alive and we still lived in Pretoria and I could stand barefoot in the kitchen in the afternoon and watch Rebecca iron the washing. I wish I could turn back the clock, be eleven years old again, and listen to the hissing of the steam iron while I make myself a peanut butter sandwich. For ever and ever.

The Voortrekker Monument

And now my mother has this stupid idea that she wants to go and look at our old house – or rather at the wall around the house, because that is all that you can see from the street. She has brought along my Granny Anna to give her "psychological support". Support to look at a wall?

"I have forgotten how dry the Highveld gets in winter," my mother says as we drive past the Voortrekker Monument. "Or maybe it just looks paler because we have become used to a place that is always green."

Because it always rains. Because the sun never shines properly, not like it shines here in Africa.

"The grass on the other side is always greener," mumbles Granny Anna. Not for me. I miss the pale grass on this side of the fence.

I am sitting in the back of the car, staring at the high, pale blue sky, drinking in the air as if it were water. When last did I see such a wide cloudless sky? The closer we get to our old suburb, the slower Mom drives. And the faster she talks, almost without breathing, her fingers clutching onto the steering wheel.

"Just look at all those fences! The burglar bars and the security gates! The alarm systems and the vicious dogs behind the gates! I'm sure it wasn't so bad three years ago."

"Three years ago you just didn't notice it because you were used to it," Granny says. "Familiarity breeds contempt."

Dad always used to say that Granny Anna had swallowed a book of idioms when she was small. I sometimes wonder if she has any of her own words left in her head.

"Three years ago I didn't feel contempt, Mom. I thought it was normal to live like this. Now I live in a village where no one hides behind security gates. Where the dogs sound friendly when they bark."

"Maybe their bite is worse than their bark," Granny says with a dry laugh.

My mother doesn't catch the joke. She doesn't even listen to what Granny is saying. She is far too worked up.

"I never want to live here again!"

"What you sow you shall reap," mumbles Granny.

Mother glares at her, irritated.

"I didn't sow the crime in this country, Mom."

"The sins of the fathers …"

I had never noticed before how much they look alike from the back. Both have short, dark and smooth hair, small ears and thin necks. Their voices also sound quite similar. They say that I also look like my mother. It's hard to believe because she always wears dark red lipstick and black kohl around her eyes, which makes her look, well, quite exotic.

I can't remember what my voice sounds like. I was never much of a chatterbox anyhow. My mother was always the talker in the house and my father and I understood each other without having to say anything – Dad, me and Rebecca.

When I was small I asked many questions, but when I was about seven I noticed that I could get more answers from books than from people. And so I started reading more and more and spoke less and less.

"Do you know what it's like to live in a country where you don't have to be scared all the time?"

"I refuse to live in fear, Anneke. The only thing to fear is fear itself."

As we turn into our old road my mother breathes in sharply. I remember the trees, many of them now pale and naked, but in summer they form a green canopy over the pavement. How I used to jump from shade to shade on my way to the café, barefoot, trying not to get my foot burnt by the cement. My heels were almost as rough as Becca's. My mother had bought me a grey stone to scrape my feet soft at night in the bath, but I never used it. I wanted to have feet like Becca's, soles that don't hurt on the cement, heels that can step on pieces of glass and thorns.

We stop in front of the house, the one on the left-hand side, on the corner. We stare at the high white wall and the red signs of two different security companies. The black steel gate that opens with a remote from inside the house. The driveway gate which also opens with a remote. My mother's shoulders are shaking. She is crying. My gran takes her hand, turns around and gives me a worried smile. As if concerned that I too will start crying.

I get out of the car. I am hot and I don't want to watch my mother cry because I can't bear the expression in Gran's eyes – as if she has forgiven me everything, will always love me, even if I never say another word.

I stumble across the pavement, all along the white wall, around the corner where they can't see me. My eyes are filled with tears, my ears are filled with the familiar sounds of the street, the sound of a lawn mower and the soft hum of the pool cleaners and the barking of the dogs behind the gates – not friendly dogs, not here. Voices from the radios in the kitchens, usually Zulu or Sesotho,

136 **to catch** *here* to understand
137 **worked up** *aufgebracht*
139 **to sow** *säen*
139 **to reap** *ernten*
140 **irritated** angry
142 **sin** *Sünde*
143 **to look alike** to look similar/the same
146 **lipstick** *Lippenstift*
157 **Anneke** ['æni:ki:]
158 **sharply** suddenly
159 **naked** *nackt*
160 **canopy** *here Blätterdach*
160 **pavement** *Bürgersteig*
161 **heel** *Ferse*
162 **rough** opposite of smooth
168 **remote** *Fernbedienung*
171 **concerned** worried
177 **lawn mower** *Rasenmäher*
179 **Zulu, Sesotho** ['zu:lu:], [sə'səʊtəʊ]

180 **siren** *Sirene*
184 **bar** *Stab*
185 **washing line** *Wäscheleine*
191 **slops** cheap shoes
191 **overall** *here Hauskleid*
200 **to shake** *rütteln*
203 **to bellow** to shout very loudly
205 **hoarse** *heiser*
209 **to cup** *here* to hold
214 **potato** *Kartoffel*
221 **profound** deep
221 **overwhelmed** *überwältigt*
228 **to hug** to put one's arms around someone

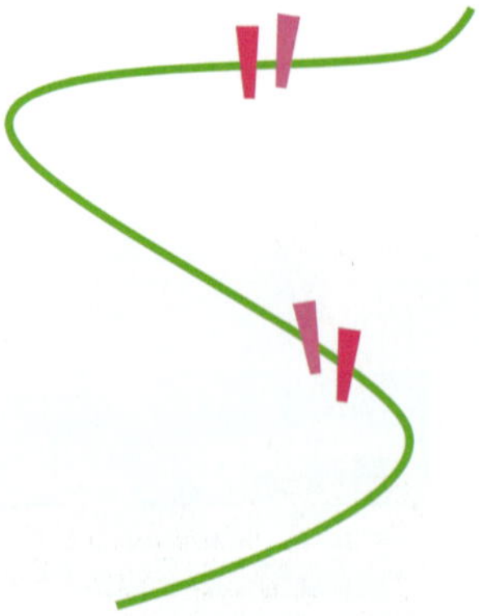

sometimes English or Afrikaans. Screaming sirens in the distance, in another suburb, or the highway. I had forgotten about all the sirens.

On the farthest side of the property there is a smaller iron gate that Rebecca used to get to her outside room. I hold onto the gate and press my face against the bars as if I want to press right through this barrier. I look at the kitchen window, the back door and the washing line full of baby clothes. Little white vests and pink jackets. I didn't know that the new people had a baby. I wonder if they know that my father was shot dead in their lounge. It's probably not the type of thing that an estate agent tells you when she wants to sell a house.

The back door opens and my heart breaks into tiny pieces as I see Rebecca walking towards the washing line. Impossible. But it is Becca's thin black body. Becca's tough feet in her slops. Becca's familiar light pink overall. It can't be. Becca doesn't work here any more. My mother helped her to find other work before we went to England. We had sent her postcards the first year and then … we had lost contact. Someone had let us know that she no longer worked at the same address.

And now she is here standing at the washing line, of course it is she, the woman who looked after me when I was a baby. The body that I know better than my mother's, busy packing the clothes of a stranger's baby into a plastic basket.

I shake the gate to get her attention. It has to be her. But she is too far to hear anything.

"Rebeccaaa!" The voice that burst out of my throat frightens me. It doesn't sound human. More like a dying animal, a cow bellowing, or something like that. The woman turns around, comes closer, uncertain.

"Becca?" I try again. A hoarse rattle. Once when my dad had laryngitis it sounded like that. "Is it you?"

"Noekie?" her face bursts open with joy. She drops the basket with the baby clothes onto the lawn and comes running towards the gate. Pushes her rough hands through the bars, cups my face in her hands, laughs in amazement.

"Noekie! It's you!"

I laugh and cry at the same time. She takes a bunch of keys out of the pocket of her pink overall and unlocks the gate. Her hands are shaking. She pulls me close to her and presses me against her. I didn't know how much I had missed this body, the smell of clean washing and spices and … potatoes? Nobody in England smelled like this. No one in the whole world smells like this.

"Anouk?" my mother calls as she appears around the corner. "Anouk? *Rebecca?*"

"It's me, Madam." She wants to let go of me, but I cling to her. "The child is very happy to see me."

"But … what are you … are you working here again?"

My mother's voice is high with profound surprise, her face overwhelmed. My gran stands behind her, her mouth wide open.

"Things didn't go too well with the other people, Madam." Rebecca sounds embarrassed, like when she had burnt the food, as if she is scared that Mom will be cross.

"And then I heard that these people were having a baby and they were looking for someone to help them. I missed having a child in the house …"

My mother hugs Rebecca, but all the time she is looking at me, at my tear-stained face and at my laughing mouth.

"Do they treat you well?" Granny wants to know from Rebecca.

"Very good, Madam. And the little one is so cute. She reminds me a lot of Noekie when she was a baby. Also has such round, curious eyes. She will probably ask just as many questions when she begins to talk."

I laugh, a breathy rattle, and my mother's hand flies to her mouth.

"Anouk has stopped talking." Her dark red lipstick is slightly smudged, her eyes hidden behind her sunglasses. "She has stopped laughing. I thought …"

"She spoke to me," Becca says proudly, teasingly, as if my mother has just made a joke. "She screamed like a mad one when she saw me."

"Anouk?"

"My name is Noekie," I say in my strange new voice. A bit less hoarse with each word. For the first time in four years it is my mother who is speechless. She stares at me, the tears dripping from under her sunglasses.

"You know I don't like to be called *Anouk*."

And with every word that comes out of my mouth I sound more like my mother.

[241] **speechless** not able to speak
[242] **to drip** *here* to fall

STEP 1 – Looking at South Africa as the story's setting

a) *Describe the events that lead to Anouk becoming mute and to her starting to speak again.*

b) [✎] *How is South Africa portrayed in the short story? Make a list of everything we learn. Compare this with how Britain is portrayed. Think about: wet/dry • colours … and the way the country influences the characters.*

STEP 2 – Looking at narrative techniques →S6, S7

a) [👥] ***Characterization:*** *The mother and daughter deal with the trauma very differently. One of you describes the mother's response, and the other Anouk's. Find words and phrases in the story to support your answers.*

b) ***Narrator's point of view:*** *Why is it important that Anouk narrates the story? Think about what would happen if the mother narrated it?*

c) ***Symbols:*** *What do the references to walls in the story mean?*

d) ***Atmosphere:*** *Describe the atmosphere in this short story.*

WORD BANK
to be traumatised • to force oneself to do sth • to work through sth • to miss sth • to be worked up about sth • to experience sth • to bear sth

STEP 3 – Looking at the genre of the short story →S4

1. *Read the TIP about short stories on page 52 and the Skills section* →S4*. Which of these elements can you identify in this short story? Think especially about 'medias in res' and say how the action is closely packed.*
2. *Describe the turning point. Why is it very important for this short story?*

STEP 4 – Your turn at creative writing →S23

[✎] *Anouk's mother is telling a friend back in London about the day when Anouk started speaking again. Write their conversation. The steps below will help you with this:*

- First, make sure you know what happened that day; a time line might help.
- Next, think about how the mother speaks. What kind of language does she use?
- Now write the conversation.
- When you have finished, read the text aloud. Does it sound natural?
- Check your work for common mistakes (spelling, word order etc.) and make any necessary changes. →S24

WORD BANK
Everyday expressions for conversations
Anyway, … • You know, … • If you ask me, … • Who knows? • To tell you the truth, …

Topic 3 The Blue Planet

[◎] Give and take

I give you clean air
You give me poisonous gas.
I give you mountains
You give me quarries.

I give you pure snow
You give me acid rain.
I give you spring fountains
You give me toxic canals.

I give you a butterfly
You give me a plastic bottle.
I give you a blackbird
You give me a stealth bomber.

I give you abundance
You give me waste.
I give you one last chance
You give me excuse after excuse.

Roger McGough

WORD BANK
climate change • to have an effect on • a result of global warming • to cause damage to • (air) pollution • to raise awareness of • (not) to waste natural resources • renewable / alternative energy sources • to recycle • to use / generate wind or solar power

1 a) *Look at all the material on these two pages. Choose a photo, fact or idea that interests you especially, and explain why.*
b) *Use the information on these two pages and describe the 'Blue Planet' for a friend. What positive or negative aspects could you mention? Note down as many ideas as you can in three minutes. (Use your own knowledge, too.)*

2 a) *In your opinion, what makes the poem 'Give and take' effective?* →S8
b) 1. *How does the title of the poem relate to its message?*
2. *Who are the 'I' and 'you'?*
3. *What environmental problems are mentioned?*
c) [⊡] [✎] *Write an extra verse that could be added to the poem before the last verse. Make sure you follow the structure of the poem.*

3 a) 1. *What problems are addressed on the Friends of the Earth website?*
2. *How does the viewpoint differ from that of the poem?*
3. *Which viewpoint appeals to you more? Why?*
b) [⊡] *Start two mind maps, one for 'problems' and one for 'solutions'. Add to them as you work through this Topic.*

Shopping at farmers' market

An offshore windfarm

Friends of the Earth International

WE STAND FOR THREE BIG IDEAS:

There is a tomorrow • We need to use the planet like there is a tomorrow. This means living within the limits of the natural world.

Everyone gets a fair share • Everyone, everywhere, now and tomorrow, deserves to have a good life.

Change the rules • We need to change the rules so that the economy works for people and the environment, not pit one against the other.

A paper recycling plant

FACT FILE

- The surface of the earth is two thirds water, but fresh water represents only one hundredth of one per cent.
- The human population of the world is expected to be tripled by the year 2100.
- Every day 50 to 100 species of plants and animals become extinct because of human influences.
- The UK has 1 per cent of the planet's population but produces 2.3 per cent of carbon dioxide emissions while the US, with 5 per cent of the population, produces 21.2 of the world's CO_2. The figures for Germany are 1.3 % (population) and 3.0 % (CO_2 emissions).
- Each person throws away about four pounds of garbage every day.

4 1. *What means are used to present the information or ideas on these two pages?*
2. *How effective do you think the different elements are in getting the message across?*
3. *How else might environmental issues be presented?*

⟨**5**⟩ [▤] *What aspects of the environment interest you most? Continue your file.*

Friends of the Earth international pressure group that campaigns to protect the environment

Bag Lady

1 [👥] [✎] ***Pre-reading:*** *Each of you lists the pros and cons of plastic. Then share and compare your ideas.*

It was the birds that finally made me break down and weep. The Hawaiian island of Midway is the main breeding ground for the Laysan albatross, as beautiful a seabird as you will ever see. But standing on a Midway beach, I was surrounded by thousands of dead and dying albatross chicks. I could not move without standing on dead birds. I was filming a Natural World documentary for the BBC about the environmental crisis facing the region's marine wildlife. But this was beyond a crisis – this was an apocalypse.

Adult albatrosses fly out over the sea for thousands of miles looking for brightly coloured squid to feed on. However, today there is so much colourful plastic in the water that they pick this up instead. They fly back and feed their chicks with it. It fills up the chicks' stomachs so they die.

Two years ago I thought I was environmentally aware. I was born on a South Devon farm where my father instilled in me the importance of thinking green. And I work as a camerawoman for the BBC Natural History Unit. But I was just sleepwalking then. I had no idea how desperate our situation really is.

My wake-up call started 18 months ago on the island chain of Hawaii at the start of my wildlife documentary. We had heard that in the North Pacific the ocean currents move in a huge circular motion, sucking in all the rubbish from the continents into the centre, where Hawaii is. We had learned that 80 per cent of all marine litter comes from land and that 90 per cent of it is plastic, but what we didn't know was the scale of the problem. Our ignorance became clear when we interviewed researcher Charles Moore.

Charlie said: "Guys, let me take you to the dirtiest beach in the world."

Kamilo beach was five miles long but wasn't the golden sand you would expect of a Hawaiian beach. It was multi-coloured as far as the eye could see. Cups, keyboards, DVDs, plates, combs, knives, forks, toys, TVs, drink bottles, sandwich wrappers, lipsticks, hair brushes, pens, shoes, plugs, clocks – every plastic item you would find in a typical house was on that beach.

"Welcome to consumer throwaway living," said Charlie. He pointed to the sand – it wasn't sand, it was tiny fragments of plastic, small enough to be eaten by animals at the bottom of the food chain. This plastic carries dangerous toxins that ascend the food chain right up to the top. Guess where we are in that food chain.

Charlie's last words to us that day haunted me. "Plastic lasts for at least 400 years and each year it's getting worse." Four centuries to clear up the mess – and that's if we start today. Over the following months we watched a whale rescue team untangling a whale from plastic ropes; I came across an old turtle and her throat was full of plastic packaging; we talked to seal scientists who told us they regularly have to rescue animals from plastic; dolphins were using a plastic bag as a football, unaware of the danger; and on Midway, the albatrosses moved me to tears. I knew I had to do something, anything.

Back home in South Devon, I wondered how on earth I was going to get people to understand what we are doing to the planet.

By March this year our documentary was finished and I lent a copy to a friend, Adam, who runs a delicatessen in my home town of Modbury. The next evening he told me he wanted to stop using plastic bags in his shop. I lent the

[2] **breeding ground** place where birds or animals have their young
[2] **Laysan albatross** type of albatross named after island in Hawaii
[7] **beyond** *here* more than
[9] **squid** *Tintenfisch*
[12] **South Devon** area in the south-west of England
[13] **to instil in** to teach sb (an idea or attitude)
[14] **BBC Natural History Unit** part of the BBC that makes programmes about wildlife
[18] **current** water moving in a definite direction
[18] **circular motion** movement around a central point
[34] **to haunt** *here* to stay in one's mind
[37] **to untangle** to make free
[37] **turtle** *Seeschildkröte*
[38] **seal** *Seehund*

film to another friend, Sue, who owns an art gallery. Her response was the same. Suddenly the penny dropped – two traders, same reaction. Why not get all the town's traders to watch the film? Sue offered her gallery as a venue and so the Modbury campaign began.

Of the town's 43 traders, 37 turned up and after the film I told them the facts and figures about marine plastic. I told them how bits of plastic act like sponges for many of the nasty chemicals we have been pouring into the oceans. These chemicals move up the food chain and end up in us. Many of these chemicals cause cancer. When I had finished, the room was silent. Everyone looked shocked. Simon, our local butcher, whispered to me to take a vote on the proposed bag ban. Every hand went up.

Over the following month, half the world's press seemed to descend on our town. Modbury wasn't just the first town in Britain to ban plastic bags, it was the first town in Europe to do so. Other towns followed our lead. Then e-mails came in from Sweden, from America, from China. They all wanted to ban plastic bags.

Six months on and in Modbury our ban has been a huge success. Trade has not suffered and the traders have saved half a million bags. They now sell reusable cotton bags and biodegradable bags.

I'm thrilled with the campaign, but walking on my local beaches provides a nasty reality check. There is throwaway plastic still littering the sand.

Water covers seven-tenths of the Earth. The oceans are the lungs of the world, providing far more oxygen than all the rainforests. We are polluting them at a terrifying rate and politicians are doing practically nothing about it.

It takes nature 300 million years to form oil. We use much of the plastic made from that oil for just a few moments before discarding it. It then takes another 400 to 1,000 years for that plastic to degrade. Is that not madness? What a waste of our planet.

Rebecca Hosking, *The Mail on Sunday*

[48] **the penny dropped** phrase used to express that sb has finally understood sth
[48] **trader** person who buys and sells things
[49] **venue** place where an event happens
[53] **sponge** *Schwamm*
[57] **to propose** to suggest (an idea or plan)
[60] **to follow sb's lead** to do the same as sb else has done
[66] **reality check** reminder of the true situation
[71] **to discard** to throw away

2 *Working with the text:*
a) *Summarize the article in a few sentences. Comment on the heading 'bag lady'.*
b) [✎] *Collect the facts and figures in the text about marine plastic. Look back at your pros and cons from exercise 1. Do the new facts make you want to change your mind?*
c) *Giving examples, analyze how Hosking tries to appeal to people's hearts.*

WORD BANK
to describe one's own emotions • to choose emotive words and phrases • to describe a sad / shocking scene • to use contrast / repetition • to add stress • to speak directly to • to ask a rhetorical question

3 [◎] *Listening: Analyze a short campaign speech about plastic.* →S29
1. *How is the speech structured?*
2. *How does the speaker try to get people's attention right away?*
3. *What can you say about the speaker's style and voice?*

4 CORE SKILL *Preparing a short speech:* →S23
a) *Think of an environmental issue you feel strongly about and what action you would like people to take. Research facts, figures, examples etc.*
b) [✎] *Plan and write a campaign speech, using the speech in exercise 3 as a model.*

5 CORE SKILL *Giving a speech:* →S28
a) *Collect Skills tips for talking to an audience (how to speak, where to look etc.)*
b) [ååå] *Working in pairs or small groups, give your speeches from exercise 4 in spoken form. Make helpful comments to each other about how to improve.*
c) [⊡] *After each speech, ask and answer questions about the issue dealt with.*

[◎] The Divide (I)

VIP FILE

Nicholas Evans
- born 1950 in England
- started career as journalist before moving into television and films
- travelled widely, especially in the US
- novels all best-sellers
- first novel 'The Horse Whisperer' (1995) also made into movie

1 *While-reading: Collect words describing landscape and the natural world.*

The following text is an extract from The Divide, a novel written by Nicholas Evans in 2005. Abbie Cooper and her family are staying at The Divide, a guest ranch in Montana. Ty Hawkins, who is working there during the college vacation, invites Abbie to go with him on a visit to his parents' ranch in Wyoming.

They loped the horses up a low bluff. From the brow Abbie could see the river. They stood the horses awhile, Ty on her right and his father on her left. Ty's father pointed east to where the river disappeared behind a distant shoulder of rock and said that this was where their land ended and their neighbor's began.

"It's so beautiful. How long have you lived here?"

"Three generations. Ty's will be the fourth."

He seemed about to say more but instead just stared in silence out across the land. High beyond the river a great bird was spiraling slowly upward. Abbie asked what it was and Ty said it was a golden eagle. Earlier, riding high in the hills, up where the forest began, they had seen a moose and a black bear.

"Let's go find those colts," Ty's father said.

He nudged his horse forward and Abbie followed down through the boulders with Ty behind her. Never had she found a horse so easy yet so alive, but then breeding such horses was how Ty's father made his living.

Ray was probably about the same age as her father, Abbie figured, though too much weather had made him look older. His eyes were the same pale blue as Ty's and he had that same quiet serenity she sometimes saw in Ty when he was concentrating on his work. In fact, so did Ty's mother and the horses and dogs and just about every living creature on the ranch. It was as if they were in on some special secret. Maybe it was simply from living in such a wondrous place.

It had been a long drive the previous evening from The Divide, east then south and into Wyoming and the Powder River Basin. They talked a lot but were comfortable enough with each other by now to be silent too. Abbie slept and when she woke they were in Sheridan.

The Hawkins ranch sat in a cleft of hills some five miles out of town. It was dark when they got there and so it wasn't until morning that Abbie got to see what a spectacular setting it was. Ty's parents had waited up to greet them and insisted on serving an epic supper of cold ham and turkey and baked potatoes. And all the while, Ray and Martha, who had eaten earlier, watched and smiled, listening as their son recounted between mouthfuls what had been going on at The Divide. He was their only child and the pride shone from them.

The colts they were now going to see had been turned loose in the meadows. They lifted their heads and watched while the three riders came closer. When he was still a hundred yards away, Ray left his horse and went on foot toward them. The colts lowered their heads and shambled to meet him. When they reached him he stroked their necks and spoke to them. He called to Abbie to come and she and Ty got off their horses and joined him. And though shier with her than with Ty and his father, they let her put her hands on them and blow into their noses.

Back at the house over lunch, another spread of cold meats and salad and home-baked bread, Abbie declared that she had never seen such a heavenly place in all her life. Ty's father smiled and nodded but his wife sighed and shrugged.

1 **to lope** *here* to ride casually
1 **bluff** land ending in a cliff
1 **brow** top (of a hill)
10 **moose** *Elch*
11 **colt** young male horse
12 **to nudge** to push gently
16 **pale** with little colour
17 **serenity** state of being calm and peaceful
19 **to be in on** to share knowledge (of sth secret)
25 **in a cleft of** between
30 **to recount** to tell
32 **to turn loose** to allow to move around freely
35 **to shamble** *trotten*

"It is now," she said. "How long it'll stay that way is another matter."

"What do you mean?" Abbie said.

Ty looked as puzzled as Abbie was.

"What is it?" he said.

"Your mom's just talking about the drilling, that's all."

"Why, what's happened?"

"It's nothing. It won't happen."

"For heaven's sake, Ray. Tell him about the letter."

Abbie felt she was intruding on some private family matter and wondered if she ought to excuse herself. Ty's father sighed and when he spoke it was to Abbie.

"There's a lot of drilling going on around here."

"For oil?"

"Gas. Methane. The land here is full of it, all across the Powder River Basin. The gas gets trapped in the coal seams. Nobody bothered too much with it until recently. But now they've found this real cheap way of drilling for it. And like most ranchers, when my granddaddy bought this land, the government only sold him the surface rights. They kept the mineral rights themselves and lately they've been leasing them off. We just found out somebody leased our land."

"Show Ty the letter," Martha said.

"Mom, it's okay. I'll read it later. Who bought the lease?"

"Some little outfit in Denver."

"And what do they plan on doing?"

Ty's father shrugged. "I guess we'll find out next week. They're sending a team to check things out."

"Don't let them."

Ray smiled. "You can't stop them. The law's on their side. They can drive around, dig, drill, do whatever they like. They give you a so-called 'surface damage agreement', which everybody around here knows isn't worth the paper it's written on. But if we don't sign it, they can just go ahead, anyhow."

"That's terrible," Abbie said.

"It probably won't come to much. A lot of these folks just buy the lease, then just sit on it and don't do a thing."

He didn't sound as if he'd convinced even himself of this but he changed the subject and asked Abbie what it was like living in New York. She said she used to like it more than she did now. The problem was, the more time she spent out West, where there was so much space, the harder it was to go home.

"Ty says you want to go to college out here," Martha said.

"Definitely."

It was the middle of the afternoon when they set off back to The Divide. As they drove out of Sheridan, Ty said he wanted to show her something and turned off the highway onto a gravel road. Ahead of them a great cloud of red dust rose into the sky and they saw two giant yellow excavators.

"They're digging a pit for the water," Ty said. "When they drill into the coal seam, it releases this huge amount of water, which you'd think, in a place as dry as this, would be a good thing. But it's salt water and where it floods onto the land nothing can grow. Kills everything. See those white patches there, down by the creek? That's salt. Those were hay meadows. Friend of my daddy owns them. Now they're good for nothing. Used to be good fishing there too, but now there's not a single fish. All died. The gas companies line these big holes with plastic. But they leak, and they don't fix them because they don't give a damn."

[50] **for heaven's sake** *um Himmels willen*
[56] **coal seam** underground layer of coal
[63] **outfit** *here (coll)* company
[73] **it won't come to much** it won't be a big problem
[83] **gravel** sand and small stones used for paths and roads
[84] **excavator** large machine used for removing earth
[85] **pit** large hole in the ground
[86] **to release** to free
[88] **patch** small piece of ground
[89] **creek** very small river
[89] **hay** grass that is dried and used to feed animals
[91] **to line** to cover the inside of sth with some material
[92] **they don't give a damn** they don't care

93 **every so often** from time to time
93 **well-head** structure over a hole drilled for oil or gas
95 **to bubble** *sprudeln*
97 **well** underground source of water
97 **happily** *here* without any problem
99 **to rupture** to break
99 **aquifer** rock through which water can pass
103 **bullshit** *(slang)* rubbish
107 **to head** to go in a specific direction
108 **sorrowful** sad
110 **forlorn** sad and lonely
113 **to spatter** to cover with drops of sth

They drove on and every so often Ty would point things out to her – well-heads, power- and pipe-lines, dirt roads across the landscape. They stopped by a low wooden bridge where the water of another creek bubbled with methane released by the drilling. In other places, like the deserted ranch house he showed her on the way back to the highway, wells that had functioned happily for forty years had suddenly started to bubble gas or run dry because some idiot gas drillers had ruptured the aquifer five miles away.

"Can't anyone stop these people doing this?"

"No. There's a pretty good protest group, but the problem is a lot of people think the drilling benefits the town. Creates jobs, brings business to the stores, that kind of deal. And that's bullshit. Often as not the companies ship in their own cheap labor and all the town gets is a whole lot of problems."

"Is this going on in Montana too?"

"Not yet. But it won't be long."

They didn't talk much after that. They headed north and west, while Steve Earle sang sorrowful songs on the stereo and a pale sun slid down ahead of them into its own coalbed of cloud. Ty said the weather looked set to change. Abbie had never seen him so forlorn and she reached out and stroked the back of his neck.

"Two more days," he said. "And then you'll be gone."

A first few drops of rain spattered the windshield.

"I'll be back," she said.

2 ***Talking about the situation:***

a) *"You can't stop them." (line 68) Who or what does 'them' refer to? What are they going to do and why can't they be stopped?*

b) *Using your notes from exercise 1, describe the Hawkins' land. Then refer to lines 82–99 and explain why they are so worried. What would you do if you were in their situation?*

3 ***Narrative techniques – Characterization and mood:*** →S5, S7

a) *Find details that help to characterize the Hawkins and their lifestyle. In what way can they be seen as archetypes? What do they stand for?*

b) *Describe the mood in different parts of the text. Give examples of the ways in which this atmosphere is created.*

4 CORE SKILL ***Holding an informal discussion (role play):*** →S26

Work in groups of at least four. You are people from Sheridan discussing the drilling in the area. Think of an equal number of roles to support the drilling (e.g. supermarket/bar owner, someone who has found work with a gas company) and to argue against it (e.g. rancher, someone who has moved to the area from a big city, 'green' politician). Choose your roles and note down arguments for your character. Then hold a discussion. Try to convince the others.

⟨5⟩ ***Listening – What happened next:***

a) *This audio extract from 'The Divide' describes a scene two years later. Abbie has not spoken to Ty for a long time. Then he calls and tells her that his father has had a stroke. Listen and make notes about the events that led to this.*

b) *Imagine Abbie's reaction to what Ty tells her. Write down what she says to express her feelings. Then compare ideas with a partner.*

WORD BANK
to have an effect on • the local economy • to create jobs • to benefit • to destroy forever • future generations • to make a living • a healthy lifestyle • (only) interested in • to cause lasting damage • to protect the land

TIP
archetype
in literature: typical character that does not change

TIP
AE: attorney = BE: lawyer

⟨The Divide (II)⟩

1 *Pre-reading: What do you associate with the word 'demonstration'?*

In this further extract from 'The Divide', Abbie, now a student at the University of Montana, has come to Seattle to take part in a demonstration together with friends Mel, Eric and Scott, and an environmental activist called Hacker.

FACT FILE
The WTO (World Trade Organization) is an international organization that decides the rules for trade between nations. During a WTO conference in Seattle in November 1999, over 40,000 people who were against its policies took part in demonstrations in the streets of the city.

Dressing up as genetically engineered fruit was Mel's idea and had once seemd a pretty funny one. They had spent every evening of the week before Thanksgiving making their costumes out of painted papier-mâché and Mel's, a strawberry with the head of a fish, was the best. Everyone who saw it just cracked up.

Abbie's was supposed to be a cross between a tomato and a sheep but in the drizzle its front legs had fallen off and the red paint had run down the front of her parka and pants. Eric and Scott had already ditched their costumes and Hacker hadn't made a costume at all, considering himself above anything so childish.

It was early morning and downtown Seattle was a sea of humanity. Thousands of demonstrators were in every street, all marching toward the convention center. And, despite the cold and the rain, everyone seemed to be having a ball, waving and shouting, laughing and chanting.

There ain't no power like the power of the people
And the power of the people won't stop!

There were people dressed as trees and elephants, turtles and whales. Above them fluttered banners denouncing the World Trade Organization. The guy in front had one with a huge picture of Dracula sinking his bloody fangs into the planet. The woman next to him was waving one that said *WTO. Fix it or Nix it.* Those who weren't chanting were blowing whistles or banging drums.

And it wasn't just students and hippies. There were people of all ages, colors, and nationalities. Word was going around that they had already succeeded in stopping the opening ceremony. It was awesome. History was being made. It was one of those world-changing events, like the Berlin Wall coming down or Martin Luther King Jr. telling the world about his dream. And Abbie was actually taking part. In years to come she would tell her children and grandchildren about it.

So here she was, soaked to the skin and dressed as a sheep-tomato, which had now gotten so soft that the time had come to ditch it.

Hey-hey! Ho-ho! WTO has got to go!

The rain seemed to be stopping now and as they marched forward, the sky began to clear. Between the buildings she could see the ocean and port, two massive ships anchored offshore. She had never been to this city before. It was even more stunning than she had heard.

Ahead there was smoke and she saw a dumpster had been set on fire. Now she heard glass being smashed but she couldn't see where or what it was. To her right, a chanting throng of demonstrators was laying siege to a McDonald's. Some were hammering on the windows and the doors. On the walls, in black paint, they had scrawled *McShit* and *McMeat Is Murder*.

The police they had so far seen had been friendly. But the ones they were now beginning to see looked different. They seemed to be some kind of special riot police. They were all in black, wearing helmets with gasmasks. They stood still as statues, blocking off the side streets, nightsticks at the ready.

"Wow," Mel said. "Who are *those* guys?"

Seattle industrial city on the north-west coast of the US
[1] **genetically engineered** *genetisch verändert*
[4] **to crack up** *(coll)* to laugh
[6] **drizzle** light rain
[7] **to ditch** *(coll)* to get rid of
[13] **to have a ball** *(coll)* to enjoy oneself greatly
[17] **to denounce** to speak publicly against sth or sb
[18] **fang** large tooth
[19] **to nix** *(coll)* to put an end to
[24] **Martin Luther King Jr.** great American civil rights leader
[27] **soaked to the skin** very wet
[33] **stunning** very attractive
[34] **dumpster** (AE) large container for rubbish
[36] **throng** crowd of people
[36] **to lay siege to** to surround in order to attack
[42] **nightstick** (AE) stick used by police officer

A helicopter suddenly thundered over their heads and they all ducked as the air vibrated. The march slowed and then stopped and for a long time they all stood there, chanting and singing.

Quite how or why it all began to go wrong, Abbie never really knew. Some later blamed it on a few nervous cops. Another dumpster had been set on fire and the black smoke kept drifting across the crowd so that sometimes it was impossible to see what was happening. Through the crowds Abbie could see a circle of chanting protesters.

Listen to the voices of the people in the street!
We don't have a vote, we don't have a seat!

And now another voice. Somebody with a megaphone was telling everyone to leave the area, and that all who refused would be arrested.

To begin with, Abbie didn't know what the smell was. Then her eyes started to sting and she saw a cannister rolling across the ground, spewing smoke. Somebody yelled that it was tear gas. A guy grabbed the cannister and hurled it back behind the lines of police who were now starting to move toward them.

In just a few minutes the whole atmosphere had changed. Panic began to spread. Abbie saw one of the protesters being beaten to his knees by the cops with their nightsticks and another being dragged away. Then a girl standing just a few yards ahead of Abbie fell and started screaming, clasping her leg.

"Holy shit!" Eric yelled. "They're shooting at us!"

"They're firing plastic," Hacker said. He probably meant to reassure them but Abbie had never felt more scared in her life. Hacker and Scott were helping Mel scramble out of her strawberry-fish.

"Come on," Hacker said. "Let's get out of here."

But it was easier said than done. Everybody was trying to leave. There were too many people and too much panic and nobody seemed to know the best way to go. With the crowd, they were swept toward a side street but those in front started ducking. Water was gushing all over them and for a moment Abbie couldn't figure out where it was coming from. Then she saw the police water cannon and in the next moment the jet caught Mel and sent her cartwheeling backward.

Abbie rushed to her and asked if she was okay, and Mel nodded but seemed too shocked to know. There was blood coming from her nose. Hacker and Scott took hold of her, one on each side, and hoisted her to her feet. As they hauled her off, Hacker yelled to Abbie over his shoulder to stay close.

Once they had gotten clear of the water cannon, Abbie stopped and looked back for Eric. There was no sign of him. She hollered to Hacker and the others to stop but they couldn't have heard her. She started to run but must have lost her bearings, because there weren't so many people now and she realized she must be heading back toward the police line. Another helicopter roared over and as she looked up at it she collided with a man who was running the other way. The impact shocked her and she just stood there, fighting for breath and trying to figure out where to run, but her head was paralyzed with panic.

That was when the tear-gas cannister knocked her clean off her feet. The back of her skull hit the ground when she fell and she saw a flash of white light. For how long she was knocked out, she had no idea, maybe only a few seconds, but when she opened her eyes again there was a helicopter directly above her and she had a sudden fearful certainty that it was going to land right on top of her. She scrambled to her knees and then to her feet and tried to run but found she couldn't because of the pain where the gas cannister had struck her. The air

[56]**to begin with** at first
[57]**to sting** to hurt with a burning pain
[58]**to hurl** to throw with force
[62]**to drag** to pull
[63]**to clasp** to hold tightly
[64]**Holy shit!** *heftiger Ausruf*
[64]**to yell** to shout loudly
[74]**jet** *here Strahl*
[74]**to cartwheel** *radschlagen*
[78]**to haul off** to pull away
[80]**to get clear of** to move away from
[81]**to holler** to shout loudly
[82]**to lose one's bearings** not to know the right direction any more and get lost
[87]**paralyzed** not able to move
[88]**to knock sb clean off one's feet** *jemanden umhauen*
[89]**skull** *Schädel*
[90]**knocked out** *bewusstlos*

all around her was filling fast with the tear gas and her eyes and lungs were on fire. Alone in the chaos, Abbie stood there and started to scream.

The next thing she knew, someone had grabbed her arm and was hauling her away. Her first thought was that it was a cop and she yelled at him.

"For Christsake, I'm trying to help you!"

Through her streaming eyes all she could see was the black snout of a gasmask, which made her think, despite what he'd said, that he had to be a cop. Then the snout lifted and she saw a thin face and a pair of intense blue eyes and long black hair under a red bandana. He was dressed all in black but he sure didn't look like a cop.

"Here, put this on," he said.

There was a trace of an accent, German or Scandinavian maybe. Before she had a chance to argue he had taken off the gasmask and was putting it on her, pulling the goggles and snouted air filter down over her face. Almost at once the air became breathable. Through the goggles she watched him take off his bandana and soak it with water from a bottle he pulled from the pocket of his parka. He tied it over his nose and mouth.

"Come on, let's go."

He put an arm around her and began to steer her off through the crowd. Her leg hurt but she soon forgot about it and surrendered, without a thought for the others or even for herself or where this stranger might be taking her.

Maybe it was simply that she was dazed from the knock to her head when she fell. Behind the mask, the helicopters and screams and sirens now muted, she felt as if the world had suddenly gone into slow motion and she was in a dream or watching it all on the TV news. All she would later remember were images in the little round lenses of the goggles: a woman lying bleeding on a bed of broken glass, a Buddhist monk on his knees in prayer, discarded banners everywhere and an African drum rolling slowly away down an empty street to the ocean.

99 **For Christsake!** *heftiger Ausruf*
100 **snout** nose and mouth (of an animal)
106 **trace** a very small sign or amount of sth
116 **dazed** not able to think clearly because of shock
117 **muted** making no or very little sound
118 **slow motion** *Zeitlupe*

2 ***First comments:*** *Give your immediate reaction to what you have read.*

3 ***Narrative techniques – Atmosphere:*** → S6, S7

a) 1. *Divide the text into parts to show how the demonstration develops for Abbie.*
   2. [⏎] *Note down keywords about the atmosphere and action.*

b) [⏎] *Analyze how the demonstration is brought to life for the reader. Think about: the narrator perspective, the use of direct speech, words with sounds that help to create a 'live' effect.*

4 ***Your opinion:***

a) *Speculate on what you think went wrong at the demonstration.*

b) *Say why you agree or do not agree with these statements:*
   1. *Abbie was naive to think that she was helping to make history.*
   2. *The demonstrators were wrong to attack the McDonald's.*
   3. *The police had no choice. The situation forced them to act that way.*

5 [✎] ***Creative writing:***

Choose one of these tasks:

- *A newspaper article the next day, reporting on the demonstration.* → S22
- *The next part of the story. (Who is the stranger? What happens to Abbie?)* → S23
- *An 'open letter' to the WTO about the need to create a fairer world.* → S16

WORD BANK

Maybe/Perhaps … • It's possible … • I get the impression … • It wouldn't surprise me if … • I could be wrong, but … • I don't think it's fair to criticize sb for … • It's understandable that … • … caught up in the moment • I don't see anything wrong with … • To me, it's (not) acceptable to … • … can't (ever) be justified

Environmental films

1 *First read only the headline of the article, and in one sentence, answer the question yourself. Then read the whole article to find out the writer's opinion.*

An inconvenient truth

Happy feet

Erin Brockovich

Movies with a message: What makes a good environmental film?

Earlier this week I spent a long lunch in Turin with fellow jury members at the environmental film festival, Cinemambiente. After three hours of debate we finally settled on a winner. *The nuclear comeback* is a documentary by New Zealand filmmaker Justin Pemberton, weighing up the pros and cons of nuclear energy in a world that urgently needs to decarbonise its economy. Like the best documentaries, it is engaging, nuanced and avoids preaching its cause.

Every filmmaker wants the viewer to care about their issue. But, sadly, good environmental films rarely make the light of day. Ask any cinema-goer to name their favourite environmental film, and you are unlikely to get much further than *An inconvenient truth*, Al Gore's Oscar-winning film about global warming.

Some of the films with the most effective green messages, however, have been big-budget movies. Children and adults have lapped up Hollywood animations such as *Happy feet*, *Finding Nemo* and *WALL-E*, without noticing that they are watching a condemnation of, say, the damage industrial-scale trawlers are doing to global fish stocks. Science fiction has also provided some strong environmental statements about where humanity might be headed if we don't address today's problems. I was transfixed by *Logan's run* as a child, and the vision it painted of a world nearly destroyed by overpopulation and pollution. Hollywood has also dramatised the real-life stories of those who have fought for environmental causes with films such as *Erin Brockovich*, *The emerald forest* and *Silkwood*.

But for me, the most powerful environmental film ever is an often-forgotten 1982 release with a near-unpronounceable title. *Koyaanisqatsi* is a haunting meditation on the relationship between humanity, technology and the natural environment. It combines striking imagery with a mind-changing message.

Any good environmental film, as we discussed in Turin, must boast such qualities if it is to truly influence its audience. Leo Hickman, *The Guardian*

Koyaanisqatsi

[2] **Turin** city in northern Italy
[5] **to settle on** to agree on
[10] **to decarbonise** to reduce carbon
[12] **to engage** to get sb's full attention
[16] **to make the light of day** to get seen
[26] **to lap up** *here* to enjoy
[31] **trawler** type of fishing boat
[36] **transfixed** unable to move, speak etc. (because of some strong emotion)

2 [✎] ***Finding out about environmental films:*** *Scan the article again and name the film genres mentioned. Using different genres as headings, list environmental films from the text. Then research and add your own ideas.* → S1

⟨3⟩ ***Film project:***

a) [ ] *Each group chooses a different genre, watches one of the films on your list from exercise 2 and presents it in class.* → S10, S11

b) [✎] *Watch more films individually and write reviews.* → S12, S23

[◎] ⟨An environmental song⟩

1 ***Before you listen:*** *What are your expectations of an environmental song?*

Down to earth was written and sung by Peter Gabriel for the animated science fiction film *WALL-E* (2008). Heard at the end of the film, the song refers to the plot about human beings returning to earth after hundreds of years of living in space. They had to leave their planet because of the environmental damage they themselves had caused. WALL-E is a robot left behind to try and clean up the heavy pollution and huge amounts of rubbish everywhere.

WALL-E

Peter Gabriel: *Down to earth*

Did you think that your feet had been bound
By what gravity brings to the ground?
Did you feel you were tricked
By the future you picked?
Well come on down

All these rules don't apply
When you're high in the sky
So come on down
Come on down

[Chorus]

We're coming down to the ground
There's no better place to go
We've got snow upon the mountains
We've got rivers down below
We're coming down to the ground
To hear the birds sing in the trees
And the land will be looked after
We send the seeds out in the breeze

Did you think you'd escaped from routine
By changing the script and the scene?
Despite all you made of it
You're always afraid of the change

You've got a lot on your chest
Well you can come as my guest
So come on down
Come on down

[Chorus]

Like the fish in the ocean
We felt at home in the sea
We learned to live off the good land
We learned to climb up a tree
Then we got up on two legs
But we wanted to fly
When we messed up our homeland
And set sail for the sky

[Chorus]

We're coming down
Comin' down to earth
Like babies at birth
Comin' down to earth

Redefine your priorities
These are extraordinary qualities

[Chorus]

Words and music: Gabriel, Peter / Newman, Thomas Montgomery

2 ***First impressions:*** *Listen to the song. Describe the general mood and tone.*

3 ***Thinking about the lyrics:*** → S9

a) 1. *Who is being addressed?* • 2. *What went wrong in the past?* • 3. *What two different meanings does 'down to earth' have in this context?* • 4. *How is the earth portrayed? Why is there 'no better place to go'?*

b) *Use your answers from a) to help you summarize the message of the song.*

4 [✎] ***Thinking about the music:*** *Comment on the sound of the instruments you hear in the introduction. Relate the loud and quiet parts of the song to the ideas expressed in those parts.*

5 [✎] [👥] ***Presenting an environmental song:*** *What other environmental songs do you know? Present a song of your choice in class.*

VIP FILE

Peter Gabriel
born 1950 in England; musician and songwriter; lead singer for rock band Genesis; then successful solo career; promotes world music; developing world activist

Environmental footprints

1 *Pre-reading: What is meant by the expression 'carbon footprint'? Who should think about this concept and why?*

2 *A first look: Skim the following two articles. Do you find them easy to understand? Explain why or why not. Say what each text is about.*

Greenhouse gases from food

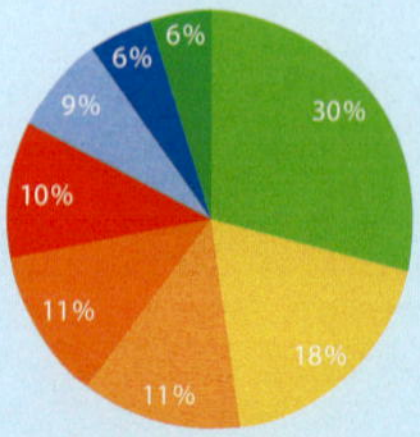

- red meat
- dairy products
- cereals
- fruit / vegetables
- chicken / fish / eggs
- other
- drinks
- oils / sweets / condiments

Red meat and dairy are responsible for nearly half of all greenhouse gas emissions from food for an average US household.

Source: Christopher Weber / Rhonda Saunders

Do food miles matter?

On a typical spring day, lunch for Seattle-based writer Sage Van Wing includes pasta with pork sausage from a small local farm. The peppers, cheese and shallots on top come from the nearby farmers' market. Van Wing is a locavore – she tries to eat only locally grown foods whenever possible.

For many people, "food miles", the distance food travels from farm to plate, are a simple way to gauge food's impact on climate change. But it's how food is produced, not how far it is transported, that matters most for global warming, according to new research. In fact, eating less red meat and dairy products can be a more effective way to lower an average US household's food-related climate footprint than buying local food, says Christopher Weber of Carnegie Mellon University.

Weber found that transportation creates only 11 % of the 8.1 metric tonnes (t) of greenhouse gases that an average US household generates annually as a result of food consumption. The agricultural and industrial practices that go into growing and harvesting food are responsible for most (83 %) of its emissions.

For perspective, food accounts for 13 % of every US household's 60 t share of total US emissions. By comparison, driving a car for 12,000 miles per year (the US average) produces about 4.4 t. Switching to a totally local diet is equivalent to driving about 1,000 miles less per year, Weber says.

A relatively small dietary shift can accomplish about the same greenhouse gas reduction as eating locally, Weber adds. Replacing red meat and dairy with chicken, fish or eggs for one day per week reduces emissions equal to 760 miles per year of driving. And switching to vegetables one day per week cuts the equivalent of driving 1,160 miles per year.

Several other recent studies have analyzed foods and poked holes in the food mile concept. For example, it can be more energy efficient for a British household to buy tomatoes and lettuce from Spain than from heated greenhouses in the UK.

Van Wing read Weber's paper and found it a "helpful" look at food miles. But she says she will continue to buy from local growers, whose production practices she can see firsthand.

Erika Engelhaupt, *Science News*

[6] **to gauge** to check (the size or amount of sth)
[13] **annually** every year
[18] **to switch** to change
[18] **to be equivalent to** to have the same effect as
[20] **dietary shift** change in what you eat
[20] **to accomplish** to achieve
[25] **to poke holes in** to show sth is not completely true
[31] **firsthand** directly or from personal experience

Forget carbon: you should be checking your water footprint

Ethical shopping just got harder. The concept of water footprints will tell consumers the amount of precious H_2O that has been used in the manufacture of products they buy. As with carbon footprints, the message is clear: less is better.

A new website run by the University of Twente in the Netherlands gives consumers a chance to work out the hidden implications of their shopping habits. Groceries, clothes, stationery and electrical goods are evaluated according to a water footprint calculator. In each case, the water footprint covers both the manufacture and transport of the goods.

The results are striking. An apple weighing 100g has a water footprint of 70 litres, while a 125 ml cup of coffee has a water footprint twice that size, 140 litres. But the water used in producing wheat or meat is much greater.

Academics have also created a worldwide league table for the water footprint of different countries. The US is the biggest offender, with a water footprint of close to 2,500 cubic metres per year per capita, while Italy is a close second. Britain's water footprint is relatively modest at 1,245 cubic metres per year per capita.

The calculations are complicated, but for consumers keen to minimise their water wastage, there remains a simple mantra to live by: always recycle. A cotton shirt, for example, has a water footprint of 2,700 litres, tallying up the water evaporated in irrigating and growing the cotton, as well as the water needed to wash away fertilisers. Recycling such products, minimising fresh production, could make the earth's water resources go much, much further.

Though it covers more than two-thirds of the earth's surface, water has never been more precious. An influential UN report published in 2003 predicted water shortages would affect 4 billion people by 2050.

Amol Rajan, *The Independent*

FACT FILE

Counting the cost
- slice of white bread: 40 l
- kg of cheese: 5,000 l
- kg of beef 15,500 l
- kg of chicken 3,900 l
- glass of wine: 120 l
- pint of milk: 1,760 l

6 **hidden implications** effects which are not obvious
7 **stationery** writing and other office materials
16 **modest** *here* small
20 **to tally up** to add together
21 **to evaporate** *verdampfen*
21 **to irrigate** to give water to land or plants
25 **UN** = **United Nations** organization working for peace between nations of the world

3 *A closer look:*

a) *Go through each article again to check that you have understood the information correctly. Note down the main idea in each paragraph.*
b) *Compare the two articles. In what way is the specific focus different? In what way is the general message the same?*
c) [✎] *Examine the style in which statistical reports like these are written. Find examples of specialist expressions, formal vocabulary, complex sentences.*

4 [👥] ***Working with the statistics:*** → S35

a) *Discuss the information given in the two articles about different kinds of food. Which produce the most greenhouse gases? Do those foods have a large or small water footprint?*
b) *Share your thoughts on which statistics in the two articles surprised you most.*
⟨c)⟩ [✎] *Turn the facts and figures in the articles into practical advice by writing a list of environmental tips for consumers.*

TIP
The next page can help you to express numbers and measurements in spoken form.

5 CORE SKILL ***Holding a formal debate:*** → S27

"We should all stop eating meat and become vegetarians."
Have a class debate and vote on the statement above. First decide who is going to be the chairperson and who is going to take the roles of the main speakers for and against. Then prepare by collecting arguments you may want to use during the debate. Think about these issues: the environment, health, the freedom to make personal choices, animal rights, the developing world.

TIP
A debate is a formal discussion, so speak in a suitable style.

⟨6⟩ [👥👥] ***Doing local research:*** *Find out where the food in your local shops, supermarkets and markets comes from. Report on what choices there are for consumers and also what kinds of food would be missing if only local food was available.* → S36

Expressing facts and figures

1 *Units of measurement:* →S35

a) [ ] *Say the figures and add the correct information.*
Start: "Four point six billion years is the …"
4.6 billion years • 7 l • 63,000 sq. miles • 200 kg • 13,000 km • 4/5 • 6°C

- the average volume of water used to flush a toilet
- the distance half of all British plastics travel to be recycled in China
- the area of rainforest destroyed each year
- the predicted rise in temperature by the end of the twenty-first century
- the length of time the earth has been in existence
- the proportion of household waste that could be recycled
- the weight of nitrogen added to the land as fertiliser for every metric tonne of cotton harvested

TIP

In English, you use …
- a decimal **point** (not a comma as in German).
- commas to separate long numbers into groups of 3 figures.

Abbreviations
- l = litre
- kg = kilogram
- km = kilometre
- °C = degree Celsius

b) [ ] *Collect groups of words used to express units of weight, length and volume. Write down the words in their full form, as you would say them, and also their abbreviations.*

c) *In the US and the UK, you might need to understand non-metric measurements. Look up the information you need and work out the metric equivalent of:*
1. *a 12-ounce steak*
2. *thirty miles an hour*
3. *a pint of beer*
4. *a ten-foot six-inch alligator*
5. *a gallon of petrol*

⟨2⟩ [ ] [ ] ***Make an environment quiz:***
Use information from this topic and also your own knowledge to write multiple choice questions about the environment (e.g. how long plastic lasts, the water footprint of an apple, the total population of the earth, …). The answers should all be measurements. Use your quiz to test other students at your school.

3 ***The language of statistics:***

a) *Look at the question on the right. What would you expect the answer to be? Explain why.*

b) *Reports giving facts and figures use special expressions. Make the answer on the right more formal by replacing the words in italics with the words below. (Two words are not needed.)*

approximately • equal to • average • add • compared to • higher • factors • total • calculate • per • the majority of • less

c) [ ] [ ] *Discuss whether the information about cotton and polyester will make you think about the clothes you buy in future.*

Question:
Which is more environmentally friendly: a T-shirt made of cotton or one made of polyester?

Answer:
Generally, people do not (**1** *work out*) the environmental cost of the clothes they wear, and (**2** *most*) consumers would probably think cotton is more environmentally friendly than polyester. Growing cotton does cost (**3** *a smaller amount of*) energy than creating the raw materials of polyester from oil. Cotton uses (**4** *about*) a quarter of the world's insecticides, however, and the land also needs fertiliser – on average, 200 kg (**5** *for every*) tonne of cotton – which releases a powerful greenhouse gas into the atmosphere. Such (**6** *things*) mean that the carbon cost of producing a new cotton T-shirt is actually (**7** *the same as*) the cost of producing a polyester one, but then wearing and using cotton has a (**8** *bigger*) cost because of the extra energy needed to wash it at a warmer temperature and also to iron it. When you (**9** *put*) all the numbers together, therefore, the (**10** *whole*) figure shows that cotton is actually the wrong choice for the environment!

4 *Mediation:* →S34

a) *A German student working on an environment project finds the article below and shows it to his group. As he has already read the whole text, he can answer his friends' questions about what they see in the grid. Scan the text and answer the questions in German.*

1. *Die Bilder und Zahlen sind soweit klar. Aber was genau ist mit CU gemeint?*
2. *Wie kann man einen Vergleich zwischen verschiedenen Verkehrsmitteln anstellen, wenn die Zahl der Passagiere nie gleich ist?*
3. *Es wundert mich, dass der Zug weniger umweltfreundlich ist als das Auto. Wieso eigentlich?*
4. *Wie ist man auf das Ergebnis für das Pferd gekommen? Das Tier hat ja keinen Motor!*

How to minimize your carbon footprint

Luis Villazon investigates

Everything we buy or do has a carbon cost. But how can you tell how much damage anything actually does? You need a simple measure of greenhouse gas contribution that can be applied, like a price tag, to any product or activity. We've devised our own Carbon Unit, or CU scale. One CU equals a kilogram of carbon dioxide released into the atmosphere.

Should we stop flying on holiday?

One of the problems with comparing the contribution of different forms of transport is that they all take different routes.

We looked at a hypothetical journey from London to Naples in Italy and calculated the CU released into the atmosphere by making the journey by air, land and sea. We also considered some more unusual options. Would travelling by horse actually be carbon neutral, for example? A horse emits about 18 kg of methane a year. This is equivalent to 378CU because methane is 21 times more powerful a greenhouse gas than CO_2. We can calculate the total CU contribution by working out the number of days it would take to make the journey and multiplying this by the methane emitted each day.

For motorised transport, average occupancy is important. Most business car journeys run at less than two people per car per mile, whereas holiday-makers average three people per car. Aeroplanes chartered by tour operators have a higher average occupancy than scheduled midweek business flights. We have assumed holiday occupancy rates here.

London to Naples

Method of transport	Distance	CU/person per km	Total CU per person
	3164 km	0.05	157
	2896 km	0.06	180
	1635 km	0.16	264
	7081 km	0.27	1892
	3164 km	0.02	59

In a nutshell

Going on holiday by horse may appeal to cowboys, but our trip to Italy would take two months each way. Surprisingly, the car is the next best choice, assuming there are three people sharing. But for a single traveller, the train would be greener. And however much the aeroplane is reviled, the cruise liner did much worse. It's less efficient per km and took the least direct route.

From: *BBC Focus magazine*

b) *Compare the figures given for the different forms of transport. Comment on the results and say if you think the investigation is a good idea or not.* →S35

WORD BANK

compared to • low / high • better / worse than • the most / least • (not) surprising • (un)realistic • a useful / helpful comparison • a waste of time

Avoiding social gaffes in the US

"If only I'd known that *before* I went to America … ."
You won't need to say that if you are well informed about the US before going there for the first time.

TIP
While visiting other countries, it helps to remember this rule of intercultural competence:
"There's no right, there's no wrong; there's just different."

1 ***The American way is to be polite:*** *Americans are very friendly and polite – and expect the same from visitors to their country.*

a) *Read these examples of typical American behaviour. How much did you already know? What was new?*

1. For special occasions (dinner at a nice restaurant, a celebration, a church visit) it is a good rule to dress up rather than down i.e. no jeans!
2. People you've just recently met might say, "We should go to lunch together!" This, though, is not the moment to say "OK, when?". It's just something nice to say, like "How are you?".
3. Americans don't like their 'body bubble' invaded i.e. they don't like it when people stand too close in conversations, at the bus stop etc.
4. Shaking hands is too formal for most Americans. This is done only when two adults meet for the first time, or if it's a business situation.
5. In America, people open doors for each other, especially men for women.

b) *Which aspects of American politeness are similar / different in your country?*

2 ***Restaurants – Know before you go:*** *American restaurants are different from European restaurants.*

a) *Explain the cartoon.*

I think he's recognized us:
I told you we should have left a tip last time…

Rule No. 1 – You must give a tip:
American waiters and waitresses receive a very low hourly wage; without tips they wouldn't be able to make a living. Every American knows this and so it is standard to leave 20% of the total bill as a tip. For very good service, leave 25%.

Rule No. 2 – 'Please wait to be seated':
When you walk into an American restaurant you will see a 'Please wait to be seated' sign. It means what it says: wait. A staff member will take you to a free table. Don't walk past that sign.

Rule No. 3 – Tables are not shared:
Americans are known to be generous. But they don't share tables in restaurants! Breaking Rule No. 2 would be bad enough, but going up to a table and asking the people already sitting there if the two remaining seats are available would be much worse; people would think you're rude and weird.

b) *Now read the rules above.*

1. *What do you think of them?*
2. *What are the restaurant rules in your country?*
3. *With a partner, discuss why you think Americans have rules like these.*

TIP
- The following topics are ***not*** suitable for small-talk situations in the US: **religion**, or America's **treatment of Native Americans**.
- Americans have a history of being wasteful with water and gasoline. But as the Fact file on the right shows, it would be wrong to think that Americans are generally ignorant of **environmental protection**.

FACT FILE
- America was the first country in the world to preserve nature by creating huge **national parks** (Yellowstone, 1872). Today there are 58. (Germany has 14 national parks.)
- 70% of Americans **recycle**. In Germany it is 90%.

At the doctor's

1 [✎] ***Reasons for going to the doctor:*** *Imagine situations when you are in a foreign country and have to see a doctor. Make a list of possible reasons.*

2 ***Useful phrases:*** *What phrases might you need at the doctor's? Think of as many as you can. The pictures and phrases on this page will help.*

Patient: I need to see a doctor. Do I have to make an appointment?
There's something the matter with my …
I've hurt my … / I've got pains in my …
I've got a stomach-ache/a headache/backache/earache/a sore throat[1].
(I think) I've broken … / sprained[2] my …
I've got a cut/bruise[3] / burn / rash[4] on my …
It won't heal up[5]. It's quite swollen / inflamed[6].
I feel sick. / I've been sick.
I've got diarrhoea[7] / flu / hay fever[8].
My nose is blocked up[9].
I've been stung[10] / bitten by a … It's very painful.
Can you give me something for my …?
Should I stay in bed?
How long will it take to clear up[11]?
Do the pills have any side effects[12]?
Is there a chemist's[13] near here?

Doctor: Have you taken your temperature[14]?
You've caught an infection. It's going round.
You've torn[15] a muscle in your …
I'll give you some pills / ointment[16] / antibiotics / homeopathic[17] medicine / an injection[18].
We'd better have it X-rayed[19].
I'll have to do some tests / take a blood sample[20].
The allergy is caused by … / You've got sunstroke / a bad sunburn.
You'll have to see a specialist.
If it's not better / cured in … days' time, come and see me again.
Here's your prescription[21].

WORD BANK

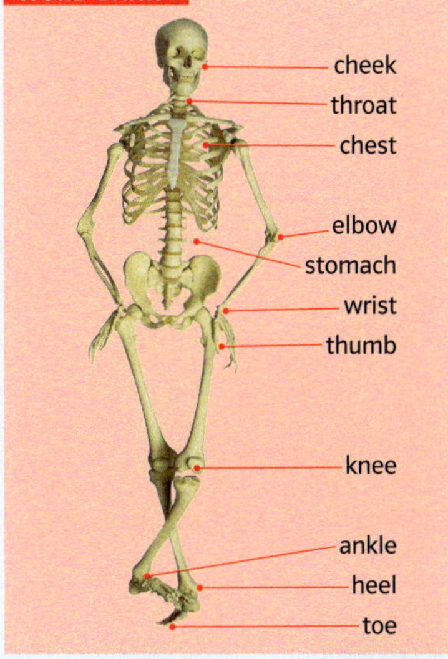

3 [◎] ***Listening:*** *What seems to be the trouble? Listen to the dialogue between Lukas, who is on holiday in Greece, and a local doctor. Then answer these questions.*
1. *What is wrong with Lukas? Explain when and how his illness started, and what his symptoms are.*
2. *What is Dr Fotopoulos's diagnosis[22]? How does she want to treat the illness?*
3. *How does Lukas react to the doctor's suggestion for treatment? Why? What plan do they finally agree on?*

4 [👥] ***Your turn:*** *Choose a situation (an illness, accident or other problem). Then use words and phrases from this page to write a dialogue between a patient and a doctor. Then act it out together.*

[1]Halsweh • [2]verstaucht • [3]Prellung • [4]Ausschlag • [5]heilen • [6]entzündet • [7][ˌdaɪəˈrɪə] Durchfall • [8]Heuschnupfen • [9]verstopft • [10]gestochen • [11]besser werden • [12]Nebenwirkungen • [13]Apotheke • [14]Fieber (gemessen) • [15]gerissen • [16]Salbe • [17][ˌhəʊmiəʊˈpæθɪk] homöopathisch • [18]Spritze • [19]geröntgt • [20]Blutprobe • [21]Rezept • [22][ˌdaɪəɡˈnəʊsɪs] Diagnose

Discussing environmental issues

1 [ ] ***Thinking about the material in the Topic:***

a) *Give your opinion on the different texts you have read. (Did you find them interesting? Do you think the issues they dealt with were important? Did you learn anything useful?)*

b) *Take turns to say whether or not you feel generally positive about the future of the earth, and why. Refer to the mind maps for 'problems' and 'solutions' which you started in exercise 3 on page 58.*

2 [ ] ***Study the cartoons on page 77:***

In each of them the caption is missing, so talk about the message you think is being given and decide together what you think the caption could be. Write down your ideas, and when you have finished, compare them with the artist's captions which you will find on page 249. → S15

⟨3⟩ ***Find out about and report on one of the following:***

- *a product that helps consumers to lower their carbon footprint.*
- *a local project to protect or improve the environment in the area where you live.*
- *interesting new research on some environmental issue.*

4 [ ] ***Watching and understanding a short film:***

a) *You are going to watch a report titled 'Mediterranean Britain'. Think about this title, look at the two pictures below and say what you expect the report to be about.* → S13

b) *Watch the video once without taking notes. Then in no more than three or four sentences, summarize the main points that are made.*

c) *Read the following questions. Then watch the video again, this time noting down the information you need to give detailed answers.*

1. *Where do a lot of tourists go at the moment? Why do they go there?*
2. *Where will tourists be going by the year 2050? What will cause this change?*
3. *What could Britain's coast look like in the future?*
4. *What is already being planned in Cornwall? What is the reaction of local people?*
5. *What positive and negative effects are mentioned in the context of the predicted changes?*

d) [ ] *Give examples of different ways in which the information and predictions are presented in the video. Think about both spoken and visual forms of presentation, and explain the effect they have.*

e) *Think – pair – share: The video concentrates on Britain and just one effect of climate change. Collect and discuss ideas about the various changes you think will happen in your own country if climate predictions are correct.*

1

2

3

4

5

6

⟨Revision for tests⟩

Minorities and stereotypes

TIP
Dictonary work:
Look up the new words of Revision B in a dictionary.

Travellers

In the UK, 'Traveller' is an umbrella term covering many communities, including Romany, Roma and circus families. Travellers are officially defined as an ethnic minority group, as their home lifestyle is significantly different to that of the majority settled community. The term 'Traveller' is acceptable to most of these groups, but 'Gypsy' is rejected by most Traveller communities because they find the word has negative connotations for the settled community.

Eadie McCarthy Orr, 15, has this to say:

"My family, friends and I are discriminated against every day, just because of the way we live and who we are. We are Travellers. I live with my parents and two brothers on a double-decker bus, and my parents have always stayed in the same area, so I don't change schools. It's not a very nice thing to grow up with the feeling that people just hate you because of the way you live, and instantly judge you before they even meet you just because they've heard something bad about a Traveller who has absolutely no connection to you. I've been called "gypo" and "thief" by children at school. It used to upset me when I was younger, but no one ever went any further than calling me names.

I won't lie – there probably are bad Travellers out there who steal and stuff, but there are also bad people out there who live in houses, and who steal and do bad things. But when I meet someone who lives in a house, I don't say, 'Oh no, not a person from a house. Stay away, you might rob me.' "

Kieran Tickner-Hinkes, 17:

"As a member of the Traveller community, I moved about a lot when I was younger. I went to 15 or 16 schools, which made it difficult to make friends. Other kids would say I was untidy and call me names, so I had a pretty hard time. Because I moved about from school to school, I was always behind with Maths and English. Every school was at a different stage in the curriculum and I always felt that I was labelled stupid.

I think that most people these days are more accepting of Travellers, but you still get some people with stereotyped opinions of the community. If people understood more about what being a Traveller actually involves, they would realize that we are just like everyone else."

1 a) *Which answer is correct?*

1. Travellers do not like the word 'Gypsy' because
   a) it has a negative meaning for them.
   b) most non-Travellers consider it negative.
   c) it is not a word for an ethnic minority.
2. Eadie experiences discrimination because
   a) she has unsuitable friends.
   b) her home is dirty.
   c) she lives the Travellers' way of life.
3. She feels people often judge her negatively because they
   a) have had bad experiences with Travellers.
   b) have heard a negative story about Travellers.
   c) have lived near a Travellers' community.
4. Kieran did not have friends at school because
   a) he was a Traveller.
   b) he did not stay at one school for long.
   c) his grades were not very good.
5. Kieran thinks that the settled community
   a) is completely against Travellers.
   b) knows that Travellers are no different from the rest of society.
   c) should be better informed about Travellers.

b) [✎] *Make a list of the problems which the two teenagers experience in society. Which are the same? Which are different?*

2 [◎] ***Listening – Travellers as neighbours?***

a) *Listen to this conversation in the Marsden family and find the right answers.*

1. The problem in the Marsdens' neighbourhood is that
   a) Travellers are living near the river.
   b) the police are having trouble with Travellers in the area.
   c) Travellers want to have a camp near the river.
2. Mr Marsden thinks
   a) there is no truth at all in the stories about Gypsies.
   b) the Gypsies' non-settled lifestyle causes problems for everyone.
   c) his wife doesn't understand how serious the problem is.
3. Mrs Marsden is worried about the Travellers' plans because
   a) she can't accept their way of life.
   b) she thinks their site will be a serious problem for the environment.
   c) she thinks life will be too hard for the Travellers in that area.
4. The Travellers want the town council to
   a) sell them some land for a site.
   b) stop complaining about illegal sites.
   c) allow them to set up a site on their own land.
5. How many members of the Marsden family are going to the meeting?
   a) 2. b) 3. c) 4.

b) [✎] ***Opinions pro and con:*** *Prepare a list like this and make notes about what is said in the conversation.*

negative statement	positive statement/explanation
• lots of caravans	• big field
• …	• …

3 [👥] ***Speaking – On the move … or not?***

With a partner, discuss the pros and cons of life in a settled community on the one hand and a 'travelling' lifestyle on the other. Make notes first.

4 ***Mediation– Stereotyping in the media:*** *Summarize the main points of this article in German.*

The media can be a powerful tool in creating or reinforcing stereotypes. An example is the public perception that youth crime is on the rise, or out of control.

This impression has been created largely through media coverage of terrible stories about high school shootings, property crimes, and incidents involving so-called youth gangs.

Statistics tell a different story. According to official research, incidences of youth homicide have been on the decrease for years, and the rate of youth charged with property offences, the most common kind of youth crime, has dropped steadily. But prompted by sensational headlines, politicians and lobby groups have called for tougher measures to deal with young offenders and to combat a perceived increase in youth crime.

Negative stereotypes not only affect how adults see teenagers, they influence how teenagers see themselves. The feeling that the rest of the world doesn't respect or understand you does little to encourage a positive feeling of self-worth.

Other minority groups in society – such as blacks, native people, women, gays and lesbians – have all experienced the effects of negative stereotyping in the media. Many of these groups have lobbied successfully to educate the media about issues that concern them, to challenge stereotypes, and to provide more balanced coverage of their communities.

Media Awareness Network, Canada

5 [✎] ***Writing – A personal view:***

Write a text about some negative stereotyping you know of, based on your own experience or that of people you know. Examples: Are you stereotyped because of … your nationality • your age • girl/boy role ("Boys are better at Maths and Science." "Girls work harder than boys.")? Say why you think such false impressions exist and what can be done to correct them.

Topic 4 Make a difference

American philosopher and social critic **Henry David Thoreau** (1817 – 1862) felt it was every citizen's duty to rebel against the state when the state was guilty of immoral or unjust behaviour e.g. in the form of bad laws. His essay on the subject, *Civil disobedience* (1849), reached a large international audience and has been a major influence on how people view their rights and their governments ever since. Thoreau himself spent a night in prison after refusing to pay taxes: he did not want to support a state which itself supported slavery. Thoreau is also the father of the ecological movement (*Walden; or, Life in the Woods*, 1854).

Emmeline Pankhurst (1858 – 1928) from Manchester was the leader of the British suffragette movement. The suffragettes' goal was to achieve the right to vote – suffrage – for the women of Britain. Although Pankhurst and her circle were often criticized for their violent tactics (e.g. physical attacks against police officers, arson), it is recognized that they played a major role in making universal suffrage possible in Britain.

Only 80 years ago, it was not unusual for many children to die before adulthood. One major reason for this was that there were no cures for common bacterial illnesses such as pneumonia, diphtheria or scarlet fever. Thanks to biologists like Scotsman **Alexander Fleming** (1881 – 1955), whose discovery of penicillin helped to launch the field of antibiotic medicine, contracting bacterial illnesses was no longer a death sentence – at least for those who had access to good medical treatment.

FACT FILE
- 36 % of all Germans 14 years and older are involved in some form of volunteer work.
- Boys in Germany are somewhat more involved (38 %) than girls (33 %).

1 [✎] ***Start-up activity:*** *What does it mean to 'make a difference'? What ways are there to make a difference? Take a few minutes to write notes on both questions before discussing your ideas in class.*

2 ***Famous people who have made a difference:***

a) *Read the six profiles. In a sentence or two, say what difference(s) these people have made in their country and/or in the world.*

b) [group] *In groups, decide on a suitable heading for each profile.*

3 ***Your ideas:*** *If you could choose one area of life to make a difference in, what would it be? Explain.*

Martin Luther King, Jr. (1929 – 1968) was a Baptist preacher from Atlanta who led the African-Americans in their fight to end racial segregation and discrimination in the US. Like Thoreau and Gandhi before him, 'MLK' stressed the importance of showing civil disobedience in non-violent ways e.g. through huge protest marches. In 1964 he was awarded the Nobel Peace Prize for his civil rights work. King made a difference in the US and the world, but he also made enemies: He was assassinated in Memphis on 3 April 1968.

In the 70s and 80s, **Bob Geldof** (b. 1951 in Ireland) was best-known as a rock musician. It is, however, his charity work in his fight against poverty in the developing world that he is best-known for now. He has raised hundreds of millions of dollars with charity songs *(Do They Know It's Christmas)* and concerts (Live Aid, 1985; Live 8, 2005). His all-star music projects have been a major factor in raising money and public awareness for his fight against poverty.

Owners of huge private fortunes can play a major role in making a difference. Microsoft founder **Bill Gates** (b. 1955) and his wife Melinda (b. 1964) donate $800 million a *year* to their foundation's Global Health Program to improve the world health situation. In other words, two people donate as much money for healthcare each year as all 193 countries in the World Health Organization have in their entire annual healthcare budget.

4 [◎] CORE SKILL *Understanding a radio interview:* →S29

a) *Before you listen to the interview with Bob Geldof, find out the meaning of these keywords: food aid • band-aid • wound • drought • to turn up at a concert • complexity of issues • level of understanding • subsidy • political lobby*

b) *Now listen and explain the gist of the interview.*

c) [✎] *Listen again, this time noting down the following details:* →S30

1. *What is the 'political issue' Geldof refers to?*
2. *What does Geldof say about Africa and subsidies?*

d) [ ] *What do you think about celebrity charities?*

⟨5⟩ [👥] [▤] ***Internet research:*** *For one of the people featured on these pages, create a time line with key life and career moments.* →S36

WORD BANK

I want to make a difference to how people … • I will / would make a difference by … • I'm not sure what to think about … • On the one hand …, but on the other hand … • to give your time / money to a charity / to a good cause • role models • trailblazers • to make the world a better place (for the current / for future generations) • celebrity charities

[◎] Looking for Alibrandi

1 *Pre-reading: What events do you know of which feature public speaking? Would any of them interest you enough to go and listen, or perhaps even to take part?*

It is 'Have a Say Day' and pupils from all over Sydney have come to a park in the city centre for a speech competition. There are even members of Australia's political elite in the audience. The story is told from the perspective of 17-year-old Josie Alibrandi, the novel's main character.

So I sat there next to a Jewish hunk, wishing he believed in Jesus so we could get married, and behind a girl resembling Poison Ivy who belonged to a Presbyterian school. Seated on my side was Jacob Coote from Cook High.

Cook High is a public school in the city area. Because it's the closest school to us we don't get on well with them. We think we're better than them. They think we're the biggest dags in the world.

When we were young, they would throw things out of their bus windows at us and in Year 10, on the last day of school, Jacob Coote and about ten of his friends, male and female, blocked both entrances of a lane we cut through to get to our bus stop. Twelve of us were bombarded with eggs, rotten fruit and vegetables. Everyone said that one day we would look back on the occasion and laugh.

Very unlikely.

"What are you going to talk about?" he whispered in my ear.

I moved away hoping nobody had seen him speaking to me. My friends think he's gorgeous. His hair is brown, shoulder-length, not cut into any particular style and his eyes are green and they always seem to be laughing at you.

He grinned and by the way his lips were twitching he looked like he was trying to control a laugh. I knew he recognised me from the lane.

"Didn't I once squash two eggs against your glasses?" he asked.

"I'm flattered you remember. I tripped over a rubbish can, you know, and cut my hand on some broken glass."

"Oh, come on. We were suspended for that. We didn't go to school for six weeks."

"Very funny. We had six weeks holiday after that."

He tapped the Presbyterian girl in front of us and asked her what she was going to speak about.

"University careers," she smiled, flirting before turning around.

1 **hunk** slang for a well-built (young) man
2 **Poison Ivy** a 'bad girl' character played by Drew Barrymore in a film
2 **Presbyterian** referring to a branch of the Protestant Church strongly associated with Scotland and which Scottish immigrants took with them to Australia
6 **dag** Austr. slang for sb who is very uncool
12 **unlikely** unrealistic
15 **gorgeous** very good-looking

"Great choice," he said looking at me and making a face at her back.

Some people spoke about the government's school cuts, others about careers. The environment was spoken about, as well as the homeless.

I decided to talk about sex education in our schools due to the AIDS issue. I had used it as an oratory speech before and had won, so I knew I couldn't go wrong.

I spoke for five minutes and accepted the Jewish hunk's hand when he offered it to me, and the nod of approval from the Presbyterian girl when I sat down. Jacob Coote nudged me, almost sending me sprawling over my neighbour.

"Great speech. Only the seniors have AIDS talks at our school, which is a waste because by that stage most of us have had sex for years."

I nodded vaguely in agreement, embarrassed that he had divulged that information to me.

"What are you going to talk about?"

He dug into his pocket and pulled out a condom.

"I'm going to show these people how to put one on," he said seriously, standing up.

I was horrified. I knew he wasn't a debater and that he probably didn't have a speech prepared. I was also worried that by sitting behind him I wouldn't see anything and was ashamed of myself for thinking it. Until he stood in front of the microphone and spoke.

"I'm speaking about the vote today," he said, digging his fingers into his pockets.

I sighed in relief but was disappointed by his boring topic.

"I think that all political parties are the same," he began, sounding a bit stilted. He had taken his fingers out of his pockets by then and was kneading his neck with one. His white sleeves were rolled up to his elbow and I could see that he was tanned. Not a beach tan, though. More like a working, outdoor tan.

"These politicians, they make the same promises. They tell the same lies and frankly, I can't understand why normal voters get influenced by a political campaign. We all know that what they're gonna say is what we wanna hear."

I could feel my Jewish neighbour cringing at the 'gonna' and 'wanna'.

"I used to think that when it came time for me to vote," he said, knocking his fist to his chest, "I'd put no effort into it. Maybe I would put in a dummy vote. Maybe I wouldn't even bother registering at all.

"Probably because until recently I wondered what the big deal was. *What's* great about our political system here? *Why* do we call ourselves the lucky country when half of us can't afford housing payments?"

He was pointing his finger now and I could feel my neighbour sitting up and taking notice.

Jacob Coote shrugged. "You know, I didn't know what to talk about today, because I was only told an hour ago that I had to say something. I was gonna speak about the freedom you feel when you ride a motor bike, but that has nothing to do with having a say. When my neighbour up here was talking about ignorance when it came to sex education I was worried. I couldn't think of anything to say that was as worthwhile as her speech. Until I looked out and saw everyone."

He shook his head and gave a little laugh.

"And I felt lucky. Because we have a choice, and I think that we vote, not to get the *best* party in, but to keep the *worst* party out. Because we can stand here

FACT FILE

Famous place for public speaking: Established in 1872, Hyde Park's **Speakers' Corner** is London's oldest public space reserved for public speaking – and probably the world's most famous. Speakers' Corner is important because even in the late 19th century, it was unusual to speak completely freely in public (though the authorities did make sure that no foul language was used at Speakers' Corner!). Today, tourists and Londoners love watching the sometimes strange but often entertaining speakers make a case for issues important to them.

[29] **cut** *Budgetkürzung*
[36] **to nudge** to push (usually gently)
[36] **to send sb sprawling** *jmdn umwerfen*
[54] **stilted** *gesteltzt*
[54] **to knead** [ni:d] *kneten*
[56] **tanned** brown from the sun
[60] **to cringe** to feel embarrassed about what is happening or being said around you

[80]**dickhead** vulgar expression to say a man is a complete idiot
[89]**People's Army** a (negative) reference to the army of any communist country
[92]**apathetic** having or showing no interest in sth
[98]**to be stunned** to be shocked

and protest. We can get all riled up about the Premier's ideas. We can say he's a dickhead even. We can call the Prime Minister and the Leader of the Opposition one as well.

"*We* can scream and shout and protest and even burn our flag if we want to. Because we're free to do whatever we want to do and if we break the law we get a fair trial.

"But in some countries, people can't do that. They can't go out into places like Martin Place and protest. In some countries people our age can't concentrate on their schoolwork or their lives because of the sound of gun-fire.

"In some countries they have one-party systems and they have things called the People's Army and when the people come out and have a say like we're doing today – scream and shout and voice their opinion – the People's Army shoots the people. Young people like us," he added almost in a whisper.

"So, great. Let's be apathetic. Let's *not* vote. Let's let *anyone* run this country. Let's all be ignorant and let's all be proud of that ignorance. And maybe we'll have a People's Army one day, too."

He sat down next to me and everyone in our row leaned forward to stare at him before they clapped. I could sense where his friends were standing because of the shouting and whistling that was coming from their direction.

I was stunned. Not about what he'd said, but the way he'd said it. I would never have thought that Jacob Coote would be passionate like that.

Abridged extract from *Looking for Alibrandi*, by Melina Marchetta

WORD BANK

Having one's say
• to have a say (on sth) • to voice one's opinion (on sth) • to make a speech • debater • oratory / debating skills

Voting & Making a difference
• the vote (= suffrage) • to vote • voter • politician • to make / break a promise • to have a choice • free country • election • democracy / democratic • one-party system • to get a fair trial • freedom • free country • dictatorship • to be apathetic • ignorant • ignorance • to feel passionate about sth

FACT FILE

Voting facts
- In Australia, all citizens 18 or older have to vote.
- In the US, voter turnout in national elections is traditionally quite low, usually between 50% and 55%.
- In Germany, voter turnout in national elections is high, on average 75%.

2 *Comprehension:*
1. *Explain who Josie and Jacob are, and how they already knew each other before the action in this scene begins.*
2. *What usually happens on Have a Say Day? Explain how this Have a Say Day is special for Josie.*
3. *Summarize Jacob's message to his audience.*

3 ***Narrative technique – Suspense:***
a) *Find the scene's climax and describe how suspense is created.*
b) *In lines 92-94, Jacob tells his audience to be apathetic and not to vote, when he actually wants them to do the opposite. Why?* →S7

4 ***Discussion:*** →S26
a) *If one Australian did not vote, would it matter?*
b) *When can one vote make a difference?*

5 [⏎] ***Your turn: What are you passionate about?***
What have you ever felt passionate enough about to want to change?
Explain whether your passion could include speaking publicly.

⟨6⟩ ***Your ideas:*** *Talk about different ways of overcoming public speaking anxiety.*

Make A Difference Day awards

1 [👥] ***Pre-reading:*** *You've seen some examples of how people can make a difference at a national or international level. With a partner, collect ideas about how people can make a difference at the* ***local*** *level.*

Created by USA WEEKEND Magazine, 'Make A Difference Day' is an event that takes place every October across the US. Read about these award-winners.

Teens show a talent for helping sick children

KENNEBEC-WATERVILLE, MAINE – The 12 Winslow High School juniors and seniors in Kendra Littlefield's service-learning class have seen the effects of cancer up close and personal: in one year, the disease took the lives of four teachers they knew in earlier school years.

"Four out of six teachers battling cancer we know have died," says Jen Bizier, 17. She and her classmates decided to spend their second Make A Difference Day helping young cancer patients. "All of us have younger siblings, and we just couldn't imagine losing a sibling to this terrible disease."

Their plan: to aid an art-therapy program at Portland's Maine Medical Center that gives pediatric patients, from infants to teens, an emotional outlet during difficult, frequent chemo treatments.

The class raised $1,000 and received donations of art supplies during a talent show in the school gym, which was decorated with children's drawings of a bright future. Their teachers would be proud.

[8]**sibling** brother / sister
[12]**chemo** chemotherapy
[13]**donation** gift for a good cause

7,000 Florida residents really clean up

DAYTONA BEACH, FLA. – The United Way definitely lives up to its name in Florida. The Volunteer Center for Volusia and Flagler counties has been helping the central coast area and its residents for years, but never quite as much as in 2006, when 7,000 volunteers helped 50,000-plus people with about 80 projects on Make A Difference Day.

In one volunteer effort, Stetson University sophomore Dave Glerum, 19, signed on 25 of his frat brothers to perform maintenance jobs at a park he frequented as a child.

Miles away, it was Guy C. Strutz's first time as a helper, and he didn't disappoint: Strutz and five employees at GCS Construction Inc. fixed up the hurricane-damaged home of a 92-year-old widow, repairing the roof and replacing plaster and painting. "I wouldn't call myself a big religious man," he says, "but I think maybe God is about everyone trying to take care of each other."

From *www.usaweekend.com*

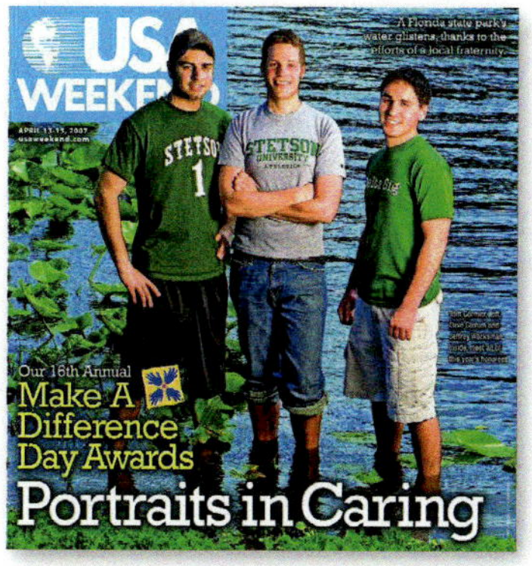

[1]**United Way** a large charitable organization in the US which focuses on fundraising for community issues
[7]**frat brother** fraternity brother *(Mitglied einer Studentenverbindung in den USA)*

2 ***Comprehension:*** *Explain the projects the people in these articles have taken part in. What are their reasons for making a change?*

3 ***Your turn:*** *What similar projects do you know in your community? Say which of them you can imagine taking part in, and why.*

⟨Daily dilemmas⟩

Make a difference quiz

1 [✎] *A quiz: Write your answers to this quiz on a piece of paper. Don't put your name on it. After everyone has done the quiz, find out how many people in class chose the different answers.*

1. At a fast-food restaurant: your bill comes to €7.50, you give the cashier a 10-euro note, and he gives you €12.50 back instead of just €2.50. What do you do?

A Keep the 10 euros.
B Give back the 10 euros.
C Keep the money at first, and then think about what you should do. You *might* give it back.

2. You feel like shopping in a different part of your city one day. Stopping for a coffee, you see your best friend's boyfriend/girlfriend kissing somebody who is definitely *not* your best friend. What do you do?

A Talk to him/her while promising not to say anything to your friend.
B Talk to him/her and say you'll tell your friend what is happening.
C Pretend you didn't see them and say nothing to your friend.

3. You've been invited to the party of the year that *everyone* wants to go to. But you've already promised a friend you'll be in the audience on the opening night of her new musical – the *same* night. What do you do?

A Tell her you can't come and give her the real reason.
B Tell her you can't come but tell her a 'white lie' ("grandmother is ill") instead of the real reason.
C Go and see your friend in her musical.

4. On a full tram: you had already found a place to sit before it got so full. Now an old and weak-looking woman is looking for a seat. What do you do?

A Wait and see if anybody else offers her a seat first; if not, you *might* offer her your seat.
B Offer her your seat.
C Look the other way, pretending you didn't see her.

5. Biology is not your favourite subject, and you're having trouble with it. One day after class you see that your Biology teacher has left behind the answers for tomorrow's test. A perfect grade on that test could really help you right now... Nobody else is in the room. What do you do?

A You take the answers directly to your teacher and say you've seen a few questions, but no more.
B You take the answers, make yourself a photocopy, and then take it back to where you found it.
C You look at all the questions, but not the answers.

6. At a good friend's house before you go out together one night: he/she wants to try out a new outfit. You are shocked at how embarrassing it looks, but you can see your friend thinks it's perfect. What do you do?

A Decide not to tell your friend, but as soon as you get to the disco you tell everyone how awful you think your friend's outfit is.
B Tell your friend what you really think.
C Ignore it and hope nobody at the club sees you together.

WORD BANK

to be caught in a dilemma • In my opinion, the right/wrong thing to do would be to ... • to have/develop a sense of right and wrong • honesty • honest/dishonest • to treat others as you would want to be treated yourself

2 *Discussion:*

a) *Look at your class's results. Find and comment on the majority reaction to each situation.*

b) [⏍] *Discuss whether doing the right thing in the situations above relates to the idea of 'making a difference'.*

3 ***Who is right?*** *Do you feel that some of your classmates definitely chose the wrong reaction? Explain why you think you are right and they aren't.*

TIP

For a closer look at the concept of 'right and wrong', do ⟨Project⟩ **Ethics**.

[◎] A song: *The theatre* by Pet Shop Boys

It's another world here
The streets are gleaming
I was even dreaming
That they're paved with gold

Seventeen, at half past ten
All the crowds are surging past
An electric display

There's another world here
Below shop windows
Upon the pavement
Where you wave goodbye

Boys and girls
Come to roost
From northern parts
And Scottish towns
Will we catch your eye?

[CHORUS]

While you pretend not to notice
All the years we've been here
We're the bums you step over
As you leave the theatre

It's another world here
Somebody is singing
I was only wishing
For a bit of cash
From a patron of the arts
Or at least the phantom of the opera
Will I catch your eye?

[REPEAT CHORUS]

Pavarotti in the Park
Then you walked back up the Strand
Did you catch my eye?

And then pretend not to notice
All the years we've been here
We're the bums you step over
As you leave the theatre

In the end, you pretend
'Cause it's so much easier
We're the bums you step over
As you leave the theatre

Words and music:
Lowe, Chris / Tennant, Neil Frances

VIP FILE

Pet Shop Boys
- famous British synthpop duo consisting of Neil Tennant (b. 1954) and Chris Lowe (b. 1959)
- known for catchy tunes and funny lyrics, often with deeper meaning
- biggest hits: *West End Girls* (1985), *Suburbia* (1986), *Go West* (1994)

4 CORE SKILL *Understanding a song:*
Listen to this song set in the streets of London's West End and summarize in a few words what the song is about. → S9

5 *Analyzing song elements:*
a) ***Mood:*** *Between which two moods does the song switch back and forth?*
b) ***Structure:*** *Describe how the songwriters create the two musical moods.*
c) ***Setting:*** *What do you think was attractive to the Pet Shop Boys about London's West End for the setting of their song?*

6 [group] *Discussion:*
a) *Why do some people 'pretend not to notice' when they see 'bums'? Discuss what else they could do and what difference it would make.*
b) *Put yourself in somebody else's shoes. How do you think a person becomes a 'bum'? Discuss whether you feel it could happen to anybody.*

7 *A cartoon:* → S15
Explain the message of the cartoon.

"Melvin? He's gone to his weekend-box in the country."

[2] **to gleam** to shine (e. g. from having just been cleaned)
[13] **to roost** *here* (of birds) to rest for the night
[16] **to catch sb's eye** to get sb's attention
[19] **bum** *(coll)* homeless person
[25] **patron of the arts** a formal expression to describe sb who supports cultural events and artists
[28] **Pavarotti** Luciano Pavarotti was a famous opera singer who gave huge concerts in places like London's Hyde Park.
[29] **Strand** street in London, famous for theatres

A historic speech

VIP FILE

Barack Obama
- born Barack Hussein Obama in 1961 in Hawaii
- his mother, from Kansas, was white; his black father was from a small village in Kenya
- attended two of America's top universities (Columbia and Harvard)
- Senator Obama of Illinois became 44th president of the United States on 20 January 2009, having won the election as the candidate for the Democratic Party
- first African-American US president

Rarely had the expectations of a new president been as high as they were when Barack Obama became president in January of 2009. America's reputation in the world was at an all-time low; the country continued to be involved in two unpopular and extremely expensive wars; the healthcare system was a disaster; and the economy was in the worst state of crisis since the 1930s.

Over the months before Obama's election, it had become clear that the majority of Americans felt he could be the person to lead the country and make a difference. Obama's campaign slogan, "Yes we can!", became a synonym for the idea of bringing change to America in many ways.

1 ***Pre-listening:*** *You're about to listen to excerpts from Barack Obama's Inauguration Speech on January 20, 2009. These are some of the keywords that come up during his speech: success • greatness • values • better life • responsibility • work*
What do you think Obama might say about these topics in his speech?

2 [◎] CORE SKILL ***Listening for gist:*** *Listen to the speech once and pick out the main ideas, especially with regard to the keywords from exercise 1.* →S29

3 ***First reactions:*** *Describe your reaction to the speech. Think about what Obama says and how he says it.*

4 CORE SKILL ***Listening for detail:*** →S30

a) *Comprehension: In your own words, explain what Obama means with these key quotes:* 1. *"We understand that greatness is never a given. It must be earned. Our journey has never been one of shortcuts and settling for less."* • 2. *"Starting today, we must pick ourselves up, dust ourselves off, and begin again the work of remaking America."* • 3. *"There is nothing so satisfying to the spirit, so defining of our character than giving our all to a difficult task."*

b) [✎] 1. *Name the values that are important for America's success, according to Obama.* • 2. *What does he say on the subject of duties?*

5 ***Discussion:*** *Say what statements / messages in Obama's speech were the most inspiring to you. And if nothing was inspiring – why not?*

6 [✎] [◎] CORE SKILL ***Examining contrasts in speaking style:*** *Go back to 'Looking for Alibrandi' and listen to the scene in which Jacob Coote takes the stage and speaks.*
1. *What differences in style are there between Jacob's speech and Obama's?*
2. *Why are there differences?*

7 [🎬] ***The visual dimension:*** →S13

a) *Watch the video of the parts of Obama's speech you have just listened to. Discuss: Is Obama the kind of speaker one has to watch to be able to appreciate? Or is he just as effective without the visual dimension?*

b) [✎] *Think of other situations where you get information without pictures on the one hand, and with pictures on the other hand. Which do you prefer, and why?*

WORD BANK

greatness • It's a given that … • shortcut • (not) to settle for less • prosperity / prosperous • freedom • to give one's all to sth • to meet the demands of sb / sth • ambition • common purpose • necessity • courage • to struggle • to sacrifice • values • a new era • challenge • task • charismatic speaker / speaking style … • to win an audience over with …

Biographical portrayals

1 *Looking at categories of biographical films:*

a) [👥] *With a partner, write down the names of cinema or TV films you know which deal with the lives of real people. You might find it helpful to think in terms of categories such as 'artists', 'rags-to-riches stories' etc.*

b) *Now share your results with the class. Make a class grid to show which films are in which categories.*

2 [👥👥] *Analyzing a biographical film:* Gorillas in the mist *(1988) – Project work:* → S10, S36

1. *Divide into 4–5 groups and read the summary below. Each group then researches the life of Dian Fossey (books, Internet, magazines) and prepares an outline of the important events and achievements in her life.*
2. *Get a copy of* Gorillas in the mist *and view it together, noting down differences you notice between Dian Fossey's real and film lives.*
3. *In a short presentation, explain where there is artistic license in the film, and why you think the film makers used artistic license. Use the facts from your research.* → S28

TIP

Don't confuse **biographical films** with **documentaries**:
- Biographical films are based on true stories, but the makers almost always take liberties with the facts e.g. for entertainment reasons, or to keep a film from becoming too long. This is called *artistic license*.
- Documentaries, on the other hand, are purely factual films which use original footage (when available).

WORD BANK

biographical film / portrayal • film adaptation of someone's life • based on a true story / a real person / a historical figure • artistic license • I think the criteria for making a successful film are …

Sigourney Weaver playing the part of Dian Fossey

It is 1967. American zoologist Dian Fossey has set up a research camp in the jungles of Rwanda to study the mountain gorillas there. But Fossey does more than just study the gorillas; she communicates with them, plays with them, even becomes 'friends' with them.

The gorillas, however, are becoming extinct: poaching has reduced the population to a dangerously small number. She decides to fight the cruel poachers and save the gorillas, but soon realizes that the Rwandan government is not interested in helping her. So she takes action of her own, though her sometimes extreme methods make her many enemies over the years.

In 1985, Fossey is found murdered – under mysterious conditions – in her camp.

Dian Fossey became an international star after appearing on the cover of *National Geographic* in 1970

Talking about the past and present

*One of the keys to expressing yourself correctly is being able to use the tenses and the progressive and simple forms correctly. Look in your Grammar (**G1 – G2**) before you do each exercise.*

Viviane West, 30, doctor; spends her holiday time as a hospital ship volunteer

Jay Vaughan, 28, film maker; does documentary films on everyday heroes

Erin O'Dea, 18, London schoolgirl; volunteers part-time at an animal shelter

1 [👥] ***Present progressive and simple present:***

a) *With a partner, ask and answer questions about the different people above.* →**G1**

Example: 1. Say what Viviane's job is. → **She's a doctor.** • 2. Say how she spends her holidays. • 3. Say how often she does it. • 4. Explain why you think she does this. • 5. Describe the action in the picture (name at least three things). • 6. Describe a typical day on a hospital ship for Viviane. • 7. Apart from the thought bubble, say what else you think is going through Viviane's mind. • 8. Say what Jay does. • 9. Say why he does it. • 10. Say what Erin does. • 11. Say why you think she does it. • 12. Describe the action in the second picture above (name at least three things).

b) [⊡] ***Role play:*** *Take on the roles of Viviane, Jay and Erin, asking and answering questions about their daily routines (jobs, hobbies) and about what is going on in their lives at the moment.*

2 ***Simple past or past progressive?*** *Describe the action in these scenes with Erin, Jay and Viviane using the simple past and past progressive wherever needed.* →**G2**

3 [✎] ***Present perfect – Simple or progressive?*** →G2

a) *Prepare interview questions for a school newspaper article about Erin. Think of questions about her volunteer work at the shelter. Use the simple and the progressive forms of the present perfect for your questions (e.g. Have you ever … • How long have you been working … • How many times … • Has one of the animals … • Have callers …).*

⟨b)⟩ *Now write an article on Erin for your school newspaper.*

4 ***Mixed bag – Tense revision:*** *Read more about Erin and put in the verbs. Pay attention to which tense is needed in each gap.*

include • not have • look • run • escape • volunteer • love • make • start • have • arrive • receive • want

"I 1 animals ever since I was a kid, and while I was growing up we had lots of pets – cats, dogs, rabbits. But my parents were really worried when they realized my love of animals 2 the not-so cuddly animals, too. At one point I really 3 my own snake – a python. 'Erin, you 4 to get on my nerves with this python idea,' my mum would say. 'I don't want to come home one day and find that your 'friend' 5 from its terrarium! What if it 6 a new home in my bed?! How about getting a job at a pet shop? Just don't bring anything home that 7 fur!'

The owner of the local pet shop didn't have a job for me – but he had an idea: 'What about the animal shelter? They 8 a lot of problems with exotic snakes lately. Too many people buy baby pythons and iguanas and ignore the fact that their babies will one day become huge. When that day finally 9, the people phone the shelter to have their 'monsters' picked up. The shelter 10 more calls in the past six months than in the previous six years. A friend of mine 11 the shelter. She'd be glad to have some help. She can't pay you. It would be volunteer work. But remember: volunteering 12 good on a CV!'

I 13 at the shelter for over two years now, and I love it. But I'm leaving soon. I'm going to Brazil to study – what else? – zoology. In the jungle!"

⟨5⟩ [▤] ***Writing a story:*** *Use your knowledge of the past tenses to write a story of your own. Here are some examples of typical phrases and tenses used to get a story started. Be creative!* →S23, S24

It all **started** last Monday …	• It's typical to start off with the **past tense**.
I'**d been doing** lots of volunteer work at the local hospital over the past few weeks and **getting** home pretty late at night.	• **Past perfect** constructions (simple and/or progressive) help to look *further* into the past.
Monday night **was** no different. It **wasn't** until midnight that I **got off** work. Anyway, while **I was driving** home, a strange feeling **came** over me.	• It's back to the **past** now for the main story.
Then, when I **walked** through my front door, the reason for my funny feeling **was** there to greet me …	• Mixing the **past** with the **past progressive** is typical for contrasting shorter and longer actions.

6 CORE SKILL ***Listening – Mediation:*** *At the dinner table, you are telling your parents that you have been listening to different types of speakers in this Topic. Your parents want to know what is being discussed. Choose one of the listening texts in this Topic and summarize for your parents, in German, what is being said.* →S34

Online-Link 547170-4003

Political correctness ('PC') in the US

Political correctness is a very important aspect of American society. This is especially true of schools, universities and the workplace, i.e. places where people from sometimes completely different backgrounds are expected to get along and not offend each other by the way they speak and behave.

1 *PC super heroes:*

a) *Examine the cartoon on the right. Say what makes the super heroes' names 'politically correct', and what the politically incorrect versions would be.*

b) [group] *In a group, look at the following politically correct expressions, along with the older expressions (in brackets) which they have gradually replaced over the years, especially in more formal contexts. Who do you think wanted politically correct versions of the expressions in brackets, and why? Share your group ideas with the class.*
- *Native American (instead of 'Indian')*
- *flight attendant (instead of 'stewardess' or 'steward')*
- *Happy Holidays! (instead of 'Merry Christmas!')*

c) *Discuss what a suitable definition for political correctness could be.*

2 [group] ***PC in the workplace:*** *In groups, decide what parts of the following statements and / or actions could be seen as politically incorrect, and explain your thoughts. Then make suggestions for politically correct alternatives.*

1. **Boss to new art director:** "I like your idea for sending all our employees different seasonal cards, but we can't send these two out: 'Happy Halloween' and 'Happy St. Patrick's Day'. We need a PC alternative for these fall and spring cards."
2. **Boss to her assistant:** "I need a new secretary. You know what qualities she'll have to have; could you please place an ad? Thanks."
3. **Woman to male colleague:** "Wow, Dave, you've really been spending a lot of time at the gym lately. Come on, let me feel your biceps."
4. **Foreign business visitor:** "There aren't many negroes in your company. Why not?"
5. **One colleague to another:** "Ugh, *another* call from someone who could hardly speak English, expecting me to speak Spanish! People have always spoken English in America, so why don't these people just learn English?!"
6. **Mixed group of male and female colleagues:** "The job for chairman has just opened up; I wonder which executive is going to get it …"
7. **Man to colleagues:** "Seen the new chick on the 4th floor yet? Pretty hot!"

3 ***Evaluating euphemistic language:***

a) *People use euphemistic language every day (e.g. saying something is 'inexpensive' instead of 'cheap'). Look at the cartoon. Can you explain what a euphemism is?*

b) *Many Americans feel that the PC movement sometimes goes too far, and the cartoon makes fun of using euphemistic language. Discuss the following:*
1. *What do you think euphemisms have to do with the PC movement?*
2. *How does euphemistic language represent 'PC going too far'?*

"Couch potato is a deeply offensive term – we prefer furniture-based leisure prioritizers."

On the telephone

1 [◎] ***Useful telephone phrases:*** *Listen for these phrases. Try to use them in the tasks below.*

WORD BANK

The kind of things you may want to say:
Hello. Is that Mr Brown speaking?
Could I speak to Mr Brown, please?
This is ... I'm calling from Germany.
I'm calling about ...
I'd like to enquire about ...
I hope I'm not calling at an inconvenient time.
I've got a few questions/a complaint about ...
I'd like to make an appointment[1] to see the doctor/dentist ...
Shall I ring back later?
Could you take a message/give her a message, please?
What time would be most convenient?
Could you repeat that, please?
I'm afraid the line[2]'s very bad/we've got a bad connection.

What you may hear at the other end of the line:
Brown and Wilson Car Rentals. Can I help you?
Speaking!
I'll just fetch him. Hang on a moment, please.
I'm afraid he's not available/he's in a meeting.
I'm afraid the line is engaged at the moment.
Could you call back later?
Can I take a message?
I'll give you his extension[3].
I'll put you through to the ... department/...
I'll connect you. Please hold the line[4].
Sorry. I think you've got the wrong number.

The person you are calling is not available at the moment.
Please leave a message after the tone.
If you wish to contact the sales/complaints/customer service department, please press ONE/TWO/...

2 [◎] ***Make a difference by using the phone:***

a) *Listen to Stefanie calling 'Shelter', a UK charity.*
   1. *What do you learn about Shelter?*
   2. *Did Stefanie get the information she wants?*

b) [👥] 1. *Listen to three messages recorded on an answering machine.*
   2. *Write and act dialogues number two and three in which you answer the messages.*

c) [👥] *You are taking part in a charity project where people have to 'make a difference'. Think of a task for yourself. After that, make a list of people, companies, institutions that you have to phone. Practise these phone calls, using fewer and fewer notes each time.* →S29, S30

NAF

I'm just opening the mail – you should see the size of my mobile phone bill!

[1]Termin • [2]Leitung • [3]Durchwahl • [4]dran bleiben

Reasons for making a difference

1 *Examining the power of pictures:*
Organizations trying to make a difference depend on the media to attract interest to their causes.
a) *Look at the posters below. Say what you think the aim behind each could be.*
b) *Analyze the differences in approach.*
c) [⏎] *Explain which approach you feel is more effective, and why.*

The American *Peace Corps*

Amnesty International

2 [⏎] ***Talking about organizations with a mission:***
1. *Do you know of any organizations that are trying to make a difference?*
   Think about causes such as these:
   - *human rights*
   - *the environment*
   - *wildlife*
   - *animal rights*
   - *aid for the developing world*
2. *Say what you know about the organizations, and whether the causes they stand for interest you. Explain.*

3 CORE SKILL ***Understanding a news report:***

a) *Look at the photo above of activists in action and answer these questions:*
   1. *Which boat do you think the activists are in, and what makes you think this?*
   2. *What kind of activists do you think they are? Give reasons for your answer.*
   3. *What kind of actions are possible at sea?*

b) [◎] [✎] *Now listen to a report about the activists and their cause. Take notes on these points:*
   1. *Who are the two opposing sides?*
   2. *What issue is causing the conflict?*
   3. *What criticism is there of whom?* →S30

c) *Compare your answers from b) to your ideas from a). What were you right about?*

d) [✎] *Summarize the content of the report in writing.*

e) *Discuss how effective you feel the organization's tactics are.*

⟨4⟩ [ååå] [✎] ***Group activity – Gallery walk:***

1. *In a group, find out more about one of the organizations you have discussed while working on these pages, or during your work on this Topic. Use the Internet.*
2. *Prepare an information poster with a short text in your own words describing the organization's mission. Use the organization's material.*
3. *Present your poster to the class in the form of a 'gallery walk'. Each group hangs up its poster, and the class walks through the 'gallery' from poster to poster, with each group explaining its organization.*

⟨Project⟩ Drama

DRAMA TIP
Putting on a play at school means involving the whole class. But how? Those of you who do not want to act on stage could take on the other important jobs of a stage production: stage manager, director, lighting experts, set and costume designer(s) and scene painter(s), make-up specialist(s), prompter, and classmates helping with any other technical things you might want (e.g. music, sound effects).

Putting on a school play
Before you can put on this play, the whole class should read Wesker's one-act play carefully. Think about this: What is the message of the play? What about 'courage' and the various characters? Who is the main character? What makes this play good drama? Discuss all this and whatever else you think is important in your group or in class.

STEP 1 – Selecting a character
Reread the play and think about which character you could imagine playing. Agree in class who should act which character! Think about this: What could his/her biography be like? Write a character outline. This way the character you'll be playing will later become your own 'creation'. To act your role convincingly, you must really understand your character. And for those of you not acting: Decide who does what, and start thinking about set design and costumes, about lighting, etc.

STEP 2 – Reading the play in character
The second step is to read the play in character – aloud and in a small group. Try to give your character the voice and typical features that you have thought about in your character outline. Don't forget: The main purpose of putting on a play is to have fun yourself and to entertain the audience, so take your job seriously, but don't put yourself under too much pressure.

STEP 3 – Creating dramatic elements
Now think about gestures, the way the characters could interact, and who should be where and when on stage. Keep trying things out until you are all satisfied. Stay polite when you criticize others, their acting and their ideas, and don't take criticism personally!

STEP 4 – Rehearsing
If you are an actor, learn your role by heart. As soon as you know it by heart, continue to try out different ways of acting, alone or with your classmates. Don't speak too fast. Speech pauses or pauses between dialogue parts can be very effective and a good way of catching the audience's attention. This is the main goal in drama.

A good way to gain confidence is 'speed-through' rehearsals, a technique very much like the fast-forward in cinema. During speed-through rehearsals you often come across lines or scenes that still cause some problems, so you can now give these smaller problems special attention. All you can do at the end is to try it and – most of all – have fun putting on the play.

act one of the parts of a show or play
to select to choose
creation *Schöpfung, Werk*
set the background for the stage
feature aspect
to entertain *unterhalten*
gesture a movement that you make with your hands, your head or your face to show a particular meaning
to interact to act or communicate with sb
satisfied happy, pleased
attention *Aufmerksamkeit, Interesse*
goal *Ziel*
to gain confidence *Selbstbewusstsein erlangen*
fast-forward *Zeitraffer*
to involve *einbeziehen, einbinden*
prompter a person who helps actors with their lines

Little old lady *by Arnold Wesker*

Carriage of an Underground train. Sound of an Underground train hurtling through its tube. Lights up on interior of a London Underground carriage. 'No Smoking' signs are in evidence. Two young people sit side by side in the length-ways section, Sam and Tracy. She is testing him from a diary full of information. It has been going on some time.

Tracy Capital of Greece?

Sam Dunno.

Tracy Athens. Capital of Japan?

Sam Dunno.

Tracy Tokyo. Capital of Russia?

Sam *(jubilantly)* Moscow!

Tracy Right! Bloody congratulations! Flaming hallelujah! At last! Genius! Hero!

Sam Alright, alright. You'll give me a big 'ead.

Tracy Now that we know the capital of Russia can we start having aitches where they belong? *H*ead. The word is '*h*ead', not 'ead'.

Sam It's quicker to say 'bigead'. Say it like *you* want and I've got to take a deep breath. Big *(breath)* *h*ead.

The train stops. Sound of doors opening. The Little old lady gets on.

Little old lady Is this the right train for South Kensington?

Sam *(Not looking at chart)* Yeah. You got King's Cross, Russell Square, Holborn, Covent Garden, Leicester Square, Piccadilly Circus, Green Park, Hyde Park Corner, Knightsbridge first. Then South Ken.

Sound of doors closing. Train moves off. She sits some seats away from them.

Tracy Capital of Hungary?

Sam Dunno.

Tracy Budapest. Capital of Portugal?

Sam I don't even know where Portugal is.

Tracy Whereas you know where Hungary is, and Finland and Norway?

Sam Don't be like that.

Tracy Well I am like that. You want to be my friend you must take me like that.

Sam Cor! Girls ain't 'alf bossy.

Tracy *(Bossily)* That's sexist.

Sam Alright, *you're* bossy then.

Tracy That's better. Here, *(showing him map)* Portugal.

Sam *(As though it's just come to him)* Lisbon.

Tracy You saw.

Sam I never. Print's too small.

Tracy Capital of New Zealand?

Sam Cor! You're getting really difficult, aren't you?

Little old lady You don't know the capital of New Zealand?

Tracy He doesn't know the capital of anywhere, missus.

Little old lady It's Wellington. Don't they teach you these things in school?

Tracy Got no time to teach us. Too busy getting us through exams.

Little old lady I don't think I understand that. Subtle.

Sam What's she on about? 'Subtle'?

VIP FILE

Arnold Wesker
- born 1932 in London
- dramatist, journalist and poet
- he is one of the important British dramatists of the 20th century

CHARACTERS

Tracy, aged 15
Sam, aged 15
Little old lady, aged 65
Harassed woman, aged 45
Unpleasant man, aged 19 or 50
Jason, aged 17

dramatist person who writes plays for the theatre, television or radio
harassed *zermürbt*
unpleasant not nice
to hurtle to move very fast
tube *Tunnel, Röhre*
interior the inside part of sth
to be in evidence *sichtbar, erkennbar sein*
length-ways section seats that are built along the walls of the carriage

[2]**dunno** = *coll* don't know
[6]**jubilantly** very happily
[7]**bloody** very rude expression
[7]**congratulations** *Glückwunsch*
[7]**flaming hallelujah** *here Super, ganz toll!*
[9]**aitch** the letter 'h'
[12]**big head** *aufgeblasenes Ego*
[15]**chart** *Anzeige(tafel), Schema*
[26]**cor** *coll* expression of surprise
[26]**ain't** *coll* are not
[26]**bossy** always telling people what to do
[36]**missus** *coll* woman, wife
[39]**subtle** *subtil*

Tracy Subtle, dum-dum, means the meaning isn't obvious *(To Little old lady)* It's simple, missus. They show us the kind of question we'll get in our exams and we just learn an assortment of answers.

Little old lady You don't seem stupid to me.

Tracy My dad's a civil servant isn't he, so I read books don't I!

Little old lady And your boyfriend doesn't?

Tracy He's not my boyfriend, he's the new next-door neighbour, and he's nicer than me.

Little old lady You mean people who read books are unpleasant, and people who don't read books are all honey and spice and everything nice?

Tracy I didn't say that.

Little old lady What's your names?

Tracy I'm Tracy he's Sam.

Sam I'm Sam she's Tracy.

Little old lady And I'm just an interfering old woman.

Sam Old? You're not old. Who says you're old?

Little old lady I think you're making fun of me. Don't young people think everyone over twenty-five is old?

Sam *(Taking book from Tracy. To Little old lady)* Capital of Turkey?

Little old lady Ankara. Used to be Constantinople, now known as Istanbul. Istanbul! Dreary old sound. Constantinople's much nicer, don't you think? More romantic. Named after the Roman Emperor Constantine who was the first Roman Emperor to convert to Christianity you know. Started another Empire. The Byzantine. Now there's a romantic sound for you. Byzantine. Produced lots of paintings and churches. I used to love history at school. But I never saw anywhere. Couldn't afford to travel. Too late now.

Sam *(Hoping for another long answer)* Capital of China?

Little old lady Peking. *(The young ones eagerly await)* I don't know anything about Chinese history.

Sam Capital of Mexico?

Little old lady Mexico City.

Sam Brazil?

Little old lady Brasilia.

Sam Peru?

Little old lady Lima.

Sam Nigeria?

Little old lady Lagos.

Sam Is there anywhere you don't know the capital of?

Little old lady I don't think I know the capital of – oh – Madagascar or the Fiji Isles, or, let me see now, Guinea-Bissau.

Tracy But she has *heard* of a place called Guinea-Bissau. Have *you*, dum-dum?

Train stops. Sound of doors opening. Two people enter. The Harassed woman with cumbersome shopping, who sits. The Unpleasant man, who stands and sways. Sound of doors closing. Train moves off. Unpleasant man lights up a cigarette. Everyone watches. Mesmerised. No one says anything. They look at one another. Helpless. He's mean and aloof. Nothing and no one exists for him. The silence is long. Unease grows. He seems to flourish in such atmospheres. Finally –

41 **dum-dum** stupid
43 **assortment** *eine Auswahl*
45 **civil servant** *Beamter*
50 **all honey and spice** wonderful
55 **to interfere** *sich einmischen*
61 **dreary** boring
63 **to convert** to change to
66 **to afford** to have enough money to buy or do sth
69 **eagerly** very interested and excited
85 **cumbersome** large and heavy; difficult to carry
85 **to sway** to move slowly from side to side
87 **mesmerised** fascinated
88 **aloof** not friendly or interested in other people
89 **unease** nervousness
89 **to flourish** *here* to be happy

Little old lady Excuse me, sir, but smoking's not permitted on the Underground. *He glares at her, then ignores her. More silence.* Well isn't anyone else going to say anything? No support? Just one old lady?

The Harassed woman turns away, deeply embarrassed to be drawn into a public scene. The young ones take up their game, voices subdued now.

Sam Capital of Egypt?
Tracy Cairo.
Sam Capital of Argentina?
Tracy Buenos Aires.
Sam Capital of South Africa?
Tracy Pretoria.
Sam Capital of USA?
Unpleasant man New York.
Tracy Washington.

The Unpleasant man has been corrected in public. He's angry. The air is now charged.

Little old lady Excuse me, sir, but smoking is a danger to health and a hazard to life and is not permitted on the Underground. *Again he glares and then ignores her.* Well you can glare all you like, sir, but experience has taught us a lesson and I'm going to keep on asking you – please put out your cigarette. There are other people in this carriage who have to be considered. *(No response)* I mean you don't live on this earth by yourself, sir. Someone's driving this train for you and someone made your jacket for you and I assume you had a good breakfast this morning. *(No response)* Can you hear me? *(No response)* Are you listening, sir?
Sam Why's she keep calling him 'sir'?
Little old lady Do you enjoy upsetting other people? *He opens his newspaper as though to escape her.* People like him make it a really depressing day. Just takes one person and you feel all human nature is rotten. *Silence.* I suppose he's imagining he's exercising his democratic rights. *No comment.* Well let me tell you, sir, if you'll forgive me lecturing you, sir, and I know I'm only a foolish old woman with everything finished and failed behind me, and you're a splendid young man with everything brave and shining ahead of him, let me tell you – democratic rights have their limitations. They have! *Your* democratic rights are limited by *our* democratic rights. And it's our democratic right not to breathe in the foul smoke of your cigarette or run the risk of going up in flames. What do you say to that?
Sam Subtle! *The Unpleasant man turns a fierce gaze upon Sam.* It's the capital of Madagascar. *(Points to book)* Subtle – capital of Madagascar.
Unpleasant man I know what 'subtle' means, sonny. I'm not stupid. Play your games and mind your own business.
Little old lady It is his business. His life's under threat because of you.
Unpleasant man And you think yourself lucky you're an old woman.
Little old lady No, you think yourself lucky I'm an old woman, and this is a poor mother, and these are only young children and that there's no one here to yank that weed from your mouth and stand ten feet taller than you.
Unpleasant man You can yank it out, lady. Be my guest. Anyone can be my guest.

DRAMA TIP
The technical equipment that you have can be important features in your production of the play. Will you have a proper stage with stage lights? Do you you need special effects, sound effects or any music for the play? If, for example, the characters in this scene are to walk through the sliding doors of the Underground train, you could use an overhead projector and move some slips of paper from the centre to the left and right and then back again.

91 **to glare** to look at sb / sth in an angry way
94 **subdued** not very loud
105 **charged** *aufgeladen, voller Spannung*
106 **hazard** danger
113 **to assume** to think
117 **to upset** to make sb feel unhappy
118 **to escape** to get away from sb / sth
119 **rotten** bad
120 **to exercise** *ausüben*
121 **to lecture** to criticize sb or tell them how they should behave
123 **failed** not successful
123 **splendid** excellent, fine
125 **limitation** *Grenze*
129 **fierce** angry and aggressive
129 **gaze** *Blick*
132 **mind your own business** *kümmere dich um dich selbst*
133 **under threat** *in Gefahr*
137 **to yank** to pull sth with a quick movement

No one takes up his invitation. The train stops. Sound of doors opening. Jason gets on. He has a Walkman plugged into his ears and is dancing to himself to music that cannot be heard other than the maddening bass beat of 'dud, dud, dud'. Sound of doors closing. Train moves off. Jason is oblivious to the tension. Dances on. All regard him except the Unpleasant man and the Little old lady who is watching the Unpleasant man. Suddenly Jason notices and slowly comes to a halt.

Jason *(To Harassed woman)* Hey, man. He's smoking.
Tracy You could've fooled me. *(together with)*
Sam Nah! You're imagining it.

The Unpleasant man turns his fierce gaze first upon Sam and Tracy who huddle down, then upon Jason who, frightened, returns to his jigging.

Jason Cool, man, cool! It's a free country. Cool.
Little old lady Free for you, too, young man.
Jason Yes, ma'am, I know that. Look *(dancing)* I'm free!
Little old lady Chained to one of those things? *(No response)* While you're dancing Rome may burn.
Jason *(To Sam and Tracy)* She do exaggerate don't she!
Little old lady And you're the only one here who's his size.
Jason Please, ma'am. My life gives me enough headaches. My brother's in jail, my girl's left me, I don't like my job and my motor bike's been nicked. I can only take on board so much or I'll sink. This gentleman here may be my size but he's not my type. My type is reasonable, co-operative, full of love and tenderness with two kind eyes in a friendly head. Know what I mean? You seen that man's eyes? Them's the unhappiest eyes I've seen in a long time. He don't like himself one little bit. That man's got an inferiority complex the size of a volcano and there ain't nothing more unpredictable and dangerous than a volcano, ma'am, I'm telling you. Now, do you mind, excuse me, I've got to get back to my therapy.

He returns to his dancing. The joy is gone, though. He's more apprehensive.

Little old lady Is no one going to stand up to this oaf?
Unpleasant man *(Steps towards her, threateningly. Defiantly)* Hit me!

He considers it. All watch. Thinks better of it. Grins. Returns to his newspaper.

Tracy Capital of India?
Sam Dunno.
Tracy New Delhi. Capital of Canada?
Sam Dunno.
Tracy Ottawa. Capital of Ireland?
Sam *(Surprised at himself)* Dublin!
Unpleasant man Thank bloody Christ!

Train stops. Sound of doors opening. His cigarette is at an end. He stubs it out with his foot. Sound of doors closing. Train moves off. Tension eases. A kind of normality returns. Only the sound of the train and the 'dud, dud, dud' from the Walkman. Very slowly and deliberately the Unpleasant man takes out his packet of cigarettes and places one in his mouth. Everyone turns to see what he'll do. Even Jason ceases moving. The tension has risen again. He takes out a lighter. Before he can strike it the Little old lady stands up.

140 **plugged** *eingestöpselt*
141 **maddening** very annoying
142 **oblivious to** *etw. nicht wahrnehmen*
143 **to regard** to look at sb / sth
143 **except** apart from
146 **to fool sb** to trick sb
148 **to huddle (down)** *sich niederkauern*
149 **to jig** to dance
152 **ma'am** = madam, polite form of address
153 **to be chained to sth** *an etw. angekettet sein*
155 **to exaggerate** to make sth seem larger, better or worse than it really is
158 **to nick** *coll* to steal
160 **reasonable** *vernünftig*
161 **tender** kind, gentle and loving
163 **inferiority complex** *Minderwertigkeitskomplex*
167 **apprehensive** worried that sth terrible may happen
168 **oaf** idiot
169 **defiantly** *herausfordernd*
177 **Thank bloody Christ!** very rude, ironic and aggressive expression
179 **to ease** *sich beruhigen, lockern*
183 **to cease** to stop
183 **lighter** *Feuerzeug*
184 **to strike** *here (an)zünden*

Little old lady You light that cigarette and I'll pull this chain.

She raises her hand to the emergency chain. Confrontation. The Unpleasant man is held. He's having second thoughts. His face is full of fury. The tension is unbearable.

Jason Oh, ma'am, give us a break, ma'am. You pull that chain and the train will stop and then all the other trains will have to stop and maybe something will go wrong and there'll be a crash and people will die or get hurt just for one man who so badly needs a drag he can't hold back.

Little old lady I smoke thirty a day. I can hold back.

Jason You're stronger than he is. Anyone can see that.

Little old lady *(To Unpleasant man)* Light it and I'll pull.

The tension is now so unbearable that the Harassed woman bursts out.

Harassed woman You pull that chain and I'll be late for my appointment. One late appointment leads to another. And there's someone looking after my children who has their own appointments. Why are you making trouble? What's in a cigarette? One cigarette in a whole carriage. No one else is smoking and no one else is complaining. Can you see anyone else smoking? Can you hear anyone else complaining? You frightened from the smoke of one cigarette? Open the windows. Look! I'll open them. This one, and this one, and this one. There! There won't be any smoke now and all of us can detect smouldering in time – only don't pull that chain or you'll upset everyone's life. For one man! One antisocial man and a lousy cigarette.

Silence. Only the train and the 'dud, dud, dud'. What will he do? What will she do?

Little old lady Light it. I pull.

The question and answer between Sam and Tracy continues, but really their concentration is on the Unpleasant man.

Tracy Capital of Denmark?
Sam Dunno.
Tracy Copenhagen. Capital of Zimbabwe?
Sam Dunno.
Tracy Harare. Capital of Israel?
Sam *(Hopefully)* Jerusalem?

He lights. She pulls. Blackout. Sound of train, now loud, screeches to a halt. A babble of complaining voices. Cut out. Silence. End.

186 **emergency chain** *Notbremse*
187 **fury** *Wut, Zorn*
188 **unbearable** *unerträglich*
192 **drag** *informal* an act of breathing in smoke from a cigarette
196 **to burst out** to speak suddenly, loudly and with strong feeling
205 **to detect** to discover or notice sth
205 **smouldering** to burn slowly without a flame, *Schwelbrand*
206 **lousy** *lausig*
218 **to screech** to make a loud high noise

DRAMA TIP
Wesker thinks Jason should be 17 years old, but no age is given for the Unpleasant man. Think about this.
Once you have studied the parts, try changing the age of the characters. Does this change the message of the play?

⟨Project⟩ Ethics

Ethics is about 'right' and 'wrong'. Philosophers of all ages and backgrounds – such as Socrates, Aristotle and Kant – have thought about questions like these: How should we lead a good life in society? What is just? And who is to judge this?

This project is about becoming aware of ethical behaviour. It is about looking at your own ethics, about how you and your classmates act.

WORD BANK

to obey / disobey the law • an act of civil disobedience • it's illegal / an offence to … • it's right / wrong to … • to commit / be guilty of a crime • to damage / destroy sth • to have a clear / guilty conscience • to rely on / trust your intuition • it's ethical / unethical to … break the law / stop a greater evil / disobey the police / damage property / hurt people • the ends justify the means

STEP 1 – Discussing an ethical problem

Look at this photo, taken in a school. The boy is having problems.

a) *What could the pupils who are watching do – if anything? Discuss the alternatives.*
b) *Explain what your arguments for or against each alternative were based on. Feelings? (What feelings?) Being ethical and practical? Both?*

STEP 2 – Defining 'ethical'

a) *Now look at the situation on the left. Describe what is happening.*
b) *Say how you feel about what the people are doing. Use the Word Bank.*
c) *Not everyone in class will feel the same way about the situation on the left. Why? Use the Ethics Skills to help you explain.*

ETHICS SKILLS

1. Your reaction to what other people say or do: The way someone acts or talks is always **interpreted** by others. This interpretation is very often an ethical **judgement** (about an action/a person, about what someone says).
2. Think about where your opinions and judgements (your ethical principles) come from: parents • education • religion • rules made by society • personal experience • an 'inner voice' • the feeling that something is "simply right".
3. Question your opinions and judgements: Do you understand how differences in religion, education etc. can influence ethical decisions and actions in ways different from your own?

FACT FILE

There are two schools of thought in ethics:
1. Absolute ethics: There are ethical values and principles which are always right / applicable under any circumstances. ("It is unethical to kill someone.") Religions are typical examples of absolute ethics – they tell you exactly what is right and what is wrong – as *they* see it.
2. Relative ethics: Two individuals or groups can disagree about whether an action is ethical or not – and they can both be right. ("For some communities it is ethical to kill someone under certain circumstances.") The ancient Greeks, for example, said it was acceptable to kill a tyrant if he destroyed their democracy.

just *gerecht*
to become aware of sth to know or realize sth
to obey / to disobey (not) to do what you are told or expected to do
an act of civil disobedience *ein Fall von zivilem Ungehorsam*
offence crime
to commit sth (usually a crime)
to be guilty of sth to be responsible for sth bad
to damage *beschädigen*
a clear / guilty conscience ein reines / unreines Gewissen
to rely on sth / sb to need or depend on sb / sth
property a thing or things that are owned by sb
the ends justify the means *der Zweck heiligt die Mittel*
judgement *Urteil*
applicable *anwendbar, geeignet*
circumstance *Umstand, Lage*
certain *bestimmt, gewiss*

STEP 3 – Doing a survey
Find out whether the pupils in your class have similar ethical principles.

a) [group] *In your group, prepare three statements on ethical issues. Choose topics which you think could be controversial. Then do a survey in your group first.* →S21

Here are some suggestions:
- Human rights come before animal rights.
- Always be friendly to other people.
- Lying is always unethical.
- …

The questionnaire could look like this:

Put a cross in the appropriate box.

Human rights come before animal rights.	☒ That's right ☐ I mostly disagree ☐ I don't know	☐ I mostly agree ☐ I completely disagree

b) *Now do your survey in the whole class. (Collect your own group's questionnaires separately so that you can discuss them later.)*
Analyze and discuss the result of the surveys in class. Are there any trends which surprise you? Are you happy with the ethical standards that everyone has? Could anything be changed for the better?

c) [group] *Finally, look at your own group's questionnaires and think again. What were your own personal opinions / judgements based on? (Look back at Step 2c).) In your group, discuss the principles behind your answers.*

STEP 4 – Preparing a presentation
Find an ethical topic you would like to research further and then present it to your class.

a) *In class, decide which group will take which of these topics:*
- Rights and duties between young people and their parents.
- Limits of solidarity with friends who are in the wrong (loyalty, keeping secrets).
- Equality in society e.g. women and equal rights or ethnic minorities and their specific cultural differences and requirements.
- Freedom of the individual e.g. to be happy, to take drugs, to damage the environment.
- …

b) [group] *In your groups, research your topic. Find out what different ethical viewpoints there are and prepare your presentation. Think what form of presentation would best suit your theme.* →S36, →S28
- a talk show or discussion on TV or radio
- a written report on a case that you have made up
- a video news report from your town, with filmed interviews and comments
- a photo exhibition in your classroom with a "guided tour" by group members

c) *Present the results of your work in class and comment on the presentations.*

to lie to say or write sth that you know is not true
cross *Kreuz*
limit a point at which sth stops
equality *Gleichheit*
requirement need
to suit *passen (zu)*
to encourage to give sb support or hope
white lie *Notlüge*
to betray *verraten*
to condone *stillschweigend dulden*
shoplifting stealing things from a shop

WORD BANK
I'm surprised how many • There doesn't seem to be any agreement about • There's a contradiction between • The general opinion seems to be … • It's quite encouraging / disappointing / shocking • to tell a white lie • to show respect for • to be in the wrong • to keep / to betray a secret • to be loyal to • a conflict of loyalites • to condone cheating / shoplifting / …

Skills

This Skills section is a reference section. It can give you *practical* help for writing essays, understanding and analyzing texts, for tests, job applications, letter-writing etc.

Table of contents

Text skills

S1 Reading techniques

Skimming, scanning and close reading

Skimming
When you skim a text you read it quickly to get the **general idea**. This is also called 'reading for gist'.

- Read the title, the headings, the first sentences of paragraphs and the last paragraph because it often summarizes the text.
- Do not read every single word – concentrate on looking for keywords.

Scanning
Scanning is a useful technique for **finding specific information** quickly. This is also called 'reading for detail'.

- Look for words in the text related to the information you are looking for.
  Example: You are reading a tourist guide text about London, but only want to find out something about London parks. Look for the word *park* or the names of parks such as *Hyde Park*, *Green Park*, *St. James's Park*, *Regent's Park*.
- Ignore unrelated information. It is not relevant for scanning.
- Headings and words in **bold** or *italics* may help you to identify the relevant sections.

Close reading
If you want to answer detailed questions about a text, you must read every line carefully.

- Skim the text a second time, this time listing the paragraphs and noting down the keywords in each of them.
  Example: *Bag Lady* in Topic 3. **1st paragraph:** *dead and dying albatrosses*. **2nd paragraph:** *albatrosses pick up plastic in the sea, feed chicks.* **3rd paragraph:** … Leave space for more notes later.
- Read the complete text slowly. While you are reading, find out and note down any words you do not know.
- Then reread the text – as often as you need to understand everything. If you want, you can make more notes.
  Example as on the left: **1st paragraph:** *dead and dying albatrosses. Hawaiian island of Midway, breeding ground of Laysan albatross, dead birds everywhere; looks like apocalypse; author filming a BBC documentary, she breaks down and weeps.*

S2 Different types of texts

Texts can be divided into two different groups: fictional and non-fictional texts.

Non-fictional texts	Fictional texts (*or* fiction) *or* literature
Important types: Newspaper article, informative text, essay, review, biography, diary, letter, instructions, advertisements, travel writing ■ These texts provide information, facts and often opinions. ■ They are usually well-structured and written in clear, direct prose.	**There are three main literary genres:** Fiction (novels, short stories, fables, fairy tales, etc.), drama (plays: tragedies, comedies and tragi-comedies) and poetry They take the reader into another world. ■ Characters and plot are invented (the range is from realism to complete fantasy). ■ The style depends on the author. Atmosphere and emotions are often more important than hard facts. ■ Some novels include letters, diary entries etc. written by the characters.

S3 Understanding texts

When you analyze a text, you will need to answer different questions about it. First of all, identify the type of text you are going to read. → S2 *Then decide which of the following questions are relevant for this text type and try to answer them.*

Understanding texts: Checklist

General
- Who is the addressee, i.e. for whom is the text written (the 'target group')?
- Who is the author (e.g. journalist, expert, private person)?
- When was it written (e.g. recently, a long time ago)?
- What is the purpose of the text (e.g. to provide information, to entertain, or both)?
- Is there a central message?

Structure, language and style

- How is the text structured? Can it be divided into chapters, acts/scenes, verses?
- How are the sentences structured (e.g. short, complex)?
- What kind of language does it use (e.g. BE, AE, formal, informal, technical)?
- Are stylistic devices used (e.g. symbols, metaphors, rhetorical questions, repetition)?
- What is the tone like (e.g. humorous, ironic, serious, emotional)?
- Does the text have any other special features?

Effect

- What effect might the text have on the reader?
- What atmosphere is created?
- What is your personal impression?
- What is the author's intention? What is the 'moral of the story'?

Additional questions for fictional texts

- Who is the narrator (e.g. first-person, third-person)? → S6, S7
- What is the setting?
- Who are the characters? What do we learn about them? → S5
- How are they portrayed?
- What is the main theme?
- What is the plot?
- Does the short story follow a traditional structure? → S4
- What narrative techniques are used? → S7

WORD BANK

General
The text is a typical example of … • The writer/author describes … • The aim/purpose of the text is to … • The writer/author uses … in order to show/illustrate … • He/she might want to show that … • On the one hand … on the other hand … • In contrast to … • That's why/ For this reason … • Personally, I feel that … • In my opinion, …

Non-fictional texts
The article/text was published in … • The text deals with … • The way the topic/problem is presented suggests that …

Fictional texts
The novel/short story/poem/play was written by … in … • He/she is famous for … • It tells the story of … • It is written from the point of view of … • It is set in … • The action takes place in … • The main characters are … • The narrator is … • At the beginning … • Later on … • At the end … • The climax is…/the turning point is …

S4 Fictional texts – an overview

Novel	Short story	Play	Poem
A long fictional prose text that often includes a large number of characters, different settings (i.e. the time and place) and a complex plot (storyline).	A short fictional text that is meant to be read in one sitting. It usually focuses on a single event and one setting. There are often only one or two main characters. A short story often starts in an unexpected way ('medias in res' = right in the middle of the action), and there is also often a turning point and a surprise ending.	A play is intended to be performed on stage by actors and actresses. The characters speak to each other in dialogue. They may also speak directly to the audience in 'asides'. A play is usually divided into acts and scenes.	A poem is usually a short piece of writing, divided into lines which may or may not be grouped into verses (stanzas). An important element of poetry is 'condensed' language. → S8

haracters of a novel or short story in different ways e.g. through

athletic, attractive, blonde, elegant, tall, ugly, young …
honest, jealous, kind, shy, sympathetic …
angry, confident, embarrassed, emotional, innocent, irresponsible, open …
polite, quiet, rude, talkative …
aristocratic, from a broken home, criminal, lonely, married, rich …
boss, boyfriend, daughter, enemy, friend, mother …

S6 Narrative point of view

The narrator is the person or voice who tells the story. The reader is strongly influenced by the narrative point of view or the perspective from which a story is told. There are three ways in which this can be done:

The **3rd person omniscient* narrator** knows everything about all of the characters' thoughts and feelings and the events. This kind of narrator tells the story from the outside, so he/she is not a character in the story.

This means that the reader often knows more than the characters. Example: *The Divide* (Topic 3)

* **omniscient** [ɒmˈnɪʃɪənt] knowing everything

! When you are talking about a text, do not confuse the narrator, the author and the characters.

The **3rd person limited narrator** seems to present the story from the outside, but only knows the thoughts and feelings of one of the characters in the story. The narrator is not, however, identical with this character.

This means that the reader only has a limited amount of information.
Example: *My son the fanatic* (Topic 2) – only Parvez's thoughts and feelings are known.

WORD BANK
The narrator influences the reader by … • The reader sees the events through the eyes of … • The narrative point of view creates suspense because … • The author has chosen a good narrative perspective because …

The **1st person narrator** is a character in the text who tells you what he/she knows, experiences and feels ('I'). The point of view is limited because the reader only gets to know what this particular character knows, and the information may not be reliable. It is easy to identify with this kind of narrator.
Example: *Slam* is narrated by Sam (Topic 1).

S7 Narrative techniques

When you analyze a story, you should not only think about the story itself, but also the ways in which it is told. These 'narrative techniques' influence the way the reader sees the story.

The effect a story has depends on the relationship between the characters, the narrator and the reader. The way the reader can identify with one or more of the characters is influenced by these factors:

Important narrative techniques

A Native American storyteller

- **Point of view** (→ S6) or **perspective**: Who is the narrator and what is his/her attitude towards the characters? Does the narrator tell the reader everything and is it really true? The point of view determines what the reader gets to know and when. The author can create suspense by not giving away too much information, which is a typical feature of crime stories.
- The **plot** is what happens in a story. There are many ways a plot can be told. For example, part of it might be told to the reader directly and other parts might be told by one character to another.
- The narrator can treat the characters **humorously** or with **irony**. The use of irony means that what is said is not actually meant, or that the reader and narrator are aware of something that the character is not. A good example of irony is when the woman in Hastings (*Slam*, Conclusion pages of Topic 1) asks, "Would you say I'm more than one day old?" What she really means is that she knows very well that Sam wants the room for a girl and himself. The irony of the whole *situation* is that this is exactly what Sam *does not* want.
- In addition to **descriptions** of characters, events and **settings**, the author can also use **dialogue** to reveal the characters' thoughts and feelings. In some cases, what a character does not say can be just as revealing as what they say. **Letters, diary entries** and **dreams** are also very effective ways of showing how the characters feel.
- In some stories you read or hear directly what a character thinks. The character's thoughts can be unstructured and chaotic, as they often are in real life. This is known as 'interior monologue'.
- Sometimes the characters are **archetypes**. An archetype is a character that always stays the same and that often symbolizes something e.g. the 'proud Indian' or the 'bad guy'. Archetypes are often based on standard personality traits and may present a cliché that often has little to do with reality. Films and novels/stories often use archetypes because they are easy for the viewer/reader to understand. Example: the secret agent who knows how to act in every situation and never gets killed.
- An author often creates an **atmosphere** (or **mood**) by using particular words and descriptions. *Slam* has very little atmosphere, but *Paranoid Park* has a lot of atmosphere. It is important for the plot. In *Slam* humour and irony are more important than atmosphere.
- It is important to look at the order in which the events are told. Many stories are **not linear** i.e. they do not start at the beginning and go straight through to the end. To make the story more interesting, an author might include a **back story**. This refers to the experiences of a character or an event that occurred before the story starts. It is extremely important in the *Harry Potter* novels, for example. Sometimes **flashbacks** are used which take the narrative back in time. *Paranoid Park* begins with a flashback. Flashbacks are often used in films, too. **Flashforwards** reveal future events. ▶

Foreshadowing on the other hand means that there are clues early on in the story that hint at future developments. This is typical of crime stories and tragedies and helps to build up **suspense**. In the first extract from *Slam*, suspense is created by hinting at what Alicia might tell Sam when they meet at Starbuck's.

- An author often uses **symbols** to say something indirectly. A symbol represents something else. In *She doesn't speak*, for example, the wall is a symbol of the distance between the narrator Noekie and the world around her. One of the main characteristics of literature is that the author says something **symbolically** and/or **metaphorically** → S8. You have to **interpret** the novel/story yourself because the author only gives the reader clues.

S8 Interpreting poetry

A poem is like a picture painted with words instead of paint. These words produce rhythms, sounds, pictures and meanings that the reader responds to. Like the different parts of a painting, every word in a poem is important. Do not worry about finding the "correct" meaning. Poems can often be interpreted in different ways.

Tips for analyzing poems

- Read the poem aloud several times. This way you get a feeling for the poem's theme and the emotions it creates. These emotions are intended to have an effect on the reader. Example: In *Give and take* in Topic 3 the reader can feel how the Blue Planet is being destroyed.
- In poems, emotions are usually very important, more so than in novels.
- What is the poem about? Does it tell a story, create an atmosphere, describe a feeling or a situation?
- Look up any words or phrases that you do not understand – in a poem, every word is important.
- Look at the form of the poem. What is its structure? Is it divided into **stanzas** (a group of lines that can be rhymed). Example: *Give and take* in Topic 3 has four stanzas. Modern free verse often has no structure and there are no stanzas.
- Listen to the sounds. Is there a particular **rhythm** or **metre**? *Metre* is the term for the pattern of accented and unaccented syllables in a poem. Example: "Dis ˊpoetry is ˊwid me/Be'low me and a'bove …" from *Dis poetry*, p. 43, lines 48/49.
- Does the poem **rhyme**? Example: "Dis poetry is not Party Political/Not designed fe dose who are critical" from *Dis poetry* in Topic 2. Is repetition used? Example: "I am not de problem" from *No problem* in Topic 2 is repeated four times. What other patterns can you find?
- What **images** and **symbols** (→ S7) does the poet use? What other **poetic devices** does the poet use? Examples: In a **metaphor** one thing is given the name of another because they both have something in common – "You are the rock on which we depend." A **simile** ['sɪmɪli:] also compares things or people, but a simile uses "like" or "as" – "You are *like* a rock."

Dis poetry is wid me,
Below me an above,
Dis poetry's from inside me
It goes to yu
WID LUV.

Benjamin Zephaniah, Dis poetry

S9 Understanding songs

Songs are similar to poems, but here the music is very important, too. Listen to the song once or twice, look at the ***lyrics*** *and structure of the song (stanzas and chorus) and think about this:*

WORD BANK
The lyrics are sad/moving/disturbing/ repetitive • The melody is striking/simple/ catchy • The chorus is repeated • The song has a complicated/simple/ repetitive rhythm

- What kind/style of music is it?
- What instruments are used?
- Are there any repeated musical patterns or rhythms? Is the rhythm slow, fast?
- What atmosphere and emotions are produced by the music and rhythm?
- What is the function of the chorus?
- What does the music do that the lyrics cannot?
- What is the melody like (soft, repetitive)? Does it change?
- Do the rhythm and melody match the lyrics (e.g. a slow, sad melody for a sad story)?
  Or is there a contrast between melody and lyrics (e.g. a sad story but fast, happy music)? If there is a contrast between melody and lyrics, is this ironic? → S7
- Background information that you research (→ S36) can help you to understand a song: information on the singer/band, the type of music, the history of the singer/band etc.
- Finally: Does the song have a message?

Dealing with visual material

S10 Working with films

A ***feature film*** *tells a story, so when you are analyzing a film, you can use the techniques you have learnt for literary texts (→ S7 narrative techniques: atmosphere, setting, characters etc.).*

The ***audio-visual*** *aspects, however, are at the centre of film-making. So you will have to consider camera operations, lighting, editing (i.e. the cutting and joining of camera shots), special effects and the way that sounds and music have been integrated.*

The way the camera is used influences how the viewer sees the action and identifies with the characters. It creates the ***cinematic point of view****. This can either be* objective, *i.e. the camera is like a window through which the viewer observes the action, or it can be* subjective, *i.e. the viewer sees the characters and events through the eyes of one particular character. The cinematic point of view often changes from one shot to the next.*
It can be helpful to use a grid like this to make notes on a film scene:

setting	characters	story	camera	lighting	editing	sound/music	special effects
contemporary? historical? the future? imaginary world? rural/urban? ...	who? relationship to others? appearance? costumes? language? body language?	plot? dialogue? point in story? interaction?	zooming? panning? static? close-up? long shots? overhead?	colours? bright/dark? soft lighting? atmosphere?	long sequences? fits action?	what about sounds/ dialogues? atmosphere? kind of music?	computer generated? slow motion?/ fast forward? flashback? animation?

Jodie Foster in *Contact*

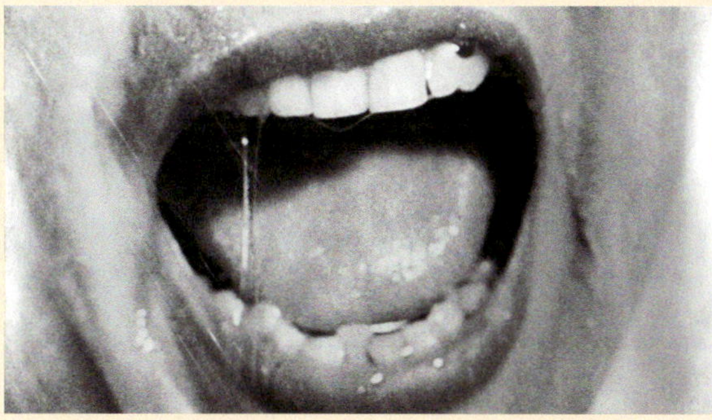

Janet Leigh in Alfred Hitchcock's classic thriller *Psycho*

S11 Presenting a film in class

1. *Before you start, give your audience some information about the film (aside from the title) to put it in context. Think about:*

Genre: Comedy, crime, western, drama, etc.?
The people: Who directed it? Who acted in it?
Background: When was it made? Where was it filmed?
The script: Is it based on a literary text? If so, which one?
Other: Is there anything special about it? Was it a success? Has it won any awards?

WORD BANK
Important genres
adventure • action • animation • biographical portrayal • comedy • crime • documentary • drama • epic/historical • fantasy • horror • melodrama • musical • romance • science fiction • teen • war • western

2. *Briefly describe the theme, the setting, characters and plot.*
3. *Introduce the scene you are going to present, saying where it comes in the film and what its function is. Present an important scene that is typical of the film. This should make it easier to talk about the characters, their relationship with one another, their role in the plot and the atmosphere of the film.*
4. *Ask the class whether they liked/disliked it and why. Discuss how effective the scene is.*

WORD BANK
Talking about camera movements
In the foreground/background there is … • The camera takes a long/medium/close-up shot • This brings … close • This creates distance between … and … • The viewer sees … from the front/from above/below/behind • The camera zooms in/out … • The viewer sees a close-up of … • The camera pans from (left) to (right) • The camera follows … • The shots follow each other quickly • There are very few cuts (at the beginning) • … is shown in slow/fast motion

S12 Watching films in English

- When you are watching a film or video in English, do not worry if it takes you a while to get used to the voices, the accents, the speed and rhythm. This happens to everyone.
- You do not have to understand every single word to be able to follow the plot. The characters' body language and other visual elements can help you, too.
- If the accents are very difficult to understand, try watching the film with English subtitles.
- If you have to analyze a particular scene, watch it several times and concentrate on different elements each time.

S13 Other audio-visual materials

You can use many of the film techniques in S10 to talk about videos, music video clips and commercials. In these cases you should also consider the target group and the purpose of the material.

- **Videos**: What kind of video is it e.g. a documentary? What is its purpose? How does it achieve this?
- **Music video clips**: In addition to looking at the song, think about how the music clip reflects the lyrics. Does it tell a story? Does it improve the song?
- **Commercials**: They *always* try to sell something. Even political party broadcasts try to 'sell' politicians. Always focus on what the 'product' is.

S14 Talking about pictures

Visual material, i.e. pictures, photographs, paintings, drawings, cartoons and diagrams, can be just as effective as written texts. When you talk about visual material, you should think about the following:

Analyzing pictures

1. First impressions

- What is your first reaction to the picture?
- What atmosphere does it create?
- If it is art: who is the photographer/artist who created it, and can you find out anything about her/him?
- Is the artwork a portrait/a group portrait/a self-portrait/a landscape/a still-life/an installation/a video …?

2. Taking a closer look

- Describe what you can see in detail. Start with the most important elements, then move on to the things or people in the background if there is a background.
- If there are people in the picture, describe their body language, facial expressions and their relationship with each other.
- Talk about the way in which colours and light are used.

Bud Fields and his family, by Walker Evans (1936)

WORD BANK

The photograph is striking/shocking/thought-provoking/moving/intense • The picture is realistic/stylized/detailed/lifelike • The picture gives the impression that … • The photograph was probably taken in … • The artist might have wanted to show • In the middle/centre … • In the bottom right-hand corner … • In the top left-hand corner … • In the foreground/background … • … is seen from the back/the front/above/below … • The people appear to be … • The colours are dark/bright/dull/vibrant • It's a black and white photograph

3. Interpreting and evaluating

Think about these questions:

- Is/Was the picture aimed at a particular target group?
- Do you think the artwork/picture has a message? If so, what do you think the message is? Give reasons.
  Examples: Why did the great American photographer Walker Evans photograph these poor people in the South of the US during the Depression? (You can research this!) Why did van Gogh paint a portrait of the psychiatrist Dr. Gachet with his head resting on his hand?
- When was the photograph made/the artwork created? For some photographs/artworks, this is very important. It is, for example, important to know that Walker Evans's photograph was taken in the 1930s during the great Depression. Other details can be important, too. It helps to know that Dr. Gachet was van Gogh's doctor in the psychiatric hospital in Auvers (northern France).
- Has the artist or photographer succeeded in making the message clear? Explain.

S15 Talking about cartoons

Cartoons often focus on something of interest in the news. The way they do this is funny and critical. As a cartoon usually combines a drawing with a short text, it is important to analyze and understand both.

The text can be in the form of

- a caption (a statement underneath the illustration). In this case it is important to work out who is speaking.
- one or more speech bubbles.
- another text e.g. a sign or a poster in the cartoon.

Cartoonists often make use of **exaggeration, puns, irony** or **symbols** to make their point. Look at this cartoon and say why the use of the word 'alien' is funny. Is it an exaggeration, pun, irony or symbol?

When you are asked to analyze a cartoon, follow the steps described in → S14. Pay special attention to the combination of text and picture.

"Just how long do you illegal aliens plan on staying in our country?"

WORD BANK

The cartoonist is making fun of … • The cartoonist is satirizing … • The cartoonist is making the point that … • The cartoon is funny because of the misunderstanding between … • I get/don't get the joke • I think/don't think the cartoon is easy to understand because …

Writing skills

S16 Writing a formal letter

A formal letter can be a letter of application, a request for information, a letter to a government office or an organization. You can use different layouts for these kinds of letters.

Whenever you write a formal letter, the language and style should be polite and factual. Do not use contractions (short forms such as didn't*) or question tags (*did you?*).*

! In application letters and in CVs **you must not make one single mistake!** A mistake could mean the difference between getting or *not* getting an interview / job.

Punctuation: In the UK commas after 'Dear Sir or Madam' and 'Yours faithfully' are often omitted. In the US you must use commas!

Addressee: Include name and position if they are known to you

After 'Dear Sir or Madam' or 'Dear …', always continue with a **capital letter.**

The **first paragraph** should say why you are writing.

Finish your letter with:
Signature
Your full name

Encl. = enclosures. This shows that you are sending something else with the letter. Write what it is.

Hauptstr. 1
70183 Stuttgart
Germany
00 49/(0) 711/123 456
E-mail: pbraun@online.de

Personnel Manager
Creative Concepts
62 Denmark Street
London WC5 10B
England

8 May 2009

Re: Your advertisement of 2 May 2009

Dear Sir or Madam

My name is Petra Braun and I am a sixteen-year old pupil at a grammar school in Stuttgart, Germany. Last week I read your advertisement in the Daily Times (2 May) and would now like to apply for a summer job with your company.

As you will see from the enclosed CV, I have learnt English at school for eight years and have been on a school exchange to Leeds twice. In addition, I have visited the UK and the USA several times with my family. In September I will be entering the sixth-form to study for my Abitur, which is similar to English A-levels. My aim is to study information science.

I am particularly interested in working in London as it is one of the most creative centres for web design and applications. I am keen to gain practical experience and would like to learn more about the services that your company offers. My computer skills are very good and I would be able to carry out the duties required.

I enclose my curriculum vitae. Please do not hesitate to contact me if you need any further information. I look forward to hearing from you.

Yours faithfully

Petra Braun

Petra Braun

Encl. CV

Tips for writing a formal letter

1. Note down the most important points you want to make.
2. Put your points in a logical order.
3. Think about how to write them in a polite manner.
4. When you write your letter, pay careful attention to the formalities listed on the previous page.
5. Check your letter for mistakes: spelling, grammar, punctuation. → S24

If you do not know the name of the person you are writing to, begin *Dear Sir or Madam* and end with *Yours faithfully*.

If you know the person's name, you write *Dear Mr Brown / Dear Ms Smith* and end with *Yours sincerely*.
A less formal ending for people you are acquainted with is *Best wishes* or *Best regards* or *Kind regards*.

WORD BANK

Starting the letter: My name is … and I am writing regarding • My name is … and I am writing to ask about • My name is … and I would like to … • With reference to your letter of … • Thank you for your letter of …
In the main part: I appreciate … • I apologize for … • I am sorry to have to tell you that … • You will be pleased to hear that … • Please send me …
Connecting ideas: Furthermore • In addition • Therefore • That is why
Coming to the end: I look forward to hearing from you • Please do not hesitate to contact me if you need any further information • Thank you very much in advance • I enclose …

Writing a letter of application

A letter of application follows the same rules as a formal letter. The letter that accompanies your CV should also contain the following information:

Opening paragraph:	Introduce yourself and say why you are writing the letter. Add where you found out about the job. Do not start your letter with 'I'. Especially in the US, this is bad style!
Paragraph 2:	Name your relevant qualifications and experience, as well as your personal qualities that make you a suitable candidate.
Paragraph 3:	Say why you are interested in the job and this company. Say why you think you can do the job.
Closing paragraph:	End with a friendly sentence which looks forward to an answer.

S17 Writing a CV

CV is short for 'curriculum vitae'. Americans call it a 'resume' ['rezju:mei]. *There are no rules about how to write a CV in English. It should, however, be well-structured and clearly arranged on the page. You should also make sure that the information in it is genuine – do not include information to impress people unless it is really true.*

How to write a CV

Here are a few other *dos* and *don'ts*:

- **Do** include skills and interests that are relevant for the job, if possible.
- **Do** explain the German terms in English, if possible.
- **Never** write more than one page.
- **Never** include a photo, unless you are asked for one.
- **Do not** write your CV by hand, unless you are asked to.
- **Do not** sign your name at the end of the CV.
- **Remember** to check your CV for mistakes before you send it. → S24

American CVs are a bit different. They start off with a "profile" of three to four lines saying something about yourself relating to work e.g. you are a teamplayer, an outgoing person, you have experience in …, you are able to work well under pressure. The American profile is *not* a personal profile as in the UK – you only mention things that are important for your work.

Here is an example of a CV in the UK:

Curriculum vitae: Petra Braun

Personal details:

Name:	Petra Braun
Address:	Hauptstr. 1 70183 Stuttgart Germany
Tel:	0049 (0)711 123456
E-mail:	pbraun@online.de
Date of birth:	17 September 1992

Education:

1998–2002 Grundschule (primary school)
Since 2002 Geschwister Scholl Gymnasium in Stuttgart
In 2010 will take Abitur (like English A-levels)

Work experience:

August 2008 ScreenDesign in Stuttgart (computer programming firm)
August 2007 volunteer work for Staatsgalerie Stuttgart

Personal profile:

I am creative and reliable, and have very good computer skills, including being able to programme.
Having friends in Leeds, my English is very good, too. I have been to Leeds twice on a school exchange.
I love travelling and meeting new people. My main hobbies are modern art, computer games and computer programming. In my free time I also play volleyball.

References available if needed

"When I grow up, I'd like to be a nurse or a manager with responsibility for the installation and management of primarily digital systems who is able to direct and plan the work of local technicians and also liaise with suppliers and senior overseas officials visiting the UK while at the same time being prepared to travel to the countries concerned to facilitate the contract completion, with a starting salary in the region of £15,000 a year."

S18 Writing e-mails

Although e-mails are considered less formal than letters, if you are writing to someone you do not know, you should …

- Always write a **subject line** so that the person you are writing to knows what the e-mail is about.
- Write the most important information first.
- Use paragraphs to structure your e-mail.
- Write short and simple sentences. Obey the **KISS** rule – **K**eep **I**t **S**hort and **S**imple.
- Never use abbreviations, emoticons (smileys ☺ etc.) or exclamation marks (!) in formal e-mails. They are considered to be very impolite.
- Use correct punctuation and grammar. It is common to write everything in lower case letters in informal e-mails (dear mike …), but avoid this if you are writing to someone you do not know. Using capital letters for whole words in e-mails is almost like shouting.
- Check your e-mail before you send it. → S24

S19 Writing an argumentative essay

An argumentative essay discusses a controversial issue from more than one point of view. Its aim can either be to win someone over to one side or to present arguments for each side and leave the readers to decide for themselves.

Reserarch: *Choose a clear issue that can be argued about. Become an expert on the topic by using all kinds of sources of information. Decide if you want to persuade the reader to agree with you or if you want to remain neutral. An argumentative essay ending with your own opinion is also called a comment.* → S36

Writing an argumentative essay: Steps 1–4

Step 1: Introduction

- You present the issue. You can include:
  - facts about the background of the problem
  - information about its relevance today
  - a quotation
  - questions that you promise to give answers to
- Decide on your opinion of the issue.
  Example: Abortion. – You think every woman should decide herself.
- Find out as much as you can about the topic: facts, statistics, examples and quotations. Look for facts that support your position. Look for arguments that criticize the opposite position. Make sure that your sources are reliable. You should always be able to name your sources. It is not good to have only Internet sources. They are often not reliable. → S36

Step 2: Main part

- There are two kinds of task:
  A You are asked to present only one particular view of the topic. Then it is best to start with the weakest argument and end with the strongest.
  B You are asked to present two or even more different views on the topic. Then you can either present the negative points first and then the positive, or the negative and positive points alternately. You can arrange the points according to their importance, from the weakest to the strongest or the other way round.
- Each statement must be supported by evidence (examples, statistics etc.).
- If you want to persuade someone, it helps to use logic, good examples and good style.
- You can write about how the problem started, who is affected by it, how serious it is, what has been done about it so far, what can be expected if there is no solution, and so on.

Step 3: Conclusion

- The presentation of your arguments should lead to a conclusion. What you can include here:
  - a summary of what you have found out
  - an outlook on further consequences
  - your own opinion
  - an appeal to the readers to reach their own conclusion

WORD BANK

Connectives: although • because • but • even if • however • in order to • in spite of • provided that … • since • so that • unless
Ordering: first of all • I would like to begin with … • firstly …, secondly …, thirdly … etc. • my main argument is … • in addition to that • furthermore • finally • to sum up
Commenting: actually • apparently • fortunately • in fact • in my opinion • it is true that • of course • perhaps • possibly • probably • unfortunately
Comparing and contrasting: equally • in the same way • likewise • as well as • on the one hand … on the other hand • unlike • in contrast to
Giving examples: for example • for instance • by way of illustration
Giving reasons: as a result • consequently • therefore
Adverbs of degree: absolutely • almost • at least • completely • extremely • hardly • particularly • rarely • rather • really

Step 4: Checking your essay

- Read through your essay and check for grammar, spelling and punctuation mistakes. → S24

positive points negative points

S20 Summarizing

A summary is a very short version of a text. In non-fictional texts it briefly restates the author's main ideas. In fictional texts you retell a story in your own words. In both cases the summary must be much shorter than the original, especially if your summary is oral. Follow these steps for writing a summary:

Non-fictional texts

1. Read the text carefully and find out the main idea or the main argument.
2. Write it down.
3. Read the text again and write down the facts and arguments that support the main idea or argument.
4. Start writing your summary. First, write the main idea/argument.
5. Then write short paragraphs summarizing the other important arguments.
6. Leave out everything else. Your own ideas or arguments or opinions do not belong in a summary.
7. Check your summary. Are you sure you have summarized the main idea/argument clearly and correctly?
   Have you summarized the other ideas correctly? Always think of the reader who does not know anything about this topic.

Fictional texts

1. Read the text once or twice.
2. Write down the main characters and the setting.
3. Divide the text into sections if the author has not already done this for you (e.g. with chapters, mini-chapters). Also think of what the main parts of the story's structure are: plot development, climax, ending etc.
4. Read the text again and write down the keywords and the main points in each section. Also write down the turning point of the plot.
5. Using the present tense, write short paragraphs to summarize the plot. Write down what happens and how the events are connected. Use your own words as much as possible. Link your sentences with connectives.
6. Leave out everything else. Your own ideas do not belong in a summary.
7. Check your summary. Are you sure you have summarized the main points correctly?
   Have you summarized the turning point clearly and correctly?
   Always think of the reader who does not know the story.

S21 Writing a survey

If you want to find out about people's opinions or habits, you can do a survey. This involves writing a questionnaire to find out what people think. Follow these two steps, then present your findings in class.

Writing a survey: Steps 1–2

Step 1: Definition

1. Define the topic: Write one or two sentences describing what you want to know, and what the aim of the survey is. The clearer you are in your own mind, the easier it will be to write the questionnaire.
2. Decide on your target group. Think about the number of people you are going to interview and whether they should belong to any particular social or interest group e.g. age? male or female?

Step 2: Writing the questionnaire

The success of your survey will depend largely on how good your questions are. The kind of questions you ask will depend on the type of information you hope to get, and on the amount of time you want the participants to spend answering the questions.

Here are some examples with a summary of the advantages (✓) and disadvantages (×):

Multiple choice questions	Yes/no questions	Graded questions	Open-ended questions
Where do you get your news from? a) newspapers b) radio c) television d) Internet	Do you read newspapers? Yes/no	How often do you read the news on the Internet? a) never b) less than once a day c) more than once a day	Where do you find information about what is going on in the world?
✓ easy to answer and evaluate × answers are not detailed/personal	✓ easy to answer and evaluate × answers are not detailed/personal	✓ easy to answer and evaluate × answers are not detailed/personal	✓ answers are detailed and personal × take longer to answer and are difficult to evaluate

A few tips

- You can, of course, use different types of questions in one survey, but it is better not to have too many different types.
- All of your questions must be clear and short. Make sure the language is simple, but not too informal.
- Do not ask too many questions – people are giving up their free time to answer them.

S22 Writing a news report

News reports inform readers about interesting and important events in a neutral way. Your personal opinion is not important here, except for 'commentary'. This means that all of the relevant points should be included, even if the writer does not agree with them. There are three types of news articles: reports *(news),* features *(news and background), and* commentaries *(writer's opinion).*

Writing a news report: Checklist

- The ABC of news writing is **Accuracy**, **Brevity**, **Clarity**. This means that the facts have to be exact, the article should be short and it should be easy to understand.
- When you write a report or feature, answer the five Ws: **W**ho? **W**hat? **W**hen? **W**here? **W**hy? and sometimes How?
- Think of a headline that will attract the reader's attention. The first sentence or paragraph, the 'lead', should contain the most important and exciting point so that the reader continues reading. Look at the headlines below. Although you know nothing about the news of this day, you can immediately say what has happened.
- Think about how to structure your article. Start with the most important point, then add more facts and more details. This way the reader can stop reading at any point after the lead without missing anything important.
- Style is very important. The only acceptable style for news is factual. The article must also be informative and short. Nothing is repeated and no unnecessary details are given. The text should be well-structured and easy to read.
- News writing often contains anecdotes, examples and quotes. Only use them if they help to make a point clear. Make sure that quotes are not taken out of context and that the speaker's intention is clear.

S23 Creative writing

Text-based writing

After you have read a text, you might be asked to continue it, or to write a similar text on a different subject, or to change the point of view.

- First, make sure you have understood the text. Make a note of any key facts that will help you to write e.g. …
  - if you are continuing a fictional text, think about characterization, how the characters speak etc.
  - if you are writing a non-fictional text, think about the target audience.
- Think about what is important for the text you are going to write. What style will you need for this type of text? If you are continuing a text, you must write in the exactly same style as the text you are continuing.
- Write a very short outline of your text so that the structure is clear for you. Or you can write the outline by only noting down keywords. If you do it this way, use every keyword in your final text.
- After you have written your text, read it and check for mistakes (grammar, spelling, punctuation) and improve it where possible. → S24
  If you have written a dialogue, read it aloud to see if it sounds natural.
- Peer editing: It might also be helpful to give your text to a partner and see if he/she has any suggestions for improvement.

Free writing

You might be asked to write freely about a topic.

- First of all, decide on the target group, the purpose of the text and the genre/text type. Look at S6 and S7 if you need help.
- Think about which techniques are most suitable for your text. S7 can give you lots of ideas e.g. what is the point of view that is most effective for this text, how can you create suspense, is atmosphere important or not?
- If you decide to tell a story, you will need to think about …
  - the **exposition**: How you are going to introduce the main characters (who?), the setting (when? where?), and the theme (what?)?
  - the **main part**: How is the plot going to develop (how? why?)?
  - **the ending**: How you can give your story an interesting ending?
- When you write the text, make sure that it is logical. But of course you can use flashbacks or foreshadowing if appropriate. So the story does not have to be told in the sequence that the events happened! Example: *Paranoid Park* starts in the present and then is told as a long flashback.
  Use connectives to connect your ideas.
- Read through your text and check for common mistakes (grammar, spelling, punctuation) and improve it where possible. → S24
  If you have written a dialogue, read it aloud to see if it sounds natural.
- Peer editing: It might also be helpful to give your text to a partner and see if he/she has any suggestions for improvement.

S24 Checking written texts

Everyone makes mistakes in written texts. Many great writers were very critical about their own texts and rewrote them many times, for example Ernest Hemingway.

Checking written texts

- If you have time, put your text aside when it is finished and check it later (best of all, the next day). Are you *really* happy with it? To judge your own text, distance is very important. If you do not have any time between writing and checking, pretend that *someone else* has written your text. Would you enjoy reading it? If you do not have a 'good feeling' about your text, a few changes here or there will not be enough. Then it is best to rewrite the complete text. A complete rewriting will give you the freedom to do a new and better job. Before you start, look at the following points:
- Is the text logical and are the arguments clear? Is the text convincing?
- Check that you have said what you really mean. Or is the way you have phrased your arguments unclear? Have you given good and sensible *reasons* for your arguments?
- If you have written a fictional text: Have you *really* used all the narrative techniques that are appropriate for the type of text? Or – even worse – have you *overused* narrative techniques e.g. symbols? This was often done in texts during the Middle Ages, and many people think they are terribly boring!
- If you are really happy with your text, you can then check your text for *small* mistakes. Look at the …
  - grammar (tenses, prepositions, word order etc.)
  - spelling
  - punctuation.
- Make sure that all the sentences are complete (subject-object-predicate) and that they make sense. Is there enough variation betweeen short and longer sentences? Careful: In English, sentences are usually not as long as German sentences!
- Make sure that you have not overused some words. (Look at the first Word bank in S25.) If you vary the words you are using, your text will sound more interesting. Think about what you really mean to say e.g. instead of saying something was nice, think about *why* it was nice. This will help you to find a more precise word to describe it. But if you decide to change a word, remember to check whether it is followed by a different preposition or whether it takes an object etc.

- Peer editing: You can also give your text to a partner and see if he/she has any suggestions for improvement.

"I.N.F.O.R.M.A.T.I.O.N, why do you ask?"

Speaking skills

S25 Having a conversation

Having a good conversation is more difficult than it looks. You need to use appropriate language. The correct register (formal or informal language), depends on …

- **the situation:** when? where? for what purpose? If it is a formal situation e.g. an interview, make sure you prepare yourself in advance. Find out any useful background information about the job and the company, and useful words and phrases.
- **the person:** age? role? The register changes for friends, parents, strangers.
- **the topic:** serious? fun?

WORD BANK

Words that are often overused:
nice: wonderful • enjoyable • great • likeable • kind • delightful
bad: awful • terrible • poor • dreadful • inadequate • unsatisfactory
to say: to state • to agree • to explain • to declare • to announce • to claim
I think: I believe • in my opinion • as far as I am concerned • I am convinced
to like: to love • to enjoy • to admire • to appreciate • to be keen on • to take an interest in

Intercultural tips

In your own language you change the style automatically, but it is more difficult in a foreign language.

- If you don't know which register to use (formal? informal?), it is better to be more formal i.e. more polite. Using language that is too informal is impolite in the UK and the US.
- When you talk to older people or people with more experience, use more polite phrases and do not be too direct. Example: If you are staying with an exchange family in the US, your language register must be extremely polite – but friendly!
- Formality and respect are also shown by intonation, body language and using appropriate expressions. Example: When invited into an American/British home, wait until you are offered a seat/something to drink. Do not put your hands in your pockets while talking.
- Be tactful when you tell someone something that affects them personally. In the UK and the US, you must know the person very well before you tell them something unpleasant e.g. criticize their appearance.
- Listen to the kind of vocabulary the other person is using. If you do not understand a phrase or word, ask politely what it means. To increase your vocabulary, you could write down all the new words in a notebook. If you are living in an exchange family, use the new words to show them that they are helping you to learn.
- Conversation is 'give and take': You must be prepared to listen, and not just talk yourself the whole time. And you must react to your conversation partner. It would be very impolite not to say anything or to change the subject to something you find more interesting.
- Modals, e.g. *May I …? Would you …? I'd like …*, sound less direct and more polite.
- Question tags are a good way to show interest e.g. *… are you? … isn't it?*
- If you are a tourist, especially in the UK or the US, *never* talk about 'sensitive' topics e.g. in the UK about the bad English meal that you just had, or in the US about the way the Americans treated the Native Americans or the black slaves.

WORD BANK

Polite phrases: please • thank you • you're welcome • not at all • please do
Toning down: not exactly • slightly • a little • rather
Concessions (and not "I disagree"): Yes, that's true, but … • I agree, but …
Responding to a suggestion: I'd love to … • That's a good idea!
Showing interest: of course • I see • really? • Are you sure? • What a pity. • That's a shame. • That's very kind of you.

S26 Having a discussion

Discussions can be fun, but it is good to know what is important when discussing a serious topic.

- Make sure you understand the issue that is to be discussed.
- Try to remember everything you know about the issue and decide what your opinion is.
- If you have time, note down arguments for the other side and try to think of counter-arguments.
- Arrange your ideas in a logical order when you present them. Support your arguments with examples.
- Speak clearly so that you can be understood easily.
- Keep to the point and do not try to be the centre of the discussion all the time. Do not repeat what other people have said. Wait until you have a *real* contribution, a real point. This is much more effective.
- Be polite. Do not interrupt. Attack the arguments of the other side, but not the people.

WORD BANK

Introducing arguments: I'd like to begin by … • First of all • Next • I think • I believe • It's important to remember that … • Another point I'd like to make is … • I'd also like to state that … • Finally …
Reacting to others: It's true that …, but … • I agree, but … • I admit that …, but … • But don't forget … • I strongly disagree • In my opinion • Surely you have to admit that … • You might think differently if …

S27 Staging a debate

A debate is a formal discussion that follows rules of procedure. The language is very formal. There are two different teams – one for and one against a statement. Example: "Abortions are morally unacceptable./The decision to have an abortion is a woman's right."
The audience is allowed to ask questions, and votes for or against the arguments at the end.
A debate can be organized like this:

Staging a debate: Steps 1–5

1. The chairperson introduces the issue and presents the statement, also known as 'the motion', to the audience (also called 'the floor').
2. In the first round, six speakers speak alternately for and against the motion. They each give a speech which must not be interrupted.
3. Now the debating begins. The two teams exchange arguments. The audience may ask questions or make comments. To do this, they must raise their hands and wait to be called on by the chairperson. At this stage, the teams do not reply to the questions.
4. One speaker from each team gives a brief summary of their arguments, answering any questions that the audience raised.
5. The chairperson asks the audience to vote for or against the motion by raising their hands.

S28 Giving a presentation

Giving a presentation: Checklist

Step one: Preparation

- Choose a topic that can be presented in 15 minutes. It should *not* be a topic that has too many dimensions and cannot be dealt with in that time e.g. 'Pros and cons of a multi-cultural society'.
- Collect material on your topic from different and reliable sources. → S36
- Decide which main points you want to deal with, and make notes on them. Choose one or two other points that are especially interesting, surprising or funny to keep your audience listening.
- Prepare the visual material you are going to use: maps, diagrams, photographs or videos. Also summarize a few key facts either in powerpoint or using an overhead projector so that the audience has something to look at. Make sure that the writing is large enough so that the people at the back can also read it. Do not include too many. *You* are the presenter, not your projector or your whiteboard. Too many visuals confuse the audience.
- Write your notes on 'prompt cards'. Use one card for each point. Only write down keywords and phrases, examples, facts and figures. Do not write down complete sentences. But write down the exact words of any quotations you want to use.
- Put the cards and the visual material in a logical order: introduction, main part (sub-divided into separate points if necessary) and conclusion.
- Photocopy anything you want to give to people as a handout. But do not give it to them until the end of the presentation so that they concentrate on what you are saying!
- Practise your speech, using your prompt cards to speak freely. Check how long your presentation is. If necessary, shorten it.

Step two: Presentation

- Speak loudly and clearly and not too fast. Vary your voice so that it does not sound boring.
- Remember to look at the audience when you are speaking. Having practised your presentation often, a quick look at your prompt cards should be enough for you to remember everything you want to say. After looking at the prompt card, look up and speak freely to your audience.
- Use words that you are comfortable with. Never try to impress people with big words you have trouble understanding – or maybe even pronouncing!
- At the end, thank your audience for listening and ask if anyone has any questions.

Before Powerpoint.

Listening skills

S29 Listening

The best way to improve your listening skills is to get as much practice as possible. Some situations are only listening situations e.g. radio programmes, music, podcasts, telephone conversations and announcements without any visual aids. In these cases, you have to listen carefully to the person's intonation so that you can interpret what is being said.

In other situations, e.g. watching television, films and videos, the action context, the speaker's body language and gestures will also help you to understand what is being said. So try to listen to as many different types of authentic recordings as possible. Podcasts are a very good way to practise your listening skills. They are authentic recordings of different lengths, and they deal with many different topics. Listening to podcasts helps you to understand different accents and different types of English. So get to know different accents in the English-speaking world – South African, Australian, from the American South …

Listening: A few tips

- Listen for keywords and key phrases to help you get the gist e.g. names, numbers, places. Also listen for repeated words. Remember you do not have to understand every single word if you are listening for gist.
- Once you have listened to a text for gist, concentrate on the details.
- Listening in stages can also be helpful because you can then concentrate on a particular section of the text.
- Take notes so you do not have to remember all of the details. Read S30 for tips on note-taking.
- If you are talking to someone face-to-face or on the telephone, do not be afraid to ask them to repeat something or to explain something.
- When you are on the phone, it can be helpful to repeat important information that was given to you by the other person. That way you are sure that you have understood it correctly. Example: You are meeting the person, so you repeat, "OK, we'll meet on Tuesday at 5 pm in front of the Odeon Cinema in Leicester Square, right?"
- Before you listen to an authentic recording, try to find out whether it is in British or American English or a dialect or a regional accent. Do not feel bad if you have problems understanding what is said. Someone from the US state of Alabama might not be able to understand a Cockney from London!

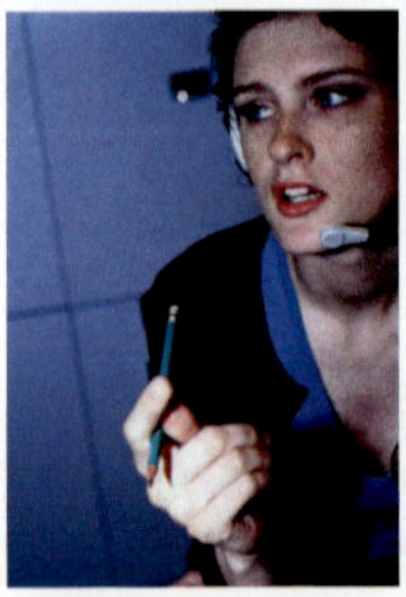

WORD BANK
Could you repeat that, please? • Could you say that again, please? • I'm sorry, I don't understand the word … What does it mean? • What does … mean? • Could you spell that for me, please? • Could you speak a little more slowly, please?

S30 Taking notes while listening

Taking notes while you are listening can help you to remember important points afterwards. → S29

Listening the right way

- Only write down the most important information – you will not have time to write everything down.
- Write down keywords, key phrases, names, times, places, but not complete sentences.

- Your notes should always be in the correct order.
- Use *symbols or abbreviations* wherever possible – but make sure that you know what they mean. You can use these symbols/abbreviations for quick note-taking:

and/yes	+
not/no	–
and so on, et cetera	etc.
with	w.
without	w/o
good/great	++
the same as, equals, means	=
not the same as, does not equal	≠
about the same as	≈
that means, id est	i.e.
for example, exempli gratia	e.g.
becomes, will be, develops into	→

- Use any other kind of symbols or abbreviations that you know or enjoy inventing.

You can also structure your notes in advance:

- If you know what a situation is going to be about, making a *grid* will help you to take notes in a systematic way.
- If you are only interested in details, a *checklist* will be useful. Before you listen, imagine which points could perhaps be mentioned, and note them down, and anything else you would like to know.
  Example: The listening text in Topic 1 from the novel *Girl* tells you about an American teenager's life. So important points could be: parents, school, boy/girlfriends, dating, clothes. Then when you are listening, you can underline some points that are mentioned, cross out other points and add anything else that is relevant.

Word skills

S31 Vocabulary

Using a dictionary

Both types of dictionary – English-English or German-English – usually contain the following information:

1 pronunciation, e.g. **adolesence** [ˌædə'lesns]

> **adolescence** /ˌæd.ə'les.ᵊnts/ ***noun*** [U] the period of time in a person's life when they are developing into an adult: *a troubled adolescence*

2 the part of speech the word is (noun, adjective, verb etc.)
3 other grammatical information e.g. irregular verb forms, whether a noun is uncountable or not, whether a verb is followed by an infinitive or gerund etc.
4 other helpful information e.g. whether the word is formal, slang, AE etc.
5 words it can be combined with e.g. certain prepositions/collocations
6 example sentences
7 different meanings of the word
8 other words in the word family
9 phrases and expressions with the word

An English-English dictionary may also often give synonyms or antonyms for the word.

! The first translation may not always be the one you need! Example: *Nerve* means 'Nerv', but it also means 'Unverschämtheit, Frechheit' as in *The nerve of that guy!* = "Der Typ da ist unverschämt!"

▶

A few tips

- Before you look up a word in your dictionary, check what part of speech it is in the context that you have found it (i.e. is it a noun?).
- Always read through the expressions because the word might be part of an idiom, e.g. *to break the law* does not mean '... brechen'; it means 'gegen das Gesetz verstoßen'.

S32 Guessing the meaning

When you read a text, you often come across new words. You already know different ways of guessing their meaning. → S33 *The more frequently you use these techniques, the easier it will become. You do not need to understand every single word if you are reading for gist.*

Here are the questions you should ask yourself when you come across a new word:

- Is the word also used in German (a 'cognate') e.g. *clown, computer, Internet?*
- Is the word similar to a German word e.g. *architect, genome, to install?*
- Is the word similar to a word in another language you may know (such as French, Italian, Latin, Spanish) e.g. *broccoli, guitar, minor, opera, phase, suburb?*
- Is the word from a word family you already know, e.g. *adventurous, deforestation, fame, to laze around, relevance?*
- Can you guess the meaning of the word from the context? Look at the word 'scrape' in this sentence – what do you think it might mean? *My heels were almost as rough as Becca's. My mother had bought me a grey stone to scrape my feet soft at night in the bath ...*

!

Watch out for **false friends!** They sound like a German word you know, but they have a different meaning. *Eventually* does not mean 'eventuell', it means 'schließlich'.
Watch out for **false false friends:**
Handy means 'geschickt' and not *mobile* (AE: *cell phone*). And the German 'Pullunder' does not exist in English, in BE it is *tank top* (AE: *vest*).

S33 Learning vocabulary with vocabulary sheets

It is very important that you find a way of learning vocabulary that suits you. To be really successful, find your own system.

The Green Line vocabulary files will help you to learn and revise the most important words and phrases from the book. All of the files can be edited with a computer, so you can easily add new words and phrases that are presented in class, or new words that you find in your own reading.

"Have some respect for my learning style."

The files are organized in three columns, all of which you can fill in.

This column is for the **word** or **phrase** to be learned. **Add notes** on pronunciation or explanation when it is necessary. Example: *to dawdle* ['dɔːdl] be slow, waste time	**You can add more notes here** e.g. words from the same word family, or pictures or phrases. Example: noun: *dawdler;* *She's always dawdling!*	This column is for the **German translation.** Example: 'trödeln'

Note down anything that helps you to remember the word or phrase and how to use it e.g.

- words from the same word family
- example sentences
- pictures or drawings
- opposites, synonyms, paraphrases
- collocations

There are many different ways of working with the files.
It might be more fun to vary what you do. Here are a few ideas:

- Complete the files using the relevant text and a dictionary.
- Add more information or vocabulary that is helpful for you.
- Print the files out and fill them in by hand.
- Partner work: Turn the files into vocabulary tests or quizzes for a partner.

Further skills

S34 Mediation

Mediation *means to help two or more people with different languages to understand each other. If you want to mediate successfully, you need to use several different skills. Never try to translate word for word, but get the gist from one language and express it in the other language.*

The way you communicate is always influenced by the context. This is why it is important to analyze the situation before you start a mediation task. Ask yourself these questions:

1. *What kind of text is it? Is it spoken or written language? What is its purpose?*
2. *Who is the author/speaker? Who is the reader/listener?*
3. *Why is mediation necessary?*

A few tips

- **Getting the gist:** First try to understand keywords, key phrases, names, numbers, dates, places and words that are often repeated. This should give you the general idea of what the one person is trying to tell the other person.
- **Scanning:** Find important details. → S1
- **Guessing new words:** Using the techniques from S32, guess the meaning of unknown words or the phrases. The body language of the speaker or the pictures – if there are any – will also help you.
- **Selecting relevant points:** You may leave out any points that are not relevant for the listener/reader.
- **Paraphrasing:** If you don't know the exact translation for a word or phrase, use other words to express it.
  Example: *We were trying to get out of the house, but my little brother was just dawdling. We were in such a rush. My little brother drove us all crazy.* „Mein kleiner Bruder war viel zu langsam, obwohl wir uns beeilen mussten. Der Kleine ging uns ganz schön auf die Nerven!"
- **Summarizing:** Sum up the relevant points in your own words. Choose the right language/register for the situation and the listener/reader. → S20

S35 Interpreting diagrams

Diagrams are a very good way to display information or statistics. They take up little space and can make information much easier to understand. First, always look at the diagram and the legend carefully to make sure you understand all of the information. You will often come across ***pie charts, bar charts*** *and* ***line graphs.***

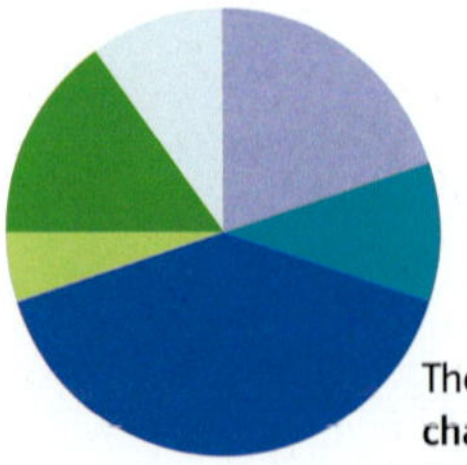

The circle of a **pie chart** represents 100 %. Each segment shows a percentage of the whole.

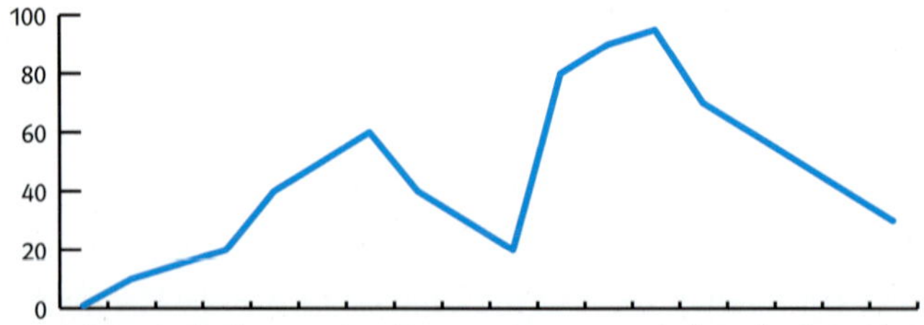

A **line graph** shows a development over a certain length of time.

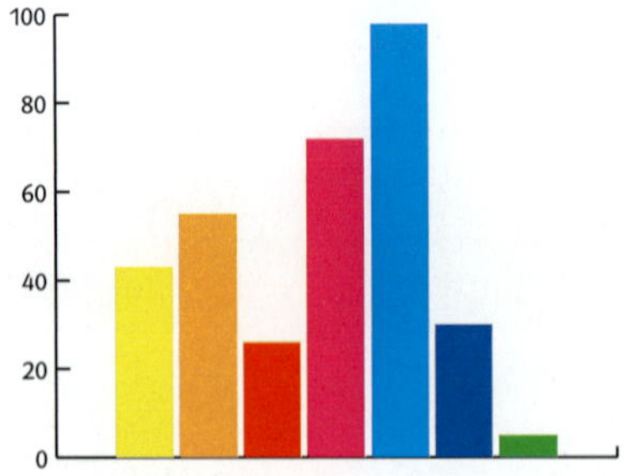

A **bar chart** is used to compare figures directly.

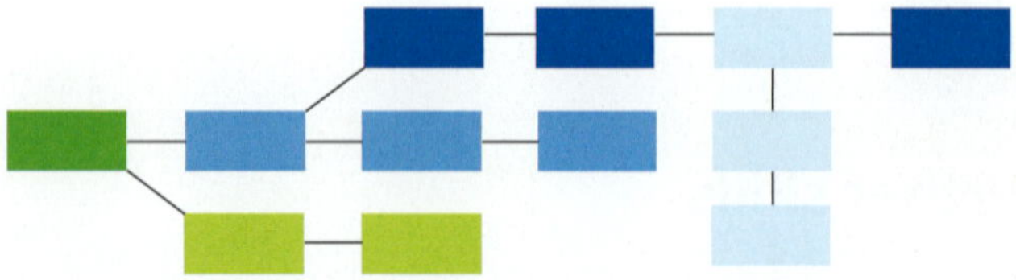

A **flow chart** shows the links between elements and their influence on each other. It is best used to describe processes that contain decisions at certain points where alternatives need to be shown.

!

- In English, decimals come after a point e.g. *2.5 % of people.* (Look at the Language page 72 of Topic 3.)
- Avoid this common mistake when using terms such as 'a third of…' or 'half of':

  Right: "A third of all Americans **have** never been to New York."
  Wrong: "A third of all Americans **has** never been to New York."

  In German, the singular is used; in English, it is the plural.

"I vote we hang the darn thing upside down and go home!"

WORD BANK

Showing an increase: to rise/increase • slowly/gradually/steadily/sharply
Describing a decrease: to decline/fall/decrease • slowly/gradually/steadily/sharply
Other useful verbs: to indicate that … • to show that … • to illustrate • to suggest that … • to prove that … • to make it clear that … • to lead to • to be due to • to result in …
Expressing numbers & figures: the latest figures • a high/low percentage of … • a significant number of …
Qualifiers: a total of • just over/under • approximately • roughly • precisely • on average
Comparing and contrasting: compared to/in comparison with … • twice/three times as many … • more/less/fewer than …

S36 Doing research

You will often have to research a topic before you can talk or write about it. There are different ways of finding out information:

- Go to your school library or local library.
- Look in books, newspapers and magazines.
- Talk to someone who knows a lot about the subject e.g. English/American friends, exchange students at your school.
- Write to an organization or an agency that might be able to send you brochures, posters or information sheets e.g. tourist offices, museums, government agencies, NGOs (= non-government organizations), political parties. Example: You want to find out more about wind and solar energy in Germany. Ask for information from Greenpeace, Bündnis 90/Die Grünen and the Ministerium für Umwelt und Verbraucherschutz.
- Research online (see below).
  Always note down your sources so that you know where the information came from.

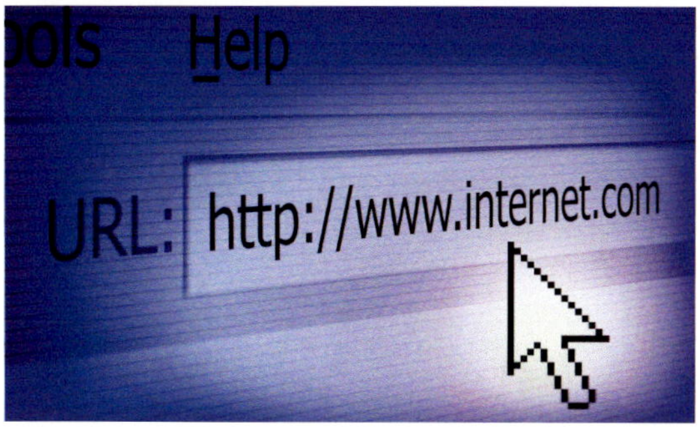

Researching online

There are two ways of doing this:

1. Use a subject guide or directory e.g. Yahoo. Choose a category, sub-category etc. This is helpful if you are researching a broad subject.
2. Use a search engine e.g. Google, and enter the expression you are looking for e.g. 'solar energy projects in Germany'. It is better if you have a specific topic and clearly defined keywords.

A few search tips for search engines

- The more clearly you define your keywords, the better results you will get. So if you are looking for a set phrase, use inverted commas so you only get this phrase e.g. 'Martin Luther King speeches'.
- Describe what you need with as few words as possible.
- You can also use '+' meaning *require* or '–' meaning *exclude*.
  If you get too many results, try changing the keywords or be less specific.
  If you do not get the results that you are looking for, try a different search word. Think of other expressions to describe the subject. If you do not get the results you want, use the *Help* support of the search engine you are using.

Finding information quickly on a website

Many websites offer a search function. If this is not given, use the search function in the edit menu ('Bearbeiten') or control+F (Strg+F) to find certain words on the page.

Checking results

Do not believe everything you read! Anyone can publish anything on the Internet, especially in Wikipedia! Some sources are more reliable than others, so always decide how trustworthy the source is. Is it an institution/government agency, expert, professor, journalist? Or did a hobby historian with a personal opinion upload the information? When was the information last updated?

Always check your website information with another source. Even if the source itself is not very reliable, it might have links to other websites that are reliable.

Grammar

This Grammar is different from the Grammar sections you have used up to now.

- It is a reference grammar. This means that the nine grammar chapters (for example **G1**) are not part of any Topic. You can refer to the relevant grammar chapter if you are unsure about a particular grammar point, for example when to use the simple past and when to use the present perfect.
- The Grammar deals with most of the grammar that you have learnt in the first five years at *Gymnasium*, so almost everything here is revision. Anything new this year is marked as ***NEW***.
- The Grammar section is designed to help your self-evaluation. Every chapter has an exercise or two after it. You can either read the chapter and then do the exercises, or first do the exercise/exercises and then see where you need more practice.
- Be especially careful when you see a box with an exclamation mark **!**. This is a tricky point!
- If you want a more detailed explanation of grammatical phenomena, you should refer to a systematic student grammar.

Table of contents

G1 Using simple and progressive forms

English, unlike German, has two **aspects** of the **verb** – **simple** and **progressive**. For each tense *(present, past, present perfect, future)* there is a **simple form** and a **progressive form**.
All English verbs can be used in the **simple form**. The **progressive form**, however, is normally only possible with verbs that can describe an action in progress.
Which of the two aspects you choose depends on the idea being expressed and the type of verb used – a **dynamic verb** or a **stative verb**.

a) Dynamic verbs

Simple form	Progressive form	
Trish swims for the school team. My brother doesn't read a lot.	Look, there she is. She's swimming in lane four – the girl with the green cap. But at the moment he's reading one of the Harry Potter books.	You can use the **simple form** and the **progressive form** with ▶ verbs that describe an **activity**: *swim, read, eat, play, walk, work* etc.
My eyes always get tired when I've been working at the computer for too long.	We've done enough work for one day. I'm getting tired now.	▶ verbs that describe a **development** or a **process**: *get, become, grow* etc.

b) Stative verbs

Stative verbs are verbs that describe a **state**. They can usually only be used in the **simple form**.

Simple form	
I've heard that Naomi and Jack have split up. –Well, I didn't notice that when I saw them last.	You **cannot** normally use the **progressive form** ▶ with verbs of perception: *feel, hear, see, notice* etc.
How long have they known each other? – I don't know. But they seem to have been together for ages.	▶ with verbs that express opinions, knowledge or suppositions: *believe, forget, imagine, mean, know, suppose, think, realize, seem* etc.
Sandra loves playing tennis, but she hates losing. She wishes she was a lot better.	▶ with verbs that express likes or dislikes and wishes: *like, love, hate, want, wish* etc.
How long have you had that bike? – Oh, that isn't mine, it belongs to John.	▶ with verbs that express a state or express that something belongs to someone: *be, belong, cost, have, own* etc.
That cake looks delicious, doesn't it? – It doesn't only look good, it tastes great, too.	▶ with *look* (aussehen), *sound, smell, taste*.

▶ *Stop and think! Can you think of two more example sentences, one for dynamic verbs and one for stative verbs?*

c) Verbs that can be used statively and dynamically

Some **stative verbs** can sometimes also express an activity and can be used in the **progressive form**. Notice the difference in meaning.

Simple form (state)	Progressive form (activity)
Their new house has a really big kitchen. *... hat ...*	They were just having supper when I called. *... waren gerade beim Abendessen ...* (also: *have a bath/shower, have fun, have a party*)

Simple form (state)	Progressive form (activity)
Sarah thinks that biology is extremely interesting. *…glaubt/denkt…*	She's even thinking of doing the subject at university. *…überlegt…, ob…*
That red pullover looks really nice. It suits you. *…sieht…aus.*	I thought you were looking at it critically. *…würdest…anschauen.*
I see that you and Bob are getting on well. *Wie ich sehe, …*	Yes, I've been seeing him a lot recently. *… habe mich … getroffen …*
What does the word 'polyglot' mean? *…bedeutet…*	I've been meaning to look up that funny word. *…habe die Absicht …*
Normally he's so reasonable. *… ist …*	But today he's being extremely silly. *…verhält sich…*

NEW: d) The progressive form to express emotion

The adverb *always* is normally a signal word for the **simple form**. But expressions of frequency like *always, constantly* and *continually* can also be used with the **progressive form**. In that case it describes the speaker's surprise, annoyance or disbelief.

She's *continually* arguing with her parents.
You're *always* criticizing me. Give me a break!
My brother's *always* taking my things and never puts them back.
My new boyfriend's a dream. He's *always* buying me flowers and giving me presents.

1 *Which form is correct?*

1. Tom **(loves/is loving)** football.
2. He **(is/is being)** a very talented and promising young player.
3. He **(plays/is playing)** for his school and the county.
4. Tom **(believes/is believing)** that there is a future for him in football and he **(thinks/is thinking of)** becoming a professional.
5. He **(has had/has been having)** this dream ever since he **(was/was being)** a small boy.
6. And, of course, he **(knows/is knowing)** that professional players **(make/are making)** a lot of money.
7. He **(doesn't often read/isn't often reading)** books. But at the moment he **(reads/is reading)** a book on the history of Manchester United.
8. He **(wants/is wanting)** to leave school next year and apply for a place at a football academy.
9. While they **(had/were having)** supper last night, his parents suddenly **(said/were saying)** that his idea **(sounded/was sounding)** good.

2 *A letter to an agony aunt: Decide whether to use the simple or the progressive form of the given verbs.*

Dear Liz,
I 1 **(realize)** that all this 2 **(sound)** rather stupid. But I 3 **(feel)** that you 4 **(be)** the only person that can help me.
I 5 **(have)** a close relationship with this fabulous girl for about two years now and I 6 **(love)** her very much. But she 7 **(get)** more and more critical and often 8 **(complain)** about all sorts of things. She 9 always **(criticize)** the way I 10 **(look)**. I 11 **(be)** really fed up. Maybe she 12 **(see)** someone else???
What 13 you **(suppose)** the reason is for the change in her? At the moment I 14 even **(think)** of breaking up the relationship. What 15 you **(think)** I should do?
Stephen (clueless) Sheffield

3 ***Express these ideas differently:***
Use the verbs in brackets. Decide whether to use the simple or the progressive form.

Example: She's behaving in a very selfish way. **(be)** → She's **being** very selfish.

1. Who is the owner of this laptop? – Who ___ **(belong to)**?
2. Some people watch TV at supper. – Some people watch TV ___ **(have)**.
3. I wonder whether I should tell her. – I ___ **(think of)**.
4. You keep saying that you're sorry, but you never change. – You ___ **(always make excuses)**.
5. How much are those black boots in the window? – How much ___ **(cost)**?
6. I like your new hairstyle. It's very nice. – I ___ your new hairstyle **(think, look)**.
7. I'm really fed up with Sarah. All she can do is complain. – She ___ **(always complain)**.
8. At the moment your behaviour is really unfair. – At the moment you ___ **(be)**.

"Move! You're blocking the TV."

G2 Talking about the present, the past and the future

a) The present

You use the **present**
- to write summaries
- to describe things and to characterize people
- to analyze and comment on texts (e.g. literature) and to describe pictures.

Simple present	
The sun **rises** in the east. Money **doesn't grow** on trees.	▶ You use the **simple present** when you express facts or what people accept as true.
The Jacksons *often* **go** to Scotland in the winter. It **doesn't** *usually* **snow** much there, or **does** it? Well, places higher up **are** *sometimes* **snowed in** for days.	▶ The **simple present** is also used when you talk about things that **happen regularly** or about **permanent states**. In this case the simple present is often used with the **signal words** *always, often, regularly, never, sometimes, usually* etc.
In William Golding's *Lord of the flies* a group of English pupils **land** on a Pacific island after their plane **is shot** down. What first **looks** like paradise soon **becomes** hell when the boys **start** fighting each other and and when the 'beast' **appears** …	▶ You can also use the **simple present** to describe a series of actions or events that happen one after another. It is often used in sports **commentaries**, in **comments** on texts and in **summaries**.

Present progressive	
I'm *just* reading a very interesting article. It says that the oceans are rising more quickly than previously predicted. It blames governments all over the world because too little is being done *at the moment* to stop this development.	▶ You use the **present progressive** to describe activities that are happening at the moment, and for gradual developments. ▶ The **present progressive** is often used with the **signal words** *at the moment, just, (just) now* and *right now.*

1 *Are you really reading a book?:*
Which is correct – the simple or the progressive form?
(You can check the rules about stative and dynamic verbs in G1.)

Trish: Hey, Zach. What are you up to these days? I **(never see/'m never seeing)** you anywhere.
Zach: Well, I **('m/'m being)** very busy at the moment. I **(do/'m doing)** a lot of revising for French, and on Saturdays I **(often help/'m often helping)** my parents in the shop. And I **(have/'m having)** a hard time putting down a terrific book!
Trish: You **(joke/'re joking)**. You **(normally don't read/'re normally not reading)** any books. You **(pull/ 're pulling my leg)**, Zach.
Zach: No, seriously. I **(forget/'m forgetting)** what the book's called, but anyway, the author **(says/'s saying)** that the world we **(know/'re knowing)** only **(looks/is looking)** like a real world. But in fact it's a computer simulation. Whether you **(believe/'re believing)** it or not, Trish. At this very moment, while we **(talk/'re talking)** to each other, these machines **(watch/are watching)** each and every of our movements. And we ourselves **(gradually turn/are gradually turning)** into machines, too. It's like this Big Brother guy in that other book.
Trish: You **(mean/'re meaning)** *1984*.
Zach: Yeah, yeah, by George Orwell.
Trish: Your book **(sounds/is sounding)** pretty weird, Zach. I **(think/'m thinking)** you've been playing too many computer games.

2 *Asking questions:*
Use the simple present or the present progressive with the given verbs to complete these questions.

1. Jenny is on holiday in France.
   – ___ she ___ a good time? **(have)**
2. Who ___ this dictionary ___? **(belong to)** –
   I've no idea. Ask Jane.
3. Why ___ you ___ me like that? **(look at)** Is anything the matter?
4. Is your grandfather really 92? Who ___ him? **(look after)**
5. ___ anyone ___ TV **(watch)** or can I switch it off?
6. How's your French, Zach? ___ it ___? **(improve)**
7. Why ___ you ___ an umbrella, Mum? **(take)** ___ it ___? **(rain)**
8. ___ Linda ___ to the same school as you, Mike? **(go)**
   – No, she's at Thomas Tallis.
9. How often a week ___ you ___ tennis, Lisa? **(play)**
   – Only once.
10. How long ___ it ___ you to get to school, Sam? **(take)**
    – About ten minutes on my bike.

b) The past

There are three tenses in English that refer to the past: **present perfect**, **past tense**, and **past perfect**. Each of them has a simple and a progressive form.

The **present perfect** connects the past to the present.

Present perfect simple	
I've *already* heard the news. → So you needn't tell me again. Tom and Sally have *just* split up. → They're no longer together. I've been told this at least *three times*. → I'm familiar with all the details of the story.	▶ The **present perfect simple** is used when you want to stress the **result** (→) of an activity. The activity itself happened in the past, but the result is still relevant in the present. The **present perfect simple** is often used with the **signal words** *already, just, (not) yet, ever, never, so far, for* and *since*, and with expressions of frequency *(three times)*.
Have you *ever* been to America? – Yes, I've visited my relatives in Florida *twice*. But I've *never* been to New York.	▶ You can also use the **present perfect simple** if you want to express that something hasn't happened yet, or to ask whether something has taken place yet.
She's known him *for* at least three years. The palace has belonged to the family *since* the Middle Ages.	▶ With **stative verbs** the **present perfect simple** can express that a state began in the past and still continues in the present.

Present perfect progressive	
Zoe's been working *for hours*. She's been sitting at her computer *since she got up this morning*.	▶ The **present perfect progressive** is normally only used with dynamic verbs. ▶ It describes an activity that began in the past and has continued until now (and may still continue). It stresses the **duration** and **continuation** of an activity. ▶ The present perfect progressive is often used with ***for*** and ***since***. ***For*** is used for a period of time *(for hours)*. ***Since*** is used for a point in time *(since she got up this morning)*.

1 *For or since?*

In German, the *Präsens* (+ *schon*) is often used when in English you would use the **present perfect** with ***for*** or ***since***.

Translate these sentences into English. Use the progressive form wherever possible.

1. Sie kennt ihn schon seit Weihnachten.
2. Der Zug hat schon wieder Verspätung. **(be late)** Wir warten jetzt schon seit über eine halbe Stunde.
3. Sie spielen schon zwei Stunden lang und haben immer noch nicht genug.
4. Ich freue mich schon lange auf meine Reise nach Australien.
5. Der Pub gehört den MacDonalds seit dem 17. Jahrhundert.
6. Mein Vater arbeitet schon zwanzig Jahre für die gleiche Firma.
7. Mike hat sein neues Fahrrad seit seinem Geburtstag.
8. Fahr' bitte vorsichtig. Es schneit schon die ganze Nacht.

Simple past	
We were in California and Nevada *last year*. – Did you go to Las Vegas, too? – Yes, we did. But we didn't win anything. And Bob wasn't allowed to play because he was still under 16 *a year ago*.	▶ You use the **simple past** to describe states, events or activities that were **completed in the past** and are now over. They are not directly related to the present. ▶ The **simple past** is often used with adverbials of past time *(last year, a year ago, in 2009, yesterday, when?* etc.).
The dusty road lay deserted in the heat of the afternoon. Johnny wondered where all the people were. He got off his horse and pushed his way into the saloon. For a moment he couldn't see clearly in the gloom of the bar. But then he heard a familiar sound …	▶ The **simple past** is also used to describe a **series of actions** or events. This makes it the basic tense in narrative texts (stories, novels) and reports about past events.

Past progressive	
We were just getting ready for the first set, *when* it suddenly started to rain heavily. *While* we were waiting for the rain to stop, we saw a wonderful rainbow over the whole valley.	▶ The **past progresssive** describes activities that were **in progress** at a certain time in the past. It is often used to describe something that was still going on when something new happened. In this case the **past progressive** is used for the **background action** and the **simple past** for the **new event**. The **past progressive** often appears in clauses with *while* and the **simple past** in clauses with *when*.
Lisa was sitting in the garden, reading a book, while her father was mowing the lawn. Her brother was playing his new computer game in his room. Clouds were slowly creeping up on the sun. It was getting colder.	▶ The **past progressive** is also used to describe several activities that were happening at the same time in the past, and for **gradual developments**.

▶ *Stop and think! Try to explain the difference in meaning between* The burglars **ran** out of the house when the police arrived. *and* The burglars **were running** out of the house when the police arrived.

"Why, Hennings, I had no idea."

The **past perfect** is the tense that goes back furthest into the past.

Past perfect simple	
After the Newmans had left the restaurant at about 10 o'clock, they took a taxi home. *As soon as* they got home they noticed that their house had been broken into. The burglars had stolen some valuable jewelry, and a lot of damage had been done to the front door and the furniture. The Newmans had *never* experienced anything like this before.	▶ The **past perfect** describes what happened before another activity or event in the past. The **past perfect** is nearly always used together with **past tense** forms. In this case the past tense describes what happened at a certain time in the past *(then, at that time)* and the past perfect states what happened before that time. ▶ Sentences in the **past perfect** often contain *after, before* and *when*. Like the present perfect, the past perfect is also often used with *ever* or *never*.

Past perfect progressive	
We had been walking *for* about three hours when the fog came down from the mountains and the first snowflakes began to fall. The path we had been following *since* early that morning soon became invisible.	▶ The **past perfect progressive** expresses that an activity was in progress before another activity in the past. ▶ Like the **present perfect progressive**, the **past perfect progressive** is often used with ***for*** and ***since***.

2 *History quiz:*
*Use the **simple past** or the **present perfect simple** to ask questions. (Do you know the answers?)*

Example: Which British explorer • the east coast of Australia. **(discover)**
→ Which British explorer **discovered** the east coast of Australia? – It was James Cook.

1. Who • England in 1066 **(invade)**?
2. How many wives • Henry VIII • **(have)**?
3. In what century • the Industrial Revolution • **(begin)**?
4. Which English monarch • Empress of India **(be called)**?
5. How long • the UK • a member of the EU **(be)**?
6. Since when • the United States • of Britain **(be independent)**?
7. Who • the first American president in 1789 **(become)**?
8. How long • the American Civil War • **(last)**?
9. When • the transcontinental railroad • **(be opened)**?
10. Since when • the present British monarch • on the throne **(be)**?

c) The future

In English the tense and aspect you choose to express future actions and events depends on the exact idea you wish to convey.

The *going to* future	
Are you going to come with us to Ireland next spring, Lisa? – No, I'm going to fly off to somewhere warmer!	▶ The ***going to* future** describes what someone wants to do in the future. It expresses a **plan** or an **intention**.
The concerts starts at 8 o'clock. Look at the time, it's already quarter to. We're going to be late.	▶ The ***going to* future** can also be used when the speaker is **sure** that something will happen in the future – because there are already **signs** that indicate this *(time on the clock).*

The *will* future	
The Southwest will have another wet and windy day, and I'm afraid it won't get any better tomorrow.	▶ The ***will* future** describes that something is **certain** to happen in the future. The speaker cannot influence these states or events (*like the weather).*
I'm sure we'll get to Heathrow on time. Harry will *probably* collect us at the airport.	▶ The ***will* future** is used after certain **verbs** (*expect, be sure* etc.) and with **adverbs** like *probably, perhaps, possibly* etc. In this case it expresses **something you think might happen**.
Will you have a look at the CD player, please? It doesn't seem to be working. – OK, I'll have a look at it.	▶ You can also use the ***will* future** to ask for help and to offer your help – **spontaneously**, without having planned to do this before.

!

Do not use the ***will* future** in *if*-clauses or in adverbial clauses with *when, as soon as* or *until*:
I'll call you ***as soon as I know*** *all the details.*

1 **Going to** ***or*** **will**? *Complete these sentences with the ideas given in the box. Decide whether to use the* ***going to*** **future** *or the* ***will*** **future**.

rain soon • let you know • win easily • do a trekking tour in Alaska • help you carry them • not have the picnic in the garden • get badly sunburnt • probably be back by six • lend you mine

1. Lisa's playing now, look. The score is 6:1, 5:0. She ...
2. If the weather is so bad tomorrow we ...
3. That girl has been in the sun for ages. Look at her pink back. She ...
4. Look at those black clouds in the west. It ...
5. What are your holiday plans, Trish? – I ...
6. Phew, these books are heavy. – I ...
7. When can I talk to Linda? – She ...
8. I've forgotten my mobile. – I ...
9. As soon as I've got the results, I ...

"Your car will be right down, Mr Lundquist."

The present progressive with future meaning	
What **are** you **doing** *this weekend*, Zach? – Well, *on Saturday morning* **I'm helping** my parents in the shop, but **I'm not doing** anything special *in the afternoon*.	▶ You use the **present progressive** when you talk about **arrangements** that have been made for the future. It is often used with adverbials like *tomorrow, this weekend, on Saturday, next week* etc. (These 'future adverbials' make it clear that the verb form refers to the future and not to the present.)

The simple present with future meaning	
When **does** our plane **leave**? – It **leaves** Los Angeles at 8.30 and **arrives** in Stuttgart at 15.59.	▶ You can use the **simple present** for **future events** when those events have been officially fixed. It normally refers to the exact times given in timetables and programmes. This 'timetable future' is often used with the verbs *arrive, begin, leave, start* and *end*.

The future progressive	
This time next month **I'll be enjoying** myself in California.	▶ The **future progressive** describes an **activity in progress at a certain time in the future** *(This time next month…)*.

The future perfect	
We'll have finished the job *by the end of this week*. We **will** already **have done** everything *when our parents come back*.	▶ You use the **future perfect** to express that **an activity or an event will be completed by a certain time in the future**. This point in time can de defined by time adverbials (*by the end of this week, by Saturday* etc.) or by an adverbial clause of time *(when our parents come back …)*.

▶ *Stop and think! Sometimes there is no time adverbial in sentences with the* **present progressive***:*
Lisa **is helping** Mike with his homework.
How can you tell whether this refers to the present or whether this is an arrangement for the future?

2 *Error spotting – Going on holiday:*
The verb forms in most of the sentences below are wrong (some are correct). Correct the mistakes.

Trish: I wonder what the weather is like next week. What do you wear on the plane tomorrow?
Zach: I think I just put on a pair of jeans and a T-shirt.
Trish: Did I tell you? I'm afraid my parents were not able to take us to the airport.
Zach: So we'll have to go by bus.
Trish: When is the bus leaving?
Zach: It leaves at 10.15 and is going to get to the airport at 11.30.
Trish: And when are you going to get up tomorrow morning?
Zach: I get up at 7.
Trish: Just think – by this time next week we'll be in San Francisco for six days!
Zach: Yep, and we're seeing all the sights and have travelled by cable car.
Trish: And we lie on a fantastic Californian beach, enjoying the sun.

3 *The big match:*
In German you very often use the Präsens *for future activities and events. In English, in most cases, you would use a form of the future. Translate these sentences:*

1. „Gegen wen spielen wir am Wochenende, Tom?“
2. „Wir spielen gegen United – das wichtigste Spiel der Saison.“
3. „Wann fängt das Spiel an?“
4. „Es fängt um 15.30 an. Und wir treffen uns um zwei Uhr am Bahnhof.“
5. „Ich hoffe, dass Mike spielt.“
6. „Ich bin sicher, dass er spielt.“
7. „Wenn wir verlieren, kommen wir nie in die erste Division.“
8. „Ja, stimmt. Sag mal, trägst du deine neuen Fußballschuhe am Samstag?“
9. „Natürlich, und ich schieße mindestens zwei Tore.“
10. „Ich sage dir, Sam, um Viertel nach Fünf sitzen wir im Clubhaus und feiern unseren Sieg.“

G3 Describing

a) Using adjectives and adverbs

You can use **adjectives** or **adverbs** to describe actions, people or things. They can make texts more interesting, more informative and more lively.

Adjective or adverb?

Undoubtedly, ‘Romeo and Juliet’ is the **best** known of Shakespeare’s plays.
It starts **very dramatically** with a **fierce** fight between some servants of the **greatest** families in Verona, the Capulets and the Montagues, who are **deadly** enemies.
Later, Romeo, a Montague, meets Juliet, the **beautiful** daughter of the Capulets, at a ball. They fall in love **immediately**. In the **most famous** scene in the play, Romeo waits under Juliet’s balcony and they arrange a **secret** marriage. They are **extremely happy**. But this happiness is not to last.

- **Adjectives** describe what someone or something is like. They can be used **attributively** (a ***fierce*** fight) or **predicatively** (They are … ***happy***.)
- **Adverbs** describe the way something happens or was done. (*They fall in love* ***immediately***.) They can modify verbs (*It starts …* ***dramatically***.), adjectives (***extremely*** *happy*) or other adverbs (**very** *dramatically*).
- **Adverbs** like *undoubtedly, obviously, unfortunately, of course* etc. can comment on a whole sentence: ***Undoubtedly***, *‘Romeo and Juliet’ is …*
- **Adverbs** like *later, soon, just* describe when something happens.

!

You know how to use regular comparative and superlative forms of adjectives and adverbs:

adjectives:	adverbs:
big, bigger, biggest	*fast, faster, fastest*
expensive, more expensive, most expensive	*clearly, more clearly, most clearly*

Remember these irregular comparative and superlative forms:

good/well: better – best ***many: more – most***
bad/badly: worse – worst ***much: more – most*** ***little: less – least***

▶ *Stop and think! Can you write an example sentence for each of these:* **more**, **most**, **less** *and* **least***?*

There are some adjectives and corresponding adverbs that are diffcult for German students to use:

Adjectives that have the same form as adverbs

There are are no special adverb forms for *fast, long, early* etc.

Adjective	Adverb
We rented a fast car when we were in the US.	But you aren't allowed to drive fast in America.
It's a long journey from Washington D.C. to San Francisco.	We didn't stay long in Chicago.
On the way home we took an early flight.	We had to get up terribly early to catch our plane.
Further examples of adverbs that have the same form as adjectives: ***far, low, daily, monthly, weekly***	

Adverbs with two different forms

Some adverbs have different forms: one with *-ly* at the end, and the other without.
Note the different meanings of the two forms.

Adverb without *-ly*	Adverb with *-ly*
We've all worked very hard. *(hart/schwer)*	We can hardly wait for the Cup Final. *(kaum)*
Our team always plays fair. *(fair)*	We're fairly sure that we'll win the match next week. *(ziemlich)*
We've just signed contracts with two promising young Brazilians. *(gerade)*	The referee awarded us a penalty quite justly. *(zu Recht)*
Their players attacked our goal, but they never got near. *(nah/in die Nähe)*	And the match was nearly over when they had their first real chance. *(fast)*
United scored the only goal late in the match. *(spät)*	Have you seen any interesting matches on TV lately? *(in letzter Zeit)*

b) The position of adverbs and adverbials in the sentence

There are three positions in the sentence where adverbs and adverbials can be placed:

- before the subject (**front position**)
- between the subject and the main verb or between the auxiliary and the main verb (**mid position**)
- after the verb or after the verb + object (**end position**).

Which position you decide on depends on the type of adverb or adverbial and the emphasis you want to give it.

▶ *Stop and think! Find the* **adverb** *in these three sentences and say which position it is in:*
We cycled hard.
Of course I love cycling.
I would never cycle without a helmet.

Front position	
Unfortunately, it was raining hard when we set off in the morning. Luckily, the sun came out a few hours later.	▶ *NEW:* **Adverbs of comment** (*actually, apparently, basically, frankly, luckily, obviously, of course, unfortunately* etc.) usually appear in **front position**.
Every morning we checked our bikes. In Canterbury we found a nice bed and breakfast place.	▶ **Adverbs** and **adverbials of time and place** can appear in **front position** for emphasis.

Mid position	
Bikers should always wear a helmet. Accidents often happen because people are not careful enough.	▶ **Adverbs of frequency** (*always, never, often, sometimes, occasionally* etc.) often take **mid position**.
Amy can easily keep up with us. They were quickly able to repair the bike.	▶ **Adverbs of manner** (*easily, quickly, carefully, hastily* etc.) can take **mid position**.

End position	
The hill was so steep that we could only go slowly. Sam had prepared the trip really well.	▶ **Adverbs of manner** (*slowly, carefully, hard, well* etc.) usually appear in **end position** (after the verb or after the verb + object). When these adverbs appear in end position, they are normally more strongly emphasized than in mid position. Very emphatic adverbs like *hard* and *well* always appear in **end position**.
We stopped for the night somewhere near Brighton. After the long ride everybody was very tired in the evening.	▶ **Adverbs and adverbials of place and time** mostly take **end position**.
Let's meet at the station tomorrow morning. We went to Scotland two years ago.	▶ If there are **two adverbials** at the end of the sentence, the normal word order is place before time.

!
Different from German:
Adverbs of manner never go between the verb and the direct object:
*We **quickly found the correct road**.* Compare: *Wir **fanden schnell die richtige Straße**.*

1 *Adjectives and adverbs:*

a) *Look at the adjectives and adverbs in the box. Which are adjectives and which are adverbs, and which can be used both as adjectives and adverbs? Make a list for each category.*

beautiful • definitely • early • easy • especially • fast • frankly • hard • hardly • gradually • immediately • late • lately • long • luckily • most • never • obviously • particularly • worse

b) ***Detective O'Brien reports**: Replace the adverbs in these sentences by adverbs from the box in a) that have a similar meaning.*

1. I saw at once that something was wrong.
2. Fortunately, the criminal hadn't worn gloves.
3. It is especially difficult to prove that people's alibis are wrong.
4. Honestly, this is one of the worst crimes I've seen.
5. It is certainly worse than the McDermott case.
6. I haven't come across anything like this recently.
7. Crime in the city is slowly getting worse.
8. Of course, the police can't be everywhere.

2 *Opposites: Use adjectives or adverbs from the box to state the opposite.*

most beautiful • most attractive • easy • fast • late • never • worse

1. We arrived in Los Angeles early in the afternoon.
2. The plane flew very slowly because of the strong wind.
3. It's hard to understand how this software works.
4. That's the ugliest car in town.
5. She always goes to school on her bike.
6. In the mixed doubles Mike played better than Tracy.
7. The one in the corner is the least attractive of the three dogs.

3 ***Error spotting – Teenage passengers**: Rewrite these sentences, correcting the mistakes.*

1. A new study on teenage driving in 2008 was in Britain published.
2. If teenage drivers travel with a group of friends apparently, can this be extreme dangerous and they are likelier to have an accident than when they alone travel.
3. British insurance companies want immediately to introduce drastically restrictions on young drivers.
4. Drivers under 20 will not be allowed to carry more than one teenage passenger for the first six months in their car after they have their driving test passed.
5. Young passengers distract often young drivers and encourage them to drive in a more riskier way.
6. Several states have already in the USA limited the number of passengers a teenage driver can in the first six or twelve months carry.
7. Fatal crashes fell in those states actually by 37 per cent after the strictly limits were introduced.
8. The insurance companies said the limit would reduce drastically the cost of insurance because the number of multimillion-pound claims significantly would fall.

based on an article in *The Times*

G4 Using non-finite verb forms

There are **finite** and **non-finite** verb forms in English. The **finite** verb forms give you some information as to the grammatical person (*I, you, she* etc.), the number (*singular* or *plural*) and the tense (*present, past, future* etc.).
Non-finite verb forms give you no such information.
The **infinitive**, the **gerund** and the **participle** are **non-finite** verb forms.

finite verb form	non-finite forms	
Ken often plays video games.	Ken wants to play his new game on the weekend.	**infinitive**
– 3rd person singular	He enjoys playing video games with his friends.	**gerund**
– simple present	His little sister sometimes watches them playing.	**participle**

a) The infinitive with *to*

	after certain verbs:	*to*-infinitive	
Amy	doesn't want	to go	to university.
	after verb + object:		
But her mother	would like her	to become	a doctor.
	after adjectives:		
It isn't always	easy	to decide	on the right job.
	after adjectives + for + noun/pronoun:		
It was	difficult for Amy	to make	up her mind.
	after nouns:		
Her parents can't understand her	decision	to leave	school early.
	after question words:		
Students often wonder	what	to do	after school.
	after the first, the last, the only one(s):		
Kevin was	the first	to finish	his essay.

!
Different from German:
German sentences like *Ich will, dass …* or *Ich möchte, dass …* can only be translated with the **verb + object + infinitive construction**:
Lehrer möchten/wollen, dass ihre Schüler in Prüfungen gut abschneiden.
*Teachers **want their students to do** well in exams.*
You **mustn't** use *that* + subordinate clause after *want* or *would like*.

▶ *Stop and think! How would you translate these sentences into English?*
Ich will nicht, dass er das tut. Ich möchte, dass du deine Hausaufgaben machst.

b) The infinitive without *to*

	after most auxiliaries:	infinitive without *to*	
I really	must	get	myself some new shoes.
	after make + direct object (causing): after let + direct object (allowing):		
That black hat is great. It	makes you	look	like Al Capone.
Come on.	Let	me	try it on.
	after verbs of perception + direct object:		
Can I	see you	put	it on again?

1 ***What people say:***
Rewrite these sentences, using infinitive constructions.

1. Girl: This bag is too heavy. I can't carry it. **(for)** → This bag is too heavy **for me to carry**.
2. Tom: Shall I get the car out of the garage? – Do you … **(want)**
3. Sarah: You simply must meet Randy. – I … **(would like)**
4. Tracy: Who shall I invite to the party? – I'm wondering … **(invite)**
5. Learner driver to instructor: Shall I go left or right at the crossing? – Do you … **(want)**
6. Host: The Millers always arrive before anyone else. – The Millers are … **(the first)**
7. Hostess: All the others brought something to drink, but Michael didn't. – Michael was … **(only one)**

2 ***The mountain tour:***
Translate this text into English, using the appropriate infinitive constructions.

1. Wir sind die ersten, die diese Tour diese Woche machen.
2. Der Neuschnee macht es uns unmöglich, die normale Route zu nehmen.
3. Er zwingt uns, einen längeren Weg zu gehen.
4. Aber ich erwarte trotzdem, dass wir bis um 12 Uhr am Gipfel sind. *(summit)*
5. Ich möchte, dass ihr einander helft und als Team arbeitet.
6. Ich will, dass mich keiner auf dem Gletscher überholt. *(glacier, overtake)*
7. Ich will keinen von euch auf dem Berg oder auf dem Gletscher verlieren.
8. Also, gute Nacht. Ich möchte, dass ihr morgen alle fit seid und viel Spaß habt.

c) Gerund constructions

Relaxing with my friends is what I like best.	▶ Like a noun, the **gerund** can be used as the **subject** of a sentence.
Emma **enjoys reading** romantic novels.	▶ The **gerund** is often used as the **object** after certain verbs (*enjoy, imagine, suggest* etc.).

We're all looking forward to going on holiday together.	▶ You can use the **gerund** after certain **verbs + prepositions** (*dream of, look forward to, talk about* etc.).
Darren is very good at developing new computer programmes.	▶ There are a number of **adjectives + prepositions** that are followed by a **gerund** (*be afraid of, be good at, be interested in* etc).
Sharon doesn't like the idea of walking home all on her own.	▶ The **gerund** is also used after certain **nouns + prepositions** (*chance of, danger of, idea of* etc.).
But she's worried about her boyfriend driving too fast. And she absolutely hates him drinking too much.	▶ Sometimes an object *(her boyfriend, him)* comes before the *-ing* form, serving as the logical subject of the *-ing* form. This construction can be looked upon as a **gerund** with a subject of its own.

d) Gerund or infinitive? (Difference in meaning)

There are a number of English verbs that can be followed either by an **infinitive** or a **gerund**:

- *Begin, continue, start, like, love, hate* and *prefer* can be used with an **infinitive** or a **gerund** **without** any difference in meaning.
- *Mean, stop, forget* and *remember* can also be used with an **infinitive** or **gerund** – but **with** a difference in meaning.

I'll never forget seeing the Grand Canyon the first time. Do you remember flying through it in that helicopter?	I mustn't forget to put all those fantastic pictures in an album. Please remember to lend me the album when you've finished.
▶ After ***forget*** and ***remember*** the **gerund** describes an event or activity that has already taken place.	▶ After ***forget*** and ***remember*** the **infinitive** expresses an intention to do something new.

Jack has stopped taking photos. He never knows what to do with them.	Oh, look at that view. Let's stop to take a photo.
▶ After ***stop*** the **gerund** refers to something that has come (or might come) to an end.	▶ After ***stop*** the **infinitive** expresses the reason for stopping.

If you really want to go to the US, it'll mean saving up for a long time. *… bedeutet das, dass …*	I've been meaning to ask you if you'd like to go to the US with me. *… ich hatte vor …*
▶ After ***mean*** the **gerund** describes a logical consequence.	▶ After ***mean*** the **infinitive** expresses an intention to do something.

1 ***Pupils hooked on energy drinks:*** *Rewrite these sentences, using gerund constructions.*

1. Lots of pupils like to drink energy drinks at school. **(be keen on)**
2. They do so because they find it hard to concentrate. **(have difficulty in)**
3. Others are afraid that they might do badly in exams. **(worry about)**
4. Drug experts say that pupils should not drink too many of these drinks or take caffeine-based pills. **(avoid)**
5. Studies say that pupils who drink these drinks regularly might be affected badly. **(get used to)**

6. There is even the danger that they may become addicted to them. **(be in danger of)**
7. Teachers have said that pupils are becoming more and more agitated in class. **(complain about)**
8. Most schools have a drugs education programme which advises pupils not to take illegal drugs. **(warn against)**
9. But drug experts want the use of legal drugs to be checked, too. **(suggest)**

based on an article in *The Guardian*

2 *After school: Complete the sentences, deciding whether to use gerunds or infinitives.*

1. My friend Jane enjoys **(travel)**.
2. She has suggested **(spend)** a gap year together with me.
3. She plans **(go)** to Australia and **(work)** there for six months.
4. Her idea is that when we have finished **(work)** there and have succeeded in **(make)** enough money, we will see as much of the world as possible.
5. It's easy for her **(talk)** because she and John have stopped **(see)** each other.
6. But I couldn't stand **(be)** away from home for so long.
7. That would mean **(not see)** Mark all that time.
8. That's why the idea of **(stay)** in far away countries doesn't sound too attractive to me.
9. I mean **(go)** to unversity straight after school.
10. Of course I'm looking forward to **(hear)** from Jane.
11. I mustn't forget **(give)** her my e-mail address.
12. Let's hope that she'll remember **(write)** to me and **(tell)** me about her adventures.

G5 Using participles

There are two types of participles: the **present participle** *(exciting)* and the **past participle** *(unexpected)*. The **present participle** is **active** in meaning; the **past participle** is **passive** in meaning.

a) Participle constructions

I thought the film was very exciting. There were lots of frightening scenes. My feelings about the unexpected ending are somewhat mixed.	▶ You can use **participles** as **adjectives**. Like adjectives, they can be used **attributively** *(frightening)* and **predicatively** *(mixed)*.
Lots of workmen stood waiting for the doors to open. *… standen und warteten …* Two policemen came running along the road. *… kamen die Straße entlang gelaufen.* The factory will remain closed because of the strike. *… wird … geschlossen bleiben …*	▶ ***NEW:*** **Present** and **past participles** can be used after verbs that describe **rest** (a "**position**") or **motion** (*come, lie, stand, sit, stay, remain* etc.).
We watched a big black car waiting in front of the bank. *Wir beobachteten, wie ein großes schwarzes Auto vor der Bank wartete.* Then we noticed a policeman standing near the entrance of the bank. *Dann bemerkten wir, dass ein Polizist in der Nähe des Bankeingangs stand.*	▶ Verbs like *feel, hear, notice, observe, see, watch* are **verbs of perception**. You can use a **direct object** + a **present participle** *(a big black car)* after these verbs.

b) Participle or infinitive after verbs of perception?

You can use both the **present participle** and the **infinitive without *to*** after **verbs of perception**. But the two constructions have a different emphasis.

present participle: activity in progress	
We heard three men near the black car talking to each other in a strange language. Then we observed them slowly moving towards the bank.	▶ The **present participle** describes an **activity in progress**. Only part of the action is seen or heard. ▶ The **present participle** corresponds to the **progressive form**: *Three men **were talking** to each other.*

infinitive: completed activity	
Suddenly we noticed the men take out their guns, and we saw the policeman take out his gun, too. We saw the three men run across the road, saw one of them stumble and fall and then heard the film director shout: "Cut!"	▶ The **infinitive** describes a **completed action**. It is seen from its beginning to its end. This is especially the case when the activity is short or when a series of actions is described. ▶ The **infinitive** corresponds to the **simple form**: *One of the men **stumbled** and **fell**.*

1 *The accident: Fill in the correct form of the participles. Use the verbs in brackets.*

1. A big truck came **(rumble)** down the road.
2. At the same time we saw a small red car slowly **(approach)** the crossing.
3. For a moment the little red car stayed **(hide)** behind a hedge, but then it drove into the main road.
4. We watched the **(terrify)** scene, but we were **(fascinate)** at the same time.
5. We heard the truck's horn and its **(screech)** brakes.
6. The crash was terrible and the little red car ended up **(lie)** on its roof, badly **(damage)**.
7. There was **(break)** glass all over the place and we could smell something **(burn)**.
8. A few minutes later we saw a police car and an ambulance **(drive)** towards the scene of the accident.
9. The ambulance men pulled the **(injure)** driver out of the car and they carried him to the ambulance. We heard one of the policemen **(interview)** the truck driver who seemed to be too badly **(shock)** to speak.
10. The **(surprise)** news the next day was that the driver had only suffered minor injuries and would be able to leave the hospital the **(follow)** week.

2 *Underground thieves: Complete the sentences with the verbs in the box. Decide whether to use participles or infinitives. Sometimes both forms are possible. Which do you think is more appropriate?*

approach • carry • get • jump • laugh • sit • take • talk • touch

It happened on a crowded Underground train. A lot of passengers and Fiona got on the train at Piccadilly Circus. She felt someone ___ her arm as the passengers pushed past her. At the next station she saw two men ___ off. Fiona noticed one of them ___ a familiar object – her handbag. The men didn't notice her ___ off the train behind them at the last moment. When Fiona came back to the platform with two police officers, she saw the two young men just ___ there on a seat. She heard them ___ to each other and ___. From the distance she watched the two police officers slowly ___ the two men and saw one of them suddenly ___ a pair of handcuffs from his belt.

G6 Using modal auxiliaries

Can, ***may, must***, and ***needn't*** are the most common **modal auxiliaries**.
May, ***must*** and ***needn't*** can only be used in the **present tense**; ***can*** has the **past tense** form ***could***.

For all the other tenses you have to use substitutes:

Modal auxiliaries	Substitutes	past	future
can, could ↔ cannot/can't, could not/couldn't	*be able to*	*was/were able to*	*will be able to*
may, can ↔ may not/mustn't, cannot/can't	*be allowed to*	*was/were allowed to*	*will be allowed to*
must ↔ needn't	*have to*	*had to*	*will have to*
needn't	*not have to*	*didn't have to*	*won't have to*

Modal auxiliaries can express …

Ability (können)	
Surprisingly many people can't swim. Mike couldn't find his swimming trunks yesterday. Lisa has been able to swim since she was five.	▶ ***Can (cannot/can't)*** and ***could (couldn't)*** express that someone (or something) is/was able or unable to do something. ▶ The substitute form is ***be able to***.

Obligation (müssen, sollen)	
I'm sorry, but I really must leave now. Thanks, but you needn't drive me home. It's not far to walk. I'll have to do a lot of work this week for school. We're required to wear school uniform at our school. You've had too much to drink. You really shouldn't be driving.	▶ ***Must*** expresses that something is necessary or should be done (You feel you must do something). ▶ ***Needn't*** expresses that something is not necessary. The usual substitute form is ***have to***, but ***be forced to*** and ***be required to*** are also sometimes used. ▶ ***Should*** and ***ought to*** can be used to give advice or to express criticism.

Possibility (können)	
Surely this can't be Tracy's mobile, can it? – You may be right. But whose is it? Ask Sarah, she might know. I think Tracy must have left hers at home.	▶ ***Can, could, may*** and ***might*** express that something is possible or seems to be possible. ***Must*** expresses that the speaker expects something to be certain or very probable.

Permission (dürfen)	
May we take photos in the cathedral, Mrs Dent? – I don't think you're allowed to. Look, there's a sign. It says: 'Visitors are not permitted to take photos or use video-cameras in the cathedral.' So I'm afraid you can't. And you certainly mustn't take your ice-cream inside, Sam.	▶ ***May*** is used to ask politely for permission. ***Mustn't***, ***can't*** and ***may not*** (more formal) are used to refuse permission. The substitute form is ***be allowed to***. (You can also use ***be permitted to***; this applies to regulations.)

> **!**
> Be careful with **must**, **mustn't** and **needn't**:
> *Du musst das tun.* → *You **must** do that.*
> *Du darfst das nicht tun.* → *You **mustn't** do that.*
> *Du brauchst das nicht zu tun.* → *You **needn't** do that.*

"We may need to work on your emergency stop."

1 *Say it with auxiliaries:*

a) *Use **can**, **could** or a form of **be able to** to complete these sentences.*

1. Mike hopes he ___ afford a trip to New Zealand after leaving school.
2. What do you think Pete is up to? I (not) ___ contact him for weeks now.
3. Could you speak up a little? I (not) ___ understand a word back here.
4. Excuse me, ___ you tell me the way to the British Museum, please?
5. Emma ___ swim when she was only four.
6. My father has had a hip operation. But he ___ to walk again in a few days.

b) *Use **may**, **might**, **mustn't** or a form of **be allowed to** to complete these sentences.*

1. You ___ make so much noise, children. The headmaster is next door.
2. When I was small I ___ eat as many sweets as I liked.
3. ___ we use dictionaries in this test, Mrs Carter?
4. I ___ stay in the sun so long again. Look at my red back.
5. Let's try this path. It ___ take us back to the car – and it ___ not.
6. I'm really trying to lose some weight. I ___ eat so much!

2 *Error spotting – Party talk:*
*Correct the mistakes with **must**, **mustn't**, **needn't** or the substitute **have to**.*

1. Needn't Tracy and I clear everything up after the party, Mum?
2. Well yes, of course you weren't allowed to clear everything up. It's your party, kids!
3. Times have changed. When I was your age I mustn't make everything look the way my parents had left it.
4. You and your friends needn't drink any alcohol.
5. The Johnsons had to be terribly worried when the police brought Tim home after Elsa's party.
6. Your guests may not bring any food. We'll have some pizzas delivered.
7. So you really can't have bought all the sausages yesterday.
8. Emma rang up, Mum. Her brother doesn't have time to bring her here by car, so she can't be collected.
9. Hi, Emma, listen, I've only invited my closest friends, so the party is a sort of secret and you must tell anyone else about it.
10. The good thing is we might have warned the neighbours. They're away on holiday.
11. How nice, Tommy. But you couldn't have brought me flowers!

G7 Using direct and indirect speech

a) Backshift of tenses and change of adverbials of time and place

When people talk to each other, they normally use **direct speech**. But if you want to report what another person has said, you use **indirect speech**.
If the report is given later, the introductory verb is often in the simple past. In this case the tenses that were used in direct speech have to be changed. The tenses are shifted one tense further back into the past (*present* → *past*, *present perfect* → *past perfect* etc.).

If the report is made at a later time or in a different place, adverbials of time and place usually have to be changed, too:

today → that day
tomorrow/the next day → the following day
yesterday → the day before
six months ago → six months before
here → there
this → that

Direct speech *Excerpts from Joe Grimsby's speech:*	Backshift of tenses	Indirect speech *What* The Gazette *reported:*
"We're all working hard to make our dreams come true."	**present progressive → past progressive**	The Labour candidate started his speech by saying that they were all working hard to make their dreams come true.
"This is a decisive moment in time and I promise to bring about fundamental changes."	**simple present → simple past**	He went on to say that it was a decisive moment in time and he promised to bring about fundamental changes.
"Everybody in the party has been doing their very best in the past few weeks."	**present perfect progressive → past perfect progressive**	He added that everybody in the party had been doing their very best in the past few weeks.
"It was only *six months* ***ago*** that I was chosen to represent the party."	**simple past → past perfect simple**	He explained that it had only been *six months* ***before*** that he had been chosen to represent the party.
"It's amazing what the party has achieved in such a short time!"	**present perfect simple → past perfect simple**	He exclaimed that it was amazing what the party had achieved in such a short time.
"And I'm absolutely certain that we will win the election ***next*** *week*."	**will → would**	He finished by saying that he was absolutely certain that they would win the election *the* ***following*** *week*.

▶ *Stop and think!* In modern colloquial English the tenses in indirect speech often are the same tense as in direct speech: "I **joined** the Labour Party in my teens." → Joe said he **joined** the Labour Party in his teens. *Can you imagine why people often avoid the backshift of tenses?*

b) Indirect questions

Direct speech	Indirect speech
Reporter from *The Gazette:* "When did you decide to become the party's candidate, Mr Grimsby?"	The reporter wanted to know when Joe Grimsby had decided to become the party's candidate.
"Will the financial situation allow you to keep all your promises?"	She asked Mr Grimsby if/whether the financial situation would allow him to keep all his promises.

If there is a **question word** in direct speech (***When*** … ?), it is used again in indirect speech.
If there is **no question word** in direct speech, you use ***if*** or ***whether*** to introduce the clause in indirect speech.
In modern English, ***whether*** sounds slightly more formal than ***if***.

c) Indirect commands

Direct speech	Indirect speech
"So, my friends, elect the right person for the job."	Joe Grimsby ***told*** *everyone* **to elect** the right person for the job.
"And don't believe any of the rumours spread by my political opponents."	And he ***warned*** *them* **not to believe** any of the rumours spread by his political opponents.

You can use *tell, advise, ask* and *warn* to introduce indirect commands.
These introductory verbs are followed by a *direct object (everyone, them)* and an **infinitive with *to***.
For negative imperatives, you use **not + infinitive with *to***.

1 *Said at school:*
Emma has to stay at home for a week because she has flu. Lisa has come to tell her what people said at school during that time. *Change the sentences in direct speech into indirect speech.*

1. Mr Bloggs: "I want all of you to finish the project."
   – Mr Bloggs said he ___
2. Careers officer: "Do you enjoy working in a team, Lisa?"
   – The careers officer asked me if ___
3. Ms Turnbull: "I'm afraid your essay is not very good, Lisa."
   – Ms Turnbull complained that ___
4. Mr Turner (headmaster): "There will be a group of Chinese students visiting our school for a few days."
   – Mr Turner anounced that ___
5. Ms Collins (secretary): "Please collect your school identity cards from the secretary's office."
   – The secretary told us ___
6. Ms McGregor: "Don't forget to bring the money for the trip to Stratford on Wednesday."
   – Ms McGregor reminded us ___
7. Dinner lady in cafeteria: "Sorry, luv. There are no more chips. Have some salad instead."
   – On Thursday the dinner lady told me ___ and she suggested ___
8. Fireman: "If there is a fire, keep all the doors and windows shut."
   – During the fire drill on Tuesday a fireman told us ___
9. Mr Turner (headmaster): "As so many books have got lost recently, pupils are no longer allowed to take books home from the library."
   – Mr Turner explained that we ___ because ___
10. Mike: "Do you know how Emma is? I miss her a lot."
   – Oh, I almost forgot the most important thing. Mike wondered ___ and he added ___

2 *Misunderstandings:*
Use indirect speech and the words from the box to clear up misunderstandings.

Example: After school I'm going to join my parents' business. (do languages at university)
– That's odd. Only a few days ago you told me **that you were going to do languages at university**.

not speak any Spanish • buy a red Ferrari • be a vegetarian • dump him • be in bed with flu • be wet and windy all day • be in Canada • not have a driving licence

1. Emma is coming to the party tomorrow.
   – Is she really? But yesterday you said ___
2. When I was in Barcelona I had an interesting conversation with some Spanish students.
   – What? I thought you said ___

3. I love driving my sister's car.
   – Are you serious? This morning you told me you
4. Our neighbours have bought a fantastic Rolls Royce.
   – They have?! The other day you said they
5. Mike is in the US at the moment. He's doing a year at the University of Montreal.
   – Did you say the US? I always thought Montreal
6. I'm starving. Let's get some hamburgers.
   – You must be joking. You've always told everybody that you
7. I'm seeing Robert tonight.
   – Robert? Didn't you say that you
8. Let's go and have a picnic by the river tomorrow.
   – Tomorrow won't be any good. The weather forecast said that

G8 Linking ideas – forming complex sentences

You can link different ideas by combining a **main clause** with subordinate clauses to form **complex sentences**.

Napoleon said that the education of the young was more important than anything that could be done for those who were already grown up.
It happened that Jessie and Bluebell had both whelped *(Junge werfen)* soon after the hay harvest, giving birth between them to nine sturdy *(kräftig)* puppies. As soon as they were weaned *(entwöhnt)*, Napoleon took them away from their mothers, saying that he would make himself responsible for their education. From: George Orwell, *Animal Farm*

In these complex sentences there are three **main clauses** and a number of different **subordinate clauses**:

main clauses	subordinate clauses
Napoleon said	***that* clause**
	… that the education of the young was more important than anything …
	relative clause
	… that could be done for those …
	relative clause
	… who were already grown up.
It happened	***that* clause**
	… that Jessie and Bluebell had both whelped soon after the hay harvest,
	participle construction (accompanying circumstances)
	… giving birth between them to nine sturdy puppies.
	adverbial clause of time
	… As soon as they were weaned,
Napoleon took them away from their mothers,	**participle construction (accompanying circumstances)**
	… saying that he would make himself responsible for their education.

Just like in German, **subordinate clauses** can come after the main clause or before it:

*Napoleon took the puppies away from their mothers **because he wanted to bring them up himself**.*
***As Napoleon wanted to bring the puppies up himself**, he took them away from their mothers.*

!

Different from German:
The word order in affirmative subordinate clauses is the same as in main clauses (except questions and negations): subject – verb – object

English: When you write an English text, you try to avoid mistakes.
German: Wenn du einen englischen Text schreibst, versuchst du, Fehler zu vermeiden.

a) Sentences with relative clauses

Relative clauses are used to give definitions or to add extra information. There are two types of relative clauses: **defining relative clauses** and **non-defining relative clauses**.

Defining relative clauses	Non-defining relative clauses
George Orwell was the English author who criticized political injustice most strongly. In his novel *Animal Farm* the pigs are the animals that rule over all the others.	George Orwell, who was born in Bengal, wrote *Animal Farm* and *1984*. The Seven Commandments, which the pigs write on a barn wall, become law on the farm.
▶ **Defining relative clauses** give necessary information. Without them the meaning of the main clause would be unclear. ▶ ***Who*** and ***that*** are the **relative pronouns** used for people. ▶ ***Which*** and ***that*** are the **relative pronouns** used for things.	▶ **Non-defining relative clauses** add extra information. This can make the sentence more interesting. But the main clause is complete and understandable without the non-defining relative clause. ▶ ***Who*** is used for people. (The object form ***whom*** is used in formal style in BE. It is commonly used in AE.) ▶ ***Which*** is used for things.
The work *(which/that)* the animals have to do on the farm becomes harder and harder.	The tools on the farm were designed for men, which made work very difficult for the animals.
▶ The relative pronoun can be left out if it is the object of the relative clause (which then becomes a **contact clause**).	▶ A relative clause with ***which*** can also be used to **comment** on the main clause.
Different from German: ▶ There is **no comma** between main clause and defining relative clause.	Not different from German: ▶ There are **commas** – and a pause in speaking – between main clause and relative clause.
The beds (which/that) the pigs sleep in don't have any sheets.	Pilkington and Frederick, with whom Napoleon has started trading, both want to buy a pile of timber.
▶ In defining relative clauses, the **preposition** usually comes ***after*** the verb (+ object). The relative pronoun is often left out (which turns the relative clause into a contact clause).	▶ In non-defining relative clauses, the **preposition** usually comes ***before*** the relative pronoun (formal style).

You can also introduce relative clauses with ***whose*** + **noun**. ***Whose*** expresses what belongs to somebody:
*George Orwell, **whose style** is very clear and easy to understand, is very popular with young readers.*

▶ *Stop and think! Why can't you leave out the relative pronoun in:* Is this the bank **that** was robbed last year?

!
Do not use ***that*** in non-defining relative clauses:
The Seven Commandments, ~~that~~ ***which*** the pigs write on a barn wall, become law on the farm.

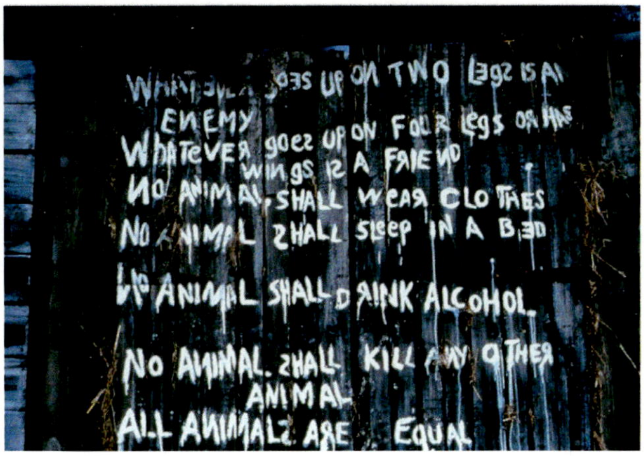

1 *Definitions: Use contact clauses with prepositions to define these words.*

Example: a washing machine → A washing machine is a machine **you (can) wash your clothes in**.

1. a cricket ball
2. a coffee cup
3. a dictionary
4. an ambulance
5. a garage
6. a tennis net
7. a primary school
8. a snack bar
9. a tent
10. a youth hostel

b) Conditional sentences

Conditional sentences consist of an ***if* clause** and a **main clause**. The *if* clause expresses a **condition** and the main clause describes the **consequence**.
Although many combinations of tenses are possible in conditional sentences, it may help you if you concentrate on these three basic types:

Type 1 realistic condition (The condition may be fulfilled in the future.)	*if* clause: **simple present** If you **park** your car in their drive,	main clause: ***will* future** our neighbours **will complain**.
Type 2 theoretical condition (The condition is unlikely to be fulfilled in the future, or is purely theoretical.)	*if* clause: **simple past** If I **had** lots of money,	main clause: **conditional** I**'d go** on a trip round the world.
Type 3 condition no longer possible (The condition can no longer be fulfilled because it refers to a situation in the past which is over now.)	*if* clause: **past perfect** If you **hadn't bought** that car last year,	main clause: **conditional perfect** you **would have been** able to afford the trip.

▶ *Stop and think! What is the difference between:*
I'll show you the photos **if** I see you on the weekend. *and* I'll show you the photos **when** I see you on the weekend?

Other frequently used combinations of tenses in conditional sentences	
simple present If it rains hard,	**simple present** you get wet without an umbrella.
If you really want to go on the world trip,	**modal auxiliary** you must try to save some money. **imperative** start to give up some of your expensive habits.
past perfect If you had accepted the job my parents offered you,	**conditional** you'd be earning a lot of money now.

!
Don't use the ***will* future**, the **conditional** or the **conditional perfect** in *if* clauses.
Remember to put in a **comma** if the *if* clause is the first part of the sentence.
If the *if* clause is the second part of the sentence, you don't need a comma:
You get wet without an umbrella if it rains hard.

"See? If Mommy had been wearing her seat belt, that wouldn't have happened."

1 *Error spotting – The* ifs *of holiday making:*
Seven of these ten conditional sentences are wrong. Spot the mistakes and correct the sentences.

1. We'd have missed the train if we didn't get up so early.
2. If I were you, I won't stay in the sun so long.
3. Anne might have invited us to her party if you'd been nicer to her.
4. If I didn't go to bed so late last night, I'd go to the beach with you now.
5. I'll go to the disco with you if I didn't have a temperature.
6. Don't buy that T-shirt if you think it's too expensive.
7. If only I hadn't played beach volleyball, I wouldn't hurt my foot.
8. I'd go in and swim with you if the water wasn't quite so cold.
9. It is much nicer on the beach if people turned their radios down.
10. If there wasn't that awful traffic jam on the motorway, we'd have caught our plane home.

2 *Situations:*
Use conditional sentences to comment on these situations. You can start either with a main clause or an if*-clause.*

Example: Wayne did badly in the exam. He didn't revise beforehand.
→ Wayne wouldn't have done badly in the exam if he had revised beforehand.
or: If Wayne had revised beforehand, he wouldn't have done badly/would have done better in the exam.

1. Jane didn't get the job. She doesn't speak French.
2. Sarah is really selfish all the time. So people don't like her much.
3. I'm not very hungry. I won't have a big meal tonight.
4. Tracy forgot to call Pete. So he didn't come to the meeting.
5. We haven't got his e-mail address. We can't contact him.
6. It was raining all day. We couldn't have the barbie on the beach.
7. Sorry, the bus was late. Otherwise I'd have been on time.
8. It's so hot today. I won't play tennis.

c) Sentences with adverbial clauses

There are **adverbial clauses** of ***time***, ***reason***, ***condition*** (*if* clauses) etc. These adverbial clauses add extra information to what is said in the main clause.
There are a number of typical **conjunctions** that can be used with the different adverbial clauses.

Before the American Revolution broke out, there were few links between the Thirteen Colonies.	▶ Adverbial clauses of *time* **conjunctions**: *when, as, after, while, as soon as, before, until/till, since*
Neighbouring colonies were often hostile to each other *because* they quarrelled over territory and trade.	▶ Adverbial clauses of *reason* **conjunctions**: *as/since, because*
Although the population of the Thirteen Colonies was only 2.5 million in 1775, the population was increasing fast. Britain wanted the colonies to pay higher taxes, *whereas* the Thirteen Colonies wanted representation in Parliament.	▶ Adverbial clauses of *concession or contrast* **conjunctions:** *although/though/even though, while/whereas*
The American rebels might have lost the War of Independence *if* the French had not helped them.	▶ Adverbial clauses of *condition* **conjunctions:** *if, even if, unless*
At the end of the war the Americans drafted a democratic constitution *so that* their newly won liberties would be protected.	▶ Adverbial clauses of *purpose and result* **conjunctions:** *so that, so/such … that*

▶ *Stop and think! Can you explain the different way* ***since*** *is used in these sentences?*
I haven't seen her **since** we met at Mike's party last month.
Since I haven't got her phone number, I find it difficult to contact her.
(Translate the sentences into German.)

1 *Cotton and slavery:*
Combine the adverbial clauses and the main clauses to form sensible sentences.

1. **Whereas** in the northern United States most people were opposed to slavery, G
2. Southern planters had concentrated more and more on cotton, ▢
3. The problem was that the fibers of cotton stuck **so** firmly to the seed ▢
4. But **after** Eli Whitney had invented a cotton gin (engine) in 1793, ▢
5. **While** a worker had only been able to clean one pound of cotton a day by hand, ▢
6. Thanks to this new machine cotton became the dominant crop – King Cotton – ▢
7. **Since** planters could make large profits ▢
8. In 1841 Ralph Waldo Emerson wrote: "**If** you put a chain around the neck of a slave, ▢

A the other end fastens itself around your own."

B **that** a worker could clean only one pound of cotton a day.

C they bought more land and more slaves.

D Eli's machine was capable of cleaning 50 pounds a day.

E **so that** more and more slaves were needed to plant and weed on the large plantations.

F production methods changed radically.

G people in the South believed that their economy depended upon slavery.

H **so** the South soon became a one-crop economy.

d) Linking sentence parts with gerunds and participles

You can use **gerunds** and **participles** to connect sentence parts.

Gerund constructions

Gerunds instead of subordinate clauses:	
Before deciding to move to America, many emigrants had suffered hardship and persecution in their home countries. On arriving in the promised land, they immediately looked for jobs.	▶ You can use a **gerund** after *before, on, for, after* and *in spite of*. ▶ These gerund constructions are used instead of subordinate clauses: *Before deciding … = Before they decided …* *On arriving… = When they arrived …*

Gerunds after certain phrases:	
Some of the newcomers hoped to get rich by finding gold. Others thought it was no use digging for gold where there was none.	▶ You can also use a **gerund** after *instead of, by, without, apart from, as well as, what about?, it's worth* and *it's no use*.

-ing form with a subject of its own:	
The white settler didn't like his little son playing with Indian children. He objected to them coming to their house.	▶ It is possible to put a noun *(his little son)* or a pronoun *(them)* between the verb and the *-ing* form. This gives the *-ing* form a 'subject of its own'.

Participle constructions

Participle constructions instead of adverbial clauses:	
Hoping to find a piece of land of their own, lots of late arrivals had to move further and further west. *(As/Since* they hoped …) Warned about hostile Indians, the settlers tried to reach the nearest fort. *(After/As/Because* they had been warned …)	▶ These **participle constructions** can be used instead of adverbial clauses.
The settlers were able to find some rest and were able to repair their wagons while staying at those forts.	▶ They can be introduced by a conjunction (*after, as, since, while, when, though* etc.)
Having lost some of their horses in the desert, the settlers were in a terrible situation.	▶ You can also use the **perfect form** of the participle *(having lost)*.

Participle constructions instead of relative clauses:	
Among the people **moving** west there were adventurers **looking** for gold, ranchers and railroad workers. (*moving* = who were moving) The circle **formed** of twenty or more wagons offered the settlers some protection at night. (*formed* = which was/had been formed)	▶ **Participle constructions** can be used to shorten relative clauses.

Participle constructions for actions/events happening at the same time:	
Sometimes the Indians attacked and rode round the circle of wagons, **waving** their tomahawks and **uttering** shrill cries. *(... wobei sie ihre Tomahawks schwangen und schrille Schreie ausstießen ...)*	▶ You can also use **participle constructions** to describe actions/events happening at the same time as actions/events described in the main clause. The participle construction expresses 'accompanying circumstances'.

Participle with a subject of its own:	
The towns on the East Coast **becoming** more and more crowded, people began to look for land further west. **With** so many *people* **moving** into Indian territory, life for the Native Americans changed dramatically.	▶ These **participle constructions** have their own subject *(The towns on the East Coast)*, which is different from the subject of the main clause *(people)*. They sound very formal. ▶ When these participle constructions are introduced by ***with***, they sound less formal and can also be used in colloquial English.

1 *Gerunds and participles:*

a) *Connect the following sentences (or sentence parts), using participle/gerund constructions introduced by the conjunctions in brackets.*

Example: People received letters from relatives or friends in the New World. And then they often decided to follow them. **(after)**
→ **After receiving** letters from relatives and friends in the New World, people often decided to follow them.

1. Many immigrants worked hard. But they still didn't get rich quickly. **(in spite of)**
2. Some rich people paid for the ocean passage of poor labourers. Then they forced them to work for them for a number of years. **(for)**
3. Before they left their homes, emigrants sold everything they possessed. **(before)**
4. Some didn't have any jobs in their home countries. And they were unfree as well. **(apart from)**
5. A few emigrants left their home country quickly. They didn't tell anyone where they were going. **(without)**

b) *Use participle constructions to connect these sentences.*

Example: The settlers knew that the journey west would be very long. So they bought lots of provisions.
→ **Knowing** that the journey west would be very long, the settlers bought lots of provisions.

1. When they moved past the Indian village, they noticed that the place was deserted.
2. In the evening everybody was busy. They collected firewood, made fires and cooked meals.
3. The trapper had never been in such a dangerous situation before. So he didn't know how to react.
4. The wagon train was surrounded by hundreds of Indians. It was unable to move on.
5. The settlers looked at their map and decided to ride back in the direction they had come.

G9 Using the passive

There is a difference in viewpoint between active and passive sentences. **Active** sentences stress who or what does something. In **passive** sentences the focus is on the activity itself. The emphasis is on what is done, while the 'doer' is either obvious, unimportant or unknown.

Active	Passive
Thousands of Chinese and Irish immigrants built the transcontinental railroad, earning one dollar a day.	The transcontinental railroad was built between 1863 and 1869.

▶ *Stop and think! Why can't you turn this sentence into the passive voice?*
The train arrived at the station five minutes late.

The same rules about which tense to use apply in both the **passive** and the **active voice**. In the **simple form** all the tenses in the **active** voice can also be formed in the passive. But there are only two tenses that can be used in the **progressive form: present progressive** and **past progressive**.

The construction of the transcontinental railroad is looked upon as a fantastic achievement.	▶ The **simple present passive** is used when something is often done, regularly done or never done. It is also used to state facts.
At the moment the tracks between Omaha and Fremont are being repaired.	▶ You use the **present progressive passive** to describe what is being done at the moment and is still going on.
A new book has been written about the men who built the railroad.	▶ The **present perfect passive** is used to stress the effect of a past action on the present.
The railroad was built by two companies: the Union Pacific Railroad from the West and the Central Pacific Railroad from the East.	▶ The **simple past passive** is used to stress that an event came to an end in the past.
While the tracks were being laid, the workers were sometimes attacked by hostile Indians.	▶ The **past progressive passive** describes what was in progress at a certain time in the past.
Before the actual work began, the railroad companies had been promised vast stretches of land along the lines.	▶ The **past perfect passive** expresses that something happened before another activity or event in the past.

Next year a new railroad connection **will be opened** between Chicago and Buffalo.	▶ The **future passive** is used to predict events in the future.
The land the railroad companies were given **could be turned** into gold by selling it to settlers and developers.	▶ The **passive infinitive** is used after modal auxiliaries and in all other cases where an infinitive is needed.
The railroad companies were also **offered** land to build towns on.	▶ The **personal passive** can be used with verbs like *give, offer, promise* etc. In most cases a person or a group of persons *(The railroad companies)* is used as the **subject** of the passive sentence. That is why this type is called the **personal passive**.
The transcontinental railroad **was built by Chinese and Irish immigrants**.	▶ When it is important to mention the person or thing that causes an action, a **by-agent** is used.

▶ *Stop and think! How would you translate* Railroads are said to be the safest means of transport*?*

1 *Forming passive sentences:*
Complete the sentences with the verbs given in the box. Use a suitable passive tense.

break into • build • empty • feed • follow around • have to cancel • repair • show • steal • take

1. Why can't you write her an e-mail? – Because my computer ___ at the moment.
2. What on earth can I do? My wallet with all my credit cards ___
3. Next month the new James Bond movie ___ in Britain.
4. The match last Saturday ___ because there was too much snow.
5. The castle ___ in the 14th century.
6. Movie stars ___ by paparazzi wherever they go.
7. When we got back from the cinema, we discovered that our house ___
8. ___ the dustbins ___ yet?
9. A car ran over a dog in the High Street. It ___ to the vet's immediately.
10. When we arrived at the zoo, the lions ___ just ___

2 *People killed in horrendous weather:*
The passive is often used in factual and historical texts, in newspaper articles and reports. *Make this report sound more natural by putting the active constructions* **(marked)** *into the passive, deciding whether to use a by-agent or not.*

1 Violent storms *have battered* the country. In Gloucestershire **2 tons of mud *buried* a workman. 3 The police *declared* him dead** at the scene, but **4 they *couldn't recover* the body** because of the horrendous conditions. As the storms moved north yesterday **5 heavy rain *caused* floods** across much of the Midlands and northern England. **6 The worst floods since the 1960s *put* hundreds of homes at risk.** Councillor Steven Bridget said: "We had no choice. **7 We *had to evacuate* people** from their homes." **8 Rising river levels badly *hit* caravan sites** all over the country. **9 The emergency services *had to rescue* two women** after their car became trapped in two feet of water. In Rothbury, Northumberland, a motorist escaped from his car only seconds before **10 the swollen river *swept* it away. 11 The Environment Agency *issued* almost 100 flood warnings.** Phil Rothwell at the Environment Agency said: "The soil is so saturated with rain that **12 it *isn't absorbing* the water any longer.**" Forecasters warn of more bad weather to come. For today **13 they *forecast* heavy showers** for the east of the country. **14** And **they *expect* the rain to continue** for at least another day.

based on an article in the *Sunday Express*

"I didn't actually *build* it, but it was based on my idea."

Vocabulary

This **Vocabulary** lists and explains all the new words of this textbook in the sequence that they appear. The column on the left lists the English words and phrases as well as the pronunciation. The central column gives you the German translation. The column on the right contains example and explanation sentences as well as tips telling you to be careful about something.
The words in **bold type** belong to the ***core vocabulary*** of obligatory texts and exercises. You have to learn, understand and use these words actively. Words not in bold type are the new words in optional texts and exercises. Other words in texts and exercises that you might not know – the ***additional vocabulary*** – you will find listed in the alphabetical word list at the back of this book. You needn't learn these words. All the words marked with a • belong to the most commonly used words in the English language.

At the start of every Topic you will find an **info box** with interesting background information about the subject matter of the respective Topic.
Aside from useful study tips, the ***Vocabulary skills*** contain small exercises so that you can apply the tip right away.
The heading ***Useful phrases*** summarizes important language phrases. They help you to express yourself when you deal with certain subjects.
Linking old and new vocabulary summarizes old and new vocabulary of a specific topic. This way you can revise old vocabulary and expand your vocabulary effectively.

After the ***Vocabulary*** you will find the alphabetical ***Dictionary***, starting on page 222. You can look up the new words of this book there.

Abbreviations and symbols

pl	*plural*	*e.g.*	*for example* (= z. B.)	8	The words appear on this page.
sing	*singular*	*coll*	*colloquial* (= ugs.)	!	Careful!
sth	*something*	*ugs.*	umgangssprachlich	↔	is the opposite of
sb	*somebody*	jmdm.	jemandem	→	is related to
AE	*American English*	jmdn.	jemanden	=	equals
BE	*British English*	etw.	etwas		

English pronunciation

Consonants

[ŋ]	morni**ng**
[r]	**r**ed
[s]	thi**s**
[z]	i**s**
[ʒ]	televi**s**ion
[dʒ]	pa**ge**
[ʃ]	**sh**e
[tʃ]	**ch**air
[ð]	**th**e
[θ]	**th**anks
[v]	**v**ideo
[w]	**w**ow, **o**ne

Vowels

[ɑː]	f**a**ther
[ʌ]	b**u**t
[e]	p**e**n
[ə]	**a** sist**er**
[ɜː]	g**ir**l
[æ]	fl**a**t
[ɪ]	**i**t
[i]	happ**y**
[iː]	t**ea**cher, sh**e**
[ɒ]	g**o**t
[ɔː]	b**a**ll
[ʊ]	b**oo**k
[u]	Jan**u**ary
[uː]	t**oo**, tw**o**

Diphthongs

[aɪ]	**I**, m**y**
[aʊ]	n**ow**, h**ou**se
[eə]	th**ere**, p**air**
[eɪ]	n**a**me, th**ey**
[ɪə]	h**ere**, id**ea**
[ɔɪ]	b**oy**
[əʊ]	hell**o**
[ʊə]	s**ure**

Additional symbols

[ˈ]	Main stress on the following syllable
[ˌ]	Secondary stress on the following syllable
[‿]	Close connection between two words

All other phonetic signs are pronounced exactly as they are written e.g. b, j, l, etc.

Topic 1: Growing up

Growing up – and behaving responsibly

- When you're growing up, it's natural to look forward to enjoying more privileges. But although on the one hand you expect to have more rights, on the other hand becoming an adult also means that you are expected to behave responsibly.
- Young Europeans visiting the USA are often surprised how different some of the legal age limits are from what they would have expected. It seems amazing that in some states kids are allowed to drive a car at the age of 14 or 15, while young people are not considered mature enough to buy alcohol or drink it in public until they are 21. Actually, this rule against alcohol became law in the US in 1984 after a campaign by 'Mothers Against Drunk Driving'. Anyone who breaks this law may have to face the consequences, and parents are considered to be responsible for their children. In some states, for example Virginia, kids of 18 are not even allowed to drink a beer with friends at a party in their own home! If they do so and the police find out, the parents are officially to blame and might even have to go to jail. All this may sound surprising in a country that is so often described as »the land of the free«.
- Basically, you might argue that it is possible to behave stupidly whether you are old or young. Of course laws are made to protect people, not only against others but also against themselves, and most teenagers would probably agree that the more grown up they become, the more responsible they begin to feel.

Introduction

8 **age limit** [ˌeɪdʒ 'lɪmɪt]	Altersgrenze	The minimum *age limit* for smoking is 18 in Germany.
• **marriage** ['mærɪdʒ]	Ehe, Eheschließung	! Watch the pronunciation Jimmy became famous after his *marriage* to a top fashion model.
FACT FILE		
to **refer to** [rɪ'fɜː tuː]	sich beziehen auf	*to refer to* → reference The numbers in brackets *refer to* the notes at the end of the book.
• **court** [kɔːt]	Gericht; Hof	He appeared in *court* yesterday.
WORD BANK		
age of consent [ˌeɪdʒ‿əv kən'sent]	(Ehe-)Mündigkeitsalter	It's illegal for young people to have sex before they reach the *age of consent*.
consent [kən'sent]	Zustimmung, Einwilligung	
compulsory [kəm'pʌlsərɪ]	verpflichtend, obligatorisch, vorgeschrieben	Everybody in the factory must wear a helmet. It's *compulsory*.
privilege ['prɪvlɪdʒ]	Privileg, Recht, Vorrecht	! Watch the pronunciation A good education should be everyone's right and not just a *privilege* of the rich.
imprisonment [ɪm'prɪznmənt]	Gefangenschaft; Haft	He was sentenced to life *imprisonment* for murder.

USEFUL PHRASES

It is always helpful to know phrases you can use when you want to react to or comment on something.

- I was surprised to see that …
- I never knew that …
- It depends on …
- In my opinion …
- On the one hand …, but on the other hand …
- I think the reason for this is …
- I think/don't think it's appropriate …
- I think it should be up to … to decide …
- I respect your opinion, but …
- You make it sound like …
- Correct me if I'm wrong, but …
- … could be dangerous.
- … should be protected.

9 **figure** ['fɪɡə]	Ziffer, Zahl	*figure* = number
WORD BANK		
On the one hand …, but on the other hand … [ɒn ðə‿'wʌn ˌhænd … bʌt‿ɒn ði‿'ʌðə ˌhænd …]	Einerseits …, andererseits …	*On the one hand* he'd like to be a better player, *but on the other hand* he doesn't want to practise hard.

Text: Paranoid Park

10 **envelope** ['envələʊp]	Umschlag, Briefumschlag	Write your letter on a piece of paper, then put it in an *envelope*.
• **rough** [rʌf]	grob, rau, derb; ungefähr	! Watch the pronunciation There's a lot of violence round here because it's a *rough* area of town.
to **go off** [ɡəʊ‿'ɒf]	explodieren	At 7.15 a bomb *went off* and destroyed the building.
All right. [ɔ:l 'raɪt]	O.k./ Also gut./ In Ordnung./ Alles klar.	*All right.* = That's OK.
Take it easy, take it slow. [ˌteɪk‿ɪt‿'i:zi, ˌteɪk‿ɪt 'sləʊ]	Nur keine Hektik. Immer mit der Ruhe.	Just relax and tell me what happened. *Take it easy, take it slow.*
accomplishment [ə'kʌmplɪʃmənt]	Errungenschaft, Leistung	Winning the Skaters' Cup was my greatest *accomplishment*.
use [ju:s]	Verwendung, Gebrauch	Do trains still stop at this station? – No, it isn't in *use* any more.
to **crawl** [krɔ:l]	kriechen	Yvonne screamed when she saw the spider *crawling* up her leg.
layout ['leɪaʊt]	Layout, Anordnung, Anlage	From the top of the tower you can see the *layout* of the town.
11 • a **couple of** [ə 'kʌpl‿əv]	ein paar	*a couple of* = a few Did you invite lots of people? – No, just *a couple* of friends.
scar [skɑ:]	Narbe	Louise was in a bad car accident last year. That's why she has that *scar* on her face.
constant ['kɒnstənt]	ständig, konstant, stetig, gleichmäßig	Can't you two stop shouting? I'm tired of your *constant* arguments!
to **run into sb** [rʌn 'ɪntə]	jmdm. über den Weg laufen	I didn't plan to meet Marco. I simply *ran into him* in town.
a **while** [ə 'waɪl]	eine Weile	*a while* = a short time
sort [sɔ:t]	Art, Sorte	What *sort* of person is Alex? Is he shy, or lonely, or maybe stupid?
to **talk sb into sth** [tɔ:k]	jmdn. zu etw. überreden	She didn't want to steal from the store, but finally her friends *talked her into it*.
to **insist (on)** [ɪn'sɪst]	bestehen (auf), insistieren	I didn't want to give up my weekend job, but my parents *insisted*.
to **rob** [rɒb]	(aus)rauben, berauben	If somebody *robs* you, they steal money or other things from you.

•**single** [sɪŋgl]	einzig, einzeln, alleinstehend	*single* = only one A *single* street light was shining.
to **pick** [pɪk]	auswählen, aussuchen; pflücken	*to pick* = to choose Which cell phone do you want? You can *pick* the one you like best.
to **keep up (with)** [ki:p‿ˈʌp‿wɪð]	mithalten (mit), Schritt halten (mit)	Slow down! You're running too fast. I can't *keep up with* you.
ladder [ˈlædə]	Leiter	Firefighters use tall *ladders* to rescue people from buildings which are on fire.
grain [greɪn]	Getreide(korn)	Bread is made from different kinds of *grain*.

WORD BANK

Linking old and new vocabulary – Arguing and fighting

You already know a lot of words to do with arguing and fighting. Now that you have learnt some more, it is useful to revise some of those you have already learnt.

Words you already know

adrenaline
aggressive
angry
argument
to attack
battle
bellow
to bleed
blood
to break
(to) bully
dangerous
to defeat
to destroy
enemy
fear
to fight (over)
furious
to grab sb
to hate
hot-headed
to hurt
(to) kick
to kill
to be mad with sb
nasty
pain
reckless
to shoot
shot
(to) shout
to tear apart
violent
weapon

New words

to damage sth
to freak out
to go mad
injury
scar
to struggle
to wreck sth

12 to **secure** [sɪˈkjʊə]	sicher befestigen, absichern	When you go rock climbing, you must *secure* all the ropes.
to **hang out** [hæŋ‿ˈaʊt]	sich hinauslehnen	Please don't *hang out* of the window. It's dangerous.
to **linger** [ˈlɪŋgə]	bleiben, verweilen	It was time to go, but she *lingered* for one last moment before she left.
•**security** [sɪˈkjʊərətɪ]	Sicherheit, Schutz; Wachdienst	If customers start causing trouble, we always call *security*.
up ahead [ʌp əˈhead]	vor	Driving along the road, Rick saw a police car *up ahead*. (= He saw it in front of him.)
to **face sth** [feɪs]	gegenüberstehen; konfrontiert werden mit; *(hier:)* mit der Vorderseite zu etw. stehen	The hotel has a café which *faces* the street.
glove [glʌv]	Handschuh	You wear shoes on your feet and *gloves* on your hands.
to **spot** [spɒt]	entdecken, erkennen	We looked all over town for Jim, then we suddenly *spotted* him in a music store.
•**immediately** [ɪˈmi:dɪətlɪ]	sofort, gleich	*immediately* = at once Can you wait a moment, please? – No, I want to be served *immediately*!

fat [fæt]	fett	*fat* ↔ thin It's not fair. Mario eats lots of chocolate and ice-cream, but he's not at all *fat*. He's really thin!
• to **swear, swore, sworn** [sweə, swɔː, swɔːn]	schwören	You can believe me. I'm telling the truth, I *swear*!
to **connect** [kə'nekt]	verbinden, vermitteln, anschließen; *(hier:)* treffen	I'm hopeless at tennis. I watch the ball, but I don't often manage to *connect*.
bone [bəʊn]	Knochen, Fischgräte	He hurt his arm in an accident, but luckily no *bones* were broken.
• **nearly** ['nɪəlɪ]	fast, annähernd	*nearly* = almost
vulnerable ['vʌlnərəbl]	verletzlich, verwundbar; gefährdet, anfällig	Young people are particularly *vulnerable* to clever advertising.
to **avoid** [ə'vɔɪd]	ausweichen, (ver-)meiden, aus dem Weg gehen	Nick drove into the field to *avoid* the car which was coming towards him.
to **tumble** ['tʌmbl]	stürzen, (hin)fallen, taumeln	*to tumble* = to fall over The box fell off the truck and *tumbled* down the hill.
to **trip** [trɪp]	stolpern	There's a bag on the floor. Be careful you don't *trip* over it.
13 **barely** ['beəli]	kaum	*barely* = hardly After her accident Denise could not walk. In fact, she could *barely* stand.
meanwhile ['miːnˌwaɪl]	währenddessen, mittlerweile, in der Zwischenzeit	Dan spent the afternoon at the skatepark. *Meanwhile* his brother was looking for him all over town.
to **freeze, froze, frozen** [friːz, frəʊz, 'frəʊzn]	erstarren; gefrieren	*to freeze* = to stay completely still. When she heard the scream, she *froze* with shock.
to **stumble** ['stʌmbl]	taumeln, stolpern	People who find it difficult to walk (because they are ill or drunk) often *stumble* and then fall over.
to **struggle** ['strʌgl]	kämpfen, Mühe haben, ringen, sich anstrengen	*to struggle* = to fight, to try very hard I *struggled* to remember the guy's name, but then I gave up.
• **coat** [kəʊt]	Mantel	In the cold weather many people wear a warm *coat* over their other clothes.
to **drag** [dræg]	schleifen, ziehen, schleppen	If something is too heavy to carry, you have to *drag* it along the floor.
to **back away** [ˌbæk‿ə'weɪ]	zurückweichen	If you want to move away from something and watch it at the same time, you must *back away*.
to **resist** [rɪ'zɪst]	widerstehen; sich widersetzen	I shouldn't spend so much money but I can't *resist* the attraction of new clothes.
to **reach** [riːtʃ]	greifen, reichen	He *reached* around with his hand, trying to find his keys.
to **unhook** [ʌn'hʊk]	losmachen, abhängen, *(hier:)* sich befreien	The guard's coat was attached to the train, so he tried to *unhook* himself from it.
all the while [ˌɔːl ðə 'waɪl]	die ganze Zeit über	She walked along the street, *all the while* talking to somebody on her cell phone.
to **skip** [skɪp]	(über)springen, hüpfen	Sometimes people *skip* along instead of walking because they feel very happy.
awkward ['ɔːkwəd]	ungünstig, ungeschickt, unbeholfen; peinlich	Ed always calls me at the most *awkward* times – when I'm in class or when I'm playing with the band.
to **stuff** [stʌf]	stopfen	I was in a hurry to catch my plane, so I quickly *stuffed* some clothes into my bag.
container [kən'teɪnə]	Container, Behälter, Behältnis	Don't leave your garbage lying around here. Put it in the *container*. That's what it's for.

to **roll up** [rəʊl ˈʌp]	zusammenrollen, aufrollen, aufkrempeln	We were getting our living room ready for a party, so the carpet was *rolled up* on one side of the room.
weed [wiːd]	Unkraut	They don't look after their garden very well. There are *weeds* growing everywhere.
dread [dred]	Angst, Furcht	A sense of *dread* is a very strong feeling of fear.
to **flood** [flʌd]	(über)fluten, überschwemmen	When he was in safety at last, a feeling of happiness *flooded* into his heart.
chest [tʃest]	Brust(korb)	Is there anything wrong with your heart? Do you have pains in your *chest*?
14 • to **touch** [tʌtʃ]	anfassen, berühren	Don't *touch* that door! The paint is still wet.
in case [ɪn ˈkeɪs]	für den Fall, dass …	The police told me to stay in town *in case* they needed to talk to me again.
• to **accuse (sb of sth)** [əˈkjuːz]	(jmdn. einer Sache) beschuldigen; anklagen	He *accused* his friends of stealing his laptop, but in fact his sister had borrowed it.
self-defense *(AE)* [ˌselfdɪˈfens]	Selbstverteidigung	She did kill the man, but it was *self-defence*, because he attacked her first.
to **process** [ˈprəʊses]	verarbeiten, aufbereiten; verstehen	I just can't believe we've broken up. I guess I need more time to *process* the situation.
to **pour** [pɔː]	fließen, strömen	Tears were *pouring* down my face.
someplace [ˈsʌmpleɪs]	irgendwo(hin)	*someplace* = somewhere Let's go *someplace* and talk about it.
to **freak out** [ˌfriːk ˈaʊt]	ausflippen	Have you heard the news? I almost *freaked out* when Steve told me.
comprehension [ˌkɒmprɪˈhenʃn]	Verständnis, Verstehen	Some exercises test students' *comprehension* of a text.
to **weigh** [weɪ]	(gegeneinander) abwägen	What are the advantages and disadvantages of the different plans? *Weigh* the pros and cons before you decide.
• **regret** [rɪˈgret]	Bedauern, Reue	Our boss expressed his *regret* at the decision.
to **make one's point** [ˌmeɪk wʌnz ˈpɔɪnt]	seinen Standpunkt deutlich machen	OK, you've *made your point*. Now let's listen to how other people see it.
character archetype [ˌkærɪktə ˈɑːkɪtaɪp]	Archetyp/-us *(Urform einer Figur)*	The 'bad police officer' is a *character archetype* in many crime novels.

Vocabulary skills

Synonyms: Different words for the same ideas

- The more English you hear – and read, the more new words and phrases you will meet that have the same meaning as words and phrases you already know.
  Look at the words/phrases (all used in 'Paranoid Park') and think of other words and phrases that mean the same.

  1. The waves were so high that we had to **struggle** to swim back to the beach.
  2. I've got three DVDs we could watch. Just **pick** the one you'd most like to see.
  3. The police officer in the warehouse **spotted** the thieves **immediately**.
  4. My cold's **nearly** better. I expect it'll be gone in **a couple of** days.
  5. Bill was so drunk that he could **barely** walk.
  6. What **sort** of books do you like reading?

- As you work through this book, notice any new words that are actually synonyms of words you've already learnt, and try to remember them together.

WORD BANK

to **be to blame for** [bleɪm]	Schuld haben an, verantwortlich gemacht werden für	It was Jim who actually stole the money, but his friends *were* also *to blame*.
to **face the consequences** [feɪs ðə 'kɒnsɪkwensɪz]	die Konsequenzen tragen	If you do something wrong and you get caught, you must *face the consequences*.
to **deny** [dɪ'naɪ]	leugnen, abstreiten	If you *deny* something, you say you didn't do or say it. He *denied* breaking into the apartment.
to **trespass**	unbefugt betreten, eindringen, überschreiten	When she walked across the field, she did not realize that she *was trespassing* on private land.

USEFUL PHRASES

These phrases can help you to take part in a discussion about a text and to express your opinion.

- ... is more to blame than ...
- It is right/wrong to ...
- In my opinion it is (not) understandable that ...
- I think it is completely right/wrong to ...
- ... have feelings of freedom/helplessness/guilt/shock.
- ... is (not) acting in self-defence.
- ... (not to) take responsibility.
- ... have to face/should have faced the consequences.
- ... is in a dilemma.
- ... have issues with ...
- ... (not to) act his/her age ...
- You have to look at it from both perspectives.
- There are two sides to every story.
- ... can be seen as a symbol of ...

FACT FILE

to **commit a crime** [kə,mɪt‿ə 'kraɪm]	ein Verbrechen/eine Straftat begehen	*to commit a crime* = to do something illegal
assault [ə'sɔ:lt]	Übergriff, Angriff, Tätlichkeit	A guy stole your camera?– Yes, and it was *assault*, too, because he pulled a gun on me.
injury ['ɪndʒərɪ]	Verletzung	After the accident she was taken to the hospital with *injuries* to her head.
theft [θeft]	Diebstahl	*theft* → thief *Theft* is the crime of stealing something.
to **account for** [ə'kaʊnt fɔ:]	ausmachen, betragen	Clothes *account for* a lot of the money spent by students in our class.
responsible [rɪ'spɒnsəbl]	verantwortlich, verantwortungsvoll	The fire was *responsible* for the death of two people.

Young people and crime in Britain

- In a recent survey of 11-16-year-olds in England, Scotland and Wales, nearly 50% (of 14,000 pupils) admitted that they had committed a crime at least once. Nearly a quarter of the older boys said they had carried a knife during the past year, which they usually explained was for self-defence. However, some admitted they had actually attacked someone and tried to cause injury.
- The authors of the survey stressed that most young people could not be accused of breaking the law, and that they usually acted responsibly. They found that forms of crime such as less serious theft (especially stealing things like beauty products or DVDs from shops) were generally committed by girls and boys around the age of 14-15. About 30% of this age group admitted committing some form of crime in the past 12 months.
- Serious crimes such as burglary were less common and usually admitted by older boys. One in ten boys aged 15-16 said they had broken into a building to steal during the past year. In general, fewer girls than boys are responsible for serious crimes.
- Who is really to blame if things go badly wrong? Most of those who were interviewed agreed there were clear rules at home and that their parents had told them it was wrong to steal or to use illegal drugs. But the survey discovered that the general atmosphere in the family, at school and in the local community plays a very important role in a child's development. Children in unhappy homes are especially vulnerable.

WORD BANK

Words to do with crime and law

law	crime	consequences
to accuse sb of sth	assault	to accuse sb of sth
act	to attack sb	to be to blame for sth
age limit	to commit a crime	to face the consequences
to ban	injury	to be responsible for
compulsory	to murder sb	to ban
independence	to rob sb	
legal/illegal	theft	
to pass/break a law	illegal	
privileges	to break a law	
rights		
self-defence		

Text: Film page

15	**troubled** [ˈtrʌbld]	mit Problemen belastet, aufgewühlt	Leroy and Cathy don't get on well together. In fact, they have a very *troubled* relationship.
	neglected [nɪˈglektɪd]	vernachlässigt	Many children have to live on the streets. They are badly *neglected* by their families and by society.
	misunderstood [ˌmɪsʌndəˈstʊd]	missverstanden	People don't realize what a nice person she is. She's *misunderstood* by everyone.
	to **look up to sb** [lʊk‿ˈʌp]	zu jmdm. aufschauen, jmdn. bewundern	If you admire somebody as your hero or your idol, you *look up to* that person.
	edge [edʒ]	Rand, Kante	She stood at the *edge* of the swimming pool, but she was afraid to jump into the water.
	• **entire** [ɪnˈtaɪə]	gesamt, ganz, komplett	the *entire* cast = the whole cast / everybody in the cast

Text: ⟨Friendship⟩

16	proverb [ˈprɒvɜːb]	Sprichwort	My dad's favourite *proverb* is 'Money doesn't grow on trees'.
	hedge [hedʒ]	Hecke	A *hedge* is a line of small trees between two fields or gardens.
	in need [ɪn ˈniːd]	in Not	On 'Make a Difference Day' we collect money for people who are *in need*.
	• indeed [ɪnˈdiːd]	in der Tat, tatsächlich; allerdings	Is this the director's office? – It is *indeed*.
	while [waɪl]	obwohl	*While* I don't want to make you scared, I think I should warn you about some dangerous criminals in this area.
	to wreck [rek]	zerstören; abwracken	*to wreck sth* = to destroy sth He was jealous of her hobbies, and that's what *wrecked* their relationship.
	to require [rɪˈkwaɪə]	erfordern; benötigen	This language course *requires* you to do a number of tests.
	to determine [dɪˈtɜːmɪn]	bestimmen, ermitteln; entschließen	Research by scientists *has determined* that this drug can be very dangerous.
	• intention [ɪnˈtenʃn]	Absicht, Intention	The director of the company has come to our town with the *intention* of opening a new factory.

	to attempt [ə'tempt]	versuchen	*to attempt* = to try Don't *attempt* to explain the problem to me. I'm not interested.
	juicy ['dʒu:si]	saftig; *(hier:)* pikant, anstößig	Have you heard about Diane and Ray? Let me tell you all the *juicy* gossip!
	• trust [trʌst]	Vertrauen	My parents won't let me go on vacation with my friends. Why don't they have any *trust* in me?
	• no matter [nəʊ 'mætə]	egal, ganz gleich	I'm going to finish this work, *no matter* how long it takes.
	significant [sɪg'nɪfɪknt]	bedeutend, signifikant, wesentlich	*significant* = important The good weather has made a *significant* difference to Jake's mood.
	to be willing to do sth ['wɪlɪŋ]	gewillt/bereit sein, etw. zu tun	*I'm willing to* help with the cooking, but I'm not going to wash up after the meal.
	• declaration [ˌdeklə'reɪʃn]	Aussage, Feststellung, Erklärung	"I love you," he said, but she wasn't interested in his *declaration*.
	to sting, stung, stung [stɪŋ, stʌŋ, stʌŋ]	stechen, *(hier:)* verletzen	*to sting* = to hurt I was really *stung* by her unkind words.
	• to damage ['dæmɪdʒ]	schaden, beschädigen	Smoking can seriously *damage* your health.
	• honest ['ɒnɪst]	ehrlich	People who tell lies or cheat are not *honest*.
	• ability [ə'bɪləti]	Fähigkeit	*ability* → able Birds have the *ability* to fly. = They are able to fly.
	commitment [kə'mɪtmənt]	Engagement, Einsatz	All the players in our team showed great *commitment*.
	to bring out [ˌbrɪŋ‿'aʊt]	ans Licht bringen	The TV interview *brought out* the actor's interest in music.
	to rank [ræŋk]	einstufen, in eine Reihenfolge bringen	When you *rank* things, you put them in a certain order on the basis of importance, quality, etc.
	• to reveal [rɪ'vi:l]	zeigen, verraten, enthüllen	Details of the murder were *revealed* by the local paper.
17	umbrella [ʌm'brelə]	Regenschirm	Take an *umbrella* with you. It looks like rain.

Text: Slam

18	**doughnut** ['dəʊnʌt]	Donut	Would you like a *doughnut* with your tea?
	previous ['pri:vɪəs]	vorig, vorherig, vorausgegangen	It wasn't his first visit to New York. He had been there the *previous* year.
	to **put sth on** [pʊt 'ɒn]	etw. überziehen, etw. anziehen; *(hier:)* ein Kondom überziehen	*Put* your pullover *on* if you're cold.
	• **even though** [ˌi:vn 'ðəʊ]	auch wenn, obwohl	*even though* = although I've never been to Greenwich, *even though* I've been living in London for five years.
	to **scribble** ['skrɪbl]	kritzeln, schmieren	My little sister says she can write, but in fact she just *scribbles*.
	to **tip sth upside down** [ˌʌpsaɪd 'daʊn]	etw. umkippen	He *tipped* the box *upside down*, and all the sweets fell onto the floor.
	to **go mad** [mæd]	verrückt werden, überschnappen	I think I'll *go mad* if Lynn tells me the same old story about her boyfriend again.
	sweetheart ['swi:thɑ:t]	Schatz, Liebling	'Don't worry, *sweetheart*,' he said to his daughter.
	deal [di:l]	Handel, Abmachung, Übereinkunft	I'll do a *deal* with you. – You stop using that awful perfume, and I'll never talk about football again.
	• **no doubt** [nəʊ 'daʊt]	zweifellos, wohl	! Watch the pronunciation We're planning a beach party for tomorrow, so it'll rain all day, *no doubt*.

19 **Say ...** [seɪ]	Angenommen ...	*Say* you had the chance to travel to the moon. – Would you go?
• **straight away** [ˌstreɪt‿əˈweɪ]	sofort, gleich	*straight away* = at once
• to **last** [lɑːst]	(an)dauern, anhalten	His happiness *lasted* just five minutes. Then the bad news came.
• **complicated** [ˈkɒmplɪkeɪtɪd]	kompliziert	These machines use a very *complicated* system, but I'll try to explain it as simply as possible.
cloth [klɒθ]	Lappen, Tuch; Gewebe, Stoff	You can brush your shoes or clean them with a *cloth*.
to **wipe up** [waɪp‿ˈʌp]	aufwischen	If there's water on the floor, somebody must *wipe* it *up*.
• **juice** [dʒuːs]	Saft	Would you like apple *juice* or water to drink?
to **spill** [spɪl]	verschütten, auslaufen	He tripped on the carpet and *spilled* his coffee all over his jeans.
• **except** [ɪkˈsept]	außer	*except* = apart from Dean likes all vegetables *except* spinach.
maturity [məˈtʃɔːrətɪ]	Erwachsensein, Reife, Mündigkeit	*maturity* → mature Most animals reach *maturity* much sooner than people do.

Vocabulary skills

Idioms with common verbs

■ Common verbs (go, come, give, get, look, put, run, etc.) are often used together with prepositions and/or other words to make idioms, each with its own special meaning.
Make your own sentences to show the meaning of these (they are all from Topic 1, up to the end of page 19).

to run into sb • to go off • to keep up (with sb) • to look up to sb • to put sth off • to put sth on • to bring sth out

■ Now use a dictionary to find out the meaning of these common idioms. (First guess – then check!)

1. I'm afraid we've **run out of** milk!
2. I used to quite like Mike, but I've **gone off** him recently.
3. Please **keep off** the grass.
4. There aren't enough chairs to **go round**.
5. Sam was trying to **get off** with your sister at the party.
6. We should be near the airport soon, so **look out for** signs!
7. The way Tom behaves is terrible! I don't know why you **put up with** it.
8. Can I talk to the manager, please? – Just a moment. I'll **put** you **through**.
9. I'd like the party to be a surprise for Julie. So please don't **give** it **away**.
10. Jack and Daisy **came round** last night.

• **humour** [ˈhjuːmə]	Humor; Komik; Stimmung	She can see something funny in any situation, but not everyone can share her *humour*.
• **suspense** [səˈspens]	Spannung	Don't keep me waiting, tell me! I can't stand the *suspense*!

WORD BANK

to **dread sth** [dred]	vor etw. große Angst haben, etw. fürchten	*to dread sth* = to be very afraid of sth, bad news, for example
to **face the truth** [ˌfeɪs ðə ˈtruːθ]	sich der Wahrheit stellen	You can't run away from the facts. You must *face the truth*.

	•to **put sth off** [pʊt‿'ɒf]	etw. aufschieben, etw. verschieben	If you don't want to do something today, maybe you can *put it off* until tomorrow.
	mature [mə'tjʊə]	erwachsen, reif, mündig	Matt is only 14, but he behaves in a very *mature* way.
	•**immature** [ˌɪmə'tjʊə]	unreif, kindisch	Tina is 28, but she behaves in a very *immature* way. She behaves in a way that is not typical of people her age.
	promiscuous behaviour [prəˌmɪskjuəs bɪ'heɪvjə]	häufiger Partnerwechsel	Adults are sometimes shocked by the *promiscuous behaviour* of some teenagers.

Text: ⟨Infinity⟩

20	infinity [ɪn'fɪnɪti]	Unendlichkeit	There's an *infinity* of stars.
	genius ['dʒi:nɪəs]	Genie	*a genius* = a very clever person That's a brilliant idea. You're a *genius*!
	•circle ['sɜ:kl]	Kreis, Ring	They sat in a *circle* round the table.
	grocery store ['grəʊsri stɔ:]	Lebensmittelgeschäft	A *grocery store* is a store where you can buy food.
	•arrow ['ærəʊ]	Pfeil	Follow the signs with the blue *arrows*.
	•exit ['eksɪt]	Ausgang, Ausfahrt	If you want to drive to the beach, take the next *exit*.
	•apparently [ə'pærəntlɪ]	anscheinend	I haven't met Jake, but *apparently* he's really cool.
	•in fact [ɪn 'fækt]	tatsächlich, eigentlich	The movie wasn't too bad, *in fact* it was quite exciting.
	to get stuck [ˌget 'stʌk]	stecken bleiben	Sorry we're late, but we *got stuck* in the crowd after the match.
	episode ['epɪsəʊd]	Episode; Folge	**!** Watch the stress That vacation in Florida is an *episode* in my life which I'd rather forget.
	•somewhat ['sʌmwɒt]	ein bisschen, einigermaßen	It wasn't a very tasty meal, but it was *somewhat* better than we had expected.
21	essentially [ɪ'sentʃli]	im Großen und Ganzen, im Wesentlichen	This book mentions some details about Leo's childhood, but *essentially* it's about his career as an actor.
	•shortcut ['ʃɔ:tkʌt]	Abkürzung	A *shortcut* is a shorter way of getting to a place.
	to reach over [ri:tʃ‿'əʊvə]	hinübergreifen	She didn't have anything to write with, so she *reached over* and took a pen from the next desk.
	to squeeze [skwi:z]	drücken, pressen; quetschen	He took her hand and *squeezed* it.
	shore [ʃɔ:]	Ufer, Küste	The *shore* is the land just next to a lake or the sea.
	parking lot ['pɑ:kɪŋ ˌlɒt]	Parkplatz	*a parking lot* = a place where you can park cars
	to pull up [pʊl‿'ʌp]	(heranfahren und) anhalten	Everybody in the car was getting hungry, so he *pulled up* at a snack bar.
	to reach up [ri:tʃ‿'ʌp]	die Hand/den Arm ausstrecken	She *reached up* to turn the light off.
	to undo, undid, undone [ʌn'du:, ʌn'dɪd, ʌn'dʌn]	aufmachen, öffnen; *(hier:)* aufknöpfen	I can't take my shirt off without *undoing* it first.
	insistent [ɪn'sɪstənt]	nachdrücklich, hartnäckig	Jenny said she wanted to be alone. She was very *insistent* about that.
	to get close [get 'kləʊs]	sich nahe kommen	They *got very close*. = They came very near to each other.
	to glare at sb ['gleər‿ət]	jmdn. (zornig) anstarren	*to glare at sb* = to stare at sb (angrily)
	•as if [əz‿'ɪf]	als ob	His face became white, *as if* he had seen a ghost or something.
22	to be close to doing sth ['kləʊs tə]	nahe daran sein, etw. zu tun	Anne *is close to giving up* her weekend job, but she hasn't decided definitely yet.
	•to give in to sth/sb [gɪv‿'ɪn]	etw./jmdm. nachgeben	Jack often feels he'd like to have an easier life, but he knows he shouldn't *give in to* this feeling.

	pleading ['pli:dɪŋ]	Flehen; Plädoyer	He kept begging her not to go, but in spite of his *pleadings* she went.
	to crop up [krɒp 'ʌp]	auftauchen, auftreten, sich zeigen	The plans for the project were going well, but then a new problem *cropped up*.
	frog [frɒg]	Frosch	The *frogs* in the lake made such a noise that he couldn't sleep.
	• to bend down, bent down, bent down [ˌbend‿'daʊn, ˌbent‿'daʊn, ˌbent‿'daʊn]	sich bücken; abknicken	If you drop something on the floor, you must *bend down* and pick it up.
	to narrow ['nærəʊ]	(sich) verengen	*to narrow* = to become narrow
	to rattle ['rætl]	klappern, klirren, rasseln	The old car *rattled* along the road.
	eventually [ɪ'ventʃʊəlɪ]	schließlich, endlich, irgendwann	Just keep trying. You'll find a job *eventually*.
	It doesn't matter. [ɪt ˌdʌzənt 'mætə]	Es ist egal.	*It didn't matter* what she said, he wouldn't change his mind.
	• even so … [ˌi:vn 'səʊ]	trotzdem, selbst dann	I know you're very busy, but *even so*, you should have remembered Tina's birthday.
23	to glance [glɑ:ns]	blicken, einen Blick werfen	*to glance* = to look quickly *He glanced* over his shoulder before he went into the building.
	to seal [si:l]	fest verschließen, versiegeln	This box is tightly *sealed* so that no water or air can get into it.
	to sympathize with ['sɪmpəθaɪz wɪð]	mitfühlen, jmdn. verstehen; sympathisieren	If you *sympathize with* people, you understand how they feel and maybe feel sorry for them.
	• similarity [ˌsɪmɪ'lærəti]	Ähnlichkeit, Gemeinsamkeit	*similarity* ↔ difference There are many *similarities* between English and French.
	WORD BANK		
	progression [prə'greʃn]	Entwicklung, Ablauf, Folge	*progression* = development He has made the *progression* from store assistant to company director.

Language: Form and function

24	to **bother** ['bɒðə]	stören, belästigen; *(hier:)* nerven	Oh shut up, Carrie! I told you not to *bother* me with your questions.
	• **anniversary** [ˌænɪ'vɜ:sərɪ]	Jahrestag, Jubiläum	I've been dating Ken for almost a year now. It's our *anniversary* next Sunday.
	to **break up** *(coll)* [breɪk 'ʌp]	Schluss machen	*to break up* = to split up Is Sue still dating Mario? – No, they *broke up* last week.
	to **crash a party** [ˌkræʃ‿ə 'pɑ:ti]	uneingeladen zu einer Party kommen	There were 50 people at my birthday, – 20 who had been invited and 30 who *crashed the party*.
25	• **basically** ['beɪsɪklɪ]	eigentlich, grundsätzlich, im Grunde genommen	She sometimes goes jogging, but *basically* she's lazy.
	frankly ['fræŋkli]	ehrlich gesagt, offen gestanden	I've just met our new coach, and – well, *frankly*, I don't think he's good enough for the job.
	honestly ['ɒnɪstli]	ehrlich gesagt	Who sent you that message? – I don't know, *honestly*.
	• **habit** ['hæbɪt]	Gewohnheit	He has got into the *habit* of drinking coffee after every meal.
	gasoline *(AE)* ['gæsli:n]	Benzin	You buy *gasoline* for your car at a gas station.
	nomination [ˌnɒmɪ'neɪʃn]	Nominierung, Ernennung	The movie awards are presented in February, but the *nominations* come out much earlier.

	• **speech** [spiːtʃ]	Rede, Sprache	At the conference the president gave an important *speech* to an audience of five hundred people.

Language: Intercultural page

26	to **give some thought to sth** [ˌɡɪv‿sʌm‿ˈθɔːt]	sich Gedanken machen über	I haven't decided about the project yet, but I*'ve given some thought to* it.
	to **illustrate** [ˈɪləstreɪt]	veranschaulichen, darstellen, illustrieren	Can you give me an example to *illustrate* what you mean?
	well-suited to [ˌwel‿ˈsuːtɪd]	geeignet für, passend für	Only very few people are *well-suited to* life in the desert.
	slip of paper [ˌslɪp‿əv ˈpeɪpə]	Zettel, Stück Papier	I wrote our names down on two *slips of paper.*

Language: Everyday English

27	• **response** [rɪˈspɒns]	Antwort, Erwiderung, Rückmeldung	*response* = reply, reaction

Conclusion

28	**attitude (to/towards)** [ˈætɪtjuːd]	Einstellung, Haltung	I don't understand why some adults have such a negative *attitude* to teenagers.
	to **confirm** [kənˈfɜːm]	bestätigen, bekräftigen	She has *confirmed* reports in the media about her role in the new movie.
	to **break down** [breɪk ˈdaʊn]	auflösen, zerstören, niederreißen, zusammenbrechen	If we want to have a better society, many negative stereotypes must be *broken down.*
	to **frown** [fraʊn]	die Stirn runzeln	I knew the phone call was bad news because Sally *frowned.*
	• **whereas** [weərˈæz]	wohingegen, während	She used to love stories about animals, *whereas* now she thinks they're boring.
	naive [naɪˈiːv]	naiv, blauäugig	Andy thinks he's going to win £1 million in a quiz show. – How *naive* can you be!
	daft *(coll)* [dɑːft]	dämlich, bescheuert	*daft* = stupid A car of your own for your birthday? Don't be *daft!*
	• **B&B (= bed and breakfast)** [biː‿ənd‿biː; ˌbed‿ənd‿ˈbrekfəst]	Frühstückspension	A *B&B* is a private house where you pay to stay the night and have breakfast.
29	to **set a good example to sb** [set‿ə‿ɡʊd‿ɪɡˈzɑːmpl]	jmdm. ein Vorbild sein	Mike is the oldest of the three brothers, so his parents expect him to *set a good example.*
	priority [praɪˈɒrəti]	Priorität, Vorrang	I'm afraid the new youth club isn't a *priority* for us at the moment.
	to **set priorities** [set praɪˈɒrətiz]	Schwerpunkte festlegen, Prioritäten setzen	You don't have enough time for three hobbies, an evening job and school. You must *set priorities.*
	valid [ˈvælɪd]	schlüssig, gültig, stichhaltig	I don't think your conclusion is *valid* because you don't know all the facts.

Topic 2: Multi-ethnic Britain

The Caribbean islands

- Many of the islands in the Caribbean are closely linked to Britain. The Caribbean Sea was actually discovered by Christopher Columbus in 1492, and for a while it was controlled by the Spanish. Other European countries later founded colonies there. Jamaica, Barbados, Trinidad and St Lucia are just a few of the islands that were once colonies belonging to the British Empire. Jamaica, one of the largest and busiest of the Caribbean islands, became independent of Britain, together with Trinidad, in 1962. Soon after that many other Caribbean islands belonging to Britain declared their independence. But, like Jamaica and Trinidad, they are still members of the Commonwealth. Because of the long-standing link with Britain, English is used as an official language in this part of the world.
- The majority of the people there are descended from slaves who were taken there by ship from Africa. During the 18th century there was a large black slave population working on the sugar plantations in Jamaica. Today Jamaica is still famous for its sugar, but other products include rum, oranges, bananas and coffee.
- Of course, as Jamaica and the other Caribbean islands have a warm climate and wonderful beaches, the tourist industry has become more and more important in recent years. Each of the islands has its own special character. Barbados, for example, is known as 'Little England' because of the many English traditions that are still kept alive there. And Trinidad, with its oil, has a more industrial economy than most of the other islands.

Introduction

32 **ethnic** [ˈeθnɪk] — ethnisch, Vielvölker- — Britain has a multi-*ethnic* society.
percentage [pəˈsentɪdʒ] — prozentualer Anteil, Prozentsatz — What *percentage* of the population comes from other countries?

WORD BANK

• **majority (of)** [məˈdʒɒrɪti‿əv] — Mehrzahl, Mehrheit — *the majority of* the population = most of the people; *majority* ⟷ minority

mass [mæs] — Masse; Massen- — At first only a few people protested, but later there were *mass* protests.

USEFUL PHRASES

Statistics give you lots of important information. These phrases can help you to discuss them and to give your opinion.

- The table/pie chart/map shows (that) …
- The statistics/numbers show (that) …
- The majority/minority of …
- Less/More than half …
- … % of the population/the people/the countries …
- Compared to (the) other countries/numbers …
- I'm (not) surprised (to see/to learn) that …
- I can/can't understand why …
- I think the results of the survey …
- I think/am of the opinion that …
- As far as I understand/can see …
- I think the results of a survey in … would be the same/different …

33 **Pakistani** [ˌpɑːkɪˈstɑːnɪ] — Pakistaner/-in; pakistanisch — Some *Pakistanis* come to the UK as students.
Bangladeshi [ˌbæŋgləˈdeʃɪ] — Bangladescher/-in; bangladeschisch — Many *Bangladeshis* came to live in one small area of London.

Black Caribbean [blæk ˌkærɪ'bi:ən]	Afrokaribe/Afrokaribin; afrokaribisch	Large numbers of *Black Caribbeans* first came to the UK from America in the 1950s.
Black African [blæk 'æfrɪkən]	Schwarzafrikaner/-in; schwarzafrikanisch	*Black Africans* have their ethnic origins in countries like Ghana and Nigeria.
perception [pə'sepʃn]	Wahrnehmung, Empfindung, Auffassung	There is a campaign to change public *perception* of politicians.
data *(pl.)* [deɪtə]	Daten, Angaben	This *data* was collected from 20 countries.
neither ['naɪðə]	weder … noch; unentschlossen; kein	"Which do you like?" – "*Neither.* I think they're both ugly."

FACT FILE

• **citizen** ['sɪtɪzn]	(Staats-)Bürger/-in, Staatsangehörige/r	Asim's parents were born in Pakistan, but they are British *citizens*.
to **descend from** [dɪ'send frəm]	abstammen von, herstammen von	Malika says she's *descended from* an Indian princess.
plantation [plæn'teɪʃn]	Plantage; Kolonie	Tea, coffee and sugar are grown on large *plantations*.
slave trade ['sleɪv ˌtreɪd]	Sklavenhandel	*the slave trade* = buying and selling people as slaves
empire ['empaɪə]	(Kaiser-)Reich	The British *Empire* was once the largest in the world.
• **gang** [gæŋ]	Gruppe, Bande, Gang	They won't let Lee play with them because he isn't a member of their *gang*.

WORD BANK

Linking old and new vocabulary – Nationalities and similar words

You already know a lot of nationalities and similar words. Now that you have learnt some more, it is useful to revise some of those you have already learnt.

Words you already know		New words
African	Indian	Afro-Caribbean
American	Italian	Bangladeshi
Asian	Mexican	Black African
British	Native American	Black Caribbean
Canadian	Polish	Caribbean
Chinese	Romanian	Pakistani
English	Russian	
French	Scottish	
German	Spanish	
Greek	Turkish	
Hispanic	Welsh	

Text: Caribbean London

34 **Caribbean**	karibisch; Karibik; Karibe/Karibin	The *Caribbean* is a region consisting of the *Caribbean* Sea and its islands.
• to **contribute** [kən'trɪbju:t]	beitragen, mitwirken	Your hard work has *contributed* to the success of the project.
• **prosperity** [prɒs'perətɪ]	Wohlstand, Gedeihen	*prosperity* = wealth They lived in an age of *prosperity*. = People had enough wealth for a good life.
post-war ['pəʊstwɔ:]	Nachkriegs-	*post-war* society = society after 1945
passion ['pæʃn]	Leidenschaft, Passion	He sang the lyrics with great *passion*.
encounter [ɪn'kaʊntə]	Begegnung, Zusammentreffen	Jamal's first *encounter* with snow was in London in 1979.

•to **rent** [rent]	mieten	They don't own the house. They *rent* it.
task [tɑːsk]	Aufgabe, Auftrag	Jane was given the difficult *task* of organising the conference.
condition [kən'dɪʃn]	Kondition, Bedingung, Zustand	You'll never sell that car. It's in terrible *condition*.
rent [rent]	Miete	How much *rent* do you pay for this flat?
abuse [ə'bjuːs]	Missbrauch	*Abuse* means the misuse of alcohol or drugs, for example.
racial abuse [ˌreɪʃl‿ə'bjuːs]	Rassendiskriminierung	He experienced *racial abuse*. = Some people hit him and told him he looked like a monkey.
•**wage** [weɪdʒ]	Lohn	*wage* = the money people are paid every week or month for their work
no one else [ˌnəʊ wʌn 'els]	niemand sonst	Steve tidied up the room because *no one else* wanted to do it.
to **object to (doing) sth** [əb'dʒekt tə]	etw. ablehnen	! Watch the pronunciation object ['ɒbdʒɪkt] ↔ to object [əb'dʒekt] I *object to wearing* this silly uniform for work.
harsh [hɑːʃ]	rau, hart, streng, scharf	He was very hurt by her *harsh* words.
treatment ['triːtmənt]	Behandlung, Versorgung	*treatment* → to treat
to **urge sb to do sth** [ɜːdʒ]	jmdn. zu etwas antreiben	She *urged me to apply* for the job before it was too late.
•**failure** ['feɪljə]	Erfolglosigkeit, Fehlschlag, Scheitern, Versagen	failure ↔ success
recognition [ˌrekəg'nɪʃn]	(An-)Erkennung	*recognition* → to recognize He has achieved *recognition* in his team. = Everybody in his team says he is a great player.
mainstream ['meɪnstriːm]	Durchschnitts-, Massen-, Hauptrichtung	*Mainstream* TV channels make programmes they think the majority of people will enjoy.
launch [lɔːntʃ]	Einführung, Start, Abschuss	*launch* = start, introduction The firm gave a big party for the *launch* of their new product.
to **aim at** ['eɪm‿ət]	zielen auf, sich richten an	*to aim at* → aim Many adverts for drinks *are aimed at* teenagers.
origin ['ɒrɪdʒɪn]	Herkunft, Abstammung, Ursprung	Melltith is a marriage custom. This has its *origins* in Wales.
to **press for sth** ['pres fə]	auf etw. drängen	We must *press for* equal rights for everyone.
Afro-Caribbean [ˈæfrəʊ ˌkærɪ'biːən]	Afrokaribe/Afrokaribin; afrokaribisch	*Afro-Caribbean* food is becoming very popular in many parts of the country.
institution [ˌɪntstɪ'tjuːʃn]	Einrichtung, Organisation, Institution	Museums, universities, churches etc. are *institutions*.
35 •**though** [ðəʊ]	obwohl	*though* = although
to **run** [rʌn]	betreiben, führen	This hotel *is run* by a young woman from Scotland.
barber ['bɑːbə]	Friseurgeschäft/-salon für Herren	A *barber* is a hairdresser for men.
service ['sɜːvɪs]	Dienstleistung	
•**throughout** [θrʊ'aʊt]	überall in	The company has shops *throughout* the world.
a **host of** [həʊst]	ein Heer an, jede Menge	*a host* = a large number
presenter [prɪ'sentə]	Moderator/-in	The *presenter* often introduces the guests on a TV show.
to **divide (into)** [dɪ'vaɪd ˌɪntuː]	teilen, aufteilen, unterteilen	The high mountains *divide* the country *into* two parts.
complexity [kəm'pleksəti]	Komplexität, Vielschichtigkeit	
content ['kɒntent]	Inhalt	Tell me about the *content* of the text in just a few sentences.
past [pɑːst]	letzte/-r/-s, vergangen	He hasn't said a word for the *past* twenty minutes.
to **include** [ɪn'kluːd]	aufnehmen, einbinden, einbeziehen	Try to *include* some useful diagrams in your presentation.
section ['sekʃn]	Sektion, Abschnitt, Paragraf	The report has a *section* on minorities in Britain.

Vocabulary skills

Expressing ideas less formally

- In informative texts, you often find abstract nouns that can sound very formal. Although in German it is quite common to use nouns, in English it is often better to express your ideas with verbs – so that your own style (especially in spoken English) doesn't sound too formal.

  Example: harsh treatment of immigrants – A lot of immigrants were treated harshly.

- Now find ways to express these ideas less formally, using verbs instead of nouns. (It won't always be possible to find a verb from the same word family as the noun.)

  1. the prosperity of Britain today
  2. feeling of passion for the »Motherland«
  3. the experience of racial abuse
  4. the failure to achieve recognition in the press

WORD BANK

subordinate clause [sə'bɔːdnɪt ˌklɔːz]	Nebensatz	
to **be homesick** ['həʊmsɪk]	Heimweh haben	When I was in England, I *was homesick* for Germany.
• **prejudice** ['predʒʊˌdɪs]	Vorurteil, Voreingenommenheit	There is little *prejudice* against workers from other EU countries.

Text: ⟨Family differences⟩

36	satirical [sə'tɪrɪkl]	satirisch; Spott-	A *satirical* presentation is critical and funny at the same time.
	• narrator [ne'reɪtə]	Erzähler/-in	The *narrator* is the person who tells the story in a book or film.
	to beat, beat, beaten [biːt, biːt, 'biːtn]	(ver)prügeln, schlagen; besiegen	The man lying on the floor had been badly *beaten*.
	attitude ['ætɪtjuːd]	Einstellung, Haltung	I don't know why she has such a negative *attitude* to school.
	to be inspired by sth/sb [ɪn'spaɪəd baɪ]	*(hier:)* hervorgerufen/geweckt werden von etw./jmdm.	His decision to go swimming *was inspired by* the warm weather.
	• husband ['hʌzbənd]	Ehemann	John and Emma live together as *husband* and wife.
	except that [ɪk'sept ðət]	abgesehen davon, dass	Justin was a fantastic coach – *except that* he couldn't play football very well.
	to age [eɪdʒ]	altern, reifen	He seemed to *age* ten years while he was taking his exams.
	to demand [dɪ'mɑːnd]	verlangen, fordern	He took the DVD player back to the shop and *demanded* his money back.
	• belief [bɪ'liːf]	Glaube, Überzeugung	*belief* → to believe
	council ['kaʊnsl]	Gemeinde-/Stadtrat	The *council* should do something about all the rubbish in the streets.
	to take sb into care [keə]	sich um jmdn. kümmern, jmdn. in Pflege nehmen	The council or the state *takes* children *into care* when their parents are not able to look after them.
	• except for [ɪk'sept fɔː]	bis auf, mit Ausnahme von	I had nothing on *except for* my socks.

	to abuse [ə'bju:z]	missbrauchen, misshandeln, beschimpfen	*to abuse sb* = to treat sb badly
	onion ['ʌnjən]	Zwiebel	I like curry with lots of *onions*.
	chilli ['tʃɪlɪ]	Chili	Some cooks use lots of *chillis* in their curries.
	What's wrong? [wɒts 'rɒŋ]	Was ist los?, Was stimmt nicht?	Linda looked very sad. "*What's wrong?*" I asked her.
37	stairs *(pl.)* [steəz]	Treppe	*stairs* = steps inside a house
	to resemble [rɪ'zembl]	ähneln	Are Amy and Susan really sisters? They don't *resemble* each other.
	before [bɪ'fɔ:]	zuvor, vorher, schon einmal	She didn't recognize Mike, although they had met a few times *before*.
	as though [əz 'ðəʊ]	als ob	He treated me *as though* I was an idiot.
	to chew [tʃu:]	kauen	Jess always finishes her dinner first because she doesn't *chew* her food properly.
	•simply ['sɪmpli]	*(hier:)* einfach nur	At first I thought I had some terrible disease, but then I realized that I was *simply* tired.
	to glare at sb ['gleə]	jmdn. (zornig) anstarren	*to glare at sb* = to stare at sb angrily
	•to touch [tʌtʃ]	berühren, anfassen	She put out her hand and *touched* him on the shoulder.
	to lean (towards) [li:n]	sich (zu jmdm. hinüber)lehnen	I *leaned towards* her so that I could hear what she was saying.
	•bit (of) [bɪt]	Stückchen (von)	*a bit* = a very small piece
	to obey sb [əʊ'beɪ]	jmdm. gehorchen	If you *obey* somebody, you do what that person tells you to.
	•to select [sə'lekt]	aussuchen, auswählen	*to select* = to choose
	to punch [pʌntʃ]	mit der Faust schlagen, boxen	*to punch* = to hit
	unmoved [ʌn'mu:vd]	unbewegt, ungerührt	He was *unmoved*. = He did not change his position or his opinion.
	•circumstance ['sɜ:kəmstɑ:ns]	Umstand, Gegebenheit	He had to leave the country earlier than expected because *circumstances* had changed.
	•to force [fɔ:s]	zwingen	She didn't want to write the letter, but they *forced* her to do it.
	to tremble ['trembl]	beben, zittern	*to tremble* = to shake
38	to be about to do sth [bi‿ə'baʊt]	im Begriff sein, etw. zu tun	He *was about to* leave the room, but then she suddenly started to speak.
	to fetch [fetʃ]	(ab)holen	*to fetch sth* = to go and get sth He wanted some coffee, so I *fetched* a cup from the kitchen.
	cloth [klɒθ]	Tuch, Lappen; Stoff, Gewebe	There's some milk on the table. We need a *cloth* to clean it up.
	to scrub [skrʌb]	schrubben, reinigen	A little water on its own won't get this floor clean. You need to *scrub* it hard.
	•to come up with sth [kʌm‿'ʌp wɪð]	sich etwas einfallen lassen, sich etw. ausdenken	Finally she *came up with something*. = She suddenly had a great idea.
	behaviour [bɪ'heɪvjə]	Verhalten, Betragen	*behaviour* → to behave
	WORD BANK		
	to convey [kən'veɪ]	vermitteln, ausdrücken	*to convey* = to express The photo *conveys* an atmosphere of fear.
	•tension ['tenʃn]	Spannung	In a situation of *tension* people feel nervous and uncertain.
	oppressive [ə'presɪv]	unterdrückerisch, gewaltsam, repressiv	An *oppressive* person does not respect other people's rights.
	•to identify with [aɪ'dentɪfaɪ]	sich identifizieren mit	I don't know him personally, but I can *identify with* his feelings.
	arranged marriage [əˌreɪndʒd 'mærɪdʒ]	arrangierte Hochzeit	In an *arranged marriage* the parents choose a marriage partner for their daughter or son.

conflicting viewpoints *(pl.)* [kənˌflɪktɪŋ 'vju:pɔɪnts]	widersprüchliche Standpunkte	It is normal for children and their parents to have *conflicting viewpoints* on some things.
responsible [rɪs'pɒnsəbl]	verantwortlich, verantwortungsvoll	Many parents feel *responsible* for their child's future.
sense of guilt [ˌsens‿əv 'gɪlt]	Schuldgefühl	! Watch the pronunciation She had a *sense of guilt* after she had run away. = She felt that she had done something wrong.
previous ['pri:vɪəs]	vorig, vorherig, vorausgegangen	the *previous* evening = the evening before When Nick came to see me, he didn't mention his *previous* visit.

Arranged marriage – and forced marriage

- Even today, arranged marriages of British Asian young girls and women are nothing unusual. In this tradition, the girls' parents often try to find a suitable partner for their daughter through an advert, for example in an Indian newspaper, or through contacts with friends or other parents they know. They usually select a partner with the same kind of background, education and beliefs and, if possible, with attitudes and interests both partners share. Normally the young people meet and have the opportunity to spend some time together before they make the final decision themselves about whether they want to get married or not. Of course, like any other husband and wife, they then hope to live together happily.
- Unfortunately, however, it sometimes happens that young British Asians are forced into marriage. Often young women are tricked into going 'on holiday' to India or Pakistan, and only discover the true reason for the trip after they arrive. Then it is usually too late, and they are forced to obey their parents' wishes. Some girls feel they should be ashamed of themselves if they try to run away from a forced marriage, and they may also fear they will have no chance to escape. Sometimes parents even use physical violence to force their daughters into the marriages they have fixed up for them.
- Naturally, for young people who were born in Britain and are used to Western traditions, the idea of any kind of arranged marriage can be hard to accept. Different opinions on this subject can cause troubled relationships between the generations in British Asian families.

39 • look ['lʊk]	Ausdruck	You should have seen the *look* of surprise on her face!
• conscience ['kɒnʃəns]	Gewissen	Your *conscience* tells you whether what you are doing is right or wrong.
to be ashamed of [ə'ʃeɪmd‿əv]	sich schämen für/wegen	Jane apologized to Jim because she *was ashamed of* what she had said to him.
on the whole [ˌɒn ðə 'həʊl]	im Großen und Ganzen	There were some boring parts, but *on the whole* I enjoyed the book.
decent ['disnt]	anständig, ehrbar	No *decent* person would get involved in a criminal activity.
in fact [ɪn 'fækt]	tatsächlich; eigentlich	I thought the work would be difficult. But *in fact*, it's very easy.
to break [breɪk]	*(hier:)* verstoßen gegen	People who *break* the law are sometimes sent to prison.
countless ['kaʊntlɪs]	unzählige, viele	*Countless* means there are so many that you can't count them.
for instance [fər‿'ɪnstəns]	zum Beispiel	*for instance* = for example
to demand [dɪ'mɑ:nd]	wissen wollen, fragen	"Where's your mobile phone?" the boy *demanded*.
• pork [pɔ:k]	Schweinefleisch	The meat from pigs is called *pork*.
to deny [dɪ'naɪ]	abstreiten, leugnen	He *denied* visiting the house. = He said he hadn't been there.

slice [slaɪs]	Scheibe, Stück, Teil	He cut four *slices* of bread.
• fried [fraɪd]	gebraten	One of the restaurant's special dishes is fish *fried* in butter.
sausage ['sɒsɪdʒ]	(Brat)wurst	! Watch the pronunciation How do you like the idea of *sausages* and eggs for breakfast?
to fit in [ˌfɪt‿'ɪn]	sich einfügen	The new neighbours never come to our parties. They don't even try to *fit in* here.
civilization [ˌsɪvlaɪ'zeɪʃn]	Kultur, Zivilisation	Some people think Indian restaurants mean the end of western *civilization* in the UK.
according to [ə'kɔ:dɪŋ tu:]	laut, gemäß	*according to sb* = in sb's opinion
to address sb [ə'dres]	sich an jmdn. wenden, jmdn. ansprechen	Ali *addressed* his father. = He spoke to his father quite formally.
to rule [ru:l]	(be)herrschen; regieren	A dictator wants to *rule* his country alone without sharing his power.
reward [rɪ'wɔ:d]	Belohnung	Anyone who manages to find the money will get a *reward* of £500.

Vocabulary skills

Learning words in groups

- You may find it helpful to learn words together with others that belong to the same context. Sort the words below into groups, then write four lists, each with its own heading, e.g. violence.

  to chew • to beat • belief • miserable • to force • to abuse • onions • to punch • attitude • pork • perplexed • inspired • sausages

- Now add more words (that you already know!) to each list. How many can you collect for each? Which of your lists is longest? Compare the results of your work with a partner's.

40 • to pray [preɪ]	beten	They went to church to *pray*.
• somehow ['sʌmhaʊ]	irgendwie	I wanted to call a friend, but *somehow* I forgot.
to be to blame for [bi: tə 'bleɪm]	Schuld haben an, verantwortlich gemacht werden für	Which driver *was to blame* for the accident?
• particular [pə'tɪkjələ]	bestimmte/-r/-s	I'd like to find out about one *particular* type of Asian music.
compromise ['kɒmprəmaɪz]	Kompromiss	We have very different points of view, but we must try to find a *compromise*.
WORD BANK		
confrontation [ˌkɒnfrʌn'teɪʃn]	Konfrontation	She wanted to avoid another *confrontation* with her father.
• miserable ['mɪzrəbl]	elend, unglücklich; armselig	*miserable* = very unhappy
perplexed [pə'plekst]	perplex, ratlos	He felt *perplexed* because he did not understand the situation he was in.
extremist [ɪk'stri:mɪst]	Extremist/-in; radikal, extremistisch	An *extremist* is a person who has very extreme ideas.
liberal ['lɪbrəl]	der Liberale; liberal	*Liberal* people are tolerant towards the ideas of others.
to reverse	tauschen, umdrehen	At first Tom was the leader and Julie was the follower, but then the roles *were reversed*.
• similar ['sɪmɪlə]	ähnlich	My opinions are not exactly the same as yours, but they're very *similar*.

Text: Film page

41 • **occasional** [ə'keɪʒənl]	gelegentlich	We don't hear much from Jason. Just the *occasional* phone call.
• to **be in charge (of)** [ɪn 'tʃɑ:dʒ]	das Sagen haben (für), die Verantwortung tragen (für), zuständig sein (für)	If you want to take photos you'll have to ask Maureen. She*'s in charge* here.
• **victim** ['vɪktɪm]	Opfer	Two boys were attacked outside their school yesterday. One of the *victims* is still in hospital.
to **be based on** [bi: 'beɪst‿ɒn]	basieren auf, beruhen auf, sich stützen auf	The country's wealth *was based on* the sugar trade.
VIP FILE		
comedian [kə'mi:dɪən]	Komiker/-in	Many *comedians* have their own show on TV.

Text: ⟨Dub poetry⟩

FACT FILE		
42 colonial [kə'ləʊniəl]	kolonial	*Colonial* times ended officially when the country became independent.
WORD BANK		
43 play on words [ˌpleɪ‿ɒn 'wɜ:dz]	Wortspiel	A *play on words* often uses words with more than one meaning, like 'patient'.
• irony ['aɪrəni]	Ironie	If I say, "Today was full of wonderful surprises, as usual", that's not the truth – it's *irony*.

USEFUL PHRASES

When you analyse a poem, it is important to know the right phrases.

- The poem describes/deals with …
- The speaker of the poem …
- The language of the poem is …
- The poet uses funny images/pairs of opposites/irony …
- The poet invents new/funny words/uses words/phrases with two meanings …
- … is a play on words/play(s) with the word(s) …
- … play(s) with a familiar phrase.
- … repeat(s) similar sounds.
- … are similar/different.

Text: English for everyone

44 • **figure** ['fɪgə]	Zahl, Ziffer	*figure* = number
resident ['rezɪdənt]	Einwohner/-in, Bewohner/-in, Ortsansässige/r, Anwohner/-in	The *residents* are the people who live in a place.
• **confused** [kən'fju:zd]	wirr, verwirrt, konfus	*confused* = not clear or easy to understand
evidence ['evɪdəns]	Beweis(material), Beleg	Scientists now have *evidence* that these chemicals cause cancer.
mosque [mɒsk]	Moschee	Bangladeshi men go to the *mosque* because it is important for their religion.

	determined [dɪ'tɜ:mɪnd]	(fest) entschlossen, entschieden	Aisha *is determined* to move to London, so she's looking for a job there now.
	• **diversity** [daɪ'vɜ:sətɪ]	Vielfalt	We mustn't lose the *diversity* of nature in our landscape.
	to **indulge (in) sth** [ɪn'dʌldʒ]	sich etw. hingeben, etw. nachgeben, sich etw. ergehen	You shouldn't *indulge* Emma's interest in computer games. She spends all day with her laptop.
	to **prevent sb from doing sth** [prɪ'vent]	jmdn. davon abhalten, etw. zu tun; verhindern, dass jmd. etw. tut	They shut all the windows to *prevent anybody from getting* into the house.
	• **service** ['sɜ:vɪs]	*(hier:)* Agentur, Büro	If I ever got a letter in Bengali, I'd take it to a translation *service* at once.
	• **compulsory** [kəm'pʌlsərɪ]	obligatorisch, verpflichtend	Driving tests are *compulsory* in the UK. You can't drive a car until you've passed.
	to **label sb (as) sth** ['leɪbl]	jmdn. als etw. abstempeln	Rob was *labelled* (as) a bully because he told kids to pick up their rubbish.
	to **speak up** [spi:k 'ʌp]	lauter sprechen; *(hier:)* den Mund aufmachen	If you disagree with what is being done, you should *speak up*.
	to **gain** [geɪn]	gewinnen	*to gain* = to win
	interpreter [ɪn'tɜ:prɪtə]	Dolmetscher/-in	An *interpreter* is a person whose job is to translate what sb is saying into another language. ↔ A translator translates writing into a different language.
45	to **encourage** [ɪn'kʌrɪdʒ]	ermutigen; unterstützen	He did not think he would get the job, but his friends *encouraged* him to apply for it.
	• **argumentative essay** [ɑ:gjəˌmentətɪv 'eseɪ]	Erörterung	In an *argumentative essay* you present the different aspects of a statement and discuss them.

Language: Form and function

46	**concise** [kən'saɪs]	präzise, kurz, prägnant	*concise* = short and exact Writing in a *concise* style, you use exactly the right words and no more of them than you need.
	parade [pə'reɪd]	Parade, Umzug	Everybody came to watch the *parade* moving along the streets.
	stall [stɔ:l]	(Verkaufs)stand, Bude	Mick bought his T-shirt at a *stall* in the market.
	to **be at sth's heart** [bi:‿æt 'hɑ:t]	im Zentrum von etw. stehen	Jane's love of nature *is at the heart of* her political activities.
	rest [rest]	Ruhe, Rast; *(hier:)* Ruhezustand	When a machine is at *rest*, it doesn't make much noise.
	hammer ['hæmə]	Hammer	I can't put up the pictures on the wall without a *hammer*.
	Youth Service ['ju:θ ˌsɜ:vɪs]	Jugendhilfe	The *Youth Service* is an official organisation which offers young people help with social problems, education, leisure, etc.
47	**edition** [ɪ'dɪʃn]	Ausgabe, Auflage, Edition	There's an article about Rick's band in the latest *edition* of 'Music Express'.
	to **print** [prɪnt]	drucken	Many books by British writers are *printed* in Asia.
	to **feel strongly about sth** [fi:l 'strɒŋli əˌbaʊt]	entschiedene Ansichten über etw. haben	Carol has joined a charity because she *feels very strongly about* the problems of the poor.
	cookery book ['kʊkəri ˌbʊk]	Kochbuch	Tanya owns twenty *cookery books*, but the food she cooks is awful.

Language: Everyday English

49 •**orange juice** ['ɒrɪndʒ ˌdʒuːs]	Orangensaft	No alcohol for me, thanks. I'd like *orange juice* or water.
•**sausage** ['sɒsɪdʒ]	(Brat)wurst	! Watch the pronunciation Would you like a *sausage* with your bacon and egg?
•**tomato** [tə'mɑːtəʊ]	Tomate	I eat lots of *tomatoes* – on pizza, with spaghetti, in salads.
•**mushroom** ['mʌʃruːm]	Pilz, Champignon	Jimmy eats the *mushrooms* which he finds in the fields.
•**jam** [dʒæm]	Konfitüre	My sister loves *jam* sandwiches, but I think they're too sweet.
porridge ['pɒrɪdʒ]	Haferbrei	You can make *porridge* with hot water, but I prefer it with hot milk.
•**baked beans** *(pl.)* [beɪkt 'biːnz]	gebackene Bohnen	Can you go to the supermarket and buy five tins of *baked beans*, please?
•**deep-fried**	frittiert; in Fett ausgebacken	*Deep-fried* chicken pieces are often served in Chinese restaurants. They usually come with rice and vegetables.
vinegar ['vɪnɪgə]	Essig	We need *vinegar* and oil for the salad.
organic [ɔː'gænɪk]	Bio-; organisch	I'm sure these eggs are OK, because it says *'organic'* on the box.
roast beef [ˌrəʊst 'biːf]	Roastbeef, Rinderbraten	*Roast beef* is meat from a cow, isn't it?
Yorkshire pudding [ˌjɔːkʃə 'pʊdɪŋ]	Yorkshirepudding *(gebackener Teig aus Eiern, Milch und Mehl, der in der englischen Küche als Beilage zu Steaks, Roastbeef und anderen Fleischgerichten serviert wird)*	Traditionally, *Yorkshire pudding* goes with roast beef.
mineral ['mɪnərəl]	Mineral(-)	Would you like a small bottle of *mineral* water or a large one?
•**rare** [reə]	rar, selten; *(hier:)* englisch *(blutig, nur leicht angebraten)*	I don't like my steak *rare*. I can't stand all that blood!
•**well-done** [ˌwel'dʌn]	gut durch(gebraten)	Some people like their meat *well-done*, but others find it too dry like that.
butter ['bʌtə]	Butter	Let's make some sandwiches with this bread. Where's the *butter*?
rice [raɪs]	Reis	Would you like chips or *rice* with your chicken?
•**spicy** ['spaɪsɪ]	würzig, pikant	I love *spicy* food, but it always makes me thirsty.
cuisine [kwɪ'ziːn]	Küche	! Watch the pronunciation '*Cuisine*' is the French word for 'kitchen', but it also means 'cooking'.

Vocabulary skills

Suffixes

With the help of suffixes, lots of different words can be formed from the same root (basic word).

- Find the new words in this topic that are formed from these roots, and underline the suffixes. How many different suffixes do you find?

  to plant • percent • to treat • to present • to behave • to confront • argument • to cook • complex • to serve

- As you work through this book, look out for more suffixes. Some typical ones are:

to form nouns:	to form adjectives:	to form verbs:
-ence	-ing	-ify
-ance	-able	-ize
-ity	-ible	-en
-ation	-ical	
-ision	-ful	
	-less	
	-ous	

- If you know the root, any new words with suffixes like these will be quite easy to understand. But be careful with the stress, which may be different from what you expect, e.g. English: **real**ist, but German: Real**ist**!

Conclusion

50	to **mark an anniversary** [ˌmɑːk‿ən‿ænɪˈvɜːsri]	ein Jubiläum feiern; einen Feiertag begehen	The ceremony *marked* the 750th *anniversary* of the town.

Topic 3: The Blue Planet

The problems of the planet we call home

- The population of our world is growing fast, so that more mouths need to be fed each day. Industries of all kinds are producing more. This has made our lives more comfortable, but at the same time it has caused pollution of the environment.
- This pollution is also growing. Carbon dioxide and other gases are causing more and more damage to the atmosphere of our planet. Cities are growing bigger and in poorer countries are often surrounded by mountains of garbage. More and more industrial waste is being produced. Environmental problems caused by traffic are getting worse. More energy is being used and natural resources are wasted. More and more species are becoming extinct.
- What we are doing to the planet is having negative effects that we can no longer ignore. The pollution of the atmosphere is leading slowly but surely to global warming. A global climate change would cause all kinds of problems in the future that are very hard to predict – and even harder to stop.
- For years now people who care about the planet have been talking about recycling, alternative forms of energy and many different ideas for protecting the environment. Now is the time to take action. That means that each one of us is responsible in some way for the future of the wonderful blue planet that we all call home.

Introduction

58 **poisonous** ['pɔɪznəs]	giftig	This plant is *poisonous*. You would die if you ate it.
gas [gæs]	Gas	There's a smell of *gas* coming from the kitchen.
pure [pjʊə]	rein, weiß	*pure* = very clean Up in the mountains the air is *purer* than in the towns.
acid rain [ˌæsɪd 'reɪn]	saurer Regen	The *acid rain* which falls on this region is caused by chemical factories.
toxic ['tɒksɪk]	giftig	*toxic* = poisonous
canal [kə'næl]	Kanal	Coal was taken along the *canals* to the factories.
butterfly ['bʌtəflaɪ]	Schmetterling	Beautiful *butterflies* were flying from one flower to another.
plastic ['plæstɪk]	Plastik(-), Kunststoff	This chair isn't made of wood. It's made of *plastic*.
blackbird ['blækbɜːd]	Amsel	Not all black birds are *blackbirds*, and not all *blackbirds* are black! Some are brown.
• **waste** [weɪst]	Müll, Abfall; Verschwendung	*waste* = rubbish, garbage
excuse [ɪk'skjuːs]	Ausrede, Entschuldigung	Stella says the bus was late, but I'm sure that's just an *excuse*.
verse [vɜːs]	Vers; Strophe	The poem has four *verses*, and each *verse* has four lines.
to **address** [ə'dres]	ansprechen; adressieren	The plans for the youth club are OK, but they don't really *address* the problem of noise.
viewpoint ['vjuːpɔɪnt]	Standpunkt	*viewpoint* = point of view
• to **differ** ['dɪfə]	sich unterscheiden; abweichen	*to differ* = to be different
to **appeal to sb** [ə'piːl tuː]	jmdm. zusagen, jmdm. gefallen	The idea of working on a farm doesn't really *appeal to* me.
to **add (to sth)** [æd]	(etw.) ergänzen, erweitern	We were able to *add to* our list of members as more and more people became interested in our club.

WORD BANK

climate change ['klaɪmət tʃeɪndʒ]	Klimawandel	Most scientists agree that *climate change* is really happening.
global warming [ˌgləʊbl 'wɔːmɪŋ]	globale Erwärmung	Because of *global warming* our winters are warmer than they used to be.
• **damage** ['dæmɪdʒ]	Schaden, Beschädigung	The storm caused serious *damage* to buildings in the area.
• **pollution** [pə'luːʃn]	Verschmutzung	If the new airport is built here, we'll have even more air *pollution* – and noise *pollution*.
to **raise awareness of** [ˌreɪz ə'weənəs]	Bewusstsein schärfen für, sensibilisieren für	We must organise a public meeting to *raise awareness of* the situation.
natural resource [nætʃrl rɪ'zɔːs]	Ressource, Rohstoff, Bodenschatz	Oil, gold and water are examples of important *natural resources*.
renewable [rɪ'njuːəbl]	erneuerbar	Energy from the sun is *renewable* because the sun is always there.
alternative [ɔːl'tɜːnətɪv]	alternativ; abwechselnd	Wind energy is an *alternative* form of energy to coal or oil.
to **generate** ['dʒenəreɪt]	generieren, erzeugen	I've heard about a new wind project to *generate* power for a whole village.
solar ['səʊlə]	Sonnen-, Solar-; solar	*Solar* energy comes from the sun.
59 **farmers' market** [ˌfɑːməz 'mɑːkɪt]	Bauernmarkt	At a *farmers' market* you can buy fresh fruit and vegetables directly from the farmers.
offshore [ˌɒf'ʃɔː]	vor der Küste gelegen	They live on an *offshore* island about five miles from the coast.
windfarm ['wɪndfɑːm]	Windpark	The tall towers of the *windfarm* can be seen from miles around.

recycling plant [ˌriːˈsaɪklɪŋ ˌplɑːnt]	Recyclinganlage, Wiederaufbereitungsanlage	Instead of throwing glass and paper away, you should make sure they go to a *recycling plant*.
international [ˌɪntəˈnæʃnl]	international	An *international* company has offices in more than one country.
pressure group [ˈpreʃə ˌɡruːp]	Interessenverband	Rachel has joined a *pressure group* which wants more rights for teenagers.
to campaign (for) [kæmˈpeɪn]	demonstrieren (für), aufmerksam machen (auf)	We *are campaigning for* smaller classes in schools.
• to protect [prəˈtekt]	(be)schützen	They want to *protect* the environment. = They want environmental protection.
tomorrow [təˈmɒrəʊ]	*(hier:)* Zukunft	I wonder what the factories of *tomorrow* will be like?
share [ʃeə]	Anteil	When we go to a restaurant, I always pay my *share* of the bill.
to deserve [dɪˈzɜːv]	verdienen	I'm glad Jason got first prize. He *deserved* to win after all his hard work.
• economy [ɪˈkɒnəmɪ]	*(hier:)* Industrie	The *economy* can only be successful if people want to buy products.

FACT FILE

surface [ˈsɜːfɪs]	Oberfläche	She jumped deep into the water and then rose up to the *surface*.
third [θɜːd]	Drittel	*Two thirds* of the people who work here are women.
fresh water [ˈfreʃ ˌwɔːtə]	Süßwasser	*Fresh water* is found in lakes and rivers, not in the great oceans.
to triple [ˈtrɪpl]	(sich) verdreifachen	Last year our club had twenty members, now we have sixty. The size of the club *has tripled*.
species pl. species [ˈspiːʃiːz, ˈspiːʃiːz]	Art, Spezies	Scientists have discovered a new *species* of fish.
to become extinct [bɪˌkʌm ɪkˈstɪŋkt]	aussterben	Dinosaurs became *extinct* millions of years ago.
carbon dioxide (CO_2) [ˌkɑːbən daɪˈɒksaɪd]	Kohlendioxid	A lot of *carbon dioxide* is created by machines which burn oil.
emission [ɪˈmɪʃn]	Emission, Ausstoß	The air quality is very bad. We must try to stop the *emissions* from this factory.
• to produce [prəˈdjuːs]	produzieren, herstellen, verursachen	Many of us *produce* far too much garbage.
• figure [ˈfɪɡə]	Ziffer, Zahl	*figure* = number
environmentally friendly [ɪnˌvaɪərənˌmentlɪ ˈfrendlɪ]	umweltfreundlich	*environmentally friendly* = good for the environment
to color *(AE)* [ˈkʌlə]	anstreichen, anmalen; färben	How long have you been *coloring* your hair?

Text: Bag Lady

60 to list [lɪst]	auflisten	*to list* = to make a list
to break down [breɪk ˈdaʊn]	zusammenbrechen	When she heard the bad news, Anna *broke down* and cried.
to weep, wept, wept [wiːp, wept, wept]	weinen, schluchzen	*to weep* = to cry
Hawaiian [həˈwaɪən]	hawaiianisch;Hawaiianer/-in	The *Hawaiian* islands are part of the US.
young *(pl.)* [jʌŋ]	Nachkommen, Junge	These birds feed their *young* on small pieces of fish.
seabird [ˈsiːbɜːd]	Seevogel	a *seabird* = a bird which lives near the sea

to **be surrounded by sth/sb** [sə'raʊndɪd]	umgeben sein von etw./jmdm.	An island *is surrounded by* water.
dying ['daɪɪŋ]	sterbend, im Sterben liegend	dying → to die
chick [tʃɪk]	Küken	A *chick* is a baby bird.
documentary [ˌdɒkju'mentri]	Dokumentarfilm, Dokumentation	I saw an interesting *documentary* about China on TV last night.
• **crisis pl. crises** ['kraɪsɪs, 'kraɪsiːz]	Krise	*a crisis* = a very difficult and dangerous situation
to **face** [feɪs]	gegenüber stehen, konfrontiert werden mit	We *are facing* a big problem at the moment.
marine [mə'riːn]	Meeres-; See-	There are special ships used for *marine* research.
wildlife ['waɪldlaɪf]	Tierwelt (in freier Wildbahn)	We can watch many forms of *wildlife* even in our cities.
• **instead** [ɪn'sted]	stattdessen	Tom didn't have any breakfast. He had an early lunch *instead*.
to **fill up** [fɪl 'ʌp]	(auf)füllen, sich füllen	You must *fill up* your water bottles before you go on your hike.
to **be aware of sth** [bɪ‿ə'weər ɒv]	sich einer Sache bewusst sein	Are you *aware* of the problems caused by our garbage?
• **attitude** ['ætɪtjuːd]	Einstellung, Haltung	I don't agree with your *attitude* towards nature.
• **desperate** ['desprət]	ernst, verzweifelt, hoffnungslos	*desperate* = seriously bad
chain [tʃeɪn]	Kette	Danny wears a gold *chain* round his neck.
• **litter** ['lɪtə]	Müll, Abfall	*litter* = garbage
scale [skeɪl]	Ausmaß; Skala	The earthquake has destroyed houses on a huge *scale*.
• **ignorance** ['ɪgnərəns]	Unwissenheit, Ignoranz	Children often behave badly out of *ignorance*.
researcher [rɪ'sɜːtʃə]	Forscher/-in	*researcher* → to research
keyboard ['kiːbɔːd]	Keyboard, Tastatur	Where can I find '@' on a computer *keyboard*?
comb [kəʊm]	Kamm	! Watch the pronunciation Your hair is in a mess. Haven't you got a *comb*?
wrapper ['ræpə]	Verpackung; Hülle	I had to take off the plastic *wrapper* before I could eat the sandwich.
lipstick ['lɪpˌstɪk]	Lippenstift	Amy doesn't use much make-up. – Just pink *lipstick* for her mouth.
brush [brʌʃ]	Bürste	You brush your teeth with a tooth*brush*.
• **plug** [plʌg]	Stecker, Stöpsel	Of course this coffee machine doesn't work. – You've forgotten to put the *plug* in.
item ['aɪtəm]	Gegenstand, Objekt	I had to make a list of all the *items* in my bag.
Welcome to consumer throwaway living. [ˌwelkəm tʊ‿kən'sjuːmə 'θrəʊəweɪ ˌlɪvɪŋ]	Willkommen in der Wegwerfgesellschaft.	We *consumers throw* everything *away* instead of buying things which can be used many times.
food chain ['fuːd ˌtʃeɪn]	Nahrungskette	Plants are eaten by small animals, small animals are eaten by big ones ... That's how the *food chain* works.
to **carry** ['kærɪ]	*(hier:)* beinhalten	The plastic *carries* dangerous chemicals. = There are dangerous chemicals in the plastic.
toxin ['tɒksɪn]	Gift(stoff), Toxin	*Toxins* in food or in the air can make you ill.
to **ascend** [ə'send]	(auf)steigen, ansteigen	*to ascend* = to move up
to **last** [lɑːst]	(an)dauern, anhalten; *(hier:)* brauchen um sich abzubauen	Plastic *lasts* much longer than wood or paper.
to **clear up** [klɪər‿'ʌp]	aufräumen, beseitigen	Who is going to *clear up* the garbage in the park?
whale [weɪl]	Wal	One type of *whale* is the largest animal in the world.

to **come across sb/sth** [kʌm əˈkrɒs]	zufällig begegnen, antreffen, vorfinden	Walking along the trail, Tim *came across* a group of teenagers camping in the forest.
throat [θrəʊt]	Rachen, Kehle, Hals	She can't sing today because her *throat* hurts.
packaging [ˈpækɪdʒɪŋ]	Verpackung	I've bought a new computer, and now I have to get rid of all the *packaging*.
dolphin [ˈdɒlfɪn]	Delfin	We didn't see any whales, but there were some *dolphins* playing together in the water.
to **be unaware of sth** [ˌʌnəˈweə]	sich einer Sache nicht bewusst sein	We *were* completely *unaware of* the danger we were in.
to **move sb to tears** [muːv tə ˈtɪəz]	jmdn. zu Tränen rühren	The birds *moved her to tears*. = She was so sad about the birds that she started to cry.
to **run** [rʌn]	betreiben, führen	They *run* a very successful Italian restaurant in the city centre.

WORD BANK

Linking old and new vocabulary – Animals

You already know a lot of animals. Now that you have learnt some more in Topic 3, it is useful to revise some of those you have already learnt.

Words you already know				New words
bear	dinosaur	horse	pigeon	blackbird
bird	dog	kangaroo	platypus	butterfly
buffalo	eagle	koala	polar bear	chick
cat	elephant	monkey	shark	dolphin
chicken	fish	mouse	sheep	seabird
cow	fox	pet	spider	species
dachshund	green ant	pig	tiger	turkey
				whale
				wildlife

61 **response** [rɪˈspɒns]	Antwort, Erwiderung, Rückmeldung	*response* = reaction
to **turn up** [tɜːn ˈʌp]	kommen, erscheinen	Hundreds of people were invited to the meeting, but only 85 *turned up*.
• **bit (of)** [bɪt]	Stückchen (von)	*a bit* = a small piece
to **act like** [ˈækt laɪk]	handeln wie, fungieren als	He tried to run quickly, but the heavy bag he was carrying *acted like* a brake.
to **pour** [pɔː]	schütten, (ein)gießen	He *poured* some coffee into a cup.
• **butcher** [ˈbʊtʃə]	Fleischer/-in, Metzger/-in	! Watch the pronunciation A *butcher* sells meat in a shop.
• to **whisper** [ˈwɪspə]	flüstern	*to whisper* = to talk very quietly
• **ban** [bæn]	Bann, Sperre, Verbot	Skateboards are not allowed in the town centre. = There's a *ban* on them.
press [pres]	Presse	There have been reports in the *press* about the protest marches.
to **descend on** [dɪˈsend]	einfallen in, herfallen über	Thousands of young people *descend* on the town every summer for the music festival.
• **trade** [treɪd]	Handel, Gewerbe	The new campsite has brought a lot of *trade* to the local shops.
reusable [ˌriːˈjuːsəbl]	Mehrweg-, wiederverwendbar	If something is *reusable*, you can use it more than once.
cotton [ˈkɒtn]	Baumwoll-, Baumwolle	T-shirts are usually made of *cotton*.
biodegradable [ˌbaɪəʊdɪˈɡreɪdəbl]	biologisch abbaubar	! Watch the pronunciation Many chemicals are OK because they're *biodegradable*.

to **be thrilled (with)** [bi 'θrɪld]	sich riesig freuen (über)	He's *thrilled with* his success. = He's very happy and excited about it.
to **litter** ['lɪtə]	verschmutzen, verunreinigen	Why do some people have to *litter* the landscape with their garbage?
oxygen ['ɒksɪdʒən]	Sauerstoff	! Watch the pronunciation There is *oxygen* in the air around us, and we need it to live.
• to **pollute** [pə'lu:t]	verschmutzen, verunreinigen	Cars *pollute* the air. = They make it dirty.
rate [reɪt]	Geschwindigkeit, Tempo	The water in the river is rising at a *rate* of 5cm an hour.
to **degrade** [dɪ'greɪd]	abbauen, zerfallen	Materials which *degrade* quickly are not so dangerous for the environment.
• **madness** ['mædnəs]	Wahnsinn, Irrsinn	You must be crazy! It's *madness* to go swimming in this storm!
• **speech** [spi:tʃ]	Rede; Sprache	At the conference Mark gave a *speech* to two hundred people about human rights.
• **speaker** ['spi:kə]	Redner/-in	A person giving a speech is a *speaker*.
to **feel strongly about sth** [fi:l 'strɒŋli əˌbaʊt]	besorgt um etw. sein, beunruhigt wegen etw. sein, wichtig sein	Janet has become a vegetarian because she *feels* very *strongly about* animals.

WORD BANK

• **emotion** [ɪ'məʊʃn]	Emotion, Gefühl	*emotion* = feeling
emotive [ɪ'məʊtɪv]	gefühlsbetont	An *emotive* topic is one which makes people have strong feelings.
repetition [ˌrepə'tɪʃn]	Wiederholung	*repetition* → to repeat
rhetorical question [rɪ'tɒrɪkl ˌkwestʃən]	rhetorische Frage	"What business is it of yours?" That's a *rhetorical question*, because what the speaker really means is "It's none of your business, so shut up!"

Vocabulary skills

Different ways of expressing opposites

- You already know a number of words that can be turned into their opposites simply by using the prefix 'un-', for example: unlucky, unaware.
- Other prefixes that are sometimes used in English are:

Prefix	Example	Prefix	Example
• in-	independent	• ir- (before r)	irregular
• im- (before b, p, m)	impossible	• dis-	to disagree
• il- (before l)	illegal		

- Note that these English prefixes are not stressed when spoken.
  Compare with German: un**happy** – **un**glücklich; il**legal** – **il**legal
- Decide which of the words in this list express opposites, and which do not.
  underground • unaffected • inappropriate • inside • unprotected • distance • dislike • universe • impure • improve • illness • impolite • important • unable • ingredient • disco
- Now use the right prefixes to turn the following words into their opposites. Use a dictionary if you are unsure.
  likely • respect • realistic • attractive • to believe • activity • advantage • personal • to tie • educated • patient • perfect
- Sometimes, of course, a completely different word is needed to express the opposite meaning.
  Do you (still) know the opposites of these words? (It's often helpful to think of them in pairs.)
  positive • low • well • full • to live • to shout • weak • upstairs • future • modern • to win • ugly • north • front • to arrive • to buy

Text: The Divide (I)

VIP FILE

62 **career** [kəˈrɪə]	Karriere	Leo is hoping for a *career* in medicine.
extract [ˈekstrækt]	Auszug, Exzerpt	This isn't the whole novel. It's only a short *extract*.
ranch [rɑːntʃ]	Farm	In North America a very big farm is called a *ranch*.
college vacation [ˌkɒlɪdʒ vəˈkeɪʃn]	Semesterferien	Students always look forward to the *college vacation* at the end of the semester.
distant [ˈdɪstnt]	entfernt	the *distant* hills = the hills in the distance
shoulder (of rock) [ˈʃəʊldə]	Felsvorsprung	The castle stood high above the village on a *shoulder* of rock.
to **breed, bred, bred** [briːd, bred, bred]	züchten	The Wilsons have a sweet little dog. They bought him from a place where they *breed* dogs.
to **make one's living** [ˌmeɪk wʌnz ˈlɪvɪŋ]	seinen Lebensunterhalt bestreiten	Shirley thinks she can *make her living* selling her paintings.
to **figure** [ˈfɪgə]	sich vorstellen; *(hier:)* schätzen	It's about five miles to the house, so I *figure* we should get there by three o'clock.
• **in fact** [ɪn ˈfækt]	genau genommen	Jim had done his work well. – *In fact*, he had done it perfectly.
creature [ˈkriːtʃə]	Kreatur, Lebewesen, Geschöpf	The area was empty. There was no living *creature* to be seen or heard anywhere.
wondrous [ˈwʌndrəs]	wundersam, erstaunlich	Every morning they looked forward to the view over the *wondrous* landscape.
• **drive** [draɪv]	(An-)Fahrt	Jake got into the car and started on the long *drive* to the coast.
previous [ˈpriːvɪəs]	vorig, vorherig, vorausgegangen	When Lucy came to the house yesterday, she didn't mention her *previous* visit.
to **sit** [sɪt]	*(hier:)* sich befinden	The castle *sits* on the top of a hill just outside the town.
spectacular [spekˈtækjələ]	spektakulär	The view from the tower was quite *spectacular*.
setting [setɪŋ]	Umgebung, Lage	This beach is the perfect *setting* for a TV commercial.
to **insist (on)** [ɪnˈsɪst ɒn]	bestehen (auf), insistieren	We wanted to walk home, but Danny *insisted on* taking a taxi.
• **supper** [ˈsʌpə]	Abendessen	*Supper* is a meal which is eaten in the evening.
• **ham** [hæm]	Schinken	*Ham* is one kind of meat from a pig.
• **turkey** [ˈtɜːkɪ]	Truthahn, Pute	A *turkey* is a very large bird. It is often eaten at Christmas.
baked potato [ˌbeɪkt pəˈteɪtəʊ]	Ofenkartoffel	Kathy loves big *baked potatoes* with lots of butter.
• **pride** [praɪd]	Stolz	*pride* → proud
meadow [ˈmedəʊ]	Wiese, Viehweide	A *meadow* is a field where grass and flowers grow wild.
yard [jɑːd]	Yard *(Längenmaß: 91,44 cm)*	
to **lower** [ˈləʊə]	(ab)senken; verringern	He lifted his hand, then he *lowered* it again.
to **stroke** [strəʊk]	streicheln	The girl picked up the cat and *stroked* it with her hand.
to **join** [dʒɔɪn]	sich anschließen, sich gesellen zu	Go to the café now, and I'll *join* you there later.
to **blow, blew, blown** [bləʊ, bluː, bləʊn]	pusten, blasen; wehen	Don't forget to *blow* the candles out before you leave the room.
spread [spred]	Aufstrich; *(hier:)* große Auswahl	Dinner was a fantastic *spread* of at least ten different dishes.
heavenly [ˈhevnli]	himmlisch	These flowers smell *heavenly*!
to **sigh** [saɪ]	seufzen	Mike thought about all his problems and *sighed* deeply.

63	**matter** ['mætə]	Thema, Angelegenheit	They had important *matters* to discuss.
	puzzled ['pʌzld]	verwirrt, verdutzt	You *look* very *puzzled*. Is there something you don't understand?
	drilling [drɪlɪŋ]	Bohren, Bohrung	The *drilling* for oil can harm the environment.
	letter ['letə]	Brief, Schreiben	Mary's parents have just received a *letter* from her school.
	to **intrude on sth** [ɪn'tru:d]	eindringen in	Don't you realize that you're *intruding on* a private conversation between Charlie and me?
	methane ['mi:θeɪn]	Methan	*Methane* gas can keep your house warm, but it's bad for the environment.
	to **get trapped** [get 'træpd]	eingeschlossen/gefangen werden	Because of an accident in the tunnel, some people *got trapped*.
	underground ['ʌndəgraʊnd]	unterirdisch	The police found the money in an *underground* car park.
	layer ['leɪə]	Lage, Schicht	! Watch the pronunciation The wall needs another *layer* of paint.
	mineral right ['mɪnərəl ˌraɪt]	Abbaurecht	The owner of the *mineral rights* owns the gold or oil which is under the fields.
	lately ['leɪtlɪ]	in letzter Zeit, kürzlich	Have you seen Chris in town *lately*?
	period of time [pɪəriəd əv 'taɪm]	Zeitraum	Twenty years is a long *period of time*.
	to **lease** [li:s]	(ver)mieten, (ver)pachten, leasen	They have *leased* the field for 25 years.
	lease [li:s]	Miete, Pacht	A *lease* is an official arrangement about leasing land or a building.
	to **check out** *(coll)* [tʃek 'aʊt]	untersuchen, überprüfen	I've just heard about some musicians who sound interesting, so I'm going to *check them out*.
	to **drill** [drɪl]	bohren	Could you do me a favour and *drill* a hole in the wall?
	whatever [wɒt'evə]	was auch immer, egal was	There are no rules in this place. Everybody does *whatever* they like.
	so-called ['səʊˌkɔ:ld]	so genannte/-r/-s	Nobody was able to help, not even the *so-called* advisers.
	anyhow ['enɪhaʊ]	trotzdem, sowieso	*anyhow* = anyway
	folks *(pl.)* [fəʊks]	Leute	*folks* = people
	to **set off** [set‿'ɒf]	aufbrechen, sich aufmachen	They *set off* for the ranch. = They started their journey to the ranch.
	to **turn off** [tɜ:n‿'ɒf]	abbiegen von	They *turned off* the road and drove into the park.
	stone [stəʊn]	Stein	Some people started to throw *stones* at the police.
	to **remove** [rɪ'mu:v]	entfernen	Where has the painting gone? Somebody must have *removed* it.
	ground [graʊnd]	(Erd-)Boden, Erde	Most of the *ground* was covered with grass.
	amount (of) [ə'maʊnt]	Menge; Betrag, Summe	a large *amount of* water = a lot of water
	salt [sɔ:lt]	Salz	The water in the ocean tastes of *salt*.
	to **flood** [flʌd]	(über)fluten, überschwemmen	! Watch the pronunciation When the wall broke, water from the river *flooded* into the streets.
	single ['sɪŋgl]	einzig, einzeln, alleinstehend	*not a single* fish = not even one fish
	to **leak** [li:k]	lecken, auslaufen, undicht sein	Sorry about the water on the table. – My plastic water bottle *is leaking*.
	to **fix** [fɪks]	reparieren; befestigen	*to fix* = to mend
64	to **drive on** [draɪv]	weiterfahren	*to drive on* = to continue driving
	deserted [dɪ'zɜ:tɪd]	verlassen, menschenleer	The house was *deserted*. = There was nobody in or near the house.

to **function** ['fʌŋkʃn]	funktionieren	There's something wrong with this machine. – It isn't *functioning* properly.
to **run dry** [rʌn 'draɪ]	austrocknen	This river always *runs dry* in summer.
gas driller ['gæs ˌdrɪlə]	Gasbohrarbeiter/-in	A *gas driller* is a worker who drills holes to look for gas.
to **pass** [pɑ:s]	hindurchdringen	No light can *pass* through these curtains.
to **benefit sb/sth** ['benɪfɪt]	jmdm./etw. zugutekommen, jmdm./etw. nutzen	The new hospital will *benefit* the whole town.
deal [di:l]	Handel, Abmachung, Übereinkunft	The company wanted to make a *deal* with local politicians.
to **ship in** [ʃɪp]	einschiffen; *(hier:)* mitbringen, importieren	*to ship in* = to bring in
labor *(AE)* ['leɪbə]	Arbeitskraft/-kräfte	Many companies use cheap *labor* to make their products.
• **not yet** [nɒt 'jet]	noch nicht	"Have you finished your work?" = "*No, not yet.*"
it won't be long [ɪt ˌwəʊnt bi 'lɒŋ]	es wird nicht (mehr) lange dauern	Lunch isn't ready yet, but *it won't be long* now.
stereo ['steriəʊ]	Stereoanlage; *(hier:)* Radio	*the stereo* = the radio
ahead of [ə'hed‿əv]	vor	*ahead of* them = in front of them
to **look set to do sth** [ˌlʊk 'set tə]	so aussehen als ob	The weather *was set to change.* = It looked like it was going to change soon.
to **reach out** [ri:tʃ 'aʊt]	(die Hand) ausstrecken	she *reached out* = she put out her hand
drop [drɒp]	Tropfen	There were some *drops* of blood on the floor.
windshield *(AE)* ['wɪndˌʃi:ld]	Windschutzscheibe	The *windshield* is the big window at the front of a car.
• **front** [frʌnt]	Front-, Vorder-	The *front* window is the window at the front of something.
to **refer (to)** [rɪ'fɜ:]	sich beziehen (auf), sprechen (von)	The numbers in the text *refer to* the notes at the end of the book.
• to **characterize** ['kærəktraɪz]	charakterisieren	*to characterize* = to describe a person's character
informal [ɪn'fɔ:ml]	informell; zwanglos	*informal* ↔ formal
bar owner ['bɑ:r‿əʊnə]	Kneipenbesitzer/-in	The *bar owner* was worried because not so many people were coming to drink in his bar.
WORD BANK		
• **future** ['fju:tʃə]	zukünftig	*future* events = events in the future
lasting ['lɑ:stɪŋ]	bleibend	The exchange student made a *lasting* impression on everyone at school.
attorney *(AE)* [ə'tɜ:ni]	(Rechts-)Anwalt/Anwältin, Staatsanwalt/-anwältin, Jurist/-in	! Watch the pronunciation *'Attorney'* is the American word for 'lawyer'.
literature ['lɪtrətʃə]	Literatur	*literature* = novels, plays and stories etc.

Text: ⟨The Divide (II)⟩

65 • to associate [ə'səʊʃieɪt]	assoziieren, verbinden	Most people *associate* California with sunny beaches and Hollywood.
demonstration [demən'streɪʃn]	Demonstration; Darstellung, Veranschaulichung	They organised a *demonstration* to protest against the new laws.
to dress up [dres‿'ʌp]	sich verkleiden	When you *dress up*, you wear a costume.
strawberry ['strɔ:brɪ]	Erdbeere	We look forward to eating *strawberries* in May and June.
a cross between [ə 'krɒs bɪˌtwi:n]	eine Kreuzung zwischen/von	Nina's job at the hospital is a *cross between* a nurse and a caretaker.

• tomato *(pl. -es)* [tə'mɑ:təʊ]	Tomate	Spaghetti with *tomatoes*. – My favourite!
front [frʌnt]	Vorderseite	Ken has a picture of Eminem on the *front* of his T-shirt.
parka ['pɑ:kə]	Anorak, Parka	It's cold and wet today. – Wear your *parka*.
to consider yourself above sth/sb [kən'sɪdə]	etw./jmdn. für unter seiner Würde halten	Paul would never throw sticks for a dog. He *considers himself above* such games.
childish ['tʃaɪldɪʃ]	kindisch; kindlich	Marco is so *childish*. It's hard to believe he's nearly 18.
demonstrator ['demənstreɪtə]	Demonstrant/-in; Vorführer/-in	A *demonstrator* is a person taking part in a demonstration.
to march [mɑ:tʃ]	marschieren; wandern	Hundreds of soldiers *marched* into the city.
convention center *(AE)* [kən'venʃən ˌsentə]	Kongresszentrum	An important political conference was held at the *convention center*.
• despite [dɪ'spaɪt]	trotz	*despite* = in spite of
• cold [kəʊld]	Kälte	in spite of *the cold* = although it was cold
dressed (as) [drest]	angezogen (wie), verkleidet (als)	She *was dressed as* a pirate. = She wore a pirate's costume.
banner ['bænə]	Transparent, Fahne, Banner	Two demonstrators were carrying a large *banner* with the words 'No to the WTO!'
• bloody ['blʌdi]	blutig	*bloody* → blood
to bang drums [bæŋ 'drʌms]	trommeln	When you play the drums, you make music. When you *bang a drum*, you just make a noise.
hippy ['hɪpi]	Hippie	You can recognize *hippies* by their unusual clothes.
to succeed in [sək'si:d‿ɪn]	Erfolg haben, erfolgreich sein	He finally *succeeded in* opening the door. You'll have to train hard to *succeed in* football.
opening ceremony ['əʊpnɪŋ ˌserɪməni]	Eröffnungsfeierlichkeiten	The *opening ceremony* was watched by millions on TV.
History was being made ['hɪstəri wɒz ˌbi:ɪŋ meɪd]	Geschichte wurde geschrieben	As they watched the doors of the building opening, they felt that *history was being made*.
to come down [kʌm 'daʊn]	herunterkommen; *(hier:)* fallen	*to come down* = to fall
grandchild pl. grandchildren ['græntʃaɪld, 'græntʃɪldrn]	Enkel/-in, Enkel(kind)	*grandchild* → grandparents
• forward ['fɔ:wəd]	vorwärts	When you walk *forward*, you walk towards something which is in front of you.
to clear [klɪə]	aufklaren, sich aufhellen	The sky began to *clear*. = The clouds started to disappear.
port [pɔ:t]	Hafen	*port* = harbour
massive ['mæsɪv]	riesig, massiv, wuchtig	*massive* = very large
to anchor offshore [ˌæŋkər‿'ɒfʃɔ:]	im Hafen liegen	When the ships reached the harbour, they *anchored offshore*.
container [kən'teɪnə]	Behälter, Container, Behältnis	Dean is moving to another apartment, so he needs some large *containers* for all his stuff.
to set on fire [faɪə]	anzünden, in Brand setzen	Three cars were burning in the street, but nobody knew who *had set* them *on fire*.
to smash [smæʃ]	zerschlagen, zertrümmern	A boy threw a rock and *smashed* the window of a café.
in order to [ɪn‿'ɔ:də tə]	mit der Absicht; um … zu	Many firms advertise on the Internet *in order to* attract more customers.
to scrawl [skrɔ:l]	kritzeln, vollschmieren	*to scrawl* = to write very badly
• murder ['mɜ:də]	Mord	His crime was *murder*. = He murdered somebody.
special riot police [ˌspeʃl 'raɪət pə'li:s]	Sondereinsatzkommando	The *special riot police* deal with especially violent situations.
gasmask ['gæsmɑ:sk]	Gasmaske	The air was so bad that they had to wear *gasmasks* over their faces.
to block off [blɒk 'ɒf]	absperren, abriegeln	The soldiers *blocked off* the road so that nobody could get through.

FACT FILE

	policy ['pɒləsɪ]	Politik, politische Linie, Grundsatz	It is this company's *policy* to hire people from minority groups if possible.
66	march [mɑ:tʃ]	Marsch, Kundgebung	*the march* = the people taking part in the protest march
	to slow [sləʊ]	langsamer werden, sich verlangsamen	*to slow* → slow
	to blame sth on sb ['bleɪm ˌɒn]	jmdn. für etw. verantwortlich machen	Most people *blamed the accident on* the driver of the van.
	to drift (across) [drɪft]	(vorbei)schweben, (vorbei)treiben	White clouds *drifted across* the landscape.
	• impossible [ɪm'pɒsəbl]	unmöglich	impossible ↔ possible
	circle ['sɜ:kl]	Kreis, Ring	They sat in a *circle* round the table.
	to refuse (to do sth) [rɪ'fju:z]	ablehnen, sich weigern (etw. zu tun)	She *refused* to go. = She said that she would definitely not go.
	• to be arrested [ə'restɪd]	festgenommen/verhaftet werden	The driver *was arrested* by police officers and taken to the police station.
	to roll [rəʊl]	rollen	The ball *rolled* across the floor.
	panic ['pænɪk]	Panik	There was a feeling of *panic* when the doors didn't open.
	• to beat, beat, beaten [bi:t, bi:t, 'bi:tn]	schlagen, (ver)prügeln; besiegen	*to beat* = to hit (with a stick)
	• to fire ['faɪə]	*(hier:)* schießen mit, abfeuern	They *fired* plastic into the crowd. = They shot small balls of plastic.
	to reassure [ˌri:ə'ʃʊə]	beruhigen, beschwichtigen	Steve was still worried about the exam, although his friends had tried to *reassure* him.
	to sweep, swept, swept [swi:p, swept, swept]	fegen, kehren; *(hier:)* mitreißen	The wind was so strong that some people *were swept* along the beach.
	to figure out [ˌfɪgər‿'aʊt]	ergründen, herausfinden	*to figure out* = to find out
	water cannon ['wɔ:tə ˌkænən]	Wasserwerfer	When the protest march became violent, the police used *water cannon*. (plural usually 'cannon')
	to rush to ['rʌʃ tə]	eilen zu, zustürzen auf	*to rush to sb* = to run very quickly to sb
	to collide [kə'laɪd wɪð]	kollidieren, zusammenstoßen	*to collide with sb/sth* = to bump into sb/sth
	impact ['ɪmpækt]	Aufprall; Auswirkung	When she ran into the wall, the *impact* made her fall over.
	to fight for breath [ˌfaɪt fə 'breθ]	nach Luft ringen	She had to *fight for breath*. = She found it difficult to take a breath.
	certainty ['sɜ:tnti]	Gewissheit	*certainty* → certain
	to strike, struck, struck [straɪk, strʌk, strʌk]	(auf)treffen, einschlagen	*to strike* = to hit
67	to fill [fɪl]	(sich) füllen	It *was filling*. = It was becoming full.
	to put on sth [pʊt‿'ɒn]	etw. anziehen, aufsetzen	The sun was very strong, so he *put on* his sunglasses.
	Scandinavian [ˌskændɪ'neɪviən]	skandinavisch	Finland is one of the *Scandinavian* countries.
	to soak [səʊk]	tränken, durchweichen, durchnässen	If you stay out in the rain, your clothes will be completely *soaked*.
	to surrender [sə'rendə]	sich ergeben	The thief hid in the woods for ten days, then he *surrendered* to the police.
	stranger ['streɪndʒə]	Fremde/-r	A *stranger* is a person you do not know.
	knock [nɒk]	Stoß, Schlag	He got a bad *knock* to the head when he fell out of the tree.
	siren ['saɪrən]	Sirene, Martinshorn	She knew the ambulance was coming because she could hear the *siren*.
	• image ['ɪmɪdʒ]	Bild	*image* = picture
	Buddhist monk [ˌbʊdɪst 'mʌŋk]	buddhistischer Mönch	The religion of *Buddhist monks* is against violence.

prayer [preə]	Gebet	In many religions, people go to a special building like a church to say their *prayers*.
to discard [dɪ'ska:d]	wegwerfen; ausziehen; ablegen	She had *discarded* her pullover because of the heat.
• immediate [ɪ'mi:dɪət]	direkt, unmittelbar, spontan	your *immediate* reaction = the reaction which you have at once
to analyze ['ænlaɪz]	analysieren, untersuchen	*to analyze sth* = to examine sth carefully We must *analyze* the results before making any statements.
to bring to life [ˌbrɪŋ tə 'laɪf]	veranschaulichen, zum Leben erwecken	The way Ron described everything really *brought* the scene *to life*.
• narrator [nə'reɪtə]	Erzähler/-in	The *narrator* is the person who tells a story.
to speculate ['spekjəleɪt]	spekulieren, vermuten	I have no idea where Leroy is at the moment, and I don't want to *speculate* on it.
naive [naɪ'i:v]	naiv, blauäugig	Sharon thought that they would ask her to join the band. How *naive* of her!
• to force [fɔ:s]	zwingen	The burglars *forced* her to give them money.
WORD BANK		
• understandable [ˌʌndə'stændəbl]	verständlich	Harry's point of view is *understandable* to me. = I can understand his point of view.
to be caught up in the moment [ˌbi kɔ:t‿'ʌp ɪn ðə 'məʊmənt]	in dem Moment gefangen sein, vertieft sein	At the match Mike was so *caught up in the moment* that he didn't notice someone taking his wallet.
to justify ['dʒʌstɪfaɪ]	rechtfertigen	He *justified* their actions. = He said they had acted in the right way.

Text: Film page

68 • **writer** ['raɪtə]	Verfasser/-in	*writer* = sb who writes texts
fellow ['feləʊ]	Mit-	Ryan is a *fellow* worker at the store. = He works at the store, like me.
jury member ['dʒʊəri ˌmembə]	Jurymitglied	At the film festival the *jury members* had to decide on the winner.
debate [dɪ'beɪt]	Debatte, Beratung	*debate* = a formal discussion
filmmaker ['fɪlmeɪkə]	Filmemacher/-in	A *filmmaker* is a person who makes films.
to **weigh up** [weɪ]	abwägen	Don't make a decision too quickly. *Weigh up* the good and bad points first.
to **reduce** [rɪ'dju:s]	reduzieren, verringern	The workers' pay *was reduced*. = They were paid less money.
carbon ['ka:bn]	Kohlenstoff	We find *carbon* in coal and in oil.
nuclear energy [ˌnju:kliə 'enədʒɪ]	Kernenergie	Some people say *nuclear energy* is clean because there is no smoke.
urgent ['ɜ:dʒənt]	dringend	We need an ambulance at once. It's very *urgent*!
• to **avoid** [ə'vɔɪd]	(ver)meiden	When you're writing a text, try to *avoid* clichés.
to **preach** [pri:tʃ]	predigen, propagieren	Carrie is a vegetarian, and she keeps *preaching* her message to us.
• **cause** [kɔ:z]	*(hier:)* Ziel	We all support the *cause* of human rights.
• **rarely** ['reəlɪ]	selten	*rarely* ↔ often
• **unlikely** [ʌn'laɪkli]	unwahrscheinlich	You're *unlikely* to see a bear here. = You probably won't see one here.
Oscar-winning ['ɒskəwɪnɪŋ]	Oscar-gekrönt	"Has Spielberg won any Hollywood awards?" – "Oh yes, he has made a number of *Oscar-winning* movies."
effective [ɪ'fektɪv]	effektiv, nachhaltig	Kelly is ill, and the medicine she's taking hasn't been very *effective* so far.

big-budget [ˈbɪɡˌbʌdʒɪt]	mit großem Budget	A *big-budget* movie costs a lot of money to make.
animation [ˌænɪˈmeɪʃn]	Animation; Zeichentrickfilm	I think modern *animations* are much better than the old Mickey Mouse films.
condemnation [ˌkɒndemˈneɪʃn]	Verurteilung, Verdammung	After the TV report Jenny wrote to the company expressing her *condemnation* of their actions.
global [ˈɡləʊbl]	global, weltweit	A *global* problem has an effect on the whole world.
stock [stɒk]	Bestand	There aren't many fish in the sea. = *Stocks* are very low.
overpopulation [ˌəuvəˌpɒpjuˈleɪʃn]	Überbevölkerung	*Overpopulation* usually means that there isn't enough food for everyone.
to **dramatise** [ˈdræmətaɪz]	verfilmen, dramatisieren	*to dramatise* = to make an event or a story into a film or play
real-life [ˈriːəˌlaɪf]	authentisch, aus dem wirklichen Leben	Is this a *real-life* story, or did somebody make it up?
• **powerful** [ˈpaʊəfl]	stark, mächtig; bedeutend, beeindruckend	A *powerful* film makes a strong impression on you.
release [rɪˈliːs]	Veröffentlichung, Herausgabe, Freigabe	They've just finished making the film, and cinema *release* will be next September.
• **humanity** [hjuːˈmænəti]	Menschheit	*humanity* = all people
to **combine** [kəmˈbaɪn]	kombinieren, verbinden	When Luke goes to Florida next month he wants to *combine* business with a vacation.
striking [straɪkɪŋ]	bemerkenswert, auffallend	Everybody noticed her because of her *striking* clothes.
• **imagery** [ˈɪmɪdʒrɪ]	Bilder, Bildsprache	*imagery* = pictures
to **boast** [bəʊst]	angeben, prahlen, sich rühmen	This town is an interesting place. It *boasts* a castle, two museums and a zoo.
film genre [ˈfɪlm ˌʒɒnrə]	Filmgattung	Helen likes animations, but her favourite *film genres* are documentaries and science fiction.

Text: ⟨An environmental song⟩

69 animated [ˈænɪmeɪtɪd]	lebhaft; *(hier:)* Zeichentrick-	an *animated* film = an animation
robot [ˈrəʊˌbɒt]	Roboter	In many factories *robots* are used instead of people.
to clean up [ˌkliːnˈʌp]	aufräumen, beseitigen	Every year we *clean up* the garbage on the beach.
gravity [ˈɡrævəti]	Schwerkraft, Schwere	The law of *gravity* says that what goes up must come down.
to be tricked [biː ˈtrɪkd]	ausgetrickst/hereingelegt werden	I *was tricked*. = Somebody played a trick on me.
to pick [pɪk]	auswählen, aussuchen; pflücken	*to pick* = to choose
to apply (to) [əˈplaɪ]	gelten (für), zutreffen (auf)	All students must wear uniform. (This does not *apply* to exchange students.)
seed [siːd]	Saat, Samen	It's amazing that big plants grow from such small *seeds*.
to escape (from) [ɪˈskeɪp]	(ent)fliehen, entkommen	She sometimes goes out hiking alone to *escape* from her family.
despite [dɪˈspaɪt]	trotz	*despite* = in spite of
to mess up sth [ˈmesˌʌp]	etw. durcheinanderbringen, etw. in Unordnung bringen	Terry *has messed up* my things. – Now they're in a mess.
• birth [bɜːθ]	Geburt	The day of your *birth* is your birthday.
to redefine [ˌriːdɪˈfaɪn]	neu definieren	Ken's job with his firm will be different in future. They've *redefined* his work.
priority [praɪˈɒrətɪ]	Priorität, Vorrang	What are the most important things you must do now? Make a list of these *priorities*.

extraordinary [ɪk'strɔ:dnri]	außergewöhnlich	*extraordinary* = very unusual
•introduction [ˌɪntrə'dʌkʃn]	Einleitung	At the beginning of the song there's a short *introduction* without any lyrics.

VIP FILE

songwriter ['sɒŋˌraɪtə]	Songschreiber/-in	A *songwriter* is a person who writes the lyrics (and sometimes the music) of songs.
lead singer ['li:d ˌsɪŋə]	Leadsänger/-in, Frontsänger/-in	*lead singer* = main singer in a group
to promote [prə'məʊt]	fördern, vorantreiben	He organised a big festival to *promote* African music and musicians.

Text: Environmental footprints

70 **footprint** ['fʊtprɪnt]	Fußabdruck	They followed the *footprints* in the snow.
•to **matter** ['mætə]	von Bedeutung sein, etw. ausmachen	Does the quality of the air *matter* to you? = Is it important to you?
-based [beɪsd]	*(hier:)* ansässig in	It's a New York-*based* company, but they have stores in many cities.
to **include** [ɪn'klu:d]	beinhalten, einschließen	The new exhibition *includes* paintings from many countries and centuries.
•**pasta** ['pæstə]	Pasta, Nudeln	Spaghetti is one type of *pasta*.
pork sausage [pɔ:k 'sɒsɪdʒ]	Fleischwurst	! Watch the pronunciation *Pork sausage* is made from the meat of a pig.
pepper ['pepə]	Pfeffer; Paprikaschote	*Peppers* can be red, green or yellow.
shallot [ʃə'lɒt]	Schalotte	*A shallot* is a small vegetable with a strong taste. It can make you cry!
whenever [wen'evə]	wann immer; immer, wenn; so oft	Tracy always buys new clothes *whenever* she's downtown.
impact ['ɪmpækt]	Einfluss, Auswirkung	The warmer winters are having a serious *impact* on winter sports.
to **produce** [prə'dju:s]	anbauen, erzeugen	*to produce* → product A lot of plants are needed to *produce* one kilo of meat.
to **transport** [træn'spɔ:t]	transportieren; überführen, bringen	! Watch the pronunciation and the stress *to transport* → transport
•**according to** [ə'kɔ:dɪŋ tə]	laut, gemäß	*According to* this report, there are dangerous chemicals in some meat products.
dairy product ['deəri ˌprɒdʌkt]	Milchprodukt, -erzeugnis	*Dairy products* are made from milk.
average ['ævrɪdʒ]	Durchschnitt, Durchschnitts-	The *average* teenager watches TV every day.
household ['haʊshəʊld]	Haushalt	There are five people in our *household* – my parents, my two brothers and me.
to **find** [faɪnd]	feststellen, herausfinden, zu dem Ergebnis kommen	*to find* = to discover His research *found* that dogs were not able to smell the drug.
•**transportation** *(AE)* [ˌtrænspɔ:'teɪʃn]	Transport	*transportation (AE)* = transport *(BE)*
•to **create** [kri'eɪt]	verursachen, ausmachen	*to create* = to cause
metric tonne [ˌmetrɪk 'tʌn]	(metrische) Tonne	*A metric tonne* is 1000 kilograms.
greenhouse gas [ˌgri:nhaʊs 'gæs]	Treibhausgas	The air above the earth is trapped by *greenhouse gases*, and so it becomes hotter.
as a result of [æz‿ə rɪ'zʌlt‿əv]	als Ergebnis von, als Folge von	*As a result of* the protests, the government's plans have been changed.
consumption [kən'sʌmpʃn]	Verbrauch, Konsum	The *consumption* of ice-cream is usually higher in summer than in winter.

agricultural [ˌægrɪ'kʌltʃrəl]	landwirtschaftlich, Agrar-	*agricultural* land = land which is used for farms
• to **grow, grew, grown** [grəʊ, gruː, grəʊn]	*(hier:)* anbauen	Farmers *grow* vegetables on this land.
to **harvest** ['hɑːvɪst]	ernten	When the fruit on the trees is ready, it is *harvested* by workers from Mexico.
responsible [rɪs'pɒnsəbl]	verantwortlich, verantwortungsvoll	Some people think that teenagers are *responsible* for most of the crime in our city.
to **account for** [ə'kaʊnt fɔː]	ausmachen, betragen	Clothes *account for* half of the money which Danny spends.
• **total** ['təʊtl]	gesamt, Gesamt-	The *total* number of visitors was 150. = There were 150 visitors altogether.
• **diet** ['daɪət]	Ernährung, Diät	Your *diet* isn't very healthy – all those sweets and chocolate.
relatively ['relətɪvlɪ]	relativ, vergleichsweise, verhältnismäßig	Modern cameras are sometimes quite difficult to use, but this one is *relatively* easy.
reduction [rɪ'dʌkʃn]	Abnahme, Verminderung, Reduzierung	Kate wants to buy a new laptop, but she's waiting for price *reductions* next month.
to **replace sb/sth (with sb/ sth)** [rɪ'pleɪs]	jmdn./etw. (durch jmdn./etw.) ersetzen	The manager has got rid of some of his older workers and *replaced them with* students.
to **be equal (to)** ['iːkwəl]	*(hier:)* entsprechen	If you want to keep fit, an hour in our fitness centre *is equal to* three hours' jogging.
• to **cut, cut, cut** [kʌt, kʌt, kʌt]	*(hier:)* reduzieren	The new planes *cut* the flight time from here to New York by twenty minutes.
• **several** ['sevrl]	einige, mehrere, verschiedene	This isn't my first visit to Seattle. I've been here *several* times.
study ['stʌdi]	Studie, Untersuchung; Studium	*study* → to study
energy efficient ['enədʒɪ ɪˌfɪʃnt]	energieeffizient	Are vegetarians more *energy efficient* than meat-eaters?
• **tomato** (*pl.* -es) [tə'mɑːtəʊ]	Tomate	You can eat *tomatoes* in salad or with spaghetti.
lettuce ['letɪs]	Kopfsalat	! Watch the pronunciation Can you do anything with *lettuce* apart from making a green salad?
heated ['hiːtɪd]	beheizt, erhitzt	Their garage is warm even in winter because it's *heated*.
greenhouse ['griːnˌhaʊs]	Gewächshaus, Treibhaus	A *greenhouse* is a shed made of glass for growing plants.
paper ['peɪpə]	Artikel, Abhandlung	Scientists often read *papers* to the audience at conferences.
grower ['grəʊə]	Erzeuger/-in, Bauer/Bäuerin	*Growers* in this area use their land for vegetables.
production [prə'dʌkʃn]	Produktion, Herstellung	Many farmers complain about the cost of milk *production*.
condiment ['kɒndɪmənt]	Aromat, Gewürz, Würzmittel	
ethical ['eθɪkl]	ethisch, moralisch	If you can't decide whether an action is right or wrong, you've got an *ethical* problem.
consumer [kən'sjuːmə]	Verbraucher/-in, Konsument/-in	A *consumer* is someone who buys things or services.
precious ['preʃəs]	wertvoll, kostbar	Water is very *precious* to people who live in a dry climate.
value ['væljuː]	Wert	What's the *value* of the dollar compared with the euro at the moment?
H_2O (= water) [ˌeɪtʃ tuː‿'əʊ]	H_2O (= Wasser)	! Watch the pronunciation 'H_2O' means 'water'.
71 • **habit** ['hæbɪt]	Gewohnheit	Some people have strange eating *habits*. – Salad for breakfast, cake for dinner.
• **groceries** *(pl.)* ['grəʊsərɪz]	Lebensmittel	*groceries* = the types of food you can buy in a supermarket

electrical goods *(pl.)* [ɪ'lektrɪkl]	Elektrogeräte	You can buy *electrical goods* to do all kinds of work – to brush your teeth, to make bread, to make rooms or water hot.
to **evaluate** [ɪ'væljʊeɪt]	bewerten, evaluieren, auswerten	*to evaluate* = to decide or judge how good or bad something is After the presentations the students *evaluated* the different projects.
calculator ['kælkjʊˌleɪtə]	(Taschen)rechner	A *calculator* is very useful for Maths homework.
case [keɪs]	Fall	Fruit from ten shops was tested, and in two *cases* the scientists found chemicals.
to **cover** ['kʌvə]	*(hier:)* berücksichtigen	The film *covers* five different points of view.
gram (g) [græm]	Gramm	A bag of sugar usually weighs 1000*g (grams)*.
litre (l) ['li:tə]	Liter	One *litre* of water weighs 1000g.
millilitre (ml) ['mɪliˌli:tə]	Milliliter	There are 1000 *millilitres* in one litre.
• **twice** [twaɪs]	zweimal, doppelt	Five people work in the office, and there are ten in the workshop. – That's *twice* as many.
• **wheat** [wi:t]	Weizen	Bread is usually made from *wheat*.
worldwide ['wɜ:ldwaɪd]	weltweit	This is a *worldwide* company. It has offices all over the world.
offender [ə'fendə]	Übeltäter/-in, Zuwiderhandelnde/-r	Many students in our class drop rubbish on the floor, but Martin is the worst *offender*.
cubic metre [ˌkju:bɪk 'mi:tə]	Kubikmeter	Guess how many *cubic metres* of water there are in this swimming pool.
per capita [pə 'kæpɪtə]	pro Kopf	*per capita* = per person
calculation [ˌkælkjə'leɪʃn]	Berechnung, Kalkulation	I'd like to know how much water my lifestyle uses, but I can't do the *calculation*.
complicated ['kɒmplɪkeɪtɪd]	kompliziert	This machine isn't easy to use, in fact it's quite *complicated*.
to **be keen to do sth** [ki:n]	sehr daran interessiert sein, etw. zu tun	I'm *keen to help* you. = I very much want to help you.
to **minimise** ['mɪnɪmaɪz]	vermindern, minimieren	If you *minimise* something, you make it as small as possible.
wastage ['weɪstɪdʒ]	Verbrauch; Verschwendung	There's a lot of food *wastage*. = We throw a lot of food away.
to **remain** [rɪ'meɪn]	bleiben	There *remains* one problem. = There is still one problem.
to **recycle** [ˌri:'saɪkl]	wiederverwerten, recyceln	We don't throw paper away. We *recycle* it.
• **shirt** [ʃɜ:t]	Hemd, Shirt	Andy works in a bank now. He always wears a suit with a white *shirt*.
• **as well as** [əz 'wel‿əz]	sowie	Ray had to pay for the drinks *as well as* the tickets.
fertiliser ['fɜ:tɪlaɪzə]	Dünger	Many farmers use *fertilisers* to make the plants grow better.
• **though** [ðəʊ]	obwohl	*though* = although
influential [ˌɪnflu'enʃl]	einflussreich, maßgebend	*influential* → influence
• to **publish** ['pʌblɪʃ]	veröffentlichen, publizieren, verlegen	The results of the scientists' research *will be published* next month.
shortage ['ʃɔ:tɪdʒ]	Mangel, Knappheit	There is a *shortage* of doctors. = There are not enough doctors.
to **affect** [ə'fekt]	beeinträchtigen, betreffen, beeinflussen	The storm *affected* transport in a large area.

FACT FILE

slice [slaɪs]	Scheibe, Stück, Teil	He cut four *slices* of bread to make sandwiches.
• **beef** [bi:f]	Rindfleisch	*beef* = the meat from cows
• **wine** [waɪn]	Wein	Would the guests like red *wine* or white *wine* with the meal?

pint [paɪnt]	Pint *(Flüssigkeitsmaß, entspricht 0.568l in Großbritannien, 0.473l in den USA)*	Could you go to the supermarket and buy a *pint* of milk, please?
focus [ˈfəʊkəs]	Schwerpunkt, Blickpunkt, Fokus	The *focus* is the topic which you concentrate on.
specialist [ˈspeʃəlɪst]	Fach-; Experte/Expertin, Spezialist/-in	Computer firms advertise in *specialist* magazines.
complex [ˈkɒmpleks]	komplexe/-r/-s	A *complex* sentence has a main clause and other clauses, too.
measurement [ˈmeʒəmənt]	Maßeinheit	'Kilo' is a *measurement* of weight.

USEFUL PHRASES

These words and phrases help you to talk or write about environmental problems.

Causes	**Effects**	**Helpful actions**
to cause damage (to)	acid rain	to raise awareness/to be aware of sth
poisonous/toxic gas	climate change	renewable/alternative energy sources
toxin	global warming	to use/generate solar/water/wind energy
(air/water) pollution	rise in temperature	to recycle
waste of natural resources	environmental crisis	recycling plant
carbon dioxide/methane emission	greenhouse gas	to campaign
to litter/pollute	to become extinct	to protect
overpopulation		to use reusable/biodegradable bags
wastage of energy/water wastage		to reduce carbon/carbon dioxide emission

to **turn into** [ˈtɜːn‿ˌɪntuː]	umformulieren, umwandeln in	Let's *turn* all these numbers *into* sentences that people can understand.
• to **vote on sth** [vəʊt]	über etw. abstimmen	Are we going to follow my plan or Amy's? Let's *vote on it.*
chairperson [ˈtʃeəˌpɜːsn]	Vorsitz, Vorsitzende/-r	The *chairperson* organises what happens in a debate or at a meeting.
to **be missing** [bi ˈmɪsɪŋ]	fehlen	"Is everybody here?" – "No, Mike *is missing*."

Language: Form and function

TIP

72 **abbreviation** [əˌbriːvɪˈeɪʃn]	Abkürzung	'UK' is the *abbreviation* for 'United Kingdom'.
kilogram (kg) [ˈkɪləgræm]	Kilogramm	This bag of sugar weighs one *kilogram*.
kilometre (km) [ˈkɪləʊˌmiːtə]	Kilometer	A marathon is more than 42 *kilometres*.
degree Celsius (°C) [dɪˈgriː ˈselsiəs]	Grad Celsius	Water becomes ice at zero *degrees Celsius*.
unit of measurement [ˈjuːnɪt‿əv ˈmeʒəmənt]	Maß-, Größeneinheit	Which *unit of measurement* is larger: kilometre or mile?
square mile (sq. mile) [ˈskweə ˌmaɪl]	Quadratmeile	The area of this park is three *square miles*.
volume [ˈvɒljuːm]	Volumen; Lautstärke; Band *(Buch)*	After heavy rain, there is a greater *volume* of water in the lake.
to **flush** [flʌʃ]	spülen, die Wasserspülung betätigen	He threw the pieces of paper into the toilet and *flushed* it.
rise in temperature [raɪz‿ɪn ˈtemprətʃə]	Temperaturanstieg	There was a *rise in temperature*. = The temperature became higher.
length [leŋθ]	Länge; *(hier:)* Dauer	What *length* of time did you spend there? = How long were you there?

to **be in existence** [ɪɡ'zɪstns]	existieren	Our band isn't very old. It's *only been in existence* for three months.
nitrogen ['naɪtrədʒən]	Stickstoff	! Watch the pronunciation A very large part of the air is *nitrogen*.
non- [nɒn]	nicht-	Tickets for the concert are £10 for members and £15 for *non*-members.
equivalent [ɪ'kwɪvələnt]	Entsprechung, Äquivalent	What's the German *equivalent* of a high school?
ounce [aʊnts]	Unze *(Maßeinheit: 28,35g)*	What's today's price for an *ounce* of gold?
steak [steɪk]	Steak	If someone else is paying for the meal, Jack usually orders a big *steak*.
inch [ɪntʃ]	Zoll *(Längenmaß: 2,54cm)*	School uniform skirts must not be shorter than three *inches* above the knee.
gallon ['ɡælən]	Gallone *(Hohlmaß: UK = 4,5l; USA = 3,8l)*	We must get ten *gallons* at the next gas station.
• **petrol** ['petrəl]	Benzin	*petrol (BE)* = gas *(AE)*
factor ['fæktə]	Faktor, Gesichtspunkt	Food is one of the most important *factors* influencing people's health.
to **calculate** ['kælkjʊleɪt]	(be)rechnen, kalkulieren	Can you *calculate* the whole cost of the vacation?
• **majority (of)** [mə'dʒɒrəti]	Mehrheit	I'm sure the *majority of* teenagers would like to have more freedom.

WORD BANK

Unit of measurement	**Abbreviation**	**Unit of measurement**	**Abbreviation**
cubic metre	m^3	kilometre	km
degree Celsius	° C	litre	l
gallon	gal	millilitre	ml
gram	g	pint	pt
inch	in	square mile	sq. mile
kilogram	kg		

73 **carbon unit** [ˌkɑ:bn 'ju:nɪt]	Kohlenstoffeinheit	*'Carbon unit'* expresses how much CO_2 is going into the air.
hypothetical [ˌhaɪpə'θetɪkl]	hypothetisch; theoretisch	All his talk about winning an Olympic gold medal is completely *hypothetical*, of course.
by sea [si:]	zu Wasser, mit dem Schiff	Are you going to fly to New York, or are you going *by sea?*
to **consider** [kən'sɪdə]	in Betracht ziehen, berücksichtigen	Linda has thought about all kind of careers, but so far she *hasn't considered* medicine.
• **option** ['ɒpʃn]	Möglichkeit, Wahl, Option	*option* = possibility, choice
neutral ['nju:trl]	neutral	I don't agree with you or your brother. I'm completely *neutral* on this issue.
to **emit** [ɪ'mɪt]	absondern, ausstoßen	Factories sometimes *emit* black smoke.
• to **multiply** ['mʌltɪplaɪ]	multiplizieren, vervielfachen	If you *multiply* 6 by 7, the result is 42.
in a nutshell [ɪn‿ə 'nʌtʃel]	kurz und bündig, zusammengefasst	Frank talked about all the things that had gone wrong. *In a nutshell* – he made a stupid mistake.
cruise liner ['kru:z laɪnə]	Kreuzfahrtschiff	! Watch the pronunciation During their vacation they travelled from one harbour to another on a luxurious *cruise liner*.

USEFUL PHRASES

Scientists often publish investigations into different topics and problems. These phrases help you to talk about the results and comment on how informative and convincing you find them.

- Compared to … the numbers/the amount …
- … is low/high …
- … is better/worse than …
- … the most/least …
- … is (not) surprising (because) …
- … is (un)realistic (because) …
- In my experience …
- I think/believe/suppose …
- … is a useful comparison …
- … is a waste of time (because) …

Language: Intercultural page

74	**occasion** [ə'keɪʒn]	Anlass, Gelegenheit	*occasion* = event
	to **dress up** [dres‿'ʌp]	sich herausputzen/feinmachen	*to dress up* = to wear special or formal clothes
	to **invade sth** [ɪn'veɪd]	in etw. eindringen, etw. überfallen	Every summer hundreds of people *invade* the village for the festival.
	tip [tɪp]	Trinkgeld	He paid $80 for the meal, then he gave the waiter a $20 *tip*.
	•**wage** [weɪdʒ]	Lohn	"Do you earn a good *wage*?" – "I get $10 an hour."
	staff [stɑ:f]	Belegschaft, Personal; Kollegium	*the staff* = all the people who work in a firm, a school etc.
	generous ['dʒenrəs]	großzügig	Steve gives a lot of money to charity. He's a very *generous* person.
	wasteful ['weɪstfl]	verschwenderisch	Amy leaves all the lights on, even when she's not at home. That's very *wasteful*.
	gasoline *(AE)* ['gæsli:n]	Benzin	He stopped at the gas station because he needed more *gasoline* for his car.
	to **preserve** [prɪ'zɜ:v]	erhalten, bewahren	We're against the new factory because we want to *preserve* this landscape for future generations.

Language: Everyday English

WORD BANK

75	**cheek** [tʃi:k]	Wange	She kissed her daughter on both *cheeks*.
	elbow ['elbəʊ]	Ell(en)bogen	Many people say it's not polite to put your *elbows* on the table while you're eating.
	wrist [rɪst]	Handgelenk	Your *wrist* is between your hand and your arm.
	thumb [θʌm]	Daumen	Do you hold your pen between your *thumb* and two fingers?
	ankle [æŋkl]	Fußgelenk/-knöchel	Your *ankle* is between your foot and your leg.
	heel [hi:l]	Ferse, Hacke	Your *heel* is the back part of your foot.
	•**-…ache** […eɪk]	-…schmerz(en)	! Watch the pronunciation I've got a head*ache*. = My head hurts.
	•**sore** [sɔ:]	schmerzhaft, wund	I've got a *sore* throat. = My throat hurts.
	to **sprain** [spreɪn]	verstauchen	He fell over and *sprained* his ankle. At least it wasn't broken.
	•**cut** [kʌt]	Schnitt(wunde)	*a cut* → to cut I had an accident with a knife, and now I've got a *cut* on my hand.
	bruise [bru:z]	Prellung, blauer Fleck	She got those *bruises* on her arm when she fell off her bike.
	allergy (to) ['ælədʒɪ]	Allergie (gegen)	I have an *allergy to* cat hair.

allergy rash ['ælədʒɪ ˌræʃ]	allergischer (Haut-)Ausschlag	! Watch the stress and pronunciation "What's wrong with Jenny's skin?" – "She gets an *allergy rash* when she drinks milk."
to **heal up** [hiːl‿'ʌp]	verheilen	I've had this cut for weeks, and it hasn't *healed up* yet.
swollen ['swəʊlən]	geschwollen	Mike can't wear his normal shoes because his feet are *swollen*.
inflamed [ɪn'fleɪmd]	entzündet	After a long hike in stormy weather Mick's eyes were red and *inflamed*.
diarrhoea [ˌdaɪə'rɪə]	Durchfall	! Watch the pronunciation "Why does Laura keep running to the toilet?" – "She's got *diarrhoea* after eating all that fruit."
hay fever ['heɪ ˌfiːvə]	Heuschnupfen	Nick hasn't got a cold. He's got *hay fever* from those flowers.
to **be blocked up** [bi‿blɒkt‿ʌp]	verstopft sein	If your nose is *blocked up*, you have to get your breath through your mouth.
to **sting, stung, stung** [stɪŋ, stʌŋ, stʌŋ]	stechen	Poor Judy got *stung* while we were having our picnic in the field.
to **bite, bit, bitten** [baɪt, bɪt, 'bɪtn]	beißen	Don't worry. Those dogs bark a lot, but they don't *bite*.
to **clear up** [klɪə‿ʌp]	*(hier:)* besser werden	"Has your cold gone now?" – "Yes, it *cleared up* completely after two days."
pill [pɪl]	Pille, Tablette	Take one of these *pills* three times a day after meals.
side effect ['said‿ɪˌfekt]	Nebenwirkung	These pills work very quickly, but they can have nasty *side effects*.
•**chemist's** ['kemɪsts]	Apotheke	The doctor has given me a prescription for some pills. Can you take it to the *chemist's* for me?
•**infection** [ɪn'fekʃn]	Infekt(ion); Ansteckung	She's gone to the doctor's because of an ear *infection*.
to **tear a muscle** [teə‿ə‿'mʌsl]	einen Muskel reißen/zerren	I can't do sports this month because I've *torn a muscle* in my leg.
ointment ['ɔɪntmənt]	Salbe	Put some of this *ointment* on your arm.
•**antibiotic** [ˌæntɪbaɪ'ɒtɪk]	Antibiotikum	You can get rid of an infection with *antibiotic* pills and ointments.
homeopathic [ˌhəʊmiə'pæθɪk]	homöopathisch	Not all doctors believe in *homeopathic* medicine.
•**injection** [ɪn'dʒekʃn]	Spritze, Injektion	Medicine can work very quickly if the doctor gives it to you as an *injection*.
•to **X-ray** ['eksreɪ]	röntgen	A doctor sometimes *x-rays* a patient to see if any bones are broken.
blood sample ['blʌd ˌsɑːmpl]	Blutprobe	A *blood sample* is blood which a doctor wants to examine or test.
specialist ['speʃəlɪst]	Facharzt, Fachärztin	A *specialist* is a doctor who has special knowledge in one field of medicine.
•**illness** ['ɪlnəs]	Krankheit	*illness* → ill
symptom ['sɪmptəm]	Symptom, Merkmal	! Watch the pronunciation and stress I'm sure Tim is suffering from flu. He's got all the *symptoms*.
diagnosis pl. diagnoses [ˌdaɪəg'nəʊsɪs, ˌdaɪəg'nəʊsiːz]	Diagnose	After the doctor had examined Lee, she gave her *diagnosis*.

Conclusion

76 **caption** ['kæpʃn]	Untertitel, Bildunterschrift	The *caption* above the picture said, 'Home at last'.
Mediterranean [ˌmedɪtər'eɪnɪən]	mediterran; Mittelmeer(-)	Italy, Spain and Greece are *Mediterranean* countries.

Vocabulary skills

Compounds

- Find the words that go together to make compound nouns.

pressure • climate • carbon • food • air • nuclear • greenhouse • energy • dioxide • group • chain • gases • change • pollution

- Now write your own example sentences that show you know their meaning.

Topic 4: Make a difference

Don't think it makes no difference

- In 2009, 30 years after Margaret Thatcher became Prime Minister, Andrew C., a British citizen, remembered serving her during his training as a hairdresser in London. In a letter to *The Times* he wrote:
- When she was leader of the opposition, she used to come in every week to have her hair done, and it was my job to wash her hair. On one occasion, while I was busy with the shampoo, she asked whether I had voted. I was a teenager who had just arrived in London and frankly, I was unaware that there were local elections that week. Without realizing how she might react, I replied that I hadn't bothered. This was a big mistake! Horrified, Mrs Thatcher turned in her chair and looked me in the eye. She told me in a quiet voice, but very clearly, how so many people had given their lives for our country to stay a democracy, and that it was my duty to vote. She told me I should never underestimate the importance of the right to vote, and that I should always use that right. She even said she didn't care which party I voted for, just as long as I did so. I felt so embarrassed, but also a bit ashamed of myself. It was an experience I have never forgotten, and a key moment in my life. Ever since I have voted at every election.

Introduction

80 **philosopher** [fɪ'lɒsəfə]	Philosoph/-in	! Watch the stress A *philosopher* studies important ideas about life, truth etc.
social critic [ˌsəʊʃl 'krɪtɪk]	Gesellschaftskritiker/-in	A *social critic* is a person who criticizes aspects of society.
• **citizen** ['sɪtɪzn]	(Staats-)Bürger/-in; Staatsangehörige/-r	There are millions of US *citizens* living outside the United States.
to **rebel against** [rɪ'bel]	rebellieren gegen, sich auflehnen gegen	*to rebel against sth* = to protest or fight against sth
to **be guilty of sth** ['gɪlti]	sich einer Sache schuldig machen	She *was guilty of* the child's death. = She caused the child's death.

behaviour [bɪ'heɪvjə]	Verhalten	*behaviour* → to behave
civil disobedience [ˌsɪvl dɪsə'bi:diəns]	ziviler Ungehorsam	Not to follow laws or pay taxes is an act of *civil disobedience*.
international [ˌɪntə'næʃnl]	international	He works for an *international* company with offices in many countries.
major ['meɪdʒə]	wichtig, bedeutend; Haupt-	*major* = important
ever since [ˌevə 'sɪns]	seitdem	*ever since* = since that time They moved to Boston in 1995, and they've lived there *ever since*.
to **refuse to do sth** [rɪ'fju:z]	sich weigern, etw. zu tun	She *refused to go*. = She said, "No, I will not go!"
tax [tæks]	Steuer, Abgabe	In some countries there are very high *taxes* on alcohol.
ecological [ˌi:kə'lɒdʒɪkl]	Ökologie-; ökologisch	
goal [gəʊl]	Ziel	His *goal* was to become a Hollywood star, but he never achieved it.
right to vote (= suffrage) [raɪt‿tə 'vəʊt; 'sʌfrɪdʒ]	Stimmrecht, Wahlrecht	Everyone over 18 has the *right to vote* in an election.
tactic ['tæktɪk]	Vorgehensweise	Violence is usually the wrong *tactic*. Try to convince people with your arguments.
•**attack** [ə'tæk]	Angriff, Übergriff	*attack* → to attack
to **recognize** ['rekəgnaɪz]	(an)erkennen	Her books *are recognized* as some of the best novels of the 20th century.
adulthood ['ædʌlthʊd]	Erwachsenenalter	*adulthood* ↔ childhood
cure for [kjʊə fɔ:]	Heilmittel gegen	Wendy is ill, but scientists have now found a *cure for* her health problem.
•**such as** ['sʌtʃ‿əz]	wie (zum Beispiel)	*such as* = like
biologist [baɪ'ɒlədʒɪst]	Biologe/Biologin	*a biologist* = a scientist who studies plants and animals
•**discovery** [dɪ'skʌvri]	Entdeckung	*discovery* → to discover
penicillin [ˌpenɪ'sɪlɪn]	Penicillin	! Watch the pronunciation Troy is ill. The doctor says he must take *penicillin*.
to **launch** [lɔ:ntʃ]	starten, einführen, in Gang setzen	*to launch sth* = to start sth important
antibiotic [ˌæntɪbaɪ'ɒtɪk]	antibiotisch, antibakteriell	*Antibiotic* medicines kill many things which could make you ill.
death sentence ['deθ ˌsentəns]	Todesurteil, Todesstrafe	Drinking this dirty water will kill you. – It's a *death sentence*.
treatment ['tri:tmənt]	Versorgung, Behandlung	Don's job is to organise the medical *treatment* of thousands of people.
FACT FILE		
to **be involved in** [ɪn'vɒlvd]	sich beteiligen an, sich engagieren bei/in	Many people *were involved in* preparing this party.
volunteer work [ˌvɒlən'tɪə]	ehrenamtliche Arbeit	A volunteer does *volunteer work*.
81 **preacher** ['pri:tʃə]	Prediger/-in	Many people go to their church to listen to what their *preacher* says.
to **lead, led, led** [li:d, led, led]	anführen	*to lead* → leader
African-American [ˌæfrɪkən‿ə'merɪkən]	Afroamerikaner/-in; afroamerikanisch	An *African-American* is an American whose ancestors came from Africa.
to **end** [end]	beenden	This argument has been going on long enough. We must *end* it.
•**discrimination** [dɪˌskrɪmɪ'neɪʃn]	Diskriminierung	Some black children suffer because of *discrimination* at school.
non-violent [ˌnɒn'vaɪələnt]	friedlich, gewaltfrei	It was a *non-violent* protest march, so no rocks were thrown and nobody was hurt.

to **award sb sth** [ə'wɔ:d]	jmdm. etw. verleihen	In 1993 the Nobel Peace Prize *was awarded* to Nelson Mandela and Frederik Willem de Klerk.
to **assassinate** [ə'sæsɪneɪt]	ermorden	"How did the president die?" – "He was *assassinated* at a meeting."
founder ['faʊndə]	Gründer/-in	*founder* → to found
to **donate** [dəʊ'neɪt]	spenden, stiften	*to donate* = to give money to help people or an organisation
foundation [faʊn'deɪʃn]	Stiftung, Gründung	A *foundation* is an organisation which raises money for charity or another good cause.
healthcare ['helθkeə]	Gesundheitsversorgung	Many countries offer free *healthcare* to everyone.
• **entire** [ɪn'taɪə]	ganz, komplett	*entire* = whole
• **annual** ['ænjʊəl]	jährlich	There is a music festival every year in July. It's an *annual* event.
budget ['bʌdʒɪt]	Haushalt, Etat, Budget	! Watch the pronunciation The government wants to raise the *budget* for education by 5%.
factor ['fæktə]	Faktor, Einfluss	When Ray looks for a new job, the pay is always the main *factor*.
• **awareness** [ə'weənəs]	Interesse, Bewusstsein	People's *awareness* of poverty has improved. = They now know more about it and are more interested.

Vocabulary skills

Related words

■ The more English you read or hear, the more you realize how many words are related to each other in some way. Write down any words you know that have the same root (= come from the same basic word) as the following words or expressions from pages 80-81. Write down the word category (e.g. noun, adjective, verb) in brackets.

Example: breakthrough (noun) – to break (verb) – breakdown (noun)

international • adulthood • discovery • healthcare • critic • death • to lead • foundation • treatment • to end • behaviour

WORD BANK

trailblazer ['treɪlbleɪzə]	Vorreiter/-in, Wegbereiter/-in	Bill Gates is one of the most important IT *trailblazers*.
current ['kʌrənt]	aktuell, derzeitig, gegenwärtig	the *current* situation = the situation at this time
• **future** ['fju:tʃə]	zukünftig	the *future* situation = the situation in the future

USEFUL PHRASES

There are many ways to make a difference in the world. These phrases can help you to talk about the topic.

- I want to make a difference to how people …
- I will/would make a difference by …
- … make the world a better place (for the current/for future generations) …
- It's a good idea to/I think people should/I would …
- … give your time/money to a charity/good cause …
- … is/are/was/were trailblazer(s) …
- … should act as (a) role model(s) …
- On the one hand, … but on the other hand …
- I'm not sure what to think about …
- … celebrity charities are/aren't a good idea …
- I think/believe celebrities should/shouldn't …

USEFUL PHRASES

Here are some words and phrases that help you to discuss the issue of 'having a say' and 'making a difference'.

Having a say
to have a say (on sth)
to have one's say (about sth)
to voice one's opinion
to make a speech
debater
debating skills

Making a difference
volunteer work
to feel passionate about sth
to rebel against
(non-violent) march
to donate/to make a donation
foundation
to aid
to clean up/to fix up sth
to take care of sb
to have/take over responsibility
to take action

Text: Looking for Alibrandi

82 • **speech** [spi:tʃ]	Rede; Sprache	At the conference Sue had to give a *speech* to a large audience.
elite [ɪ'li:t]	Elite	Karen thinks she belongs to the social *elite* just because she knows a few rich people.
Jewish ['dʒu:ɪʃ]	jüdisch	They're very interested in the *Jewish* religion and culture.
to **resemble sb** [rɪ'zembl]	jmdm. ähnlich sehen, jmdm. ähneln	*to resemble sb* = to look like sb
to **belong to** [bɪ'lɒŋ]	gehören zu	She *belongs to* a club. = She is a member of a club.
branch [brɑ:nʃ]	Zweig, Ast; Zweigstelle	This firm is planning to open a new *branch* in Australia.
to **be associated with** [ˌbi_ə'səʊʃieɪtɪd]	verbunden sein mit	A certain type of music *is* often *associated with* Spanish culture.
public school [ˌpʌblɪk 'sku:l]	öffentliche Schule *(AE/AUS)*, Privatschule *(BE)*	a *public school* = In the US and Australia it is a free school for everybody.
• **male** [meɪl]	männlich	*Male* friends are boys and men.
• **female** ['fi:meɪl]	weiblich	*Female* friends are girls and women.
to **block** [blɒk]	blockieren, verstellen	They couldn't go into the building because three people *were blocking* the door.
lane [leɪn]	Weg, Gasse; Fahrspur	*a lane* = a narrow road or path
to **cut through** [kʌt 'θru:]	*(hier:)* eine Abkürzung nehmen durch/über	We *cut through* the park to get to the main road quicker.
to **bombard** [bɒm'bɑ:d]	bombardieren	A violent crowd *bombarded* the police with bottles.
rotten ['rɒtn]	faulig, schlecht geworden	*Rotten* eggs smell really terrible!
• **occasion** [ə'keɪʒn]	*(hier:)* Ereignis	*occasion* = event
• **unlikely** [ʌn'laɪkli]	unwahrscheinlich	It's very *unlikely*. = I'm pretty sure it won't happen.
• to **whisper** ['wɪspə]	flüstern	Steve *whispered* the news in Linda's ear so that nobody else could hear.
• **particular** [pə'tɪkjələ]	bestimmte/-r/-s	*particular* = special "I'm looking for a white T-shirt." – "Any *particular* brand?"
lip [lɪp]	Lippe	Lauren's make-up is so cool. Those brilliant red *lips*!
• **laugh** [lɑ:f]	Lachen	*laugh* → to laugh
to **be flattered** [bi 'flætəd]	geschmeichelt sein	She *was* very *flattered* when everybody said such nice things about her paintings.

to **trip over** [trɪp]	stolpern über	I fell because I *tripped over* a bag which was lying on the ground.
rubbish can ['rʌbɪʃ ˌkæn]	Mülleimer	Don't leave all those bits of food on the table. Put them in the *rubbish can*.
to **be suspended** [ˌbi sə'spendɪd]	suspendiert werden, *(hier:)* zeitweilig vom Unterricht ausgeschlossen werden	When Rebecca broke those windows, she *was suspended* from school for two weeks.
to **tap** [tæp]	antippen	If you want to speak to somebody in front of you, you can *tap* him or her on the shoulder.
to **flirt** [flɜ:t]	flirten	Mary wasn't seriously interested in Pete. She *was* just *flirting*.

Vocabulary skills

Past participles used as adjectives

- You will very often find past participle forms of verbs that are used as adjectives.

  Examples from 'Looking for Albrandi': embarrassed, horrified, disappointed

- Choosing from the verbs in the list below, use suitable past participle forms to complete these sentences. Sometimes you may need a negative form, e.g. **un**known. If this is the case, you will see a negative symbol (–) in brackets.

  to surprise • to recommend • to love • to speak • to expect • to mix •
  to lose • to break • to frighten • to want • to write • to embarrass

  1. It's normal to use more formal style in … English.
  2. The burglars got in through a … window.
  3. I'm not sure which party to vote for. I've got … feelings about both of them.
  4. We were terribly … when our cousin from America suddenly arrived. It was a completely … (–) visit!
  5. People who had an unhappy childhood often feel … (–) and … (–) as adults.
  6. Where's that list of … hotels in Devon that you picked up at the tourist office?

- Which four verbs haven't you used yet? Make your own sentences with adjectives made from the past participle forms of these verbs.

83 • **due to** ['dju: tu:]	infolge von, wegen	*Due to* the bad weather we couldn't have a party on the beach.
stage [steɪdʒ]	Zeitpunkt, Alter	She started telling me about her health problems, but *by that stage* I wasn't listening anyway.
• **embarrassed** [ɪm'bærəst]	verlegen	It was an embarrassing situation, and I felt *embarrassed*.
condom ['kɒndɒm]	Kondom	! Watch the stress Don't risk getting AIDS. Use a *condom*.
to **put sth on** [pʊt‿'ɒn]	etw. überziehen; etw. anziehen	Matt took out the condom, but he didn't know how to *put it on*.
horrified ['hɒrɪfaɪd]	entsetzt	*to be horrified* = to be extremely shocked
to **be ashamed of** [ˌbi‿ə'ʃeɪmd‿əv]	sich schämen für/wegen	He told his sister she was stupid and boring. Later he *was ashamed of* what he had said.
• **vote** [vəʊt]	Abstimmung, Wahl; Wahlrecht	*vote* → to vote In a democracy all adults have the *vote*.
to **sigh in relief** [ˌsaɪ‿ɪn rɪ'li:f]	erleichtert aufatmen/seufzen	When the plane landed safely, everybody *sighed in relief*.

• **disappointed** [dɪsə'pɔɪntɪd]	enttäuscht	The show was disappointing, so the people in the audience were *disappointed*.
party ['pɑ:tɪ]	Partei	Which political *party* will form the next government?
• **promise** ['prɒmɪs]	Versprechen	*promise* → to promise
frankly ['fræŋkli]	offen gestanden, ehrlich gesagt	I don't watch nature films because *frankly*, I think they're boring.
• **voter** ['vəʊtə]	Wähler/-in	A *voter* is a person who votes.
to **get influenced by** [get‿'ɪnflʊənst baɪ]	beeinflusst werden von	Tom has no opinions of his own, so he easily *gets influenced by* other people.
to **knock** [nɒk]	klopfen	Please *knock* at the door before you come in.
to **put no effort into sth** [ˌpʊt nəʊ‿'efət‿ˌɪntə]	sich keine Mühe mit etw. geben	She *put no effort into* her presentation, so it wasn't very good.
dummy vote ['dʌmi vəʊt]	ungültige Stimme	More than ten thousand people voted in the election, and there were only 37 *dummy votes*.
to **bother** ['bɒðə]	sich die Mühe machen, etw. zu tun	He never wants to go out with us. I don't know why you *bother* asking him.
to **register** ['redʒɪstə]	sich registrieren lassen, sich eintragen, sich anmelden	If you want to take part in this course, you must *register* at the office first.
What's the big deal? [ˌwɒts ðə bɪg 'di:l]	Was ist das Problem?, Was ist so wichtig (daran)?	*What's the big deal?* Do you want to go to the cinema or not?
to **call oneself lucky** [ˌkɔ:l wʌnself 'lʌki]	sich glücklich schätzen	You can *call yourself lucky* that you weren't injured in that accident.
to **afford** [ə'fɔ:d]	sich leisten	I'd like to buy a car but I can't *afford* it.
to **take notice** [teɪk 'nəʊtɪs]	beachten, zur Kenntnis nehmen, *(hier:)* aufmerksam werden	When Julie began to sing, everybody in the audience started to *take notice*.
• **motor bike** ['məʊtə baɪk]	Motorrad	Riding a *motor bike* is more exciting than driving a car.
to **have a say** [ˌhæv‿ə 'seɪ]	etw. zu sagen haben, zu Wort kommen; *(hier:)* Mitspracherecht haben	Under a dictator the people *have no say* in the government of their country.
to **get the best party in** [ˌget ðə best 'pɑ:ti ɪn]	die beste Partei an die Macht wählen	When people vote in an election, they hope to *get the best party in*.

FACT FILE

to **establish**	einrichten, gründen, eröffnen	*to establish* = to found
reserved	reserviert, vorbehalten	You can't sit here. These seats *are reserved* for journalists.
entertaining	unterhaltsam	The programme at the theatre was very *entertaining*.
84 **vulgar** ['vʌlgə]	vulgär	*vulgar* = not polite
Prime Minister [ˌpraɪm 'mɪnɪstə]	Premierminister/-in, Ministerpräsident/-in	The *Prime Minister* is the most important member of the government.
leader of the opposition [ˌli:dər‿əv ði‿ˌɒpə'zɪʃn]	Oppositionsführer/-in	The *leader of the opposition* hopes to become the Prime Minister after the next election.
flag [flæg]	Fahne, Flagge	You often see a big *flag* on the top of an official building.
to **break the law** [breɪk ðə 'lɔ:]	gegen das Gesetz verstoßen	*to break the law* = to do sth illegal
trial [traɪəl]	Gerichtsverfahren/ -verhandlung	The police have caught two drug dealers. Their *trial* will begin next month.
one-party system ['wʌnˌpɑ:ti 'sɪstəm]	Einparteiensystem	In countries with a *one-party system* there is no party to criticize or control the government.
to **voice one's opinion** [ˌvɔɪs wʌnz‿ə'pɪnjən]	die eigene Meinung äußern	If you *voice your opinion*, you say what you think.

to **run a country** [rʌn‿ə ˈkʌntri]	ein Land regieren	Not everybody likes the way the government *runs this country.*
• **ignorant** [ˈɪgnərnt]	ahnungslos, unwissend, ignorant	Lewis doesn't know anything about politics, so don't listen to his *ignorant* opinions.
row [rəʊ]	Reihe	! Watch the pronunciation There are thirty *rows* of seats in this cinema.
to **lean forward** [liːn ˈfɔːwəd]	sich nach vorn lehnen	Hazel couldn't see the stage from her seat, so she *leaned forward.*
to **sense** [sens]	spüren, fühlen	*to sense* = to feel
passionate [ˈpæʃənət]	leidenschaftlich	Mark is very interested in Aboriginal culture. He's really *passionate* about it.
• **passion** [ˈpæʃn]	Leidenschaft, Passion	Jenny organises a website about children's rights. That's her *passion.*

WORD BANK

dictatorship [ˌdɪkˈteɪtəʃɪp]	Diktatur	*dictatorship* → dictator

WORD BANK

Linking old and new vocabulary – Politics

You already know a lot of words to do with politics. Now that you have learnt some more, it is useful to revise some of those you have already learnt.

Words you already know		**New words**
activist	government	campaign slogan
Apartheid	to integrate	dictatorship
authoritarian	integration	leader of the opposition
to authorize	law	to make a political speech
to ban	monarch	to make/break a promise
campaign	to pass a law	one-party system
charity	political career	opposition
community	political system	party
consulate	politically active	political aim
democracy	politician	Prime Minister
democratic	politics (*pl.* politics)	right to vote (= suffrage)
dictator	position of power	to run a country
to elect	press conference	senator
election	protest	vote
empire	segregation	voter
empress	superpower	
federal	to vote (for)	

Text: Make A Difference Day awards

85	**level** [ˈlevl]	Ebene	Our drama club takes part in theatre festivals on a regional *level.*
	• to **take place** [teɪk ˈpleɪs]	stattfinden	The Olympic Games *take place* once every four years.
	award-winner [əˈwɔːd ˌwɪnə]	Preisträger/-in	An *award-winner* wins an award or a prize.
	talent [ˈtælənt]	Talent	Laura wants to go to drama school, although she has no *talent* for acting.
	to **take the life of sb** [ˌteɪk ðə ˈlaɪf‿əv]	jmdn. das Leben kosten	The disease *took the lives of* hundreds of people. = It killed them.
	• **out of** [ˈaʊt‿əv]	von	Nine *out of* ten students enjoy sports.
	sibling [ˈsɪblɪŋ]	Bruder/Schwester, Geschwisterkind	*a sibling* = a brother or a sister

• to **aid** [eɪd]	unterstützen, helfen	*to aid* = to support
infant ['ɪnfənt]	Säugling, Kleinkind	*an infant* = a very young child
• **frequent** ['friːkwənt]	häufig	He's a *frequent* customer at our café. = He comes to our café very often.
donation [də'neɪʃn]	Spende; Schenkung, Stiftung	Mike made a *donation* of $100 to a children's charity.
talent show ['tælənt ˌʃəʊ]	Talentwettbewerb	She sang to an audience for the first time at a *talent show* last year.
to **decorate** ['dekreɪt]	dekorieren, schmücken	Tina always *decorates* her room with posters of music groups.
resident ['rezɪdnt]	Anwohner/-in, Einwohner/-in, Bewohner/-in, Ortsansässige/-r	The children's playground was closed because the *residents* didn't like the noise.
to **clean up** [ˌkliːn‿'ʌp]	aufräumen, sauber machen	The morning after the party we had to *clean up*.
to **live up to one's name** [lɪv‿'ʌp tə]	seinem Namen alle Ehre machen	"Can Tom Quick run very fast?" – "Oh yes, he really *lives up to his name*!"
county ['kaʊnti]	Bezirk, (Land-)Kreis	In the US a *county* is part of a state.
• **central** ['sentrl]	zentral	*central* → centre
• **effort** ['efət]	Arbeitsaufwand, Bemühung, Mühe	Everybody made a great *effort* to raise enough money.
to **sign on** [saɪn]	(sich) anmelden, (sich) einschreiben, anheuern	Do you want to come on the Youth Club trip? I'll *sign you on*.
to **perform** [pə'fɔːm]	*(hier:)* leisten, machen	William's boss said he had *performed* all his jobs well.
maintenance ['meɪntənəns]	Instandhaltung, Erhaltung, Pflege	The caretaker does most of the *maintenance* work at our school.
• **helper** ['helpə]	Helfer/-in	*helper* → to help
• to **disappoint** [ˌdɪsə'pɔɪnt]	enttäuschen	I found the movie disappointing. = It *disappointed* me.
• to **fix up** [fɪks‿'ʌp]	in Ordnung bringen, renovieren	Parts of their car were broken, but they managed to *fix it up*.
to **repair** [rɪ'peə]	reparieren	*to repair* = to mend
God [gɒd]	Gott	Many people go to a church to speak to their *God*.
to **take care of sb** [teɪk 'keər‿əv]	sich um jmdn. Kümmern, für jmdn. sorgen	*to take care of sb* = to look after sb

Text: ⟨Daily dilemmas⟩

86 dilemma [daɪ'lemə]	Dilemma, Zwickmühle	I don't know whether to tell my sister the secret or not. It's a real *dilemma*.
• note [nəʊt]	Geldschein	*a note* = a piece of paper money
tram [træm]	Straßenbahn	Public transport is quite good in our town. We have buses and *trams*.
photocopy ['fəʊtəʊˌkɒpi]	Fotokopie	I can't give you my text, but you can make a *photocopy* of it if you like.
• majority (of) [mə'dʒɒrəti]	Mehrheit, Mehrzahl	the *majority* reaction = the reaction of most of the people

WORD BANK

to be caught in a dilemma [ˌbiː 'kɔːt‿ɪn‿ə daɪ'lemə]	in einer Zwickmühle stecken	*I'm caught in a dilemma.* I don't know what to do.
to develop a sense of sth [dɪˌveləp‿ə 'sens‿əv]	ein Gefühl/Gespür für etw. entwickeln	Lee *has developed a strong sense of* right and wrong. He always feels what action is the right one.
honesty ['ɒnɪsti]	Ehrlichkeit	Anna never says anything which isn't true. I admire her *honesty*.

• honest ['ɒnɪst] dishonest [dɪ'sɒnɪst]	ehrlich unehrlich	A person who is *honest* doesn't tell lies. *dishonest* ↔ honest

USEFUL PHRASES

There are situations in which it is very clear what the right thing to do is, but in others, it is harder to decide. These phrases can help you discuss this problem:

- It's important to have/develop a sense of right and wrong.
- In my opinion, the right/wrong thing to do would be …
- I (don't) believe people are born with a sense of right and wrong.
- My role models have always been …
- … treat others as you would want to be treated yourself.
- I (don't) think people should …
- It's a problem if …
- I think/believe/am of the opinion that it is important to …
- … to be honest/dishonest …

VIP FILE

87	• to consist of [kən'sɪst‿əv]	bestehen aus	Our *family* consists of five people: my parents, my two brothers and me.
	catchy ['kætʃi]	eingängig, einprägsam	A commercial often has a short *catchy* song that everybody can remember.
	tune [tju:n]	Melodie	I know the lyrics of the song but I've forgotten the *tune*.
	shop window [ˌʃɒp 'wɪndəʊ]	Schaufenster	Most people look at the *shop windows* as they walk along the street.
	pavement ['peɪvmənt]	Bürgersteig	On both sides of a road there is usually a *pavement* for people to walk on.
	• to rest [rest]	ausruhen; rasten; übernachten	*to rest* = to stop moving and relax
	• northern ['nɔ:ðn]	nördlich	He lives in a *northern* city. = He's from a city in the north.
	part [pɑ:t]	Stadtteil, Gegend	*part* = region
	attention [ə'tenʃn]	Aufmerksamkeit	Kerry always gets people's *attention* because of her crazy clothes.
	• cash [kæʃ]	Bargeld	He looked in his pockets and found that he had only £2.45 in *cash*.
	opera ['ɒprə]	Oper	Rob often goes to the theatre to see plays, but he's never been to an *opera*.
	to be set in [bi 'set‿ɪn]	spielen in	The movie *is set in* New York. = The action happens in New York.
	to switch back and forth [swɪtʃ 'bæk‿ənd ˌfɔ:θ]	hin und her wechseln/schalten	She *switched back and forth* between two TV channels.
	songwriter ['sɒŋˌraɪtə]	Liedermacher/-in	A *songwriter* writes the lyrics and the music of a song.

Text: A historic speech

88	**historic** [hɪ'stɒrɪk]	historisch	A *historic* event is important in history.
	rarely ['reəli]	selten	*rarely* ↔ often
	reputation [ˌrepjə'teɪʃn]	Ruf, Ansehen	Their new English teacher had a *reputation* for being very strict.
	• **unpopular** [ʌn'pɒpjələ]	unpopulär, unbeliebt	*unpopular* ↔ popular
	• **majority (of)** [mə'dʒɒrəti]	Mehrheit, Mehrzahl	the *majority of* Americans = most Americans

campaign slogan [kæm'peɪn ˌsləʊgən]	Wahlkampfparole	If they want to win the next election, they need a good *campaign slogan*.
• **synonym** ['sɪnənɪm]	Synonym	! Watch the pronunciation and stress Two words which have the same meaning are *synonyms*, for example 'big' and 'large'.
• **responsibility** [rɪˌspɒnsə'bɪləti]	Verantwortung	James is a hospital doctor with *responsibility* for hundreds of patients.
quote [kwəʊt]	Zitat	When you're writing about celebrities, don't forget to use *quotes* from their interviews.
• **shortcut** ['ʃɔ:tkʌt]	Abkürzung	If we take a *shortcut* through the park, we can get to the main road quicker.
satisfying ['sætɪsfaɪɪŋ]	befriedigend, zufriedenstellend	It's a *satisfying* feeling when you know you've done your work well.
• **task** [tɑ:sk]	Aufgabe; Auftrag	Organising a student conference is not an easy *task*.
to **remake, remade, remade** [ˌri:'meɪk, ˌri:'meɪd, ˌri:'meɪd]	erneuern	Obama wants to *remake* America. = He wants to create the country again in a better form.
• **according to** [ə'kɔ:dɪŋ tə]	laut, gemäß	*According to* this website, most people have a positive opinion about the future.
inspiring [ɪn'spaɪərɪŋ]	inspirierend, anregend	I feel I could achieve anything after listening to those words. They're so *inspiring*.
to **appreciate** [ə'pri:ʃieɪt]	würdigen, anerkennen, schätzen	Everybody *appreciated* the students' hard work, but some people thought they had not been very successful.
effective [ɪ'fektɪv]	effektiv, nachhaltig	The new medicine didn't make Carrie feel better. It wasn't very *effective*.

VIP FILE

senator ['senətə]	Senator/-in	! Watch the pronunciation Two *senators* represent each state in the US government.

WORD BANK

It's a given that ... [ɪts‿ə 'gɪvn ðæt]	Es ist offensichtlich, dass ...	*It's a given that* everybody would like to live in peace.
• **prosperity** [prɒs'perətɪ]	Wohlstand, Gedeihen	In times of *prosperity* people have enough money and can have a good life.
• **prosperous** ['prɒsprəs]	wohlhabend; blühend	! Watch the pronunciation and stress *prosperous* → prosperity
to **meet the demands of sb/sth** [ˌmi:t ðə dɪ'mɑ:ndz‿əv]	den Anforderungen von jmdm./etw. nachkommen	Sharon left college because she couldn't *meet the demands of* the course.
common purpose [ˌkɒmən 'pɜ:pəs]	gemeinsames Ziel	The people in the group were very different from each other, but they had a *common purpose*.
necessity [nə'sesətɪ]	Notwendigkeit	! Watch the pronunciation We really need more help from the state. That's a *necessity*.
• to **struggle** ['strʌgl]	kämpfen, Mühe haben, ringen, sich anstrengen	*to struggle* = to fight
to **sacrifice** ['sækrɪfaɪs]	opfern	Would you *sacrifice* your career to look after the poor?
era ['ɪərə]	Ära, Zeitalter	The invention of the steam engine meant the start of a new *era*.
charismatic [ˌkærɪz'mætɪk]	charismatisch	Speeches can be boring – but not if they are given by a *charismatic* speaker.
to **win sb over** [wɪn‿'əʊvə]	jmdn. für sich gewinnen, jmdn. überzeugen	At first we were against Dean's plan, but finally he *won us over* with his arguments.

Text: Film page

	TIP		
89	to **confuse sth/sb with sth/sb** [kən'fju:z wɪð]	etw./jmdn. mit etw./jmdm. verwechseln	Don't *confuse* American football *with* rugby. They're two different games.
	to **be based on** [bi 'beɪst‿ɒn]	basieren auf, beruhen auf, sich stützen auf	Helen's novel *is based on* her own experiences in India.
	maker ['meɪkə]	Macher/-in	Politicians are decision and policy *makers*.
	to **take liberties with** [teɪk 'lɪbətiz wɪð]	es nicht so genau nehmen mit	Don't *take liberties with* my words! Please tell Harry exactly what I said!
	to **keep from** ['ki:p frəm]	bewahren vor; abhalten; fernhalten	I hope I'm not *keeping* you *from* your work. I think we should *keep* the truth *from* her until she's feeling better.
	pure [pjʊə]	rein	This is 100 % *pure* apple juice.
	original footage [eˌrɪdʒnl 'fʊtɪdʒ]	originales Filmmaterial	People see live *footage* of the war at home on their televisions.
	WORD BANK		
	film adaptation [ˌfɪlm ə'dæpʃn]	Verfilmung	This is a *film adaptation* of a book.
	criterion pl. criteria [kraɪ'tɪəriən, kraɪ'tɪəriə]	Kriterium, Argument	What are your *criteria* for judging a person's character?
	to **set up** [set‿'ʌp]	errichten, aufbauen; gründen	Before they started to climb the mountains, they *set up* a new campsite.
	research camp [rɪ'sɜ:tʃ ˌkæmp]	Forschungslager, -station	*a research camp* = a campsite for people doing research
	jungle ['dʒʌŋgl]	Dschungel	Many different kinds of animals and plants live in the *jungles* of Asia and South America.
	to **communicate with** [kə'mju:nɪkeɪt wɪð]	kommunizieren mit	I use my phone and the Internet to *communicate with* my friends.
	to **become extinct** [bɪˌkʌm‿ɪk'stɪŋkt]	aussterben	There are very few of these animals still alive. We must save them before they become *extinct*.
	to **poach** [pəʊtʃ]	wildern	*to poach* = to catch or kill animals illegally
	to **reduce** [rɪ'dju:s]	reduzieren, verringern	If you *reduce* something, you make it smaller.
	• **cruel** ['kru:əl]	grausam	I'm against all forms of entertainment which are *cruel* to animals.
	• to **take action** [teɪk‿'ækʃn]	handeln, eingreifen	It's not enough just to think about these problems. We must *take action*.
	• **method** ['meθəd]	Methode, Art	Jacky learns new vocabulary with her book, but Daniel has a different *method*.
	to **appear** [ə'pɪə]	erscheinen; auftauchen	His article *appeared* in a science magazine last month.
	cover ['kʌvə]	Cover, Titelblatt	Some people decide to buy a CD or a magazine because the *cover* looks interesting.
	part [pɑ:t]	Rolle	Have you learned your *part* yet?

Language: Form and function

90	**animal shelter** ['ænɪml ˌʃeltə]	Tierheim	*an animal shelter* = a home for animals which have been rescued
	routine [ru:'ti:n]	*(hier:)* Tagesablauf	Going swimming isn't part of Connie's *routine*. She just does it when she's on vacation.
91	to **include** [ɪn'klu:d]	beinhalten, einschließen	Our trip to Australia will *include* a week in the outback and two days in Sydney.

to **escape (from)** [ɪ'skeɪp]	entkommen, (ent)fliehen	Fiona had to listen to her uncle's boring story for twenty minutes before she managed to *escape* to her room.
rabbit ['ræbɪt]	Kaninchen	Jimmy's first pet was a white *rabbit* with long ears.
snake [sneɪk]	Schlange	*Snakes* are often very beautiful, but they can be dangerous.
pet shop ['pet ʃɒp]	Zoogeschäft, -handlung	You can buy food and toys for your pets at a *pet shop*.
fur [fɜː]	Fell	Most people like animals with *fur* like dogs, cats and horses. But some people are allergic to them!
• **past** [pɑːst]	letzte/-r/-s, vergangen	the *past* two weeks = the two weeks before now
• **previous** ['priːviəs]	vorherig, vorausgegangen, vorig	Linda went to London last Saturday. She spent the *previous* three weekends with her parents.

Language: Intercultural page

92 **expression** [ɪk'spreʃn]	Ausdruck, Wendung, Äußerung	*expression* → to express Do you know a polite *expression* for 'shut up'?
gradually ['grædʒʊəli]	allmählich, langsam	*gradually* ↔ suddenly I think our climate is *gradually* becoming warmer.
flight attendant ['flaɪt əˌtendnt]	Flugbegleiter/-in	*Flight attendants* look after the passengers on a plane.
holiday ['hɒlədeɪ]	Feiertag	*Happy Holidays!* instead of Merry Christmas!
significant [sɪg'nɪfɪkənt]	bedeutend, signifikant, wesentlich	*significant* = important
art director ['ɑːt dɪˌrektə]	künstlerischer Leiter/ künstlerische Leiterin	The *art director* decides about the photos and pictures in a magazine or on a website.
employee [ɪm'plɔɪiː]	Angestellte/-r; Mitarbeiter/-in; Arbeitnehmer/-in	*employee* ↔ employer
secretary ['sekrətri]	Sekretär/-in	The boss's *secretary* has to make phone calls, plan meetings and book flights.
• **ad (= advertisement)** [æd, əd'vɜːtɪsmənt]	Anzeige, Annonce; Werbespot	If you're looking for a weekend job, you should read the *ads* in the local newspaper.
colleague ['kɒliːg]	Kollege/Kollegin	The people you work with are your *colleagues*.
• **lately** ['leɪtlɪ]	in letzter Zeit, kürzlich	*lately* = recently
chairman pl. **chairmen** ['tʃeəmən, 'tʃeəmæn]	Vorsitzender, Präsident	*chairman* ↔ chairwoman Larry hopes to become the new *chairman* of the organisation.
to **open up** [ˌəʊpn‿'ʌp]	sich auftun, sich bieten, sich eröffnen	Matt thought he would never be successful, but then a new possibility *opened up* for him.
executive [ɪg'zekjətɪv]	Direktor/-in, Geschäftsführer/-in	! Watch the stress and pronunciation *an executive* = a manager in a company
offensive [ə'fensɪv]	angreifend, beleidigend; anstößig	*offensive* = extremely rude

Language: Everyday English

WORD BANK

93 to **enquire about sth/sb** [ɪn'kwaɪə]	sich nach etw./jmdm. erkundigen	*to enquire about sth* = to ask for information about sth/sb
inconvenient [ˌɪnkən'viːniənt]	unbequem, lästig	'An *inconvenient* truth' is the title of Al Gore's film.
complaint [kəm'pleɪnt]	Beschwerde	I'd like to make a *complaint* about the noise.
• **dentist** ['dentɪst]	Zahnarzt/Zahnärztin	A *dentist* looks after your teeth.

convenient [kən'vi:nɪənt]	angenehm, passend	Is one o'clock a *convenient* time to meet, or are you busy then?
to **ring back** [rɪŋ 'bæk]	zurückrufen	Sorry, Julia isn't here at the moment. Would you like her to *ring back?*
car rental ['kɑ:ˌrentl]	Autovermietung, -verleih	We can travel by train, or we can use a car from a *car rental* firm.
to **fetch** [fetʃ]	(ab)holen	Could you go to the kitchen and *fetch* Tony, please? I want to speak to him.
•to **hang on** [hæŋ'ɒn]	(einen Augenblick) warten	*Hang on*, please. = Wait a moment.
meeting ['mi:tɪŋ]	Besprechung, Treffen	I'm afraid you can't talk to her because she's in a *meeting* with important customers.
engaged [ɪn'geɪdʒd]	besetzt, belegt	The line *was engaged* when Laura called Jim because he was calling Amy at the same time.
•to **take a message** [ˌteɪk ə 'mesɪdʒ]	eine Nachricht entgegennehmen/notieren	Did Mr Sanchez ask you to *take a message* when he called?
to **put sb through** [pʊt'θru:]	jmdn. durchstellen/verbinden	Max phoned the hotel, and somebody *put him through* to the restaurant.
department [dɪ'pɑ:tmənt]	Abteilung	He works in the marketing *department* of a big computer company.
shelter ['ʃeltə]	Obdach, Unterstand	After the terrible earthquake many people were without food and *shelter.*
•to **learn** [lɜ:n]	erfahren, herausfinden	*to learn* = to find out
answering machine ['ɑ:nsrɪŋ məˌʃi:n]	Anrufbeantworter	Tanya was out when I called, so I left a message on her *answering machine.*
institution [ˌɪnstɪ'tju:ʃn]	Einrichtung, Institution, Organisation	*an institution* = an organisation

Conclusion

94 •**aim** [eɪm]	Absicht, Ziel	"What's the *aim* behind all this advertising?" – "We want to get people interested in the environment."
•to **analyze** ['ænəlaɪz]	analysieren, untersuchen	*to analyze* = to examine carefully
approach [ə'prəʊtʃ]	Herangehensweise, Annäherung, Ansatz	She still hadn't managed to convince Terry, so she decided to try a different *approach.*
mission ['mɪʃn]	Mission, Auftrag	Our *mission* is to save this landscape for future generations.
95 •**criticism** ['krɪtɪsɪsm]	Kritik	If you criticize something, you express *criticism.*
opposing side [ə'pəʊzɪŋ saɪd]	gegenüberstehende/gegnerische Seite/Partei/Mannschaft	A player from the *opposing side* suffered an injury during the match.

Dictionary

The following alphabetical word list contains the entire vocabulary of *Green Line 6 Transition*. A separate list of names can be found at the end of the Dictionary. Verbs marked with an asterisk * are irregular.

The numbers and letters of each entry tell you where a word or phrase occurs for the first time e.g. **abuse** Missbrauch **T2**, 34 occurs first in Topic 2, page 34. Angle brackets ⟨ ⟩ indicate that the word is optional.

A

a couple of [ə 'kʌpl‿əv] einige, ein paar **T1**, 11
a host of [ə 'həʊst‿əv] ein Heer an, jede Menge **T2**, 35
abbreviation [əˌbri:vi'eɪʃn] Abkürzung **T3**, 72
ability [ə'bɪləti] Fähigkeit **T1**, 16
abortion [ə'bɔ:ʃn] Abtreibung ⟨**T1**, 19⟩
*to be **absorbed into sth** [bi‿əb'zɔ:bd‿ˌɪntə] in etw. integriert werden ⟨**T2**, 44⟩
abundance pl. **abundance** [ə'bʌndəns] Fülle, Reichtum ⟨**T3**, 58⟩
abuse [ə'bju:s] Missbrauch **T2**, 34
racial abuse [ˌreɪʃl‿ə'bju:s] Rassendiskriminierung **T2**, 34
to **abuse** [ə'bju:z] missbrauchen, misshandeln; beschimpfen **T2**, 36
academic [ˌækə'demɪk] Akademiker/-in, Gelehrte/-r; akademisch ⟨**T2**, 43⟩; ⟨**T3**, 71⟩
acceptable [ək'septəbl] akzeptabel, annehmbar **T3**, 67
to **accomplish** [ə'kʌmplɪʃ] vollbringen, erreichen, bewerkstelligen ⟨**T3**, 70⟩
accomplishment [ə'kʌmplɪʃmənt] Errungenschaft, Leistung **T1**, 10
according to [ə'kɔ:dɪŋ tə] laut, gemäß **T2**, 39; **T3**, 70; **T4**, 88
to **account for** [ə'kaʊnt fə] ausmachen, betragen **T1**, 14; **T3**, 70
to **accuse** (sb of sth) [ə'kju:z] (jmdn. einer Sache) beschuldigen; anklagen **T1**, 14
... ache [...eɪk] ... schmerz(en) **T3**, 75
acid rain [ˌæsɪd 'reɪn] saurer Regen **T3**, 58
*to make no **acknowledgement of sth** [ˌmeɪk nəʊ ək'nɒlɪdʒmənt‿əv] etw. nicht an die große Glocke hängen ⟨**T2**, 44⟩
right **across** [ˌraɪt‿ə'krɒs] quer über ⟨**T2**, 35⟩
to **act like** ['ækt laɪk] handeln wie; fungieren als **T3**, 61
to act one's age [ˌækt wʌnz‿'eɪdʒ] altersgemäß handeln ⟨**T1**, 19⟩
to act responsibly [ækt rɪs'pɒnsəbli] verantwortlich handeln ⟨**T1**, 9⟩
*to take **action** [teɪk‿'ækʃn] handeln, eingreifen **T4**, 89
ad (= advertisement) [æd, əd'vɜ:tɪsmənt] Anzeige, Annonce; Werbespot **T4**, 92
film **adaption** [ˌfɪlm‿ə'dæpʃn] Verfilmung **T4**, 89
to **add** (to sth) [æd] (etw.) ergänzen **T3**, 58
to **address** [ə'dres] ansprechen; adressieren **T3**, 58
to address sb [ə'dres] sich an jmdn. wenden, jmdn. ansprechen **T2**, 39
adequate ['ædɪkwət] ausreichend, adäquat, angemessen ⟨**T2**, 34⟩
*to give a baby up for **adoption** [ˌgɪv‿ə beɪbi‿'ʌp fər‿ə'dɒpʃn] ein Baby zur Adoption freigeben ⟨**T1**, 19⟩
adrenaline rush [ə'drenlɪn ˌrʌʃ] Adrenalinstoß ⟨**T1**, 11⟩
adulthood ['ædʌlthʊd] Erwachsenenalter **T4**, 80
aeroplane ['eərəpleɪn] Flugzeug ⟨**T3**, 73⟩
to **affect** [ə'fekt] beeinflussen, beeinträchtigen; betreffen **T3**, 71
to **afford** [ə'fɔ:d] sich leisten **T4**, 83
African-American [ˌæfrɪkənə'merɪkən] Afroamerikaner/-in; afroamerikanisch **T4**, 81
Black African [blæk 'æfrɪkən] Schwarzafrikaner/-in; schwarzafrikanisch **T2**, 33
Afro-Caribbean [ˌæfrəʊkærɪ'bi:ən] Afrokaribe/Afrokaribin; afrokaribisch **T2**, 34
age limit [ˌeɪdʒ 'lɪmɪt] Altersgrenze **T1**, 8
age of consent [ˌeɪdʒ‿əv kən'sent] (Ehe-)Mündigkeitsalter **T1**, 8
to act one's age [ˌækt wʌnz‿'eɪdʒ] altersgemäß handeln ⟨**T1**, 19⟩
to **age** [eɪdʒ] altern, reifen **T2**, 36
in **agreement** [ˌɪn‿ə'gri:mənt] zustimmend, voller Zustimmung ⟨**T4**, 82⟩
surface damage agreement [ˌsɜ:fɪs ˌdæmɪdʒ ə'gri:mənt] Vereinbarung für Oberflächenschäden ⟨**T3**, 63⟩
agricultural [ˌægrɪ'kʌltʃrl] landwirtschaftlich, Agrar- **T3**, 70
ahead of [ə'hed‿əv] vor **T3**, 64
up ahead [ˌʌp‿ə'hed] vor **T1**, 12
to **aid** [eɪd] unterstützen, helfen **T4**, 85
aim [eɪm] Ziel, Absicht **T4**, 94
to **aim at** ['eɪm‿ət] zielen auf, sich richten an **T2**, 34
All right. [ɔ:l 'raɪt] O.k., Also gut., In Ordnung., Alles klar. **T1**, 10
all-star ['ɔ:lstɑ:] Gala-, Star-, Spitzen- ⟨**T4**, 81⟩
all the rage [ˌɔ:l ðə 'reɪdʒ] der letzte Schrei, der Hit ⟨**T2**, 44⟩
all the while [ˌɔ:l ðə 'waɪl] die ganze Zeit über **T1**, 13; ⟨**T3**, 62⟩
all-time low [ˌɔ:ltaɪm 'ləʊ] historisches Tief, historischer Tiefpunkt ⟨**T4**, 88⟩
allergy (to) ['ælədʒi] Allergie (gegen) **T3**, 75
allergy rash ['ælədʒi ˌræʃ] allergischer (Haut-)Ausschlag **T3**, 75
alligator ['ælɪgeɪtə] Alligator ⟨**T3**, 72⟩
let **alone** [ˌlet‿ə'ləʊn] geschweige denn ⟨**T2**, 44⟩
alternative [ɔ:l'tɜ:nətɪv] alternativ; abwechselnd **T3**, 58
amount (of) [ə'maʊnt] Menge; Betrag, Summe **T3**, 63
analysis [ə'næləsɪz] Analyse, Untersuchung ⟨**T2**, 35⟩
to **analyze** ['ænlaɪz] analysieren, untersuchen **T3**, 67; **T4**, 94
to **anchor offshore** [ˌæŋkər‿'ɒfʃɔ:] im Hafen liegen **T3**, 65
animal shelter ['ænɪml ˌʃeltə] Tierheim **T4**, 90
animated ['ænɪmeɪtɪd] lebhaft; Zeichentrick- **T3**, 69
animation [ˌænɪ'meɪʃn] Animation, Zeichentrickfilm **T3**, 68
ankle ['æŋkl] Fußgelenk/-knöchel **T3**, 75
anniversary [ˌænɪ'vɜ:sri] Jahrestag, Jubiläum **T1**, 24

to mark an anniversary [ˌmɑ:k‿ən‿ænɪ'vɜ:sri] ein Jubiläum feiern, einen Feiertag begehen **T2,** 50
annual ['ænjuəl] jährlich **T4,** 81
one **another** [ˌwʌn‿ə'nʌðə] einander, gegenseitig ⟨**T1,** 22⟩
answering machine ['ɑ:nsrɪŋ məˌʃi:n] Anrufbeantworter **T4,** 93
antibiotic [ˌæntɪbaɪ'ɒtɪk] Antibiotikum **T3,** 75; antibiotisch, antibakteriell **T4,** 80
*to overcome **anxiety** [əʊvəˌkʌm‿æŋ'zaɪəti] Angst überwinden ⟨**T4,** 84⟩
anyhow ['enihaʊ] trotzdem, sowieso **T3,** 63
apocalypse [ə'pɒkəlɪps] Apokalypse, Weltuntergang ⟨**T3,** 60⟩
apparently [ə'pærntli] anscheinend **T1,** 20
to **appeal to sb** [ə'pi:l] jmdm. zusagen, jmdm. gefallen **T3,** 58
to **appear** [ə'pɪə] auftauchen; erscheinen **T4,** 89
to **apply** (to) [ə'plaɪ] gelten (für), zutreffen (auf) ⟨**T2,** 48⟩; **T3,** 69; anwenden (bei) ⟨**T3,** 73⟩
to **appreciate** [ə'pri:ʃieɪt] schätzen, würdigen, anerkennen **T4,** 88
approach [ə'prəʊtʃ] Annäherung, Ansatz, Herangehensweise **T4,** 94
nod of **approval** [ˌnɒd‿əv‿ə'pru:vl] zustimmendes Nicken ⟨**T4,** 82⟩
aquifer ['ækwɪfə] Grundwasserleiter, Grundwasser führende Schicht ⟨**T3,** 64⟩
archetype ['ɑ:kɪtaɪp] Archetyp/-us *(Urform einer Figur)* ⟨**T3,** 64⟩
character archetype [ˌkærəktə 'ɑ:kɪtaɪp] Archetyp/-us *(Urform einer Figur)* **T1,** 14
argumentative essay [ɑ:gjəˌmentətɪv 'eseɪ] Erörterung **T2,** 45
people's **army** ['pi:plz‿ɑ:mi] Bürgerwehr, Volksarmee ⟨**T4,** 84⟩
arranged marriage [əˌreɪndʒd 'mærɪdʒ] arrangierte Hochzeit **T2,** 38
*to be **arrested** [ˌbi ə'restɪd] festgenommen/verhaftet werden **T3,** 66
arrow ['ærəʊ] Pfeil **T1,** 20
arson ['ɑ:sn] Brandstiftung ⟨**T1,** 14⟩; ⟨**T4,** 80⟩
art director ['ɑ:t dɪˌrektə] künstlerischer Leiter/künstlerische Leiterin **T4,** 92
art supply ['ɑ:t səˌplaɪ] Künstlerbedarf ⟨**T4,** 85⟩
art-therapy ['ɑ:t ˌθerəpi] Kunsttherapie ⟨**T4,** 85⟩
artistic license [ɑ:ˌtɪstɪk 'laɪsns] künstlerische Freiheit ⟨**T4,** 89⟩
as if [əz‿'ɪf] als ob **T1,** 21
as though [əz 'ðəʊ] als ob **T2,** 37
. . . as well as . . . [əz 'wel‿əz] sowohl … als auch … **T3,** 71
to **ascend** [ə'send] (auf)steigen, ansteigen **T3,** 60
*to be **ashamed of** [bi‿ə'ʃeɪmd‿əv] sich schämen für/wegen **T2,** 39; **T4,** 83
aspiration [ˌæspɪ'reɪʃn] Hoffnung; (Be-)Streben ⟨**T2,** 44⟩
to **assassinate** [ə'sæsɪneɪt] ermorden **T4,** 81
assault [ə'sɔ:lt] Übergriff, Angriff, Tätlichkeit **T1,** 14
personal assault [ˌpɜ:snl‿ə'sɔ:lt] Körperverletzung ⟨**T1,** 14⟩
sexual assault [ˌsekʃʊəl‿ə'sɔ:lt] Vergewaltigung, sexuelle Nötigung ⟨**T1,** 14⟩
to **associate** [ə'səʊʃieɪt] assoziieren, verbinden **T3,** 65
to be associated with [ˌbi‿ə'səʊʃieɪtɪd] verbunden sein mit **T4,** 82
at that point [ət ðæt 'pɔɪnt] in diesem Moment ⟨**T1,** 11⟩
attack [ə'tæk] Angriff, Übergriff **T4,** 80
to **attempt** [ə'tempt] versuchen **T1,** 16
flight **attendant** ['flaɪt əˌtendnt] Flugbegleiter/-in **T4,** 92
attention [ə'tenʃn] Aufmerksamkeit **T4,** 87
attitude (to/towards) ['ætɪtju:d] Einstellung, Haltung **T1,** 28; **T2,** 36; **T3,** 60
attorney *(AE)* [ə'tɜ:ni] (Rechts-)Anwalt/Anwältin, Staatsanwalt/-anwältin, Jurist/-in **T3,** 64
authority [ɔ:'θɒrəti] Autorität; Behörde ⟨**T4,** 83⟩
average ['ævrɪdʒ] Durchschnitt; Durchschnitts- **T3,** 70
to **avoid** [ə'vɔɪd] ausweichen, (ver)meiden, aus dem Weg gehen **T1,** 12; (ver)meiden **T3,** 68
award-winner [ə'wɔ:d ˌwɪnə] Preisträger/-in **T4,** 85
to **award sb sth** [ə'wɔ:d] jmdm. etw. verleihen **T4,** 81
*to be **aware of sth** [bi‿ə'weə] sich einer Sache bewusst sein **T3,** 60
awareness [ə'weənəs] Bewusstseinsbildung, Sensibilisierung ⟨**T2,** 44⟩; Bewusstsein, Interesse **T4,** 81
awareness-raising [ə'weənəsˌreɪzɪŋ] bewusstseinsbildend, sensibilisierend ⟨**T2,** 44⟩
to raise awareness of [ˌreɪz‿ə'weənəs] das Bewusstsein schärfen für, sensibilisieren für **T3,** 58
awhile [ə'waɪl] für eine Weile ⟨**T3,** 62⟩
awkward ['ɔ:kwəd] ungünstig, ungeschickt, unbeholfen; peinlich **T1,** 13

B

b. (= born) [bɔ:n] geb. (= geboren) ⟨**T4,** 81⟩
to **back away** [ˌbæk‿ə'weɪ] zurückweichen **T1,** 13
bacterial illness [bækˌtɪəriəl 'ɪlnəs] bakterielle Erkrankung ⟨**T4,** 80⟩
baked beans *(pl.)* [ˌbeɪkt 'bi:nz] gebackene Bohnen **T2,** 49
baked potato [ˌbeɪkt pə'teɪtəʊ] Ofenkartoffel **T3,** 62
ban [bæn] Bann, Sperre, Verbot **T3,** 61
bandana *(AE)* [bæn'dænə] Kopftuch, Schal ⟨**T3,** 67⟩
to **bang drums** [bæŋ 'drʌmz] trommeln **T3,** 65
Bangladeshi [ˌbæŋglə'deʃi] Bangladescher/-in; bangladeschisch **T2,** 33
banner ['bænə] Transparent, Fahne, Banner **T3,** 65
Baptist ['bæptɪst] baptistisch; Baptist/-in ⟨**T4,** 81⟩
bar [bɑ:] Bar, Imbiss(stube) ⟨**T2,** 49⟩
bar owner ['bɑ:r‿əʊnə] Kneipenbesitzer/-in **T3,** 64
safety bar ['seɪfti bɑ:] Sicherheitsbügel ⟨**T1,** 22⟩
barber ['bɑ:bə] Friseurgeschäft/-salon für Herren **T2,** 35
barely ['beəli] kaum **T1,** 13
*to be **based on** [bi 'beɪst‿ɒn] basieren auf; beruhen auf, sich stützen auf **T2,** 41; **T4,** 89
-based [beɪst] ansässig in **T3,** 70; -bezogen ⟨**T4,** 92⟩
basically ['beɪsɪkli] eigentlich, grundsätzlich, im Grunde genommen **T1,** 25
to **battle** ['bætl] (be)kämpfen ⟨**T4,** 85⟩
B&B *(= bed and breakfast)* [ˌbi:‿ənd 'bi:; ˌbed‿ənd‿'brekfəst] Frühstückspension **T1,** 28
*to **be about to do sth** [bi‿ə'baʊt tə] im Begriff sein, etw. zu tun **T2,** 38
to be absorbed into sth [bi‿əb'zɔ:bd‿ɪntə] in etw. integriert werden ⟨**T2,** 44⟩
to be arrested [ˌbi ə'restɪd] festgenommen/verhaftet werden **T3,** 66
to be ashamed of [bi‿ə'ʃeɪmd‿əv] sich schämen für/wegen **T2,** 39; **T4,** 83

to be associated with [ˌbiˌəˈsəʊʃieɪtɪd] verbunden sein mit **T4,** 82
to be at sth's heart [hɑːt] im Zentrum von etw. stehen **T2,** 46
to be aware of sth [biˌəˈweə] sich einer Sache bewusst sein **T3,** 60
to be based on [bi ˈbeɪstˌɒn] basieren auf; beruhen auf, sich stützen auf **T2,** 41; **T4,** 89
to be blocked up [ˌbiˌblɒktˈʌp] verstopft sein **T3,** 75
to be caught in a dilemma [ˌbi ˈkɔːtˌɪnˌə daɪˈlemə] in einer Zwickmühle stecken **T4,** 86
to be caught up in the moment [ˌbi kɔːtˈʌp ɪn ðə ˈməʊmənt] in dem Moment gefangen sein, vertieft sein **T3,** 67
to be close to [ˈkləʊs tə] in der Nähe sein von, nahe sein an ⟨**T2,** 36⟩
to be close to doing sth [ˈkləʊs tə] nahe daran sein, etw. zu tun **T1,** 22
to be confined (to) [kənˈfaɪnd] beschränkt sein (auf) ⟨**T2,** 35⟩
to be dumb scared [dʌm ˈskeəd] Todesängste ausstehen ⟨**T1,** 23⟩
to be equal (to) [ˈiːkwəl] entsprechen **T3,** 70
to be equivalent to sth [ɪˈkwɪvlənt] etw. entsprechen ⟨**T3,** 70⟩
to be flattered [bi ˈflætəd] geschmeichelt sein **T4,** 82
to be guilty of sth [ˈgɪlti] sich einer Sache schuldig machen **T4,** 80
to be homesick [ˈhəʊmsɪk] Heimweh haben **T2,** 35
to be illiterate [bi ɪˈlɪtrət] Analphabet/-in sein ⟨**T2,** 44⟩
to be in charge (of) [ˌbiˌɪn ˈtʃɑːdʒ] das Sagen haben (für), die Verantwortung tragen (für), zuständig sein (für) **T2,** 41
to be in existence [ɪgˈzɪstns] existieren **T3,** 72
to be inspired by sth/sb [ɪnˈspaɪəd baɪ] hervorgerufen/geweckt werden von etw./jmdm. **T2,** 36
to be intent on doing sth [ɪnˈtentˌɒn] fest entschlossen sein, etw. zu tun ⟨**T2,** 44⟩
to be in the big leagues [ˌbiːˌɪn ðə ˈbɪg liːgz] zur Spitzenklasse gehören ⟨**T1,** 11⟩
to be involved (in) [bi ɪnˈvɒlvdˌɪn] sich beteiligen an, sich engagieren bei/in **T4,** 80
to be keen to do sth [bi ˈkiːn] sehr daran interessiert sein, etw. zu tun **T3,** 71
to be missing [bi ˈmɪsɪŋ] fehlen **T3,** 71
to be set in [bi ˈsetˌɪn] spielen in **T4,** 87
to be stereotyped [bi ˈsteriətaɪpt] in eine Schublade gesteckt werden ⟨**T2,** 43⟩
to be surrounded by sth/sb [səˈraʊndɪd] umgeben sein von etw./jmdm. **T3,** 60
to be suspended [ˌbi səˈspendɪd] suspendiert werden; zeitweilig vom Unterricht ausgeschlossen werden **T4,** 82
to be the matter with [biˌðə ˈmætə wɪð] nicht stimmen mit, los sein mit ⟨**T3,** 75⟩
to be thrilled (with) [bi θrɪld] sich riesig freuen (über) **T3,** 61
to be to blame for [biː tə ˈbleɪm fɔː] Schuld haben an, verantwortlich gemacht werden für **T1,** 14; **T2,** 40
to be tricked [bi ˈtrɪkt] ausgetrickst/hereingelegt werden **T3,** 69
to be unaware of sth [ˌbiˌʌnəˈweə] sich einer Sache nicht bewusst sein **T3,** 60
to be willing to do sth [biː ˈwɪlɪŋ] gewillt/bereit sein, etw. zu tun **T1,** 16
while we are about it [ˌwaɪl wiˌɑːrˌəˈbaʊtˌɪt] wo wir schon dabei sind ⟨**T2,** 41⟩
baked **beans** *(pl.)* [ˌbeɪkt ˈbiːnz] gebackene Bohnen **T2,** 49
black **bear** [ˌblæk ˈbeə] Schwarzbär ⟨**T3,** 62⟩
*to **bear the brunt** [beə ðə ˈbrʌnt] harte Arbeit leisten, die Hauptlast tragen ⟨**T2,** 43⟩
beat [biːt] Takt, Rhythmus ⟨**T2,** 42⟩
*to **beat** [biːt] schlagen, (ver)prügeln; besiegen **T2,** 36; **T3,** 66
beat to hell [ˌbiːt tə ˈhel] total ramponiert ⟨**T1,** 11⟩
*to take a **beating** [ˌteɪkˌə ˈbiːtɪŋ] Prügel einstecken, verprügelt werden ⟨**T1,** 19⟩
*to **become extinct** [bɪˌkʌmˌɪkˈstɪŋkt] aussterben **T3,** 59; **T4,** 89
bed-sheet [ˈbedʃiːt] Bettlaken ⟨**T2,** 38⟩
beef [biːf] Rindfleisch **T3,** 71
roast beef [ˌrəʊst ˈbiːf] Roastbeef, Rinderbraten **T2,** 49
before [bɪˈfɔː] zuvor, vorher; schon einmal **T2,** 37
behaviour [bɪˈheɪvjə] Verhalten, Betragen **T2,** 38; **T4,** 80
promiscuous behaviour [prəˌmɪskjuəs bɪˈheɪvjə] häufiger Partnerwechsel **T1,** 19
belief [bɪˈliːf] Glaube, Überzeugung **T2,** 36
to **belong to** [bɪˈlɒŋ tə] gehören zu **T4,** 82
*to **bend down** [ˌbendˈdaʊn] sich bücken; abknicken **T1,** 22
to **benefit sb/sth** [ˈbenɪfɪt] jmdm./etw. zugutekommen, jmdm./etw. nutzen **T3,** 64
Bengali [beŋˈgɔːli] bengalisch; Bengale/Bengalin ⟨**T2,** 44⟩
biceps pl. **biceps** [ˈbaɪseps] Bizeps ⟨**T4,** 92⟩
big-budget [ˈbɪgˌbʌdʒɪt] mit großem Budget **T3,** 68
motor **bike** [ˈməʊtə baɪk] Motorrad **T4,** 83
*to **bind** [baɪnd] (ver)binden; festhalten ⟨**T3,** 69⟩
biodegradable [ˌbaɪəʊdɪˈgreɪdəbl] biologisch abbaubar **T3,** 61
biologist [baɪˈɒlədʒɪst] Biologe/Biologin **T4,** 80
birth [bɜːθ] Geburt **T3,** 69
bit (of) [bɪt] Stückchen (von) **T2,** 37; **T3,** 61
*to **bite** [baɪt] beißen **T3,** 75
Black African [blæk ˈæfrɪkən] Schwarzafrikaner/-in; schwarzafrikanisch **T2,** 33
black bear [ˌblæk ˈbeə] Schwarzbär ⟨**T3,** 62⟩
Black Caribbean [blæk ˌkærɪˈbiːən] Afrokaribe/Afrokaribin; afrokaribisch **T2,** 33
blackbird [ˈblækbɜːd] Amsel **T3,** 58
to **blame sth on sb** [ˈbleɪmˌɒn] jmdn. für etw. verantwortlich machen, jmdm. für etw. die Schuld geben **T3,** 66
to be to blame for [biː tə ˈbleɪm fɔː] Schuld haben an, verantwortlich gemacht werden für **T1,** 14; **T2,** 40
to **blare** [bleə] schmettern, plärren ⟨**T1,** 11⟩
to **blaze** [bleɪz] strahlen, funkeln, (auf)lodern ⟨**T1,** 22⟩
to **block** [blɒk] blockieren, verstellen **T4,** 82
to block off [blɒkˈɒf] absperren, abriegeln **T3,** 65
*to be **blocked up** [ˌbiˌblɒktˈʌp] verstopft sein **T3,** 75
blood sample [ˈblʌd ˌsæmpl] Blutprobe **T3,** 75
bloody [ˈblʌdi] blutig **T3,** 65
*to **blow** [bləʊ] pusten, blasen; wehen **T3,** 62
to **boast** [bəʊst] angeben, prahlen, sich rühmen **T3,** 68
body bubble [ˈbɒdi ˌbʌbl] persönlicher körperlicher Toleranzbereich ⟨**T3,** 74⟩
to **bombard** [bɒmˈbɑːd] bombardieren **T4,** 82

stealth **bomber** ['stelθ bɒmə] Tarnkappenbomber ⟨**T3,** 58⟩
bone [bəʊn] Knochen, Fischgräte **T1,** 12
cookery **book** ['kʊkri ˌbʊk] Kochbuch **T2,** 47
to **bother** ['bɒðə] stören, belästigen; nerven **T1,** 24; sich die Mühe machen, etw. zu tun **T4,** 83
to bother (with) ['bɒðə] sich kümmern (um) ⟨**T3,** 63⟩
weekend **box** ['wi:kend bɒks] Wochenendschachtel ⟨**T4,** 87⟩
bra strap ['brɑ: stræp] BH-Träger ⟨**T1,** 21⟩
brainstorming ['breɪnˌstɔ:mɪŋ] Brainstorming *(Sammlung von Ideen)* ⟨**T2,** 34⟩
branch [brɑ:nʃ] Zweig, Ast; Zweigstelle **T4,** 82
*to **break** [breɪk] verstoßen gegen **T2,** 39
to break down [ˌbreɪk‿'daʊn] auflösen, zerstören, niederreißen; zusammenbrechen **T1,** 28; **T3,** 60
to break into a run [breɪk‿ˌɪntʊ‿ə 'rʌn] plötzlich loslaufen ⟨**T1,** 11⟩
to break the law [ˌbreɪk ðə 'lɔ:] gegen das Gesetz verstoßen **T4,** 84
to break up *(coll)* [ˌbreɪk‿'ʌp] Schluss machen **T1,** 24
*to fight for **breath** [ˌfaɪt fə 'breθ] nach Luft ringen **T3,** 66
breathable ['breθəbl] frisch *(Luft)* ⟨**T3,** 67⟩
*to **breed** [bri:d] züchten **T3,** 62
breeze [bri:z] Brise ⟨**T3,** 69⟩
bridge [brɪdʒ] Nasenrücken ⟨**T1,** 20⟩
bright [braɪt] leuchtend, strahlend ⟨**T3,** 60⟩
to **bring business to the stores** [brɪŋ 'bɪznɪs tə ðə ˌstɔ:z] in (den) Geschäften für Umsatz sorgen ⟨**T3,** 64⟩
to bring out [ˌbrɪŋ‿'aʊt] ans Licht bringen **T1,** 16
to bring to life [ˌbrɪŋ tə 'laɪf] veranschaulichen, zum Leben erwecken **T3,** 67
fraternity **brother** (= frat brother) [frə'tɜ:nəti ˌbrʌðə] Bundesbruder ⟨**T4,** 85⟩
bruise [bru:z] Prellung, blauer Fleck **T3,** 75
*to bear the **brunt** [beə ðə 'brʌnt] harte Arbeit leisten, die Hauptlast tragen ⟨**T2,** 43⟩
brush [brʌʃ] Bürste **T3,** 60
bubble ['bʌbl] Blase ⟨**T1,** 19⟩
body bubble ['bɒdi ˌbʌbl] persönlicher körperlicher Toleranzbereich ⟨**T3,** 74⟩
buck *(AE) (coll)* [bʌk] Dollar ⟨**T1,** 22⟩
Buddhist monk [ˌbʊdɪst 'mʌŋk] buddhistischer Mönch **T3,** 67
budget ['bʌdʒɪt] Haushalt, Etat, Budget **T4,** 81
to **burp** [bɜ:p] rülpsen ⟨**T2,** 39⟩
to bring **business to the stores** [brɪŋ 'bɪznɪs tə ðə ˌstɔ:z] in (den) Geschäften für Umsatz sorgen ⟨**T3,** 64⟩
butcher ['bʊtʃə] Fleischer/-in, Metzger/-in **T3,** 61
butter ['bʌtə] Butter **T2,** 49
butterfly ['bʌtəflaɪ] Schmetterling **T3,** 58
by contrast [baɪ 'kɒntrɑ:st] im Gegenteil, im Gegensatz dazu ⟨**T2,** 44⟩
by myself [baɪ maɪ'self] allein ⟨**T1,** 10⟩
by sea [baɪ 'si:] zu Wasser, mit dem Schiff **T3,** 73

C

to **calculate** ['kælkjəleɪt] (be)rechnen, kalkulieren **T3,** 72
calculation [ˌkælkjə'leɪʃn] Berechnung, Kalkulation **T3,** 71
calculator ['kælkjəleɪtə] (Taschen-)Rechner **T3,** 71
call [kɔ:l] Aufruf, (An-)Ruf ⟨**T2,** 34⟩
to **call oneself lucky** [ˌkɔ:l wʌnself 'lʌki] sich glücklich schätzen **T4,** 83
research **camp** [ri:'sɜ:tʃ ˌkæmp] Forschungslager, -station **T4,** 89
campaign slogan [kæm'peɪn ˌsləʊgən] Wahlkampfparole **T4,** 88
to **campaign (for)** [kæm'peɪn fə] sich engagieren (für) ⟨**T2,** 41⟩; demonstrieren (für), aufmerksam machen (auf) **T3,** 59
rubbish **can** ['rʌbɪʃ ˌkæn] Mülleimer **T4,** 82
canal [kə'næl] Kanal **T3,** 58
cotton **candy** [ˌkɒtn 'kændi] Zuckerwatte ⟨**T1,** 22⟩
cannister ['kænɪstə] Kanister, Behälter, Büchse ⟨**T3,** 66⟩
water **cannon** ['wɔ:tə ˌkænən] Wasserwerfer **T3,** 66
feathered **cap** [ˌfeðəd 'kæp] Trachtenhut ⟨**T1,** 26⟩
caption ['kæpʃn] Untertitel, Bildunterschrift **T3,** 76
car [kɑ:] Waggon ⟨**T1,** 11⟩
car rental ['kɑ: ˌrentl] Autovermietung, -verleih **T4,** 93
carbon ['kɑ:bn] Kohlenstoff **T3,** 68
carbon dioxide (CO_2) [ˌkɑ:bn daɪ'ɒksaɪd] Kohlendioxid **T3,** 59
carbon unit [ˌkɑ:bn 'ju:nɪt] Kohlenstoffeinheit **T3,** 73
*to take sb into **care** [ˌteɪk‿ɪntə 'keə] sich um jmdn. kümmern, jmdn. in Pflege nehmen **T2,** 36
career [kə'rɪə] Karriere **T3,** 62
Caribbean [ˌkærɪ'bi:ən] karibisch; Karibik; Karibe/Karibin **T2,** 34
Afro-Caribbean [ˌæfrəʊkærɪ'bi:ən] Afrokaribe/Afrokaribin; afrokaribisch **T2,** 34
Black Caribbean [blæk ˌkærɪ'bi:ən] Afrokaribe/Afrokaribin; afrokaribisch **T2,** 33
to **carry** ['kæri] beinhalten **T3,** 60
case [keɪs] Fall **T3,** 71
in case [ɪn 'keɪs] für den Fall, dass … **T1,** 14
to make a case for [ˌmeɪk‿ə 'keɪs fə] plädieren für ⟨**T4,** 83⟩
cash [kæʃ] Bargeld **T4,** 87
cashew nut ['kæʃu: ˌnʌt] Cashewnuss ⟨**T2,** 37⟩
to **castigate** ['kæstɪgeɪt] hart bestrafen, rügen ⟨**T2,** 38⟩
*to **catch** [kætʃ] treffen ⟨**T3,** 66⟩
to catch sb's eye [kætʃ] jmdm. auffallen ⟨**T4,** 87⟩
catchy ['kætʃi] eingängig, einprägsam **T4,** 87
cause [kɔ:z] Ziel **T3,** 68
degree **Celsius (°C)** [ˌdɪgri: 'selsiəs] Grad Celsius **T3,** 72
convention **center** *(AE)* [kən'venʃn ˌsentə] Kongresszentrum **T3,** 65
central ['sentrl] zentral **T4,** 85
opening **ceremony** ['əʊpnɪŋ ˌserɪməni] Eröffnungsfeierlichkeiten **T3,** 65
certainty ['sɜ:tnti] Gewissheit, Sicherheit **T3,** 66
chai [tʃaɪ] Chai *(indischer Gewürztee)* ⟨**T2,** 49⟩
chain [tʃeɪn] Kette **T3,** 60
chain-link fence [ˌtʃeɪnlɪŋk 'fens] Maschendrahtzaun ⟨**T1,** 10⟩
food chain ['fu:d tʃeɪn] Nahrungskette **T3,** 60
chairman pl. **chairmen** ['tʃeəmən; 'tʃeəmen] Vorsitzender, Präsident **T4,** 92
chairperson ['tʃeəˌpɜ:sn] Vorsitzende/-r, Vorsitz **T3,** 71
climate **change** ['klaɪmət tʃeɪndʒ] Klimawandel **T3,** 58
to **chant** [tʃɑ:nt] singen *(Sprechgesang)* ⟨**T2,** 42⟩; ⟨**T3,** 65⟩
chapati [tʃə'pæti] *(dünner Fladen aus Weizenmehl)* ⟨**T2,** 36⟩
character archetype [ˌkærəktə 'ɑ:kɪtaɪp] Archetyp/-us *(Urform einer Figur)* **T1,** 14

to **characterize** ['kærəktraɪz] charakterisieren **T3,** 64
*to be in **charge** (of) [ˌbi‿ɪn 'tʃɑ:dʒ] das Sagen haben (für), die Verantwortung tragen (für), zuständig sein (für) **T2,** 41
to **charge** [tʃɑ:dʒ] verlangen, erheben, berechnen ⟨**T2,** 34⟩
charismatic [ˌkærɪz'mætɪk] charismatisch **T4,** 88
charitable ['tʃærɪtəbl] wohltätig ⟨**T4,** 85⟩
pie **chart** ['paɪ ˌtʃɑ:t] Tortendiagramm ⟨**T2,** 32⟩
to **charter** ['tʃɑ:tə] chartern, anheuern ⟨**T3,** 73⟩
Check. [tʃek] Abgehakt. ⟨**T1,** 21⟩
to **check out** *(coll)* [tʃek‿'aʊt] untersuchen, überprüfen **T3,** 63
cheek [tʃi:k] Wange **T3,** 75
chemist's ['kemɪsts] Apotheke **T3,** 75
chemo treatment ['ki:məʊ ˌtri:tmənt] Chemotherapie ⟨**T4,** 85⟩
chemotherapy [ˌki:məʊ'θerəpi] Chemotherapie ⟨**T4,** 85⟩
chest [tʃest] Brust(korb) **T1,** 13; ⟨**T3,** 69⟩; ⟨**T4,** 83⟩
to **chew** [tʃu:] kauen **T2,** 37
chick [tʃɪk] Küken **T3,** 60
chicken ['tʃɪkɪn] Angsthase ⟨**T1,** 15⟩
chicken tikka masala [ˌtʃɪkɪn tɪkə mə'sɑ:lə] *(Currygericht aus gegrillten marinierten Hähnchenfleischstücken in einer würzigen Soße)* ⟨**T2,** 47⟩
childish ['tʃaɪldɪʃ] kindlich; kindisch **T3,** 65
chilli ['tʃɪli] Chili **T2,** 36
to **choke** [tʃəʊk] sich verschlucken; keine Luft bekommen ⟨**T2,** 39⟩
chorus ['kɔ:rəs] Refrain ⟨**T3,** 69⟩; ⟨**T4,** 87⟩
circle ['sɜ:kl] Kreis, Ring **T1,** 20; **T3,** 66; Kreis von Anhängern ⟨**T4,** 80⟩
to **circle** (around) ['sɜ:kl] (herum)kreisen ⟨**T1,** 10⟩
circular ['sɜ:kjələ] Kreislauf ⟨**T1,** 23⟩
circular motion [ˌsɜ:kjələ 'məʊʃn] Kreisbewegung ⟨**T3,** 60⟩
circumstance ['sɜ:kəmstæns] Umstand, Gegebenheit **T2,** 37
citizen ['sɪtɪzn] (Staats-)Bürger/-in; Staatsangehörige/-r **T2,** 33; **T4,** 80
civil disobedience [ˌsɪvl dɪsə'bi:diəns] ziviler Ungehorsam **T4,** 80
civilization [ˌsɪvlaɪ'zeɪʃn] Kultur, Zivilisation **T2,** 39
service-learning **class** ['sɜ:vɪs lɜ:nɪŋ ˌklɑ:s] *(Unterricht, der den Nutzen gemeinnütziger Arbeit vermitteln soll)* ⟨**T4,** 85⟩
classic ['klæsɪk] Klassiker; klassisch ⟨**T2,** 49⟩

subordinate **clause** [səˌbɔ:dnət 'klɔ:z] Nebensatz **T2,** 35
to **claw one's way** [ˌklɔ:‿wʌnz 'weɪ] krabbeln ⟨**T1,** 13⟩
to **clean up** [ˌkli:n‿'ʌp] beseitigen **T3,** 69; aufräumen, sauber machen **T4,** 85
to **clear** ['klɪə] aufklaren, sich aufhellen **T3,** 65
to clear up [ˌklɪər‿'ʌp] aufräumen, beseitigen **T3,** 60; besser werden **T3,** 75
climate change ['klaɪmət tʃeɪndʒ] Klimawandel **T3,** 58
close to ['kləʊs tə] fast ⟨**T3,** 71⟩
to be close to ['kləʊs tə] in der Nähe sein von, nahe sein an ⟨**T2,** 36⟩
to be close to doing sth ['kləʊs tə] nahe daran sein, etw. zu tun **T1,** 22
to get close [get 'kləʊs] sich nahe kommen **T1,** 21
cloth [klɒθ] Lappen, Tuch; Gewebe, Stoff **T1,** 19; **T2,** 38; Tischdecke ⟨**T2,** 39⟩
club [klʌb] Schlagstock, Keule, Knüppel ⟨**T1,** 13⟩
coalbed of cloud ['kəʊlbed‿əv klaʊd] dunkle Staubwolke ⟨**T3,** 64⟩
coat [kəʊt] Mantel **T1,** 13
cold [kəʊld] Kälte **T3,** 65
colleague ['kɒli:g] Kollege/Kollegin **T4,** 92
collective [kə'lektɪv] gemeinsam, zusammen; Ober- ⟨**T1,** 16⟩
college vacation ['kɒlɪdʒ vəˌkeɪʃn] Semesterferien **T3,** 62
to **collide** [kə'laɪd] kollidieren, zusammenstoßen **T3,** 66
colonial [kə'ləʊniəl] kolonial **T2,** 42
to **color** *(AE)* ['kʌlə] anstreichen, anmalen; färben **T3,** 59
comb ['kəʊm] Kamm **T3,** 60
combination [ˌkɒmbɪ'neɪʃn] Kombination, Verbindung ⟨**T2,** 49⟩
to **combine** [kəm'baɪn] kombinieren, verbinden **T3,** 68
*to **come across** (sb/sth) [ˌkʌm‿ə'krɒs] zufällig begegnen, antreffen, vorfinden **T3,** 60
to come down [kʌm 'daʊn] herunterkommen; fallen **T3,** 65
to come even with [kʌm‿'i:vn wɪð] dieselbe Höhe erreichen wie ⟨**T1,** 11⟩
to come up with sth [kʌm‿'ʌp wɪð] sich etw. einfallen lassen, sich etw. ausdenken **T2,** 38
comedian [kə'mi:diən] Komiker/-in **T2,** 41
to **commit a crime** [kəˌmɪt‿ə 'kraɪm] ein Verbrechen/eine Straftat begehen **T1,** 14

commitment [kə'mɪtmənt] Engagement, Einsatz **T1,** 16
common purpose [ˌkɒmən 'pɜ:pəs] gemeinsames Ziel **T4,** 88
to **communicate with** [kə'mju:nɪkeɪt wɪð] kommunizieren mit **T4,** 89
communist ['kɒmjənɪst] kommunistisch; Kommunist/-in ⟨**T4,** 84⟩
intercultural **competence** [ɪntəˌkʌltʃrl 'kɒmpɪtns] interkulturelle Kompetenz/ Fähigkeit ⟨**T1,** 26⟩; ⟨**T3,** 74⟩
complaint [kəm'pleɪnt] Beschwerde **T4,** 93
the **complete works** [kəmˌpli:t 'wɜ:ks] die gesammelten Werke ⟨**T2,** 36⟩
complex ['kɒmpleks] komplexe/-r/-s **T3,** 71
complexity [kəm'pleksəti] Komplexität, Vielschichtigkeit **T2,** 35
complicated ['kɒmplɪkeɪtɪd] kompliziert **T1,** 19; **T3,** 71
comprehension [ˌkɒmprɪ'henʃn] Verständnis, Verstehen **T1,** 14
compromise ['kɒmprəmaɪz] Kompromiss **T2,** 40
compulsory [kəm'pʌlsri] verpflichtend, obligatorisch, vorgeschrieben **T1,** 8; **T2,** 44
concise [kən'saɪs] präzise, kurz, prägnant **T2,** 46
condemnation [ˌkɒndem'neɪʃn] Verurteilung, Verdammung **T3,** 68
condiment ['kɒndɪmənt] Aromat, Gewürz, Würzmittel **T3,** 70
condition [kən'dɪʃn] Kondition, Bedingung; Zustand **T2,** 34
under mysterious conditions [ˌʌndə mɪˌstɪəriəs kən'dɪʃnz] unter mysteriösen Umständen ⟨**T4,** 89⟩
condom ['kɒndɒm] Kondom **T4,** 83
in **confidence** [ɪn 'kɒnfɪdns] im Vertrauen ⟨**T1,** 29⟩
*to be **confined** (to) [kən'faɪnd] beschränkt sein (auf) ⟨**T2,** 35⟩
to **confirm** [kən'fɜ:m] bestätigen, bekräftigen **T1,** 28
conflicting viewpoints *(pl.)* [kənˌflɪktɪŋ 'vju:pɔɪnts] widersprüchliche Standpunkte **T2,** 38
confrontation [ˌkɒnfrʌn'teɪʃn] Konfrontation **T2,** 40
to **confuse sth/sb with sth/sb** [kən'fju:z] etw./jmd. mit etw./jmdm. verwechseln **T4,** 89
confused [kən'fju:zd] wirr, verwirrt, konfus **T2,** 44
to **connect** [kə'nekt] verbinden, vermitteln, anschließen; treffen **T1,** 12
conscience ['kɒnʃns] Gewissen **T2,** 39

consent [kən'sent] Zustimmung, Einwilligung **T1,** 8
age of consent [ˌeɪdʒ‿əv kən'sent] (Ehe-)Mündigkeitsalter **T1,** 8
parental consent [pəˌrentl kən'sent] Einverständnis der Eltern ⟨**T1,** 8⟩
to face the **consequences** [feɪs ðə 'kɒnsɪkwənsɪz] die Konsequenzen tragen **T1,** 14
to **consider** [kən'sɪdə] in Betracht ziehen, berücksichtigen **T3,** 73
to consider yourself above sth/sb [kən'sɪdə] etw./jmdn. für unter seiner Würde halten **T3,** 65
to **consist of** [kən'sɪst‿əv] bestehen aus **T4,** 87
consistent [kən'sɪstnt] gleich bleibend, stetig, konsistent ⟨**T1,** 29⟩
constant ['kɒnstənt] ständig, konstant, stetig, gleichmäßig **T1,** 11
consumer [kən'sju:mə] Verbraucher/-in, Konsument/-in **T3,** 70
Welcome to consumer throwaway living. [ˌwelkəm tʊ kənˌsju:mə 'θrəʊəweɪ ˌlɪvɪŋ] Willkommen in der Wegwerfgesellschaft. **T3,** 60
consumption [kən'sʌmpʃn] Verbrauch; Konsum **T3,** 70
container [kən'teɪnə] Container, Behälter, Behältnis **T1,** 13; **T3,** 65
content ['kɒntent] Inhalt **T2,** 35
to **contract sth** [kən'trækt] an etw. erkranken, sich mit etw. infizieren ⟨**T4,** 80⟩
by **contrast** [baɪ 'kɒntrɑ:st] im Gegenteil, im Gegensatz dazu ⟨**T2,** 44⟩
to **contrast** [kən'trɑ:st] kontrastieren, gegenüberstellen ⟨**T4,** 91⟩
to **contribute** (to) [kən'trɪbju:t] beitragen; mitwirken **T2,** 34
contribution [ˌkɒntrɪ'bju:ʃn] Beitrag, Beteiligung ⟨**T3,** 73⟩
convenient [kən'vi:niənt] passend, angenehm **T4,** 93
convention center *(AE)* [kən'venʃn ˌsentə] Kongresszentrum **T3,** 65
to **convey** [kən'veɪ] vermitteln, ausdrücken **T2,** 38
cookery book ['kʊkri ˌbʊk] Kochbuch **T2,** 47
environmental **cost** [ɪnˌvaɪərnˌmentl 'kɒst] Umweltbelastung ⟨**T3,** 72⟩
cotton ['kɒtn] Baumwolle, Baumwoll- **T3,** 61
cotton candy [ˌkɒtn 'kændi] Zuckerwatte ⟨**T1,** 22⟩
council ['kaʊnsl] Gemeinde-/Stadtrat **T2,** 36
countless ['kaʊntləs] unzählige, viele **T2,** 39
*to run a **country** [ˌrʌn‿ə 'kʌntri] ein Land regieren **T4,** 84
county ['kaʊnti] (Land-)Kreis, Bezirk **T4,** 85
a **couple of** [ə 'kʌpl‿əv] einige, ein paar **T1,** 11
court [kɔ:t] Gericht; Hof **T1,** 8
to take sb to court [teɪk tə 'kɔ:t] jmdn. vor Gericht bringen, verklagen ⟨**T1,** 8⟩
cover ['kʌvə] Cover, Titelblatt **T4,** 89
to **cover** ['kʌvə] berücksichtigen **T3,** 71
cowboy ['kaʊbɔɪ] Cowboy ⟨**T3,** 73⟩
crab [kræb] Krebs, Krabbe ⟨**T1,** 13⟩
to **crackle** ['krækl] knistern, knacken, prasseln ⟨**T1,** 13⟩
to **crash a party** [ˌkræʃ‿ə 'pɑ:ti] uneingeladen zu einer Party kommen **T1,** 24
to **crawl** [krɔ:l] kriechen **T1,** 10
to **create** [kri'eɪt] verursachen, ausmachen **T3,** 70
creative [kri'eɪtɪv] kreativ ⟨**T4,** 91⟩
creature ['kri:tʃə] Kreatur, Lebewesen; Geschöpf **T3,** 62
juvenile **crime** [ˌdʒu:vnaɪl 'kraɪm] Jugendkriminalität ⟨**T1,** 14⟩
to commit a crime [kəˌmɪt‿ə 'kraɪm] ein Verbrechen/eine Straftat begehen **T1,** 14
criminal responsibility [ˌkrɪmɪnl rɪˌspɒnsə'bɪləti] Strafmündigkeit ⟨**T1,** 8⟩
crisis pl. **crises** ['kraɪsɪs; 'kraɪsi:z] Krise **T3,** 60
criterion pl. **criteria** [kraɪ'tɪəriən; kraɪ'tɪəriə] Kriterium, Argument **T4,** 89
social **critic** [ˌsəʊʃl 'krɪtɪk] Gesellschaftskritiker/-in **T4,** 80
criticism ['krɪtɪsɪsm] Kritik **T4,** 95
to **croak** [krəʊk] krächzen ⟨**T2,** 37⟩
to **crop up** [krɒp‿'ʌp] auftauchen, auftreten, sich zeigen **T1,** 22
a **cross between** [ə 'krɒs bɪˌtwi:n] eine Kreuzung zwischen/von **T3,** 65
cruel ['kru:əl] grausam **T4,** 89
cruise liner ['kru:z ˌlaɪnə] Kreuzfahrtschiff **T3,** 73
to **crunch** [krʌntʃ] zermalmen; geräuschvoll essen ⟨**T2,** 38⟩
cubic metre [ˌkju:bɪk 'mi:tə] Kubikmeter **T3,** 71
cuddly ['kʌdli] knuddelig ⟨**T4,** 91⟩
cuisine [kwɪ'zi:n] Küche **T2,** 49
to **curb** [k3:b] einschränken; drosseln ⟨**T2,** 44⟩
cure for [kjʊə fɔ:] Heilmittel gegen **T4,** 80
ocean **current** [ˌəʊʃn 'kʌrnt] Meeresströmung ⟨**T3,** 60⟩
current ['kʌrnt] aktuell, derzeitig, gegenwärtig **T4,** 81
cut [kʌt] Schnitt(wunde) **T3,** 75
school cut ['sku:l ˌkʌt] Kürzung/ Einsparung an Schulen ⟨**T4,** 82⟩
*to **cut** [kʌt] reduzieren **T3,** 70
to cut through [kʌt 'θru:] eine Abkürzung nehmen über/durch **T4,** 82

D

daft *(coll)* [dɑ:ft] dämlich, bescheuert **T1,** 28
dairy product ['deəri ˌprɒdʌkt] Milchprodukt, -erzeugnis **T3,** 70
damage ['dæmɪdʒ] Schaden, Beschädigung **T3,** 58
property damage ['prɒpəti dæmɪdʒ] Sachschaden, Sachbeschädigung ⟨**T1,** 14⟩
to **damage** ['dæmɪdʒ] schaden, beschädigen **T1,** 16
damn [dæm] verdammt ⟨**T2,** 37⟩
dance hall style ['dɑ:ns hɔ:l ˌstaɪl] *(schnelle Reggae-Musik, über die der DJ improvisierte Texte spricht)* ⟨**T2,** 42⟩
data pl. **data** ['deɪtə] Daten, Angaben **T2,** 33
have a say **day** [ˌhæv‿ə 'seɪ deɪ] *(Tag, an dem man zu Wort kommt)* ⟨**T4,** 82⟩
deal [di:l] Handel, Abmachung, Übereinkunft **T1,** 18; **T3,** 64
What's the big deal? [ˌwɒts ðə bɪg 'di:l] Was ist das Problem?, Was ist so wichtig (daran)? **T4,** 83
death sentence ['deθ ˌsentəns] Todesstrafe, Todesurteil **T4,** 80
debate [dɪ'beɪt] Debatte, Beratung **T3,** 68
debater [dɪ'beɪtə] Debattierer/-in ⟨**T4,** 83⟩
decent ['di:snt] anständig, ehrbar **T2,** 39
decimal point [ˌdesɪml 'pɔɪnt] Dezimalpunkt, Kommastelle ⟨**T3,** 72⟩
declaration [ˌdeklə'reɪʃn] Aussage, Feststellung, Erklärung **T1,** 16
to **decorate** ['dekreɪt] dekorieren, schmücken **T4,** 85
deep-fried [ˌdi:p'fraɪd] frittiert, in Fett ausgebacken **T2,** 49
defining [dɪ'faɪnɪŋ] prägend ⟨**T4,** 88⟩
to **degrade** [dɪ'greɪd] abbauen, zerfallen **T3,** 61
degree Celsius (°C) [ˌdɪgri: 'selsiəs] Grad Celsius **T3,** 72
dread degree [dred dɪ'gri:] *(erfundener Ausdruck für einen Abschluss in "Ghettology", bei dem das Ghetto studiert wird)* ⟨**T2,** 43⟩

delicatessen [ˌdelɪkəˈtesn] Feinkostgeschäft ⟨**T3,** 60⟩
*to meet the **demands of sb/sth** [ˌmi:t ðə dɪˈmɑ:ndz‿əv] den Anforderungen von jmdm./etw. nachkommen **T4,** 88
to **demand** [dɪˈmɑ:nd] verlangen, fordern **T2,** 36; wissen wollen, fragen **T2,** 39
demonstration [ˌdemənˈstreɪʃn] Demonstration; Darstellung, Veranschaulichung **T3,** 65
demonstrator [ˈdemənstreɪtə] Demonstrant/-in; Vorführer-/in **T3,** 65
dentist [ˈdentɪst] Zahnarzt/Zahnärztin **T4,** 93
to **deny** [dɪˈnaɪ] leugnen, abstreiten **T1,** 14; **T2,** 39
department [dɪˈpɑ:tmənt] Abteilung **T4,** 93
to **descend from** [dɪˈsend frɒm] abstammen von, herstammen von **T2,** 33
to descend on [dɪˈsend‿ɒn] einfallen in, herfallen über **T3,** 61
deserted [dɪˈzɜ:tɪd] verlassen, menschenleer ⟨**T1,** 21⟩; **T3,** 64
to **deserve** [dɪˈzɜ:v] verdienen **T3,** 59
desperate [ˈdesprət] ernst, verzweifelt, hoffnungslos **T3,** 60
despite [dɪˈspaɪt] trotz **T3,** 65; **T3,** 69
to **determine** [dɪˈtɜ:mɪn] bestimmen, ermitteln; entschließen **T1,** 16
determined [dɪˈtɜ:mɪnd] (fest) entschlossen, entschieden **T2,** 44
to **develop a sense of** [dɪˌveləp‿ə ˈsens‿əv] ein Gespür/Gefühl entwickeln für **T4,** 86
to **devise** [dɪˈvaɪz] entwickeln, erfinden ⟨**T3,** 73⟩
diagnosis pl. **diagnoses** [ˌdaɪəgˈnəʊsɪs; ˌdaɪəgˈnəʊsi:z] Diagnose **T3,** 75
diarrhoea [ˌdaɪəˈrɪə] Durchfall **T3,** 75
*to keep a **diary** [ˌki:p‿ə ˈdaɪəri] ein Tagebuch/einen Terminkalender führen ⟨**T1,** 27⟩
dictatorship [dɪkˈteɪtəʃɪp] Diktatur **T4,** 84
diet [daɪət] Diät, Ernährung **T3,** 70
dietary shift [ˌdaɪətri ˈʃɪft] Ernährungsumstellung ⟨**T3,** 70⟩
to **differ** [ˈdɪfə] sich unterscheiden; abweichen **T3,** 58
dilemma [daɪˈlemə] Dilemma; Zwickmühle **T4,** 86
to be caught in a dilemma [ˌbi ˈkɔ:t‿ɪn‿ə daɪˈlemə] in einer Zwickmühle stecken **T4,** 86
dimension [daɪˈmenʃn] Dimension, Ausmaß ⟨**T4,** 88⟩

carbon **dioxide** (CO_2) [ˌkɑ:bn daɪˈɒksaɪd] Kohlendioxid **T3,** 59
diphtheria [dɪfˈθɪəriə] Diphtherie ⟨**T4,** 80⟩
art **director** [ˈɑ:t dɪˌrektə] künstlerischer Leiter/künstlerische Leiterin **T4,** 92
dirt road [ˈdɜ:t ˌrəʊd] Schotterstraße ⟨**T3,** 64⟩
to **disappoint** [ˌdɪsəˈpɔɪnt] enttäuschen **T4,** 85
disappointed [ˌdɪsəˈpɔɪntɪd] enttäuscht **T4,** 83
to **discard** [dɪˈskɑ:d] wegwerfen; ausziehen; ablegen **T3,** 67
discovery [dɪˈskʌvri] Entdeckung **T4,** 80
discrimination [dɪˌskrɪmɪˈneɪʃn] Diskriminierung **T4,** 81
dishonest [dɪˈsɒnɪst] unehrlich **T4,** 86
civil **disobedience** [ˌsɪvl dɪsəˈbi:diəns] ziviler Ungehorsam **T4,** 80
electric **display** [ɪˌlektrɪk dɪˈspleɪ] elektronische Anzeige ⟨**T4,** 87⟩
distant [ˈdɪstnt] entfernt, distanziert **T3,** 62
diversity [daɪˈvɜ:səti] Vielfalt **T2,** 44
to **divide (into)** [dɪˈvaɪd] teilen, aufteilen, unterteilen **T2,** 35
to **divulge** [daɪˈvʌldʒ] weitergeben, ausplaudern ⟨**T4,** 83⟩
dizzy [ˈdɪzi] schwindelig ⟨**T1,** 22⟩
documentary [ˌdɒkjəˈmentri] Dokumentarfilm, Dokumentation **T3,** 60
rag **doll** [ˌræg ˈdɒl] Stoffpuppe ⟨**T1,** 13⟩
dolphin [ˈdɒlfɪn] Delfin **T3,** 60
to **donate** [dəˈneɪt] spenden, stiften **T4,** 81
donation [dəˈneɪʃn] Spende; Schenkung, Stiftung **T4,** 85
no **doubt** [nəʊ ˈdaʊt] zweifellos, wohl **T1,** 18
doughnut [ˈdəʊnʌt] Donut *(frittierter Teigkringel)* **T1,** 18
to **drag** [dræg] schleifen, ziehen, schleppen **T1,** 13
to **dramatise** [ˈdræmətaɪz] verfilmen; dramatisieren **T3,** 68
*to **draw** [drɔ:] ziehen ⟨**T1,** 26⟩
dread [dred] Angst, Furcht **T1,** 13
to **dread sth** [dred] vor etw. große Angst haben, etw. fürchten **T1,** 19
dread degree [dred dɪˈgri:] *(erfundener Ausdruck für einen Abschluss in "Ghettology", bei dem das Ghetto studiert wird)* ⟨**T2,** 43⟩
dreadlocks *(pl.)* [ˈdredlɒks] Rastalocken ⟨**T2,** 41⟩
to **dress up** [dres‿ˈʌp] sich verkleiden **T3,** 65; sich herausputzen/feinmachen **T3,** 74

dressed (as) [drest] angezogen (wie), verkleidet (als) **T3,** 65
to **drift** (across) [ˌdrɪft‿əˈkrɒs] (vorbei)schweben, (vorbei)treiben **T3,** 66
to **drill** [drɪl] bohren **T3,** 63
gas **driller** [ˈgæs ˌdrɪlə] Gasbohrarbeiter/-in **T3,** 64
drilling [ˈdrɪlɪŋ] Bohren, Bohrung **T3,** 63
drive [draɪv] (An-)Fahrt **T3,** 62
*to **drive on** [draɪv‿ˈɒn] weiterfahren **T3,** 64
drop [drɒp] Tropfen **T3,** 64
to **drop sb** [drɒp] jmdn. umfallen lassen ⟨**T1,** 13⟩
to bang **drums** [bæŋ ˈdrʌmz] trommeln **T3,** 65
dub poetry [dʌb ˈpəʊɪtri] *(eine aus Jamaica stammende Form der Performance Poetry, bei der Text über Reggae-Rhythmen gesprochen wird)* ⟨**T2,** 42⟩
to **duck** [dʌk] (sich) ducken ⟨**T3,** 66⟩
to duck through [dʌk ˈθru:] hindurchschlüpfen ⟨**T1,** 10⟩
due to [ˈdju: tə] infolge von, wegen **T4,** 82
*to be **dumb scared** [dʌm ˈskeəd] Todesängste ausstehen ⟨**T1,** 23⟩
dummy vote [ˈdʌmi vəʊt] ungültige Stimme **T4,** 83
duo [ˈdju:əʊ] ⟨**T4,** 87⟩
dust [dʌst] Staub ⟨**T3,** 63⟩
to **dust oneself off** [dʌst‿ˈɒf] sich den Staub abklopfen ⟨**T4,** 88⟩
dying [ˈdaɪɪŋ] sterbend, im Sterben liegend **T3,** 60

E

golden **eagle** [ˌgəʊldn ˈi:gl] Goldadler ⟨**T3,** 62⟩
how on **earth** [ˌhaʊ‿ɒn ˈɜ:θ] wie in aller Welt ⟨**T3,** 60⟩
to **ease out** [i:z‿ˈaʊt] sich vorsichtig in den Kreisverkehr einfädeln ⟨**T1,** 21⟩
Take it **easy, take it slow.** [ˌteɪk‿ɪt‿ˈi:zi, ˌteɪk‿ɪt ˈsləʊ] Nur keine Hektik., Immer mit der Ruhe. **T1,** 10
ecological [ˌi:kəˈlɒdʒɪkl] Ökologie-, ökologisch **T4,** 80
economy [ɪˈkɒnəmi] Industrie **T3,** 59
edge [edʒ] Rand, Kante **T1,** 15
edition [ɪˈdɪʃn] Ausgabe, Auflage, Edition **T2,** 47
sex **education** [ˈseks‿edʒʊˌkeɪʃn] Sexualkunde ⟨**T4,** 82⟩

side effect ['saɪd‿ɪˌfekt] Nebenwirkung **T3,** 75
effective [ɪ'fektɪv] effektiv, nachhaltig, schlagkräftig **T3,** 68; **T4,** 88
energy **efficient** ['enədʒi ɪˌfɪʃnt] energieeffizient **T3,** 70
effort ['efət] Mühe, Bemühung, Arbeitsaufwand **T4,** 85
to put no effort into sth [ˌpʊt nəʊ‿'efət‿ˌɪntə] sich keine Mühe mit etw. geben **T4,** 83
e.g. (= for example) [ˌiː'dʒiː] z. B. (= zum Beispiel) ⟨**T4,** 80⟩
not … **either** [nɒt … 'aɪðə; nɒt … 'iːðə] auch nicht ⟨**T2,** 38⟩
elbow ['elbəʊ] Ell(en)bogen **T3,** 75; ⟨**T4,** 83⟩
electric display [ɪˌlektrɪk dɪ'spleɪ] elektronische Anzeige ⟨**T4,** 87⟩
electrical goods *(pl.)* [ɪˌlektrɪkl 'gʊdz] Elektrogeräte **T3,** 71
elite [ɪ'liːt] Elite **T4,** 82
embarrassed [ɪm'bærəst] verlegen **T4,** 83
emission [ɪ'mɪʃn] Emission, Ausstoß **T3,** 59
to **emit** [ɪ'mɪt] ausstoßen, absondern **T3,** 73
emotion [ɪ'məʊʃn] Gefühl, Emotion **T3,** 61
emotive [ɪ'məʊtɪv] gefühlsbetont **T3,** 61
emphasis ['empfəsɪs] Betonung ⟨**T1,** 24⟩
empire ['empaɪə] (Kaiser-)Reich **T2,** 33
employee [ɪm'plɔɪiː] Angestellte/-r, Mitarbeiter/-in, Arbeitnehmer/-in **T4,** 92
encounter [ɪn'kaʊntə] Begegnung, Zusammentreffen **T2,** 34
to **encourage** [ɪn'kʌrɪdʒ] ermutigen; unterstützen **T2,** 45
to **end** [end] beenden **T4,** 81
energy efficient ['enədʒi ɪˌfɪʃnt] energieeffizient **T3,** 70
nuclear energy [ˌnjuːkliə 'enədʒi] Kernenergie **T3,** 68
engaged [ɪn'geɪdʒd] besetzt, belegt **T4,** 93
genetically **engineered** [dʒəˌnetɪkli endʒɪ'nɪəd] gentechnisch verändert ⟨**T3,** 65⟩
enjoyment [ɪn'dʒɔɪmənt] Vergnügen, Freude ⟨**T2,** 39⟩
to **enquire about sth/sb** [ɪŋ'kwaɪə] sich nach etw./jmdm. erkundigen **T4,** 93
entertaining [ˌentə'teɪnɪŋ] unterhaltsam **T4,** 83
entire [ɪn'taɪə] gesamt, ganz, komplett **T1,** 15; **T4,** 81
You're part of my **entity.** [ˌpɑːt‿əv maɪ‿'entɪti] Du bist ein Teil von mir. ⟨**T1,** 17⟩
envelope ['envələʊp] (Brief-)Umschlag **T1,** 10
environmental cost [ɪnˌvaɪərnˌmentl 'kɒst] Umweltbelastung ⟨**T3,** 72⟩
environmentally friendly [ɪnˌvaɪərnˌmentli 'frendli] umweltfreundlich **T3,** 59
epic ['epɪk] episch; gewaltig, unglaublich ⟨**T3,** 62⟩
episode ['epɪsəʊd] Episode; Folge **T1,** 20
*to be **equal** (to) ['iːkwəl] entsprechen **T3,** 70
equivalent [ɪ'kwɪvlənt] Entsprechung, Äquivalent **T3,** 72
*to be **equivalent to sth** [ɪ'kwɪvlənt] etw. entsprechen ⟨**T3,** 70⟩
era ['ɪərə] Ära, Zeitalter **T4,** 88
to **escape** (from) [ɪ'skeɪp] (ent)fliehen, entkommen **T3,** 69; **T4,** 91
argumentative **essay** [ɑːgjəˌmentətɪv 'eseɪ] Erörterung **T2,** 45
essentially [ɪ'sentʃli] im Großen und Ganzen, im Wesentlichen **T1,** 21
to **establish** [ɪ'stæblɪʃ] einrichten, gründen, eröffnen **T4,** 83
to establish as [ɪ'stæblɪʃ] machen zu, etablieren als ⟨**T1,** 15⟩
well-**established** [ˌwelɪ'stæblɪʃt] bekannt, etabliert ⟨**T2,** 34⟩
ethical ['eθɪkl] ethisch, moralisch **T3,** 70
ethics *(sg.)* ['eθɪks] Ethik, Moral ⟨**T4,** 86⟩
ethnic ['eθnɪk] ethnisch; Vielvölker- **T2,** 32
euphemistic [ˌjuːfə'mɪstɪk] euphemistisch, beschönigend ⟨**T4,** 92⟩
to **evaluate** [ɪ'væljueɪt] evaluieren, auswerten, bewerten **T3,** 71
to **evaporate** [ɪ'væpreɪt] verdampfen, verdunsten ⟨**T3,** 71⟩
*to come **even with** [kʌm‿'iːvn wɪð] dieselbe Höhe erreichen wie ⟨**T1,** 11⟩
even so [ˌiːvn 'səʊ] trotzdem, selbst dann **T1,** 22
even though [ˌiːvn‿'ðəʊ] auch wenn; obwohl **T1,** 18
eventually [ɪ'ventʃuəli] schließlich, endlich, irgendwann **T1,** 22
ever since [ˌevə 'sɪns] seitdem **T4,** 80
evidence ['evɪdns] Beweis(material), Beleg **T2,** 44
*to set a good **example to sb** [ˌset‿ə gʊd ɪg'zɑːmpl] jmdm. ein Vorbild sein **T1,** 29
excavator ['ekskəveɪtə] Bagger ⟨**T3,** 63⟩
except [ɪk'sept] außer **T1,** 19
except for [ɪk'sept fə] bis auf, mit Ausnahme von **T2,** 36
except that [ɪk'sept ðæt] abgesehen davon, dass … **T2,** 36
excerpt ['eksɜːpt] Auszug ⟨**T4,** 88⟩
excuse [ɪk'skjuːs] Ausrede, Entschuldigung **T3,** 58
executive [ɪg'zekjətɪv] Direktor/-in, Geschäftsführer/-in **T4,** 92
to **exercise** ['eksəsaɪz] trainieren, üben ⟨**T2,** 36⟩
exhilarating [ɪg'zɪləreɪtɪŋ] berauschend, aufregend ⟨**T1,** 23⟩
*to be in **existence** [ɪg'zɪstns] existieren **T3,** 72
exit ['eksɪt] Ausgang, Ausfahrt **T1,** 20
expression [ɪk'spreʃn] Ausdruck, Wendung; Äußerung **T4,** 92
*to become **extinct** [bɪˌkʌm‿ɪk'stɪŋkt] aussterben **T3,** 59; **T4,** 89
extortionate [ɪk'stɔːʃnət] ungeheuer hoch/teuer ⟨**T2,** 34⟩
extract ['ekstrækt] Auszug; Exzerpt **T3,** 62
extraordinary [ɪk'strɔːdnri] außergewöhnlich **T3,** 69
extremist [ɪk'striːmɪst] extremistisch, radikal; Extremist/-in **T2,** 40
his **eyes were sunken** [hɪz‿aɪz wə 'sʌŋkən] seine Augen lagen tief in den Augenhöhlen ⟨**T2,** 37⟩
to catch sb's eye [kætʃ] jmdm. auffallen ⟨**T4,** 87⟩
to meet sb's eyes [ˌmiːt sʌmbədiz‿'aɪz] jmdm. in die Augen sehen ⟨**T2,** 37⟩

F

to **face** [feɪs] gegenüber stehen; konfrontiert werden mit; mit der Vorderseite zu etw. stehen **T1,** 12; **T3,** 60
to face the consequences [feɪs ðə 'kɒnsɪkwənsɪz] die Konsequenzen tragen **T1,** 14
to face the truth [ˌfeɪs ðə 'truːθ] sich der Wahrheit stellen **T1,** 19
in **fact** [ɪn 'fækt] tatsächlich; eigentlich **T1,** 20; **T2,** 39; genau genommen **T3,** 62
factor ['fæktə] Faktor; Gesichtspunkt; Einfluss **T3,** 72; **T4,** 81
failure ['feɪljə] Erfolglosigkeit, Fehlschlag, Scheitern, Versagen **T2,** 34
fancy ['fæntsi] schick, ausgefallen ⟨**T1,** 17⟩
farmers' market [ˌfɑːməz 'mɑːkɪt] Bauernmarkt **T3,** 59
fat [fæt] fett **T1,** 12

feathered cap [ˌfeðəd ˈkæp] Trachtenhut ⟨**T1,** 26⟩
*to **feed into** [fiːd‿ˈɪntə] münden in ⟨**T1,** 20⟩
*to **feel** [fiːl] der Ansicht sein, die Meinung vertreten ⟨**T4,** 80⟩
to feel strongly about sth [ˌfiːl ˈstrɒŋli‿əˌbaʊt] entschiedene Ansichten über etw. haben **T2,** 47; besorgt um etw. sein, beunruhigt wegen etw. sein, wichtig sein **T3,** 61
fellow [ˈfeləʊ] Mit- **T3,** 68
female [ˈfiːmeɪl] weiblich **T4,** 82
chain-link **fence** [ˌtʃeɪnlɪŋk ˈfens] Maschendrahtzaun ⟨**T1,** 10⟩
fertiliser [ˈfɜːtɪlaɪzə] Dünger **T3,** 71
to **fetch** [fetʃ] (ab)holen **T2,** 38; **T4,** 93
hay **fever** [ˈheɪ ˌfiːvə] Heuschnupfen **T3,** 75
scarlet fever [ˌskɑːlət ˈfiːvə] Scharlach ⟨**T4,** 80⟩
*to **fight for breath** [ˌfaɪt fə ˈbreθ] nach Luft ringen **T3,** 66
figure [ˈfɪgə] Ziffer, Zahl **T1,** 9; **T2,** 44; **T3,** 59
public figure [ˌpʌblɪk ˈfɪgə] Person des öffentlichen Lebens ⟨**T2,** 44⟩
to **figure** [ˈfɪgə] sich vorstellen; schätzen **T3,** 62
to figure out [ˌfɪgər‿ˈaʊt] herausfinden, ergründen **T3,** 66
to **fill** [fɪl] (sich) füllen **T3,** 67
to fill up [fɪl‿ˈʌp] (auf)füllen, sich füllen **T3,** 60
film adaption [ˌfɪlm əˈdæpʃn] Verfilmung **T4,** 89
film genre [ˈfɪlm ˌʒɑ̃ːnrə] Filmgattung **T3,** 68
filmmaker [ˈfɪlmˌmeɪkə] Filmemacher/-in **T3,** 68
financial [faɪˈnænʃl] finanziell ⟨**T1,** 26⟩
*to **find** [faɪnd] herausfinden, feststellen, zu dem Ergebnis kommen **T3,** 70
fingernail [ˈfɪŋgəneɪl] Fingernagel ⟨**T1,** 18⟩
*to set on **fire** [ˌset‿ɒn ˈfaɪə] anzünden, in Brand setzen **T3,** 65
to **fire** [faɪə] schießen mit, abfeuern **T3,** 66
fist [fɪst] Faust ⟨**T4,** 83⟩
to **fit in** [ˌfɪt‿ˈɪn] sich einfügen **T2,** 39
to **fix** [fɪks] reparieren; befestigen **T3,** 63
to fix up [fɪks‿ˈʌp] in Ordnung bringen, renovieren **T4,** 85
flag [flæg] Flagge, Fahne **T4,** 84
flash [flæʃ] (Licht-)Blitz ⟨**T3,** 66⟩
*to be **flattered** [bi ˈflætəd] geschmeichelt sein **T4,** 82
fleshy [ˈfleʃi] fleischig, fleischartig ⟨**T1,** 13⟩
flight attendant [ˈflaɪt əˌtendnt] Flugbegleiter/-in **T4,** 92
to **flirt** [flɜːt] flirten **T4,** 82
to **flood** [flʌd] (über)fluten, überschwemmen **T1,** 13; **T3,** 63
hot **flush** [hɒt ˈflʌʃ] Hitzewallung ⟨**T1,** 21⟩
to **flush** [flʌʃ] die Wasserspülung betätigen, spülen ⟨**T1,** 18⟩; **T3,** 72
to **flutter** [ˈflʌtə] flattern ⟨**T3,** 65⟩
focus [ˈfəʊkəs] Blickpunkt, Schwerpunkt, Fokus **T3,** 71
to **fold up** [fəʊld] zusammenfalten, zusammenlegen, hochklappen ⟨**T1,** 13⟩
folks *(pl.)* [fəʊks] Leute **T3,** 63
food chain [ˈfuːd tʃeɪn] Nahrungskette **T3,** 60
foolish [ˈfuːlɪʃ] dumm, töricht ⟨**T2,** 42⟩
original **footage** [əˌrɪdʒnl ˈfʊtɪdʒ] originales Filmmaterial **T4,** 89
footprint [ˈfʊtprɪnt] Fußabdruck **T3,** 70
for instance [fər‿ˈɪnstəns] zum Beispiel **T2,** 39
forbidden [fəˈbɪdn] verboten ⟨**T2,** 39⟩
ripple of **force** [ˌrɪpl‿əv ˈfɔːs] Stoßwelle ⟨**T1,** 22⟩
to **force** [fɔːs] zwingen **T2,** 37; **T3,** 67
private **fortune** [ˌpraɪvɪt ˈfɔːtʃuːn] Privatvermögen ⟨**T4,** 81⟩
forward [ˈfɔːwəd] vorwärts **T3,** 65
to lean forward [liːn ˈfɔːwəd] sich nach vorn lehnen ⟨**T1,** 11⟩; **T4,** 84
foul [faʊl] verdorben, schmutzig ⟨**T4,** 83⟩
foundation [faʊnˈdeɪʃn] Stiftung, Gründung **T4,** 81
founder [ˈfaʊndə] Gründer/-in **T4,** 81
spring **fountains** *(pl.)* [ˌsprɪŋ ˈfaʊntənz] Quellwasser ⟨**T3,** 58⟩
four-letter word [ˌfɔːletə ˈwɜːd] Schimpfwort, unanständiges Wort ⟨**T1,** 29⟩
fragment [ˈfrægmənt] Fragment, Bruchstück, Teil ⟨**T3,** 60⟩
frankly [ˈfræŋkli] ehrlich gesagt; offen gestanden **T1,** 25; **T4,** 83
frantic [ˈfræntɪk] außer sich, rasend, wild ⟨**T1,** 12⟩
fraternity brother (= frat brother) [frəˈtɜːnəti ˌbrʌðə] Bundesbruder ⟨**T4,** 85⟩
to **freak out** [ˌfriːk‿ˈaʊt] ausflippen **T1,** 14
*to **freeze** [friːz] erstarren; gefrieren **T1,** 13
to **frequent** [frɪˈkwent] häufig aufsuchen ⟨**T4,** 85⟩
frequent [ˈfriːkwənt] häufig **T4,** 85
fresh water [ˈfreʃ ˌwɔːtə] Süßwasser **T3,** 59
fried [fraɪd] gebraten **T2,** 39
environmentally **friendly** [ɪnˌvaɪərnˌmentli ˈfrendli] umweltfreundlich **T3,** 59
frog [frɒg] Frosch **T1,** 22
front [frʌnt] Front-, Vorder- **T3,** 64; Vorderseite **T3,** 65
to **frown** [fraʊn] die Stirn runzeln **T1,** 28
to **function** [ˈfʌŋkʃn] funktionieren **T3,** 64
fundraising [ˈfʌndˌreɪzɪŋ] Spendensammlung ⟨**T4,** 85⟩
fur [fɜː] Fell **T4,** 91
future [ˈfjuːtʃə] zukünftig **T3,** 64; **T4,** 81

G

gaffe [gæf] Ausrutscher, Fauxpas ⟨**T2,** 48⟩; ⟨**T3,** 74⟩
to **gain** [geɪn] gewinnen **T2,** 44
gallery walk [ˈgælri ˌwɔːk] Museumsrundgang, Vernissage ⟨**T4,** 95⟩
gallon [ˈgælən] Gallone *(Hohlmaß: USA: 3,8 l, UK: 4,5 l)* **T3,** 72
gambling [ˈgæmblɪŋ] Glücksspiel, Wetten ⟨**T2,** 39⟩
gang [gæŋ] Gruppe, Bande, Gang **T2,** 33
gas [gæs] Gas **T3,** 58
gas driller [ˈgæs ˌdrɪlə] Gasbohrarbeiter/-in **T3,** 64
greenhouse gas [ˌgriːnhaʊs ˈgæs] Treibhausgas **T3,** 70
tear gas [ˈtɪə ˌgæs] Tränengas ⟨**T3,** 66⟩
gasmask [ˈgæsmɑːsk] Gasmaske **T3,** 65
gasoline *(AE)* [ˈgæsliːn] Benzin **T1,** 25; **T3,** 74
to **generate** [ˈdʒenreɪt] generieren, erzeugen **T3,** 58
generous [ˈdʒenrəs] großzügig **T3,** 74
genetically engineered [dʒəˌnetɪkli endʒɪnɪəd] gentechnisch verändert ⟨**T3,** 65⟩
genius [ˈdʒiːniəs] Genie **T1,** 20
film **genre** [ˈfɪlm ˌʒɑ̃ːnrə] Filmgattung **T3,** 68
genuine [ˈdʒenjuɪn] echt, aufrichtig; authentisch ⟨**T1,** 16⟩
*to **get away from sb** [ˌget‿əˈweɪ frɒm] von jmdm. wegkommen, jmdm. entkommen ⟨**T1,** 12⟩
to get close [get ˈkləʊs] sich nahe kommen **T1,** 21
to get influenced by [get‿ˈɪnfluənst baɪ] beeinflusst werden von **T4,** 83
to get off sth [get‿ˈɒf] wegkommen von etw. ⟨**T4,** 91⟩
to get riled up *(coll)* [ˌget raɪld‿ˈʌp] sich ärgern ⟨**T4,** 84⟩

to get stuck [ˌget 'stʌk] stecken bleiben **T1,** 20
to get the best party in [ˌget ðə best 'pɑ:ti ɪn] die beste Partei an die Macht wählen **T4,** 83
to get trapped [get 'træpt] eingeschlossen/gefangen werden **T3,** 63
to **giggle** ['gɪgl] kichern, lachen ⟨**T1,** 29⟩
*It's a **given that ...** [ɪts‿ə‿'gɪvn ðæt] Es ist offensichtlich, dass ... **T4,** 88
to give a baby up for adoption [ˌgɪv‿ə beɪbi‿'ʌp fər‿ə'dɒpʃn] ein Baby zur Adoption freigeben ⟨**T1,** 19⟩
to give in to sth/sb [gɪv‿'ɪn] etw./jmdm. nachgeben **T1,** 22
to give some thought to sth [ˌgɪv‿sʌm 'θɔ:t tə] sich Gedanken machen über **T1,** 26
to **glance** [glɑ:ns] blicken, einen Blick werfen **T1,** 23
to **glare at sb** ['gleər‿ət] jmdn. (zornig) anstarren **T1,** 21; **T2,** 37
global ['gləʊbl] global, weltweit **T3,** 68
global warming [ˌgləʊbl 'wɔ:mɪŋ] globale Erwärmung **T3,** 58
glove [glʌv] Handschuh **T1,** 12
*to **go for sb** ['gəʊ fɔ:] sich jmdn. vornehmen, auf jmdn. losgehen ⟨**T1,** 12⟩
to go mad [gəʊ 'mæd] verrückt werden, überschnappen **T1,** 18
to go off [gəʊ‿'ɒf] explodieren **T1,** 10
to go on [gəʊ‿'ɒn] weitergehen, weitermachen, geschehen, ablaufen ⟨**T2,** 37⟩
goal [gəʊl] Ziel **T4,** 80
God [gɒd] Gott **T4,** 85
goggles *(pl.)* ['gɒglz] Schutzbrille ⟨**T3,** 67⟩
golden eagle [ˌgəʊldn 'i:gl] Goldadler ⟨**T3,** 62⟩
electrical **goods** *(pl.)* [ɪˌlektrɪkl 'gʊdz] Elektrogeräte **T3,** 71
gorgeous ['gɔ:dʒəs] großartig, hinreißend, wunderschön ⟨**T4,** 82⟩
gradually ['grædʒuəli] allmählich, langsam **T4,** 92
grain [greɪn] Getreide(korn) **T1,** 11
gram (g) [græm] Gramm **T3,** 71
grandchild pl. **grandchildren** ['græntʃaɪld; græn'tʃɪldrn] Enkel/-in, Enkelkind **T3,** 65
*to take sth for **granted** [ˌteɪk fə 'grɑ:ntɪd] etw. als selbstverständlich betrachten, etw. voraussetzen ⟨**T1,** 22⟩
gravel ['grævl] Schotter, Kies ⟨**T1,** 11⟩
gravity ['grævəti] Schwerkraft; Schwere **T3,** 69
greasy ['gri:si] fettig, schmierig ⟨**T2,** 49⟩
greatness ['greɪtnəs] Größe, Bedeutung ⟨**T4,** 88⟩
greenhouse ['gri:nhaʊs] Gewächshaus, Treibhaus **T3,** 70
greenhouse gas [ˌgri:nhaʊs 'gæs] Treibhausgas **T3,** 70
to **grin** [grɪn] grinsen ⟨**T4,** 82⟩
*to **grind** [graɪnd] (zer)mahlen, schleifen ⟨**T1,** 13⟩
grocer ['grəʊsə] Lebensmittelhändler/-in; Lebensmittelgeschäft ⟨**T2,** 35⟩
groceries *(pl.)* ['grəʊsriz] Lebensmittel **T3,** 71
grocery store ['grəʊsri stɔ:] Lebensmittelgeschäft **T1,** 20
ground [graʊnd] (Erd-)Boden, Erde **T3,** 63
pressure **group** ['preʃə ˌgru:p] Interessenverband **T3,** 59
*to **grow** [grəʊ] anbauen **T3,** 70
grower ['grəʊə] Erzeuger/-in, Bauer/Bäuerin **T3,** 70
guerrilla war [gəˌrɪlə 'wɔ:] Guerrillakrieg, Kleinkrieg ⟨**T2,** 36⟩
sense of **guilt** [ˌsens‿əv 'gɪlt] Schuldgefühl **T2,** 38
*to be **guilty of sth** ['gɪlti] sich einer Sache schuldig machen **T4,** 80
gun-fire ['gʌnfaɪə] Kanonenfeuer ⟨**T4,** 84⟩
to **gush** [gʌʃ] strömen, quellen, sprudeln ⟨**T3,** 66⟩
guts *(pl.)* [gʌts] Darm; Bauch ⟨**T1,** 18⟩

H

habit ['hæbɪt] Gewohnheit **T1,** 25; **T3,** 71
ham [hæm] Schinken **T3,** 62
hammer ['hæmə] Hammer **T2,** 46
to **hammer** ['hæmə] hämmern ⟨**T3,** 65⟩
hand [hænd] Blatt *(Kartenspiel)* ⟨**T1,** 17⟩
On the one hand ... , but on the other hand ... [ɒn ðə‿'wʌn ˌhænd ... bʌt‿ɒn ði‿'ʌðə ˌhænd ...] Einerseits ... , andererseits ... **T1,** 8
*to **hang off** [hæŋ‿'ɒf] herunterhängen (von) ⟨**T1,** 13⟩
to hang on [hæŋ‿'ɒn] (einen Augenblick) warten **T4,** 93
to hang out [hæŋ‿'aʊt] sich hinauslehnen **T1,** 12
to live **happily ever after** [lɪv ˌhæpɪli‿evər‿'ɑ:ftə] glücklich bis ans Ende seiner Tage/seines Lebens leben ⟨**T2,** 36⟩
harsh [hɑ:ʃ] rau, hart, streng, scharf **T2,** 34; ⟨**T2,** 38⟩
to **harvest** ['hɑ:vɪst] ernten **T3,** 70
to **haul** [hɔ:l] wegziehen, wegzerren ⟨**T3,** 67⟩
*to **have a say** [ˌhæv‿ə 'seɪ] etw. zu sagen haben, zu Wort kommen; Mitspracherecht haben **T4,** 83
have a say day [ˌhæv‿ə 'seɪ deɪ] *(Tag, an dem man zu Wort kommt)* ⟨**T4,** 82⟩
Hawaiian [hə'waɪən] hawaiianisch; Hawaiianer/-in **T3,** 60
hay fever ['heɪ ˌfi:və] Heuschnupfen **T3,** 75
headlight ['hedlaɪt] Scheinwerfer ⟨**T1,** 11⟩
to **heal up** [hi:l‿'ʌp] verheilen **T3,** 75
world **health situation** [ˌwɜ:ld ˌhelθ sɪtju'eɪʃn] Gesundheitszustand der Weltbevölkerung ⟨**T4,** 81⟩
healthcare ['helθkeə] Gesundheitsversorgung **T4,** 81
*to be at sth's **heart** [hɑ:t] im Zentrum von etw. stehen **T2,** 46
heated ['hi:tɪd] beheizt, erhitzt **T3,** 70
heavenly ['hevnli] himmlisch **T3,** 62
hedge [hedʒ] Hecke **T1,** 16
heel [hi:l] Ferse, Hacke **T3,** 75
beat to **hell** [ˌbi:t tə 'hel] total ramponiert ⟨**T1,** 11⟩
to run like hell [ˌrʌn laɪk 'hel] um sein Leben rennen ⟨**T1,** 13⟩
helper ['helpə] Helfer/-in **T4,** 85
hippy ['hɪpi] Hippie **T3,** 65
historic [hɪ'stɒrɪk] historisch **T4,** 88
history was being made ['hɪstri wəz bi:ɪŋ ˌmeɪd] Geschichte wurde geschrieben. **T3,** 65
H_2O (= water) [ˌeɪtʃtu:'əʊ] H_2O (= Wasser) **T3,** 70
to **hoist** [hɔɪst] hochziehen, hochheben ⟨**T3,** 66⟩
holiday ['hɒlədeɪ] Feiertag **T4,** 92
homeland ['həʊmlænd] Heimat(land) ⟨**T3,** 69⟩
homeopathic [ˌhəʊmiə'pæθɪk] homöopathisch **T3,** 75
*to be **homesick** ['həʊmsɪk] Heimweh haben **T2,** 35
honest ['ɒnɪst] ehrlich **T1,** 16; **T4,** 86
honestly ['ɒnɪstli] ehrlich gesagt **T1,** 25
honesty ['ɒnɪsti] Ehrlichkeit **T4,** 86
horrified ['hɒrɪfaɪd] entsetzt **T4,** 83
a **host of** [ə 'həʊst‿əv] ein Heer an, jede Menge **T2,** 35
household ['haʊshəʊld] Haushalt **T3,** 70
housing payment ['haʊzɪŋ ˌpeɪmənt] Miete ⟨**T4,** 83⟩
how on earth [ˌhaʊ‿ɒn 'ɜ:θ] wie in aller Welt ⟨**T3,** 60⟩
humanity [hju:'mænəti] Menschheit **T3,** 68

a sea of humanity [ˌsiː‿əv hjuːˈmænəti] ein Meer an Menschlichkeit ⟨**T3,** 65⟩

humour [ˈhjuːmə] Humor; Komik; Stimmung **T1,** 19

one **hundredth** [wʌn ˈhʌndrədθ] ein Hundertstel ⟨**T3,** 59⟩

hunk *(coll)* [hʌŋk] *(gut aussehender Mann mit gutem Körperbau)* ⟨**T4,** 82⟩

hurricane-damaged [ˈhʌrɪkənˌdæmɪdʒd] von einem Wirbelsturm beschädigt ⟨**T4,** 85⟩

hypothetical [ˌhaɪpəˈθetɪkl] hypothetisch, theoretisch **T3,** 73

I

I can't wait [aɪ ˌkɑːnt ˈweɪt] ich kann es kaum erwarten ⟨**T2,** 41⟩

to **identify with** [aɪˈdentɪfaɪ] sich identifizieren mit **T2,** 38

to **idle** [aɪdl] im Leerlauf laufen; faulenzen ⟨**T1,** 13⟩

ignorance [ˈɪgnərns] Unwissenheit, Ignoranz **T3,** 60; ⟨**T4,** 83⟩

ignorant [ˈɪgnərnt] ignorant, unwissend, ahnungslos **T4,** 84

iguana [ɪˈgwɑːnə] Leguan ⟨**T4,** 91⟩

*to be **illiterate** [bi ɪˈlɪtrət] Analphabet/-in sein ⟨**T2,** 44⟩

illness [ˈɪlnəs] Krankheit **T3,** 75

bacterial illness [bækˌtɪəriəl ˈɪlnəs] bakterielle Erkrankung ⟨**T4,** 80⟩

to **illustrate** [ˈɪləstreɪt] veranschaulichen, darstellen, illustrieren **T1,** 26

image [ˈɪmɪdʒ] Bild **T3,** 67

imagery [ˈɪmɪdʒri] Bilder, Bildsprache **T3,** 68

immature [ˌɪməˈtjʊə] unreif, kindisch **T1,** 19

immediate [ɪˈmiːdiət] direkt, unmittelbar, spontan **T3,** 67

immediately [ɪˈmiːdiətli] sofort, gleich **T1,** 12

immoral [ɪˈmɒrl] unmoralisch ⟨**T4,** 80⟩

impact [ˈɪmpækt] Aufprall **T3,** 66; Einfluss, Auswirkung **T3,** 70

implication [ˌɪmplɪˈkeɪʃn] Auswirkung, Folge ⟨**T1,** 20⟩

impossible [ɪmˈpɒsəbl] unmöglich **T3,** 66

imprisonment [ɪmˈprɪznmənt] Gefangenschaft, Haft **T1,** 8

in agreement [ˌɪn‿əˈgriːmənt] zustimmend, voller Zustimmung ⟨**T4,** 82⟩

in a nutshell [ˌɪn‿ə ˈnʌtʃel] zusammengefasst, kurz und bündig **T3,** 73

in fact [ɪn ˈfækt] tatsächlich; eigentlich **T1,** 20; **T2,** 39; genau genommen **T3,** 62

in order to [ɪn‿ˈɔːdə tə] um … zu, mit der Absicht **T3,** 65

inauguration speech [ɪˌnɔːgjəˈreɪʃn ˌspiːtʃ] Amtseinführungsrede ⟨**T4,** 88⟩

inch [ɪntʃ] Zoll *(Längenmaß: 2, 54 cm)* **T3,** 72

to **inch out** [ɪntʃ‿ˈaʊt] sich ganz langsam hinausbewegen ⟨**T1,** 20⟩

to **include** [ɪnˈkluːd] aufnehmen, einbinden, einbeziehen **T2,** 35; beinhalten, einschließen **T3,** 70; **T4,** 91

inconvenient [ˌɪnkənˈviːniənt] unbequem, lästig **T4,** 93

indeed [ɪnˈdiːd] in der Tat, tatsächlich, allerdings **T1,** 16

indescribable [ˌɪndɪˈskraɪbəbl] unbeschreiblich ⟨**T1,** 27⟩

to **indulge (in) sth** [ɪnˈdʌldʒ] sich etw. hingeben, etw. nachgeben, sich in etw. ergehen **T2,** 44

industrial-scale trawler [ɪnˌdʌstriəlskeɪl ˈtrɔːlə] Fischereiboot für den industriellen Fischfang ⟨**T3,** 68⟩

inevitable [ɪnˈevɪtəbl] unvermeidlich, unabwendbar ⟨**T1,** 21⟩

infant [ˈɪnfənt] Säugling, Kleinkind **T4,** 85

infection [ɪnˈfekʃn] Infekt(ion); Ansteckung **T3,** 75

infidel [ˈɪnfɪdl] Ungläubige/-r ⟨**T2,** 39⟩

infinity [ɪnˈfɪnəti] Unendlichkeit **T1,** 20

inflamed [ɪnˈfleɪmd] entzündet **T3,** 75

*to get **influenced by** [get‿ˈɪnfluənst baɪ] beeinflusst werden von **T4,** 83

influential [ˌɪnfluˈenʃl] einflussreich, maßgebend **T3,** 71

informal [ɪnˈfɔːml] informell; zwanglos **T3,** 64

injection [ɪnˈdʒekʃn] Spritze, Injektion **T3,** 75

injury [ˈɪndʒri] Verletzung **T1,** 14

insane [ɪnˈseɪn] verrückt, irre, wahnsinnig; unsinnig ⟨**T1,** 10⟩

insecticide [ɪnˈsektɪsaɪd] Insektenvernichtungsmittel ⟨**T3,** 72⟩

to **lean inside** [ˌliːn‿ɪnˈsaɪd] sich hineinbeugen ⟨**T1,** 14⟩

to **insist** (on) [ɪnˈsɪst] bestehen (auf), insistieren **T1,** 11; **T3,** 62

insistent [ɪnˈsɪstnt] nachdrücklich, hartnäckig **T1,** 21

insolent [ˈɪnslənt] unverschämt, frech, anmaßend ⟨**T2,** 38⟩

*to be **inspired by sth/sb** [ɪnˈspaɪəd baɪ] hervorgerufen/geweckt werden von etw./jmdm. **T2,** 36

inspiring [ɪnˈspaɪərɪŋ] inspirierend, anregend **T4,** 88

to **install** [ɪnˈstɔːl] anschließen, installieren, einrichten ⟨**T2,** 36⟩

for **instance** [fər‿ˈɪnstəns] zum Beispiel **T2,** 39

instead [ɪnˈsted] stattdessen **T3,** 60

institution [ˌɪnstɪˈtjuːʃn] Einrichtung, Organisation, Institution **T2,** 34; **T4,** 93

torture **instrument** [ˈtɔːtʃə ˌɪnstrəmənt] Folterwerkzeug ⟨**T2,** 37⟩

insurance [ɪnˈʃʊərns] Versicherung ⟨**T1,** 20⟩

insurance rate [ɪnˈʃʊərns reɪt] Versicherungsbeitrag ⟨**T1,** 20⟩

intense [ɪnˈtens] ernsthaft; heftig ⟨**T3,** 67⟩

*to be **intent on doing sth** [ɪnˈtent‿ɒn] fest entschlossen sein, etw. zu tun ⟨**T2,** 44⟩

intention [ɪnˈtenʃn] Absicht, Intention **T1,** 16

intentional [ɪnˈtenʃnl] absichtlich, vorsätzlich ⟨**T1,** 16⟩

intercultural competence [ɪntəˌkʌltʃrl ˈkɒmpɪtns] interkulturelle Kompetenz/Fähigkeit ⟨**T3,** 74⟩; ⟨**T1,** 26⟩

international [ˌɪntəˈnæʃnl] international **T3,** 59; **T4,** 80

interpretation [ɪnˌtɜːprɪˈteɪʃn] Interpretation, Auslegung ⟨**T2,** 40⟩

interpreter [ɪnˈtɜːprɪtə] Dolmetscher/-in **T2,** 44

interpreting [ɪnˈtɜːprɪtɪŋ] Dolmetschen, Verdolmetschung ⟨**T2,** 44⟩

introduction [ˌɪntrəˈdʌkʃn] Einleitung **T3,** 69

to **intrude on** [ɪnˈtruːd] eindringen in **T3,** 63

to **invade sth** [ɪnˈveɪd] in etw. eindringen, etw. überfallen **T3,** 74

to **investigate** [ɪnˈvestɪgeɪt] ermitteln, untersuchen; recherchieren ⟨**T3,** 73⟩

*to be **involved** (in) [bi ɪnˈvɒlvd‿ɪn] sich beteiligen (an), sich engagieren (bei/in) **T4,** 80

to **iron** [aɪən] bügeln ⟨**T3,** 72⟩

irony [ˈaɪərəni] Ironie **T2,** 43

irrationality [ɪˌræʃnˈæləti] Unvernünftigkeit, Irrationalität ⟨**T2,** 37⟩

to **irrigate** [ˈɪrɪgeɪt] bewässern ⟨**T3,** 71⟩

It's a given that … [ɪts‿ə‿ˈgɪvn ðæt] Es ist offensichtlich, dass … **T4,** 88

it won't be long [ɪt ˌwəʊnt bi ˈlɒŋ] es wird nicht (mehr) lange dauern **T3,** 64

item [ˈaɪtəm] Gegenstand, Objekt **T3,** 60

J

jam [dʒæm] Konfitüre **T2,** 49
to **jerk** [dʒɜ:k] reißen, schleudern, werfen; zucken ⟨**T1,** 12⟩
Jewish ['dʒu:ɪʃ] jüdisch **T4,** 82
to **join** [dʒɔɪn] sich anschließen, sich gesellen zu **T3,** 62
juice [dʒu:s] Saft **T1,** 19
orange juice ['ɒrɪndʒ ˌdʒu:s] Orangensaft **T2,** 49
juicy ['dʒu:si] saftig; pikant, anstößig **T1,** 16
to **jump for sth** [dʒʌmp] auf etw. zuspringen ⟨**T1,** 11⟩
jungle ['dʒʌŋgl] Dschungel **T4,** 89
junior ['dʒu:niə] Schüler/-in im dritten Schuljahr ⟨**T4,** 85⟩
jury member ['dʒʊəri ˌmembə] Jurymitglied **T3,** 68
to **justify** ['dʒʌstɪfaɪ] rechtfertigen **T3,** 67
juvenile crime [ˌdʒu:vnaɪl 'kraɪm] Jugendkriminalität ⟨**T1,** 14⟩

K

*to be **keen to do sth** [bi 'ki:n] sehr daran interessiert sein, etw. zu tun **T3,** 71
*to **keep a diary** [ˌki:p‿ə 'daɪəri] ein Tagebuch/einen Terminkalender führen ⟨**T1,** 27⟩
to keep from ['ki:p frəm] bewahren vor, abhalten, fernhalten **T4,** 89
to keep up (with) [ki:p‿'ʌp] mithalten (mit), Schritt halten (mit) **T1,** 11
keyboard ['ki:bɔ:d] Keyboard; Tastatur **T3,** 60
kilogram (kg) ['kɪləgræm] Kilogramm **T3,** 72
kilometre (km) ['kɪləʊˌmi:tə; kɪ'lɒmɪtə] Kilometer **T3,** 72
that **kind of thing** ['ðæt kaɪnd‿əv θɪŋ] solche Sachen, so etwas ⟨**T2,** 37⟩
kipper ['kɪpə] Räucherhering ⟨**T2,** 49⟩
knock [nɒk] Stoß, Schlag **T3,** 67
to **knock** [nɒk] stoßen; schlagen ⟨**T2,** 40⟩; klopfen **T4,** 83

L

to **label sb (as) sth** ['leɪbl] jmdn. als etw. abstempeln **T2,** 44
labor *(AE)* ['leɪbə] Arbeitskraft/-kräfte **T3,** 64
ladder ['lædə] Leiter **T1,** 11
lane [leɪn] Weg, Gasse; Fahrspur **T4,** 82
lap [læp] Schoß ⟨**T1,** 18⟩
lassi ['lasɪ] Lassi *(indisches Jogurtgetränk)* ⟨**T2,** 49⟩
to **last** [lɑ:st] (an)dauern, anhalten **T1,** 19; Zeit brauchen, um sich abzubauen **T3,** 60
lasting ['lɑ:stɪŋ] bleibend, dauerhaft **T3,** 64
lately ['leɪtli] in letzter Zeit, kürzlich **T3,** 63; **T4,** 92
laugh [lɑ:f] Lachen **T4,** 82
launch [lɔ:ntʃ] Einführung; Start, Abschuss **T2,** 34
to **launch** [lɔ:ntʃ] einführen, starten, in Gang setzen **T4,** 80
*to break the **law** [ˌbreɪk ðə 'lɔ:] gegen das Gesetz verstoßen **T4,** 84
layer ['leɪə] Schicht, Lage **T3,** 63
layout ['leɪaʊt] Layout, Anordnung, Anlage **T1,** 10
*to **lead** [li:d] anführen **T4,** 81
lead singer ['li:d ˌsɪŋə] Leadsänger/-in, Frontsänger/-in **T3,** 69
leader of the opposition [ˌli:dər‿əv ði‿ˌɒpə'zɪʃn] Oppositionsführer/-in **T4,** 84
league table ['li:g ˌteɪbl] Tabelle ⟨**T3,** 71⟩
out of my league [ˌaʊt‿əv maɪ 'li:g] nicht meine Kragenweite ⟨**T1,** 10⟩
to be in the big leagues [ˌbi:‿ɪn ðə 'bɪg li:gz] zur Spitzenklasse gehören ⟨**T1,** 11⟩
to **leak** [li:k] lecken, auslaufen, undicht sein **T3,** 63
to **lean (towards)** [li:n] sich (zu jmdm. hinüber)lehnen **T2,** 37
to lean forward [li:n 'fɔ:wəd] sich nach vorn lehnen ⟨**T1,** 11⟩; **T4,** 84
to lean inside [ˌli:n‿ɪn'saɪd] sich hineinbeugen ⟨**T1,** 14⟩
*to **learn** [lɜ:n] erfahren, herausfinden **T4,** 93
lease [li:s] Miete, Pacht **T3,** 63
to **lease** [li:s] (ver)mieten, (ver)pachten, leasen **T3,** 63
leather shorts *(pl.)* ['leðə ʃɔ:ts] Lederhose ⟨**T1,** 26⟩
It seemed to be all that was **left to us.** [ɪt ˌsi:md‿tə bi‿'ɔ:l ðæt wɒz ˌleft tə ʌs] Es schien, als bliebe uns nichts anderes übrig. ⟨**T2,** 37⟩
length [leŋθ] Länge; Dauer **T3,** 72
lens [lenz] Linse ⟨**T3,** 67⟩
let alone [ˌlet‿ə'ləʊn] geschweige denn ⟨**T2,** 44⟩
letter ['letə] Brief, Schreiben **T3,** 63
lettuce ['letɪs] Kopfsalat **T3,** 70
level ['levl] Ebene **T4,** 85
liberal ['lɪbrl] liberal; Liberale/-r **T2,** 40
*to take **liberties with** [teɪk 'lɪbətiz wɪð] es nicht so genau nehmen mit **T4,** 89
artistic **license** [ɑ:ˌtɪstɪk 'laɪsns] künstlerische Freiheit ⟨**T4,** 89⟩
white **lie** [ˌwaɪt 'laɪ] Notlüge ⟨**T4,** 86⟩
real-**life** ['rɪəlaɪf] authentisch, aus dem wirklichen Leben **T3,** 68
to bring to life [ˌbrɪŋ tə 'laɪf] veranschaulichen, zum Leben erwecken **T3,** 67
to take the life of sb [ˌteɪk ðə 'laɪf‿əv] jmdn. das Leben kosten **T4,** 85
lifeguard stand ['laɪfgɑ:d stænd] Rettungsstation ⟨**T1,** 21⟩
age **limit** [ˌeɪdʒ 'lɪmɪt] Altersgrenze **T1,** 8
to live within the limits of sth [ˌlɪv wɪˌðɪn ðə 'lɪmɪts] innerhalb der Grenzen von etw. leben ⟨**T3,** 59⟩
to **line up a shot** [ˌlaɪn‿ʌp‿ə 'ʃɒt] zielen ⟨**T1,** 22⟩
cruise **liner** ['kru:z ˌlaɪnə] Kreuzfahrtschiff **T3,** 73
to **linger** ['lɪŋgə] bleiben, verweilen **T1,** 12
lip [lɪp] Lippe **T4,** 82
lipstick ['lɪpstɪk] Lippenstift **T3,** 60
to **list** [lɪst] auflisten **T3,** 60
literature ['lɪtrətʃə] Literatur **T3,** 64
litre (l) ['li:tə] Liter **T3,** 71
litter ['lɪtə] Müll, Abfall **T3,** 60
to **litter** ['lɪtə] verschmutzen, verunreinigen **T3,** 61
to **live happily ever after** [lɪv ˌhæpɪli‿evər‿'ɑ:ftə] glücklich bis ans Ende seiner Tage/seines Lebens leben ⟨**T2,** 36⟩
to live up to one's name [lɪv‿'ʌp tə] seinem Namen alle Ehre machen **T4,** 85
to live within the limits of sth [ˌlɪv wɪˌðɪn ðə 'lɪmɪts] innerhalb der Grenzen von etw. leben ⟨**T3,** 59⟩
*to make one's **living** [ˌmeɪk‿wʌnz 'lɪvɪŋ] seinen Lebensunterhalt bestreiten **T3,** 62
location [ləʊ'keɪʃn] Aufenthaltsort, Lage, Standort ⟨**T1,** 26⟩
locavore ['ləʊkəvɔ:] *Person, die nur regionale Produkte konsumiert* ⟨**T3,** 70⟩
it won't be **long** [ɪt ˌwəʊnt bi 'lɒŋ] es wird nicht (mehr) lange dauern **T3,** 64
longing ['lɒŋɪŋ] Verlangen, Sehnsucht ⟨**T1,** 21⟩
loo *(coll)* [lu:] Klo, Toilette ⟨**T1,** 18⟩
look [lʊk] Ausdruck **T2,** 39
to **look set to do sth** [ˌlʊk 'set tə] so aussehen als ob **T3,** 64
to look up to sb [lʊk‿'ʌp tə] zu jmdm. aufschauen, jmdn. bewundern **T1,** 15

*to shake **loose** [ʃeɪk lu:z] abschütteln ⟨**T1,** 12⟩
to tear oneself loose [teə 'lu:z] sich losreißen ⟨**T1,** 13⟩
to **loosen** ['lu:sn] lockern ⟨**T2,** 38⟩
Lordship ['lɔ:dʃɪp] Lordschaft ⟨**T4,** 93⟩
all-time **low** [ˌɔ:ltaɪm 'ləʊ] historisches Tief, historischer Tiefpunkt ⟨**T4,** 88⟩
to **lower** ['ləʊə] (ab)senken; verringern **T3,** 62
to call oneself **lucky** [ˌkɔ:l wʌnself 'lʌki] sich glücklich schätzen **T4,** 83
ludicrous ['lu:dɪkrəs] irrsinnig, lächerlich ⟨**T2,** 36⟩

M

answering **machine** ['ɑ:nsrɪŋ məˌʃi:n] Anrufbeantworter **T4,** 93
*to go **mad** [gəʊ 'mæd] verrückt werden, überschnappen **T1,** 18
madness ['mædnəs] Wahnsinn, Irrsinn **T3,** 61
mail [meɪl] Post ⟨**T4,** 93⟩
mainstream ['meɪnstrɪ:m] Durchschnitts-; Massen-; Hauptrichtung **T2,** 34
maintenance ['meɪntnəns] Instandhaltung, Erhaltung, Pflege **T4,** 85
major ['meɪdʒə] wichtig, bedeutend; Haupt- **T4,** 80
majority (of) [mə'dʒɒrəti] Mehrheit, Mehrzahl **T2,** 32; **T3,** 72; **T4,** 86; **T4,** 88
*history was being **made** ['hɪstri wəz bi:ɪŋ ˌmeɪd] Geschichte wurde geschrieben. **T3,** 65
to make a case for [ˌmeɪk‿ə 'keɪs fə] plädieren für ⟨**T4,** 83⟩
to make no acknowledgement of sth [ˌmeɪk nəʊ ək'nɒlɪdʒmənt‿əv] etw. nicht an die große Glocke hängen ⟨**T2,** 44⟩
to make one's living [ˌmeɪk‿wʌnz 'lɪvɪŋ] seinen Lebensunterhalt bestreiten **T3,** 62
to make one's point [ˌmeɪk wʌnz 'pɔɪnt] seinen Standpunkt deutlich machen **T1,** 14
maker ['meɪkə] Macher/-in **T4,** 89
male [meɪl] männlich **T4,** 82
old **man** *(coll)* [əʊld 'mæn] Vater ⟨**T2,** 37⟩
mantra ['mæntrə] Mantra, Motto ⟨**T3,** 71⟩
manufacture [ˌmænjə'fæktʃə] Herstellung, Produktion, Fertigung ⟨**T3,** 70⟩

march [mɑ:tʃ] Marsch, Kundgebung **T3,** 66
to **march** [mɑ:tʃ] marschieren; wandern **T3,** 65
marine [mə'ri:n] Meeres-, See- **T3,** 60
to **mark an anniversary** [ˌmɑ:k‿ən‿ænɪ'vɜ:sri] ein Jubiläum feiern, einen Feiertag begehen **T2,** 50
farmers' **market** [ˌfɑ:məz 'mɑ:kɪt] Bauernmarkt **T3,** 59
marriage ['mærɪdʒ] Ehe, Eheschließung **T1,** 8
arranged marriage [əˌreɪndʒd 'mærɪdʒ] arrangierte Hochzeit **T2,** 38
chicken tikka **masala** [ˌtʃɪkɪn tɪkə mə'sɑ:lə] *(Currygericht aus gegrillten marinierten Hähnchenfleischstücken in einer würzigen Soße)* ⟨**T2,** 47⟩
mass [mæs] Masse; Massen- **T2,** 32
massive ['mæsɪv] riesig, massiv, wuchtig **T3,** 65
matter ['mætə] Angelegenheit, Thema **T3,** 63
no matter [nəʊ 'mætə] egal, ganz gleich **T1,** 16
to be the matter with [bi‿ðə 'mætə wɪð] nicht stimmen mit, los sein mit ⟨**T3,** 75⟩
to **matter** ['mætə] von Bedeutung sein, etw. ausmachen **T3,** 70; ⟨**T4,** 84⟩
It doesn't matter. ['mætə] Es ist egal. **T1,** 22
mature [mə'tjʊə] erwachsen, reif, mündig **T1,** 19
maturity [mə'tjʊərəti] Erwachsensein, Reife, Mündigkeit **T1,** 19
meadow ['medəʊ] Wiese, Viehweide **T3,** 62
meanwhile [ˌmi:n'waɪl] währenddessen, mittlerweile, in der Zwischenzeit **T1,** 13
measure ['meʒə] Maß, Größenwert ⟨**T3,** 73⟩
measurement ['meʒəmənt] Maß(einheit) **T3,** 71
unit of measurement ['ju:nɪt‿əv ˌmeʒəmənt] Maß-, Größeneinheit **T3,** 72
mediator ['mi:dieɪtə] Mediator/-in, Schlichter/-in, Vermittler/-in ⟨**T1,** 9⟩
meditation [ˌmedɪ'teɪʃn] Meditation; Betrachtung ⟨**T3,** 68⟩
Mediterranean [ˌmedɪtr'eɪniən] mediterran, Mittelmeer(-) **T3,** 76
*to **meet sb's eyes** [ˌmi:t sʌmbədiz‿'aɪz] jmdm. in die Augen sehen ⟨**T2,** 37⟩
to meet the demands of sb/sth [ˌmi:t ðə dɪ'mɑ:ndz‿əv] den Anforderungen von jmdm./etw. nachkommen **T4,** 88

meeting ['mi:tɪŋ] Treffen, Besprechung **T4,** 93
jury **member** ['dʒʊəri ˌmembə] Jurymitglied **T3,** 68
to **mend one's ways** [mend] sich bessern ⟨**T2,** 39⟩
to **mess up sth** [ˌmes‿'ʌp] etw. durcheinanderbringen; etw. in Unordnung bringen **T3,** 69
*to take a **message** [ˌteɪk‿ə 'mesɪdʒ] eine Nachricht entgegennehmen/notieren **T4,** 93
methane ['mi:θeɪn] Methan **T3,** 63
method ['meθəd] Methode, Art ⟨**T3,** 73⟩; **T4,** 89
cubic **metre** [ˌkju:bɪk 'mi:tə] Kubikmeter **T3,** 71
metric tonne [ˌmetrɪk 'tʌn] (metrische) Tonne **T3,** 70
microphone ['maɪkrəfəʊn] Mikrofon ⟨**T4,** 83⟩
square **mile (= sq. mile)** [ˌskweə 'maɪl] Quadratmeile **T3,** 72
millilitre (ml) ['mɪlɪˌli:tə] Milliliter **T3,** 71
mineral ['mɪnrl] Mineral(-) **T2,** 49
mineral right ['mɪnrl raɪt] Abbaurecht **T3,** 63
to **minimise** ['mɪnɪmaɪz] vermindern, minimieren **T3,** 71
Prime **Minister** [ˌpraɪm 'mɪnɪstə] Premierminister/-in, Ministerpräsident/-in **T4,** 84
rearview **(mirror)** [ˌrɪəvju: 'mɪrə] Rückspiegel ⟨**T1,** 23⟩
wing mirror ['wɪŋ mɪrə] Außenspiegel ⟨**T2,** 40⟩
miserable ['mɪzrəbl] elend, unglücklich; armselig **T2,** 40
*to be **missing** [bi 'mɪsɪŋ] fehlen **T3,** 71
mission ['mɪʃn] Mission, Auftrag **T4,** 94
misunderstood [ˌmɪsʌndə'stʊd] missverstanden **T1,** 15
to be caught up in the **moment** [ˌbi kɔ:t‿'ʌp ɪn ðə 'məʊmənt] in dem Moment gefangen sein, vertieft sein **T3,** 67
Buddhist **monk** [ˌbʊdɪst 'mʌŋk] buddhistischer Mönch **T3,** 67
monotonous [mə'nɒtnəs] monoton, eintönig ⟨**T2,** 39⟩
mosque [mɒsk] Moschee **T2,** 44
circular **motion** [ˌsɜ:kjələ 'məʊʃn] Kreisbewegung ⟨**T3,** 60⟩
motor bike ['məʊtə baɪk] Motorrad **T4,** 83
motorised ['məʊtraɪzd] motorbetrieben, motorisiert ⟨**T3,** 73⟩
mouldy-looking ['məʊldiˌlʊkɪŋ] schäbig aussehend ⟨**T2,** 37⟩

mouthful ['maʊθfʊl] Bissen; Schluck ⟨**T3,** 62⟩
to **move sb to tears** [ˌmu:v tə 'tɪəz] jmdn. zu Tränen rühren **T3,** 60
to **multiply** ['mʌltɪplaɪ] multiplizieren, vervielfachen **T3,** 73
murder ['mɜ:də] Mord **T3,** 65
mushroom ['mʌʃrʊm] Pilz, Champignon **T2,** 49
by **myself** [baɪ maɪ'self] allein ⟨**T1,** 10⟩
under **mysterious conditions** [ˌʌndə mɪˌstɪəriəs kən'dɪʃnz] unter mysteriösen Umständen ⟨**T4,** 89⟩

N

naan (bread) [nɑ:n] Naanbrot *(indisches Fladenbrot)* ⟨**T2,** 47⟩; ⟨**T2,** 49⟩
naive [naɪ'i:v] naiv, blauäugig **T1,** 28; **T3,** 67
to live up to one's **name** [lɪv‿'ʌp tə] seinem Namen alle Ehre machen **T4,** 85
narrative technique [ˌnærətɪv tek'ni:k] Erzähltechnik ⟨**T1,** 14⟩; ⟨**T3,** 64⟩
narrator [nə'reɪtə] Erzähler/-in ⟨**T1,** 20⟩; **T2,** 36; **T3,** 67
to **narrow** ['nærəʊ] (sich) verengen **T1,** 22
natural resource [ˌnætʃrl rɪ'zɔ:s] Ressource, Rohstoff, Bodenschatz **T3,** 58
near-unpronounceable [ˌnɪərʌnprə'naʊnsəbl] fast unaussprechbar ⟨**T3,** 68⟩
nearly ['nɪəli] fast, annähernd **T1,** 12
necessity [nə'sesəti] Notwendigkeit **T4,** 88
in **need** [ɪn 'ni:d] in Not **T1,** 16
neglected [nɪ'glektɪd] vernachlässigt **T1,** 15
negro pl. **negroes** ['ni:grəʊ] Neger ⟨**T4,** 92⟩
neither ['naɪðə] weder noch, unentschlossen, kein **T2,** 33
neutral ['nju:trl] neutral **T3,** 73
opening **night** ['əʊpnɪŋ ˌnaɪt] Premierenabend ⟨**T4,** 86⟩
nightstick ['naɪtstɪk] Schlagstock ⟨**T1,** 12⟩
nitrogen ['naɪtrədʒən] Stickstoff **T3,** 72
no doubt [nəʊ 'daʊt] zweifellos, wohl **T1,** 18
no matter [nəʊ 'mætə] egal, ganz gleich **T1,** 16
no one else ['nəʊ‿wʌn els] niemand sonst **T2,** 34
nod of approval [ˌnɒd‿əv‿ə'pru:vl] zustimmendes Nicken ⟨**T4,** 82⟩
nomination [ˌnɒmɪ'neɪʃn] Nominierung, Ernennung **T1,** 25
non- [nɒn] nicht- **T3,** 72
non-violent [ˌnɒn'vaɪəlnt] friedlich, gewaltfrei **T4,** 81
northern ['nɔ:ðn] nördlich **T4,** 87
not ... either [nɒt ... 'aɪðə; nɒt ... 'i:ðə;] auch nicht ⟨**T2,** 38⟩
not (...) yet [nɒt 'jet] noch nicht **T3,** 64
note [nəʊt] Geldschein **T4,** 86
spiral **notebook** [ˌspaɪərl 'nəʊtbʊk] Ringbuch ⟨**T1,** 10⟩
*to take **notice** [teɪk 'nəʊtɪs] beachten, zur Kenntnis nehmen; aufmerksam werden **T4,** 83
nuanced ['nju:ɑ:nst] nuanciert, nuancenreich ⟨**T3,** 68⟩
nuclear energy [ˌnju:kliə 'enədʒi] Kernenergie **T3,** 68
cashew **nut** ['kæʃu: ˌnʌt] Cashewnuss ⟨**T2,** 37⟩
in a **nutshell** [ˌɪn‿ə 'nʌtʃel] zusammengefasst, kurz und bündig **T3,** 73
to present sth in a nutshell [prɪˌzent‿ɪn‿ə 'nʌtʃel] etw. zusammenfassend/in aller Kürze darstellen ⟨**T2,** 38⟩

O

to **obey sb** [əʊ'beɪ] jmdm. gehorchen **T2,** 37
to **object to (doing) sth** [əb'dʒekt] etw. ablehnen **T2,** 34
occasion [ə'keɪʒn] Gelegenheit, Anlass **T3,** 74; Ereignis **T4,** 82
occasional [ə'keɪʒnl] gelegentlich **T2,** 41
occupancy ['ɒkjəpənsi] Besetzung, Belegung ⟨**T3,** 73⟩
ocean current [ˌəʊʃn 'kʌrnt] Meeresströmung ⟨**T3,** 60⟩
offender [ə'fendə] Übeltäter/-in, Zuwiderhandelnde/-r **T3,** 71
offensive [ə'fensɪv] angreifend, beleidigend; anstößig **T4,** 92
offshore [ˌɒf'ʃɔ:] vor der Küste gelegen **T3,** 59
to anchor offshore [ˌæŋkər‿'ɒfʃɔ:] im Hafen liegen **T3,** 65
ointment ['ɔɪntmənt] Salbe **T3,** 75
old man *(coll)* [əʊld 'mæn] Vater ⟨**T2,** 37⟩
On the one hand ..., but on the other hand ... [ɒn ðə 'wʌn ˌhænd ... bʌt‿ɒn ði‿'ʌðə ˌhænd ...] Einerseits ..., andererseits ... **T1,** 8
on the spot [spɒt] umgehend, sofort ⟨**T1,** 26⟩
on the whole [ˌɒn ðə 'həʊl] im Großen und Ganzen **T2,** 39
onion ['ʌnjən] Zwiebel **T2,** 36
to **open up** [ˌəʊpn‿'ʌp] sich auftun, sich bieten, sich eröffnen **T4,** 92
opening ceremony ['əʊpnɪŋ ˌserɪməni] Eröffnungsfeierlichkeiten **T3,** 65
opening night ['əʊpnɪŋ ˌnaɪt] Premierenabend ⟨**T4,** 86⟩
opera ['ɒprə] Oper **T4,** 87
tour **operator** ['tʊər‿ˌɒpreɪtə] Reiseveranstalter ⟨**T3,** 73⟩
to voice one's **opinion** [ˌvɔɪs wʌnz‿ə'pɪnjən] die eigene Meinung äußern **T4,** 84
opposing side [əˌpəʊzɪŋ 'saɪd] gegenüberstehende/gegnerische Seite/Partei/Mannschaft **T4,** 95
leader of the **opposition** [ˌli:dər‿əv ði‿ˌɒpə'zɪʃn] Oppositionsführer/-in **T4,** 84
oppressive [ə'presɪv] unterdrückerisch, gewaltsam, repressiv **T2,** 38
option ['ɒpʃn] Möglichkeit, Wahl, Option **T3,** 73
orange juice ['ɒrɪndʒ ˌdʒu:s] Orangensaft **T2,** 49
oratory speech [ˌɒrətri 'spi:tʃ] mündlicher Vortrag ⟨**T4,** 82⟩
in **order to** [ɪn‿'ɔ:də tə] um ... zu, mit der Absicht **T3,** 65
to **order sb to do sth** ['ɔ:də] jmdn. anweisen, etw. zu tun ⟨**T2,** 39⟩
organic [ɔ:'gænɪk] Bio-; organisch **T2,** 49
origin ['ɒrɪdʒɪn] Ursprung, Herkunft, Abstammung **T2,** 34
original footage [əˌrɪdʒnl 'fʊtɪdʒ] originales Filmmaterial **T4,** 89
Oscar-winning ['ɒskəˌwɪnɪŋ] Oscar-gekrönt **T3,** 68
ounce [aʊnts] Unze *(Maßeinheit: 28,35 Gramm)* **T3,** 72
out of ['aʊt‿əv] von **T4,** 85
out of my league [ˌaʊt‿əv maɪ 'li:g] nicht meine Kragenweite ⟨**T1,** 10⟩
outlet ['aʊtlet] Abfluss, Ausguss; Ventil ⟨**T4,** 85⟩
overcoat ['əʊvəkəʊt] Mantel ⟨**T2,** 36⟩
*to **overcome anxiety** [əʊvəˌkʌm‿æŋ'zaɪəti] Angst überwinden ⟨**T4,** 84⟩
overpopulation [ˌəʊvəpɒpjə'leɪʃn] Überbevölkerung **T3,** 68
bar **owner** ['bɑ:r‿əʊnə] Kneipenbesitzer/-in **T3,** 64
oxygen ['ɒksɪdʒən] Sauerstoff **T3,** 61

P

packaging [ˈpækɪdʒɪŋ] Verpackung **T3,** 60
painting [ˈpeɪntɪŋ] Farbe **T4,** 85
Pakistani [ˌpɑːkɪˈstɑːni] Pakistaner/-in; pakistanisch **T2,** 33
pan [pæn] Pfanne; Kochtopf mit Stiel ⟨**T2,** 37⟩
panic [ˈpænɪk] Panik **T3,** 66
paper [ˈpeɪpə] Abhandlung, Artikel **T3,** 70
slip of paper [ˌslɪp‿əv ˈpeɪpə] Zettel, Stück Papier **T1,** 26
papier-mâché [ˌpæpieɪˈmæʃeɪ] Pappmaché ⟨**T3,** 65⟩
parade [pəˈreɪd] Parade, Umzug **T2,** 46
Paradise [ˈpærəˌdaɪs] Paradies ⟨**T2,** 39⟩
parental consent [pəˌrentl kənˈsent] Einverständnis der Eltern ⟨**T1,** 8⟩
parka [ˈpɑːkə] Anorak, Parka **T3,** 65
parking lot [ˈpɑːkɪŋ ˌlɒt] Parkplatz **T1,** 21
part [pɑːt] Gegend, Stadtteil **T4,** 87; Rolle **T4,** 89
particular [pəˈtɪkjələ] bestimmte/-r/-s **T2,** 40; ⟨**T2,** 50⟩; **T4,** 82
party [ˈpɑːti] Partei **T4,** 83
one-party system [ˈwʌnˌpɑːti ˈsɪstəm] Einparteiensystem **T4,** 84
to get the best party in [ˌget ðə best ˈpɑːti ɪn] die beste Partei an die Macht wählen **T4,** 83
to crash a party [ˌkræʃ‿ə ˈpɑːti] uneingeladen zu einer Party kommen **T1,** 24
to **pass** [pɑːs] hindurchdringen **T3,** 64
passion [ˈpæʃn] Leidenschaft, Passion **T2,** 34; **T4,** 84
passionate [ˈpæʃnət] leidenschaftlich **T4,** 84
past [pɑːst] letzte/-r/-s, vergangen **T2,** 35; **T4,** 91
pasta [ˈpæstə] Pasta, Nudeln **T3,** 70
pathetic [pəˈθetɪk] erbärmlich, armselig ⟨**T1,** 24⟩
paved [peɪvd] gepflastert ⟨**T4,** 87⟩
pavement [ˈpeɪvmənt] Bürgersteig **T4,** 87
*to **pay sb back** [ˌpeɪ ˈbæk] jmdm. Geld zurückzahlen; es jmdm. heimzahlen ⟨**T1,** 29⟩
housing **payment** [ˈhaʊzɪŋ ˌpeɪmənt] Miete ⟨**T4,** 83⟩
to **pedal** [ˈpedl] in die Pedale treten ⟨**T2,** 42⟩
pediatric [ˌpiːdiˈætrɪk] pädiatrisch, Kinder- ⟨**T4,** 85⟩
penicillin [ˌpenɪˈsɪlɪn] Penicillin **T4,** 80
people's army [ˈpiːplz‿ˌɑːmi] Bürgerwehr, Volksarmee ⟨**T4,** 84⟩
pepper [ˈpepə] Pfeffer; Paprikaschote **T3,** 70
per capita [pəˈkæpɪtə] pro Kopf **T3,** 71
percentage [pəˈsentɪdʒ] prozentualer Anteil, Prozentsatz **T2,** 32
perception [pəˈsepʃn] Wahrnehmung, Empfindung, Auffassung **T2,** 33
to **perform** [pəˈfɔːm] leisten, machen **T4,** 85
period of time [ˌpɪəriəd əv ˈtaɪm] Zeitraum **T3,** 63
permanently [ˈpɜːmnəntli] ständig, dauerhaft, permanent ⟨**T2,** 37⟩
permit [ˈpɜːmɪt] Erlaubnis, Genehmigung; vorläufige Fahrerlaubnis ⟨**T1,** 21⟩
perplexed [pəˈplekst] perplex, ratlos **T2,** 40
persecution [ˌpɜːsɪˈkjuːʃn] Verfolgung ⟨**T2,** 39⟩
to **persist** [pəˈsɪst] bleiben, verharren ⟨**T2,** 44⟩
personal assault [ˌpɜːsnl‿əˈsɔːlt] Körperverletzung ⟨**T1,** 14⟩
for **perspective** [fə pəˈspektɪv] zum Vergleich ⟨**T3,** 70⟩
pet shop [ˈpet ʃɒp] Zoogeschäft, -handlung **T4,** 91
petrol [ˈpetrl] Benzin **T3,** 72
philosopher [fɪˈlɒsəfə] Philosoph/-in **T4,** 80
photocopy [ˈfəʊtəʊˌkɒpi] Fotokopie **T4,** 86
to **pick** [pɪk] auswählen, aussuchen; pflücken **T1,** 11; **T3,** 69
to pick out [pɪk‿ˈaʊt] aussuchen, auswählen; heraushören, herausfiltern ⟨**T4,** 88⟩
pie chart [ˈpaɪ ˌtʃɑːt] Tortendiagramm ⟨**T2,** 32⟩
multicar **pileup** [ˌmʌltikɑː ˈpaɪlʌp] Massenkarambolage ⟨**T1,** 22⟩
pill [pɪl] Pille, Tablette **T3,** 75
pinpoint [ˈpɪnpɔɪnt] winziger Punkt, Nadelspitze ⟨**T1,** 22⟩
pint [paɪnt] Pint *(Flüssigkeitsmaß, entspricht 0.568l in Großbritannien, 0.473l in den USA)* **T3,** 71
piss *(coll)* [pɪs] Pisse *(ugs.)* ⟨**T2,** 37⟩
to **pit sb/sth against sb/sth** [pɪt] jmdn./etw. gegen jmdn./etw. ausspielen ⟨**T3,** 59⟩
*to take **place** [teɪk ˈpleɪs] stattfinden ⟨**T1,** 20⟩; **T4,** 85
plain [pleɪn] klar, deutlich, einfach ⟨**T2,** 44⟩
plantation [plænˈteɪʃn] Plantage; Kolonie **T2,** 33
plaster [ˈplɑːstə] Putz; Gips ⟨**T4,** 85⟩
plastic [ˈplæstɪk] Plastik(-), Kunststoff **T3,** 58
play on words [ˌpleɪ‿ɒn ˈwɜːdz] Wortspiel **T2,** 43
pleading [ˈpliːdɪŋ] Flehen; Plädoyer **T1,** 22
plug [plʌg] Stecker; Stöpsel **T3,** 60
pneumonia [njuːˈməʊniə] Lungenentzündung ⟨**T4,** 80⟩
to **poach** [pəʊtʃ] wildern **T4,** 89
dub **poetry** [dʌb ˈpəʊɪtri] *(eine aus Jamaica stammende Form der Performance Poetry, bei der Text über Reggae-Rhythmen gesprochen wird)* ⟨**T2,** 42⟩
at that **point** [ət ðæt ˈpɔɪnt] in diesem Moment ⟨**T1,** 11⟩
decimal point [ˌdesɪml ˈpɔɪnt] Dezimalpunkt, Kommastelle ⟨**T3,** 72⟩
to make one's point [ˌmeɪk wʌnz ˈpɔɪnt] seinen Standpunkt deutlich machen **T1,** 14
poisonous [ˈpɔɪznəs] giftig **T3,** 58
special riot **police** [ˌspeʃl ˈraɪət pəˌliːs] Sondereinsatzkommando **T3,** 65
policy [ˈpɒlɪsi] Politik, politische Linie, Grundsatz **T3,** 65
to **pollute** [pəˈluːt] verschmutzen, verunreinigen **T3,** 61
pollution [pəˈluːʃn] Verschmutzung **T3,** 58
polyester [ˌpɒliˈestə] Polyester ⟨**T3,** 72⟩
popadom [ˈpɒpədəm] Papadam *(dünner, frittierter Teigfladen aus Linsenmehl, der in Indien als Vorspeise gegessen wird)* ⟨**T2,** 38⟩; ⟨**T2,** 47⟩
pork [pɔːk] Schweinefleisch **T2,** 39
pork sausage [ˌpɔːk ˈsɒsɪdʒ] Fleischwurst **T3,** 70
porridge [ˈpɒrɪdʒ] Haferbrei **T2,** 49
port [pɔːt] Hafen **T3,** 65
portrayal [pɔːˈtreɪəl] Porträt, Darstellung ⟨**T4,** 89⟩
post-war [ˌpəʊstˈwɔː] Nachkriegs- **T2,** 34
pot [pɒt] Topf; Nachttopf ⟨**T2,** 37⟩
baked **potato** [ˌbeɪkt pəˈteɪtəʊ] Ofenkartoffel **T3,** 62
to **pour** [pɔː] fließen, strömen **T1,** 14; schütten, (ein)gießen **T3,** 61
powerful [ˈpaʊəfl] stark; mächtig; bedeutend, beeindruckend **T3,** 68
practice [ˈpræktɪs] Ansatz, Vorgehensweise, Gewohnheit, Praktik ⟨**T3,** 70⟩
to **pray** [preɪ] beten **T2,** 40
prayer [preə] Gebet **T3,** 67
to **preach** [priːtʃ] predigen, propagieren **T3,** 68

preacher ['pri:tʃə] Prediger **T4,** 81
precious ['preʃəs] wertvoll, kostbar **T3,** 70
prediction [prɪ'dɪkʃn] Vorhersage, Voraussage ⟨**T3,** 76⟩
pregnancy ['pregnənsi] Schwangerschaft ⟨**T1,** 19⟩
prejudice ['predʒədɪs] Vorurteil; Voreingenommenheit **T2,** 35
Presbyterian [ˌprezbɪ'tɪəriən] presbyterianisch; Presbyterianer/-in ⟨**T4,** 82⟩
to **present sth in a nutshell** [prɪˌzent‿ɪn‿ə 'nʌtʃel] etw. zusammenfassend/in aller Kürze darstellen ⟨**T2,** 38⟩
presenter [prɪ'zentə] Moderator/-in **T2,** 35
to **preserve** [prɪ'zɜ:v] bewahren, erhalten **T3,** 74
press [pres] Presse **T3,** 61
to **press for sth** [pres] auf etw. drängen **T2,** 34
pressure group ['preʃə ˌgru:p] Interessenverband **T3,** 59
to **prevent sb from doing sth** [prɪ'vent] jmdn. davon abhalten, etw. zu tun; verhindern, dass jmd. etw. tut **T2,** 44
previous ['pri:viəs] vorig, vorherig, vorausgegangen **T1,** 18; **T2,** 38; **T3,** 62; **T4,** 91
price tag ['praɪs ˌtæg] Preisschild ⟨**T3,** 73⟩
pride [praɪd] Stolz **T3,** 62
Prime Minister [ˌpraɪm 'mɪnɪstə] Premierminister/-in, Ministerpräsident/-in **T4,** 84
to **print** [prɪnt] drucken **T2,** 47
prioritizer *(Kunstwort)* [praɪ'ɒrɪtaɪzə] Bevorzuger/-in, Priorisierer/-in ⟨**T4,** 92⟩
priority [praɪ'ɒrəti] Priorität, Vorrang **T1,** 29; **T3,** 69
to set priorities [ˌset praɪ'ɒrətiz] Schwerpunkte festlegen, Prioritäten setzen **T1,** 29
private fortune [ˌpraɪvɪt 'fɔ:tʃu:n] Privatvermögen ⟨**T4,** 81⟩
privilege ['prɪvlɪdʒ] Privileg; Recht, Vorrecht **T1,** 8
to **process** [prə'səs] verarbeiten, aufbereiten, verstehen **T1,** 14
to **produce** [prə'dju:s] herstellen, produzieren, verursachen **T3,** 59; anbauen, erzeugen **T3,** 70
dairy **product** ['deəri ˌprɒdʌkt] Milchprodukt, -erzeugnis **T3,** 70
production [prə'dʌkʃn] Herstellung, Produktion **T3,** 70
progression [prə'greʃn] Entwicklung, Ablauf, Folge **T1,** 23
promiscuous behaviour [prəˌmɪskjuəs bɪ'heɪvjə] häufiger Partnerwechsel **T1,** 19
promise ['prɒmɪs] Versprechen **T4,** 83
to **promote** [prə'məʊt] fördern, vorantreiben **T3,** 69
property damage ['prɒpəti dæmɪdʒ] Sachschaden, Sachbeschädigung ⟨**T1,** 14⟩
to **propose** [prə'pəʊz] vorschlagen ⟨**T3,** 61⟩
prosperity [prɒs'perəti] Wohlstand, Gedeihen **T2,** 34; **T4,** 88
prosperous ['prɒsprəs] wohlhabend; blühend **T4,** 88
prostitute ['prɒstɪtju:t] Prostituierte ⟨**T2,** 39⟩
to **protect** [prə'tekt] (be)schützen **T3,** 59
proverb ['prɒvɜ:b] Sprichwort **T1,** 16
public figure [ˌpʌblɪk 'fɪgə] Person des öffentlichen Lebens ⟨**T2,** 44⟩
public school [ˌpʌblɪk 'sku:l] Privatschule *(BE)*; staatliche Schule *(AE/AUS)* **T4,** 82
to **publish** ['pʌblɪʃ] veröffentlichen, publizieren, verlegen **T3,** 71
Yorkshire **pudding** [ˌjɔ:kʃə 'pʊdɪŋ] Yorkshirepudding *(gebackener Teig aus Eiern, Milch und Mehl, der in der englischen Küche als Beilage zu Steaks, Roastbeef und anderen Fleischgerichten serviert wird)* **T2,** 49
to **pull up** [pʊl‿'ʌp] (heranfahren und) anhalten **T1,** 21
to **punch** [pʌntʃ] mit der Faust schlagen; boxen **T2,** 37
pure [pjʊə] rein, pur; weiß **T3,** 58; **T4,** 89
common **purpose** [ˌkɒmən 'pɜ:pəs] gemeinsames Ziel **T4,** 88
pushy ['pʊʃi] aufdringlich, penetrant, aggressiv ⟨**T1,** 15⟩
*to **put all one's weight into sth** [ˌpʊt‿ɔ:l wʌnz weɪt 'ɪntə] sein ganzes Gewicht einsetzen ⟨**T1,** 13⟩
to put no effort into sth [ˌpʊt nəʊ‿'efət‿ˌɪntə] sich keine Mühe mit etw. geben **T4,** 83
to put sb through [pʊt‿'θru:] jmdn. durchstellen/verbinden **T4,** 93
to put sth off [pʊt‿'ɒf] etw. aufschieben, etw. verschieben **T1,** 19
to put sth on [pʊt‿'ɒn] ein Kondom überziehen **T1,** 18; etw. überziehen, etw. anziehen **T3,** 67; **T4,** 83
puzzled ['pʌzld] verwirrt, verdutzt **T3,** 63
pyjama [pɪ'dʒɑ:mə] Schlafanzug, Pyjama ⟨**T2,** 37⟩
python ['paɪθn] Python ⟨**T4,** 91⟩

Q

quarry ['kwɒri] Steinbruch ⟨**T3,** 58⟩
rhetorical **question** [rɪˌtɒrɪkl 'kwestʃən] rhetorische Frage **T3,** 61
quote [kwəʊt] Zitat **T4,** 88

R

rabbit ['ræbɪt] Kaninchen **T4,** 91
racial abuse [ˌreɪʃl‿ə'bju:s] Rassendiskriminierung **T2,** 34
rag doll [ˌræg 'dɒl] Stoffpuppe ⟨**T1,** 13⟩
all the **rage** [ˌɔ:l ðə 'reɪdʒ] der letzte Schrei, der Hit ⟨**T2,** 44⟩
acid **rain** [ˌæsɪd 'reɪn] saurer Regen **T3,** 58
to **raise awareness of** [ˌreɪz‿ə'weənəs] das Bewusstsein schärfen für, sensibilisieren für **T3,** 58
awareness-raising [ə'weənəsˌreɪzɪŋ] bewusstseinsbildend, sensibilisierend ⟨**T2,** 44⟩
ranch [rɑ:ntʃ; ræntʃ] Ranch **T3,** 62
to **rank** [ræŋk] einstufen, in eine Reihenfolge bringen **T1,** 16
ranking ['ræŋkɪŋ] Rangliste, Rangfolge ⟨**T2,** 44⟩
rare [reə] rar, selten; englisch *(blutig, nur leicht angebraten)* **T2,** 49
rarely ['reəli] selten **T3,** 68; **T4,** 88
rarity ['reərəti] Seltenheit, Rarität ⟨**T2,** 44⟩
allergy **rash** ['ælədʒi ˌræʃ] allergischer (Haut-)Ausschlag **T3,** 75
rate [reɪt] Geschwindigkeit, Tempo **T3,** 61; Quote ⟨**T3,** 73⟩
insurance rate [ɪn'ʃʊərnts reɪt] Versicherungsbeitrag ⟨**T1,** 20⟩
to **rattle** ['rætl] klappern, klirren, rasseln **T1,** 22
to rattle (by) ['rætl] (vorbei)rattern ⟨**T1,** 10⟩
to **reach** [ri:tʃ] greifen, reichen **T1,** 13
to reach out [ri:tʃ‿'aʊt] (die Hand) ausstrecken **T3,** 64
to reach over [ri:tʃ‿'əʊvə] hinübergreifen **T1,** 21
to reach up [ri:tʃ‿'ʌp] die Hand ausstrecken **T1,** 21
real-life ['rɪəlaɪf] authentisch, aus dem wirklichen Leben **T3,** 68
to **rear back** [rɪə 'bæk] ausholen, zurückziehen ⟨**T1,** 13⟩
rearview (mirror) [ˌrɪəvju: 'mɪrə] Rückspiegel ⟨**T1,** 23⟩
to **reassure** [ˌri:ə'ʃʊə] beruhigen, beschwichtigen **T3,** 66

to **rebel against** [rɪ'bel] rebellieren gegen, sich auflehnen gegen **T4,** 80
recognition [ˌrekəg'nɪʃn] (An-)Erkennung **T2,** 34
to **recognize** ['rekəgnaɪz] (an)erkennen **T4,** 80
to **recycle** [ˌri:'saɪkl] recyceln, wiederverwerten **T3,** 71
recycling plant [ˌri:'saɪklɪŋ ˌplɑ:nt] Recyclinganlage, Wiederaufbereitungsanlage **T3,** 59
to **redefine** [ˌri:dɪ'faɪn] neu definieren **T3,** 69
to **reduce** [rɪ'dju:s] reduzieren, verringern **T3,** 68; **T4,** 89
reduction [rɪ'dʌkʃn] Reduzierung, Abnahme, Verminderung **T3,** 70
to **refer (to)** [rɪ'fɜ:] (sich) beziehen (auf); sprechen (von) **T1,** 8; **T3,** 64
to **refuse** (to do sth) [rɪ'fju:z] ablehnen, sich weigern (etw. zu tun) **T3,** 66; **T4,** 80
with **regard to** [ˌwɪð rɪ'gɑ:d tə] im Hinblick auf ⟨**T4,** 88⟩
to **register** ['redʒɪstə] sich registrieren lassen, sich eintragen, sich anmelden **T4,** 83
regret [rɪ'gret] Bedauern, Reue **T1,** 14
to **reinforce** [ˌri:ɪn'fɔ:s] verstärken, bestärken ⟨**T2,** 44⟩
relatively ['relətɪvli] relativ, vergleichsweise, verhältnismäßig **T3,** 70
release [rɪ'li:s] Veröffentlichung, Herausgabe, Freigabe **T3,** 68
to sigh in **relief** [ˌsaɪ ɪn rɪ'li:f] erleichtert seufzen/aufatmen **T4,** 83
to **relish** ['relɪʃ] genießen, gern mögen ⟨**T2,** 39⟩
to **remain** [rɪ'meɪn] bleiben **T3,** 71
*to **remake** [ˌri:'meɪk] erneuern **T4,** 88
to **remove** [rɪ'mu:v] entfernen **T3,** 63
renewable [rɪ'nju:əbl] erneuerbar **T3,** 58
rent [rent] Miete **T2,** 34
to **rent** [rent] mieten **T2,** 34
car **rental** ['kɑ: ˌrentl] Autovermietung, -verleih **T4,** 93
to **repair** [rɪ'peə] reparieren **T4,** 85
repetition [ˌrepɪ'tɪʃn] Wiederholung **T3,** 61
to **replace sb/sth** (with sb/sth) [rɪ'pleɪs] jmdn./etw. (durch jmdn./etw.) ersetzen **T3,** 70
reputation [ˌrepjə'teɪʃn] Ruf, Ansehen **T4,** 88
to **require** [rɪ'kwaɪə] erfordern, benötigen **T1,** 16
research [ri:'sɜ:tʃ] Erkenntnisse, Forschungsergebnisse ⟨**T3,** 76⟩
research camp [ri:'sɜ:tʃ ˌkæmp] Forschungslager, -station **T4,** 89
researcher [rɪ'sɜ:tʃə] Forscher/-in **T3,** 60
to **resemble** [rɪ'zembl] ähneln **T2,** 37
to resemble sb [rɪ'zembl] jmdm. ähneln, jmdm. ähnlich sehen **T4,** 82
reserved [rɪ'zɜ:vd] reserviert, vorbehalten **T4,** 83
resident ['rezɪdnt] Anwohner/-in, Einwohner/-in, Bewohner/-in, Ortsansässige/-r **T2,** 44; **T4,** 85
to **resist** [rɪ'zɪst] widerstehen; sich widersetzen **T1,** 13
natural **resource** [ˌnætʃrl rɪ'zɔ:s] Ressource, Rohstoff, Bodenschatz **T3,** 58
response [rɪ'spɒns] Antwort, Erwiderung, Rückmeldung **T1,** 27; **T3,** 61
responsibility [rɪˌspɒnsə'bɪləti] Verantwortung ⟨**T1,** 8⟩; **T4,** 88
criminal responsibility [ˌkrɪmɪnl rɪˌspɒnsə'bɪləti] Strafmündigkeit ⟨**T1,** 8⟩
responsible [rɪs'pɒnsəbl] verantwortlich; verantwortungsvoll **T1,** 14; **T2,** 38; **T3,** 70
to act responsibly [ækt rɪs'pɒnsəbli] verantwortlich handeln ⟨**T1,** 9⟩
rest [rest] Ruhe, Rast; Ruhezustand **T2,** 46
to **rest** [rest] ausruhen, rasten; übernachten **T4,** 87
as a **result of** [æz‿ə rɪ'zʌlt‿əv] als Ergebnis von, als Folge von **T3,** 70
reusable [ˌri:'ju:zəbl] wiederverwendbar, Mehrweg- **T3,** 61
to **reveal** [rɪ'vi:l] zeigen, verraten, enthüllen **T1,** 16
to **reverse** [rɪ'vɜ:s] tauschen, umdrehen **T2,** 40
to **revile** [rɪ'vaɪl] (ver)schmähen ⟨**T3,** 73⟩
reward [rɪ'wɔ:d] Belohnung **T2,** 39
rhetorical question [rɪˌtɒrɪkl 'kwestʃən] rhetorische Frage **T3,** 61
rib [rɪb] Rippe ⟨**T1,** 13⟩
rice [raɪs] Reis **T2,** 49
mineral **right** ['mɪnrl raɪt] Abbaurecht **T3,** 63
right to vote (= suffrage) [ˌraɪt tə 'vəʊt; 'sʌfrɪdʒ] Stimmrecht, Wahlrecht **T4,** 80
All **right.** [ɔ:l 'raɪt] O.k., Also gut., In Ordnung., Alles klar. **T1,** 10
right across [ˌraɪt‿ə'krɒs] quer über ⟨**T2,** 35⟩
*to **ring back** [rɪŋ 'bæk] zurückrufen **T4,** 93
special **riot police** [ˌspeʃl 'raɪət pəˌli:s] Sondereinsatzkommando **T3,** 65
to **rip** [rɪp] (zer)reißen; herunterreißen ⟨**T2,** 39⟩
ripple of force [ˌrɪpl‿əv 'fɔ:s] Stoßwelle ⟨**T1,** 22⟩
rise in temperature [ˌraɪz‿ɪn 'temprətʃə] Temperaturanstieg **T3,** 72
dirt **road** ['dɜ:t ˌrəʊd] Schotterstraße ⟨**T3,** 64⟩
to **roam** [rəʊm] durchschweifen, umherstreifen, herumstreunen ⟨**T2,** 36⟩
roast beef [ˌrəʊst 'bi:f] Roastbeef, Rinderbraten **T2,** 49
to **rob** [rɒb] (aus)rauben, berauben **T1,** 11
robot ['rəʊbɒt] Roboter **T3,** 69
to **roll** [rəʊl] rollen **T3,** 66
to roll up [rəʊl‿'ʌp] zusammenrollen, aufrollen, aufkrempeln **T1,** 13; hochkrempeln ⟨**T4,** 83⟩
rotary *(AE)* ['rəʊtri] Kreisverkehr ⟨**T1,** 20⟩
rotten ['rɒtn] faulig, schlecht geworden ⟨**T2,** 37⟩; **T4,** 82
rough [rʌf] grob, rau, derb; ungefähr **T1,** 10
routine [ru:'ti:n] Tagesablauf **T4,** 90
row [rəʊ] Reihe **T4,** 84
rowdy ['raʊdi] rüpelhaft, gewalttätig ⟨**T2,** 39⟩
rubbish can ['rʌbɪʃ ˌkæn] Mülleimer **T4,** 82
to **rule** [ru:l] (be)herrschen, regieren **T2,** 39
rumble ['rʌmbl] Rumpeln, Rattern, Grollen ⟨**T1,** 11⟩
*to break into a **run** [breɪk‿ˌɪntʊ‿ə 'rʌn] plötzlich loslaufen ⟨**T1,** 11⟩
*to **run** [rʌn] betreiben, führen **T2,** 35; **T3,** 60
to run a country [ˌrʌn‿ə 'kʌntri] ein Land regieren **T4,** 84
to run dry [ˌrʌn‿'draɪ] austrocknen **T3,** 64
to run into sb [rʌn‿'ɪntə] jmdm. über den Weg laufen **T1,** 11
to run like hell [ˌrʌn laɪk 'hel] um sein Leben rennen ⟨**T1,** 13⟩
rung [rʌŋ] Sprosse *(einer Leiter)* ⟨**T1,** 11⟩
adrenaline **rush** [ə'drenlɪn ˌrʌʃ] Adrenalinstoß ⟨**T1,** 11⟩
to **rush to** [rʌʃ] eilen zu, zustürzen auf **T3,** 66
Rwandan [ru'ændən] ruandisch; Ruander/-in ⟨**T4,** 89⟩

S

to **sacrifice** ['sækrɪfaɪs] opfern **T4,** 88
safety bar ['seɪfti bɑ:] Sicherheitsbügel ⟨**T1,** 22⟩
*to **set sail** [set 'seɪl] in See stechen ⟨**T3,** 69⟩

salt [sɔ:lt] Salz **T3,** 63
blood **sample** ['blʌd ˌsæmpl] Blutprobe **T3,** 75
satirical [sə'tɪrɪkl] satirisch; Spott- **T2,** 36
satisfying ['sætɪsfaɪɪŋ] zufriedenstellend, befriedigend **T4,** 88
sausage ['sɒsɪdʒ] (Brat-)Wurst **T2,** 39; **T2,** 49
pork sausage [ˌpɔ:k 'sɒsɪdʒ] Fleischwurst **T3,** 70
Say ... [seɪ] Angenommen ... **T1,** 19
scale [skeɪl] Ausmaß; Skala **T3,** 60
Scandinavian [ˌskændɪ'neɪviən] Skandinavier/-in; skandinavisch **T3,** 67
scar [skɑ:] Narbe **T1,** 11
*to be dumb **scared** [dʌm 'skeəd] Todesängste ausstehen ⟨**T1,** 23⟩
scarlet fever [ˌskɑ:lət 'fi:və] Scharlach ⟨**T4,** 80⟩
to **scatter over** [ˌskætər‿'əʊvə] (sich) verstreuen über ⟨**T2,** 37⟩
scenario [sɪ'nɑ:riəʊ] Szenario ⟨**T1,** 22⟩
scene [si:n] Situation ⟨**T3,** 64⟩
scheduled ['ʃedju:ld; 'skedʒu:ld] planmäßig, regulär ⟨**T3,** 73⟩
public **school** [ˌpʌblɪk 'sku:l] Privatschule *(BE)*; staatliche Schule *(AE/AUS)* **T4,** 82
school cut ['sku:l ˌkʌt] Kürzung/Einsparung an Schulen ⟨**T4,** 82⟩
Scotsman pl. **Scotsmen** ['skɒtsmən; 'skɒtsmen] Schotte ⟨**T4,** 80⟩
to **scramble** ['skræmbl] sich hochrappeln; kraxeln, klettern ⟨**T1,** 13⟩
to scramble (out of sth) ['skræmbl] (heraus)klettern (aus) ⟨**T3,** 66⟩
to **scrawl** [skrɔ:l] kritzeln, vollschmieren **T3,** 65
to **scribble** ['skrɪbl] kritzeln, schmieren **T1,** 18
to **scrub** [skrʌb] schrubben, reinigen **T2,** 38
a **sea of humanity** [ˌsi:‿əv hju:'mænəti] ein Meer an Menschlichkeit ⟨**T3,** 65⟩
by sea [baɪ 'si:] zu Wasser, mit dem Schiff **T3,** 73
seabird ['si:bɜ:d] Seevogel **T3,** 60
to **seal** [si:l] fest verschließen, versiegeln **T1,** 23
seat [si:t] politische Vertretung ⟨**T3,** 66⟩
secretary ['sekrətri] Sekretär/-in **T4,** 92
section ['sekʃn] Sektion, Abschnitt, Paragraf **T2,** 35
to **secure** [sɪ'kjuə] sicher befestigen, absichern **T1,** 12
security [sɪ'kjʊərəti] Sicherheit, Schutz; Wachdienst **T1,** 12
*to **see past** [si: 'pɑ:st] außer Acht lassen ⟨**T2,** 41⟩

seed [si:d] Saat, Samen **T3,** 69
It **seemed to be all that was left to us.** [ɪt ˌsi:md‿tə bi‿'ɔ:l ðæt wəz ˌleft tə ʌs] Es schien, als bliebe uns nichts anderes übrig. ⟨**T2,** 37⟩
to **select** [sɪ'lekt] auswählen, aussuchen **T2,** 37
self-defense *(AE)* [ˌselfdɪ'fens] Selbstverteidigung **T1,** 14
senator ['senətə] Senator/-in **T4,** 88
senior ['si:niə] Schüler/-in im letzten Schuljahr ⟨**T4,** 82⟩
sense of guilt [ˌsens‿əv 'gɪlt] Schuldgefühl **T2,** 38
to develop a sense of [dɪˌveləp‿ə 'sens‿əv] ein Gespür/Gefühl entwickeln für **T4,** 86
to **sense** [sens] spüren, fühlen **T4,** 84
death **sentence** ['deθ ˌsentəns] Todesstrafe, Todesurteil **T4,** 80
service ['sɜ:vɪs] Dienstleistung **T2,** 35; Agentur, Büro **T2,** 44
service-learning class ['sɜ:vɪs lɜ:nɪŋ ˌklɑ:s] *(Unterricht, der den Nutzen gemeinnütziger Arbeit vermitteln soll)* ⟨**T4,** 85⟩
Youth Service ['ju:θ ˌsɜ:vɪs] Jugendhilfe **T2,** 46
session ['seʃn] Einheit, Sitzung, Stunde ⟨**T2,** 36⟩
*to be **set in** [bi 'set‿ɪn] spielen in **T4,** 87
to set a good example to sb [ˌset‿ə gʊd ɪg'zɑ:mpl] jmdm. ein Vorbild sein **T1,** 29
to set off [set‿'ɒf] aufbrechen, sich aufmachen **T3,** 63
to set on fire [ˌset‿ɒn 'faɪə] anzünden, in Brand setzen **T3,** 65
to set priorities [ˌset praɪ'ɒrətiz] Schwerpunkte festlegen, Prioritäten setzen **T1,** 29
to set sail [set 'seɪl] in See stechen ⟨**T3,** 69⟩
to set up [set‿'ʌp] errichten, aufbauen; gründen **T4,** 89
setting ['setɪŋ] Umgebung, Lage **T3,** 62
to **settle for less** [ˌsetl fə 'les] sich mit weniger zufrieden geben ⟨**T4,** 88⟩
several ['sevrl] einige, mehrere; verschiedene **T3,** 70
sex education ['seks‿edʒʊˌkeɪʃn] Sexualkunde ⟨**T4,** 82⟩
sexual assault [ˌsekʃʊəl‿ə'sɔ:lt] Vergewaltigung, sexuelle Nötigung ⟨**T1,** 14⟩
*to **shake loose** [ʃeɪk lu:z] abschütteln ⟨**T1,** 12⟩
shallot [ʃə'lɒt] Schalotte **T3,** 70
shape [ʃeɪp] Form ⟨**T1,** 13⟩

share [ʃeə] Anteil **T3,** 59
bed-**sheet** ['bedʃi:t] Bettlaken ⟨**T2,** 38⟩
shelter ['ʃeltə] Obdach, Unterstand **T4,** 93
animal shelter ['ænɪml ˌʃeltə] Tierheim **T4,** 90
dietary **shift** [ˌdaɪətri 'ʃɪft] Ernährungsumstellung ⟨**T3,** 70⟩
to **shift into second (gear)** [ˌʃɪft‿ɪntə seknd 'gɪə] in den zweiten Gang schalten ⟨**T1,** 23⟩
to **ship in** [ʃɪp‿'ɪn] einschiffen; mitbringen, importieren **T3,** 64
shirt [ʃɜ:t] Hemd, Shirt **T3,** 71
pet **shop** ['pet ʃɒp] Zoogeschäft, -handlung **T4,** 91
shop window [ˌʃɒp 'wɪndəʊ] Schaufenster **T4,** 87
shore [ʃɔ:] Ufer, Küste **T1,** 21
shortage ['ʃɔ:tɪdʒ] Knappheit, Mangel **T3,** 71
shortcut ['ʃɔ:tkʌt] Abkürzung **T1,** 21; **T4,** 88
leather **shorts** *(pl.)* ['leðə ʃɔ:ts] Lederhose ⟨**T1,** 26⟩
to line up a **shot** [ˌlaɪn‿ʌp‿ə 'ʃɒt] zielen ⟨**T1,** 22⟩
shoulder (of rock) ['ʃəʊldə] Felsvorsprung **T3,** 62
shoulder-length ['ʃəʊldəleŋθ] schulterlang ⟨**T4,** 82⟩
to **shove out sb** [ʃʌv‿'aʊt] jmdn. hinausdrängen ⟨**T2,** 37⟩
talent **show** ['tælənt ˌʃəʊ] Talentwettbewerb **T4,** 85
sibling ['sɪblɪŋ] Bruder/Schwester, Geschwisterkind **T4,** 85
opposing **side** [əˌpəʊzɪŋ 'saɪd] gegenüberstehende/gegnerische Seite/Partei/Mannschaft **T4,** 95
side effect ['saɪd‿ɪˌfekt] Nebenwirkung **T3,** 75
sideways ['saɪdweɪz] seitwärts, seitlich ⟨**T1,** 13⟩
to **sigh** [saɪ] seufzen **T3,** 62
to sigh in relief [ˌsaɪ‿ɪn rɪ'li:f] erleichtert seufzen/aufatmen **T4,** 83
to **sign on** [saɪn‿'ɒn] (sich) anmelden, (sich) einschreiben, anheuern **T4,** 85
significant [sɪg'nɪfɪkənt] bedeutend, signifikant, wesentlich **T1,** 16; **T4,** 92
similar ['sɪmɪlə] ähnlich **T2,** 40
similarity [ˌsɪmɪ'lærəti] Ähnlichkeit, Gemeinsamkeit **T1,** 23
simply ['sɪmpli] einfach nur **T2,** 37
lead **singer** ['li:d ˌsɪŋə] Leadsänger/-in, Frontsänger/-in **T3,** 69
to **single out** [ˌsɪŋgl‿'aʊt] auswählen, herausgreifen ⟨**T2,** 35⟩

single ['sɪŋgl] einzig, einzeln, alleinstehend **T1,** 11; **T3,** 63
sink [sɪŋk] (Abwasch-)Becken ⟨**T2,** 39⟩
*to **sink** [sɪŋk] versenken ⟨**T3,** 65⟩
siren ['saɪrən] Sirene, Martinshorn **T3,** 67
*to **sit** [sɪt] sich befinden **T3,** 62
world health **situation** [ˌwɜ:ld ˌhelθ sɪtju'eɪʃn] Gesundheitszustand der Weltbevölkerung ⟨**T4,** 81⟩
to **skip** [skɪp] (über)springen, hüpfen **T1,** 13
to **slam** [slæm] schlagen; rammen ⟨**T1,** 13⟩
slave trade ['sleɪv treɪd] Sklavenhandel **T2,** 33
to **sleepwalk** ['sli:pwɔ:k] schlafwandeln ⟨**T3,** 60⟩
sleeve [sli:v] Ärmel ⟨**T4,** 83⟩
slice [slaɪs] Scheibe, Stück, Teil **T2,** 39; **T3,** 71
*to **slide down** [slaɪd 'daʊn] hinuntergleiten; untergehen ⟨**T3,** 64⟩
slip of paper [ˌslɪp‿əv 'peɪpə] Zettel, Stück Papier **T1,** 26
to **slip on sth** [slɪp‿'ɒn] etw. überziehen ⟨**T2,** 36⟩
campaign **slogan** [kæm'peɪn ˌsləʊgən] Wahlkampfparole **T4,** 88
to **slow** [sləʊ] langsamer werden, sich verlangsamen **T3,** 66
Take it easy, take it **slow.** [ˌteɪk‿ɪt‿'i:zi, ˌteɪk‿ɪt 'sləʊ] Nur keine Hektik., Immer mit der Ruhe. **T1,** 10
to **smash** [smæʃ] zerschlagen, zertrümmern **T3,** 65
snake [sneɪk] Schlange **T4,** 91
to **snap at sb** ['snæp‿ət] jmdn. anfahren, jmdn. anschnauzen *(ugs.)* ⟨**T1,** 22⟩
to **snatch** (up) [snætʃ] (sich) schnappen, (er)greifen ⟨**T1,** 13⟩; ⟨**T2,** 37⟩
*to **sneak into** [sni:k‿'ɪntʊ] (sich) hineinschleichen ⟨**T1,** 10⟩
so-called [ˌsəʊ'kɔ:ld] so genannte/-r/-s **T3,** 63
to **soak** [səʊk] tränken, durchweichen, durchnässen **T3,** 67
social critic [ˌsəʊʃl 'krɪtɪk] Gesellschaftskritiker/-in **T4,** 80
soft [sɒft] weich; aufgeweicht ⟨**T3,** 65⟩
solar ['səʊlə] Sonnen-, Solar-, solar **T3,** 58
Somalian [sə'mɑ:liən] somalisch; Somali ⟨**T2,** 41⟩
somehow ['sʌmhaʊ] irgendwie **T2,** 40
someplace ['sʌmpleɪs] irgendwo(hin) **T1,** 14
somewhat ['sʌmwɒt] ein bisschen; einigermaßen **T1,** 20; ⟨**T4,** 80⟩
songwriter ['sɒŋˌraɪtə] Songschreiber/-in **T3,** 69; Liedermacher/-in **T4,** 87
sophomore ['sɒfəmɔ:] *(Student/-in im 2. Studienjahr)* ⟨**T4,** 85⟩
sore [sɔ:] schmerzhaft, wund **T3,** 75
sort [sɔ:t] Sorte, Art **T1,** 11
sort of ['sɔ:t‿əv] irgendwie ⟨**T1,** 11⟩
space [speɪs] Ort, Platz ⟨**T4,** 83⟩
*to **speak up** [ˌspi:k‿'ʌp] lauter sprechen; den Mund aufmachen **T2,** 44
speaker ['spi:kə] Redner/-in **T3,** 61
special riot police [ˌspeʃl 'raɪət pəˌli:s] Sondereinsatzkommando **T3,** 65
specialist ['speʃlɪst] Spezialist/-in, Experte/Expertin; Fach- **T3,** 71; Facharzt/-ärztin **T3,** 75
species pl. **species** ['spi:ʃi:z] Art, Spezies **T3,** 59
spectacular [spek'tækjələ] spektakulär **T3,** 62
to **speculate** ['spekjəleɪt] spekulieren, vermuten **T3,** 67
speech [spi:tʃ] Rede; Sprache **T1,** 25; **T3,** 61; **T4,** 82
inauguration speech [ɪˌnɔ:gjə'reɪʃn ˌspi:tʃ] Amtseinführungsrede ⟨**T4,** 88⟩
oratory speech [ˌɒrətri 'spi:tʃ] mündlicher Vortrag ⟨**T4,** 82⟩
to **spew** [spju:] (aus)spucken, ausspeien ⟨**T3,** 66⟩
spicy ['spaɪsi] würzig; pikant **T2,** 49
to **spill** [spɪl] verschütten; auslaufen **T1,** 19
to **spiral upward** [ˌspaɪərl 'ʌpwəd] spiralförmig aufsteigen ⟨**T3,** 62⟩
spiral notebook [ˌspaɪərl 'nəʊtbʊk] Ringbuch ⟨**T1,** 10⟩
on the **spot** [spɒt] umgehend, sofort ⟨**T1,** 26⟩
to **spot** [spɒt] entdecken; erkennen **T1,** 12
to **sprain** [spreɪn] verstauchen **T3,** 75
to **spray** [spreɪ] spritzen, sprühen ⟨**T2,** 38⟩
spread [spred] Aufstrich; große Auswahl **T3,** 62
spring fountains *(pl.)* [ˌsprɪŋ 'faʊntənz] Quellwasser ⟨**T3,** 58⟩
spur [spɜ:] Ansporn ⟨**T2,** 34⟩
square mile (= sq. mile) [ˌskweə 'maɪl] Quadratmeile **T3,** 72
to **squash sth against sth** [skwɒʃ‿ə'genst] etw. an etw. zerquetschen ⟨**T4,** 82⟩
to **squeeze** [skwi:z] drücken, pressen; quetschen **T1,** 21
squid [skwɪd] Tintenfisch ⟨**T3,** 60⟩
to **stab sb** [stæb] jmdn. erstechen ⟨**T1,** 10⟩
staff [stɑ:f] Personal, Belegschaft; Kollegium **T3,** 74
stage [steɪdʒ] Zeitpunkt, Alter **T4,** 82
stagnation [stæg'neɪʃn] Stagnation, Stockung ⟨**T2,** 44⟩
stairs *(pl.)* [steəz] Treppe **T2,** 37
stall [stɔ:l] (Verkaufs-)Stand, Bude **T2,** 46
lifeguard **stand** ['laɪfgɑ:d stænd] Rettungsstation ⟨**T1,** 21⟩
*to **stand for sth** ['stænd fə] etw. hinnehmen, etw. tolerieren ⟨**T2,** 39⟩
station wagon *(AE)* ['steɪʃn ˌwægən] Kombi ⟨**T1,** 20⟩
stationery ['steɪʃnri] Schreibwaren ⟨**T3,** 71⟩
statistical [stə'tɪstɪkl] statistisch ⟨**T3,** 71⟩
steak [steɪk] Steak **T3,** 72
stealth bomber ['stelθ bɒmə] Tarnkappenbomber ⟨**T3,** 58⟩
to **steer sb off** [stɪər‿'ɒf] jmdn. bugsieren *(ugs.)*, jmdn. wegbringen ⟨**T3,** 67⟩
to **step over sth/sb** [ˌstep‿'əʊvə] über etw./jmdn. hinwegsteigen ⟨**T4,** 87⟩
stereo ['steriəʊ] Stereoanlage; Radio **T3,** 64
*to **be stereotyped** [bi 'steriətaɪpt] in eine Schublade gesteckt werden ⟨**T2,** 43⟩
*to **sting** [stɪŋ] verletzen **T1,** 16; stechen **T3,** 75
stock [stɒk] Bestand **T3,** 68
to **stomp** [stɒmp] stampfen ⟨**T1,** 22⟩
stone [stəʊn] Stein **T3,** 63
grocery **store** ['grəʊsri stɔ:] Lebensmittelgeschäft **T1,** 20
straight away [ˌstreɪt‿ə'weɪ] sofort, gleich **T1,** 19
stranger ['streɪndʒə] Fremde/-r **T3,** 67
bra **strap** ['brɑ: stræp] BH-Träger ⟨**T1,** 21⟩
strawberry ['strɔ:bri] Erdbeere **T3,** 65
streaming ['stri:mɪŋ] tränend ⟨**T3,** 67⟩
strength [streŋθ] Stärke, Kraft ⟨**T2,** 34⟩
*to **strike** [straɪk] (auf)treffen, einschlagen **T3,** 66
striking ['straɪkɪŋ] bemerkenswert, auffallend **T3,** 68
stroke [strəʊk] Schlaganfall ⟨**T3,** 64⟩
to **stroke** [strəʊk] streicheln **T3,** 62
*to feel **strongly about sth** [ˌfi:l 'strɒŋli‿əˌbaʊt] entschiedene Ansichten über etw. haben **T2,** 47; besorgt um etw. sein, beunruhigt wegen etw. sein, wichtig sein **T3,** 61
to **struggle** ['strʌgl] kämpfen, Mühe haben, ringen, sich anstrengen **T1,** 13; **T4,** 88
*to get **stuck** [ˌget 'stʌk] stecken bleiben **T1,** 20
study ['stʌdi] Studie, Untersuchung; Studium **T3,** 70

to **study** ['stʌdi] prüfen ⟨**T1,** 11⟩
to **stuff** [stʌf] stopfen **T1,** 13
stuffed [stʌft] ausgestopft; gefüllt ⟨**T1,** 22⟩
to **stumble** ['stʌmbl] taumeln, stolpern **T1,** 13
dance hall **style** ['dɑ:ns hɔ:l ˌstaɪl] *(schnelle Reggae-Musik, über die der DJ improvisierte Texte spricht)* ⟨**T2,** 42⟩
subordinate clause [səˌbɔ:dnət 'klɔ:z] Nebensatz **T2,** 35
suburbia [sə'bɜ:biə] Vorstadt, Vorort, Stadtrand ⟨**T2,** 36⟩
to **succeed in** [sək'si:d‿ɪn] Erfolg haben, erfolgreich sein **T3,** 65
such as ['sʌtʃ‿əz] wie (zum Beispiel) **T4,** 80
to **suck in** [sʌk‿'ɪn] einsaugen, ansaugen, aufsaugen ⟨**T3,** 60⟩
suffragette [ˌsʌfrə'dʒet] Frauenrechtlerin ⟨**T4,** 80⟩
well-**suited to** [wel'su:tɪd] geeignet für, passend für **T1,** 26
his eyes were **sunken** [hɪz‿aɪz wə 'sʌŋkən] seine Augen lagen tief in den Augenhöhlen ⟨**T2,** 37⟩
supper ['sʌpə] Abendessen **T3,** 62
art **supply** ['ɑ:t səˌplaɪ] Künstlerbedarf ⟨**T4,** 85⟩
surf [sɜ:f] Brandung ⟨**T1,** 10⟩
surface ['sɜ:fɪs] Oberfläche **T3,** 59
surface damage agreement [ˌsɜ:fɪs ˌdæmɪdʒ ə'gri:mənt] Vereinbarung für Oberflächenschäden ⟨**T3,** 63⟩
to **surge past** [sɜ:dʒ 'pɑ:st] vorbeiströmen ⟨**T4,** 87⟩
to **surrender** [sə'rendə] sich ergeben **T3,** 67
*to be **surrounded by sth/sb** [sə'raʊndɪd] umgeben sein von etw./jmdm. **T3,** 60
*to be **suspended** [ˌbi sə'spendɪd] suspendiert werden; zeitweilig vom Unterricht ausgeschlossen werden **T4,** 82
suspense [sə'spens] Spannung **T1,** 19
*to **swear** [sweə] schwören **T1,** 12
*to **sweep** [swi:p] fegen, kehren; mitreißen **T3,** 66
sweetheart ['swi:thɑ:t] Schatz, Liebling **T1,** 18
*to **swing** [swɪŋ] schwingen; schwenken ⟨**T1,** 11⟩
to **switch back and forth** [swɪtʃ 'bæk‿ənd ˌfɔ:θ] hin und her wechseln **T4,** 87
swollen ['swəʊlən] geschwollen **T3,** 75
to **sympathize with** ['sɪmpəθaɪz wɪð] mitfühlen, jmdn. verstehen; sympathisieren **T1,** 23
symptom ['sɪmtəm] Symptom, Merkmal **T3,** 75
synonym ['sɪnənɪm] Synonym **T4,** 88
synthpop ['sɪnθpɒp] synthetische Popmusik ⟨**T4,** 87⟩
one-party **system** ['wʌnˌpɑ:ti 'sɪstəm] Einparteiensystem **T4,** 84

T

league **table** ['li:g ˌteɪbl] Tabelle ⟨**T3,** 71⟩
tactic ['tæktɪk] Vorgehensweise **T4,** 80
price **tag** ['praɪs ˌtæg] Preisschild ⟨**T3,** 73⟩
*to **take** [teɪk] ertragen, erleiden ⟨**T2,** 39⟩
Take it easy, take it slow. [ˌteɪk‿ɪt‿'i:zi, ˌteɪk‿ɪt 'sləʊ] Nur keine Hektik., Immer mit der Ruhe. **T1,** 10
to take a beating [ˌteɪk‿ə 'bi:tɪŋ] Prügel einstecken, verprügelt werden ⟨**T1,** 19⟩
to take action [teɪk‿'ækʃn] handeln, eingreifen **T4,** 89
to take a message [ˌteɪk‿ə 'mesɪdʒ] eine Nachricht entgegennehmen/notieren **T4,** 93
to take a vote on [ˌteɪk‿ə 'vəʊt] abstimmen über ⟨**T3,** 61⟩
to take care of sb [teɪk 'keər‿əv] sich um jmdn. kümmern, für jmdn. sorgen **T4,** 85
to take liberties with [teɪk 'lɪbətiz wɪð] es nicht so genau nehmen mit **T4,** 89
to take notice [teɪk 'nəʊtɪs] beachten, zur Kenntnis nehmen; aufmerksam werden **T4,** 83
to take place [teɪk 'pleɪs] stattfinden ⟨**T1,** 20⟩; **T4,** 85
to take sb into care [ˌteɪk‿ɪntə 'keə] sich um jmdn. kümmern, jmdn. in Pflege nehmen **T2,** 36
to take sb to court [teɪk tə 'kɔ:t] jmdn. vor Gericht bringen, verklagen ⟨**T1,** 8⟩
to take sth for granted [ˌteɪk fə 'grɑ:ntɪd] etw. als selbstverständlich betrachten, etw. voraussetzen ⟨**T1,** 22⟩
to take the life of sb [ˌteɪk ðə 'laɪf‿əv] jmdn. das Leben kosten **T4,** 85
talent ['tælənt] Talent **T4,** 85
talent show ['tælənt ˌʃəʊ] Talentwettbewerb **T4,** 85
to **talk sb into sth** [tɔ:k] jmdn. zu etw. überreden **T1,** 11
tanned [tænd] gebräunt ⟨**T4,** 83⟩
to **tap** [tæp] antippen **T4,** 82
task [tɑ:sk] Aufgabe; Auftrag **T2,** 34; **T4,** 88
tax [tæks] Steuer, Abgabe **T4,** 80
tear gas ['tɪə ˌgæs] Tränengas ⟨**T3,** 66⟩
to move sb to tears [ˌmu:v tə 'tɪəz] jmdn. zu Tränen rühren **T3,** 60
*to **tear a muscle** [ˌteər‿ə 'mʌsl] einen Muskel reißen **T3,** 75
to tear oneself loose [teə 'lu:z] sich losreißen ⟨**T1,** 13⟩
narrative **technique** [ˌnærətɪv tek'ni:k] Erzähltechnik ⟨**T1,** 14⟩; ⟨**T3,** 64⟩
rise in **temperature** [ˌraɪz‿ɪn 'temprətʃə] Temperaturanstieg **T3,** 72
tension ['tentʃn] Spannung **T2,** 38
terrarium [tə'reəriəm] Terrarium ⟨**T4,** 91⟩
that kind of thing ['ðæt kaɪnd‿əv θɪŋ] solche Sachen, so etwas ⟨**T2,** 37⟩
That would be that. ['ðæt wʊd bi: 'ðæt] Das wär's gewesen. ⟨**T1,** 19⟩
theft [θeft] Diebstahl **T1,** 14
art-**therapy** ['ɑ:t ˌθerəpi] Kunsttherapie ⟨**T4,** 85⟩
there and then ['ðeər‿ən ˌðen] auf der Stelle, sofort ⟨**T2,** 36⟩
There was something about it. [ˌðeə wəz sʌmθɪŋ ə'baʊt‿ɪt] Das hatte was. ⟨**T1,** 10⟩
third [θɜ:d] Drittel **T3,** 59
though [ðəʊ] obwohl **T2,** 35; **T3,** 71
even though [ˌi:vn‿'ðəʊ] auch wenn; obwohl **T1,** 18
*to give some **thought to sth** [ˌgɪv‿sʌm 'θɔ:t tə] sich Gedanken machen über **T1,** 26
*to be **thrilled** (with) [bi θrɪld] sich riesig freuen (über) **T3,** 61
throat [θrəʊt] Rachen, Kehle, Hals **T3,** 60
throughout [θru'aʊt] überall in **T2,** 35
thumb [θʌm] Daumen **T3,** 75
to **thunder** ['θʌndə] donnern ⟨**T3,** 66⟩
ticket ['tɪkɪt] Strafzettel ⟨**T1,** 20⟩
tie [taɪ] Krawatte, Schlips ⟨**T2,** 38⟩
period of **time** [ˌpɪəriəd əv 'taɪm] Zeitraum **T3,** 63
tip [tɪp] Trinkgeld **T3,** 74
to **tip sth upside down** [ˌtɪp ʌpsaɪd 'daʊn] etw. umkippen **T1,** 18
toenail ['təʊneɪl] Fußnagel, Zehennagel ⟨**T2,** 37⟩
tomato pl. **tomatoes** [tə'mɑ:təʊ] Tomate **T2,** 49; **T3,** 65; **T3,** 70
tomorrow [tə'mɒrəʊ] Zukunft **T3,** 59
metric **tonne** [ˌmetrɪk 'tʌn] (metrische) Tonne **T3,** 70
torture instrument ['tɔ:tʃə ˌɪnstrəmənt] Folterwerkzeug ⟨**T2,** 37⟩
total ['təʊtl] gesamt, Gesamt- **T3,** 70
to **touch** [tʌtʃ] anfassen, berühren **T1,** 14; **T2,** 37
tour operator ['tʊər‿ɒpreɪtə] Reiseveranstalter ⟨**T3,** 73⟩

toxic ['tɒksɪk] giftig, toxisch **T3,** 58
toxin ['tɒksɪn] Gift(stoff), Toxin **T3,** 60
trace [treɪs] Spur ⟨**T3,** 67⟩
trade [treɪd] Handel, Gewerbe **T3,** 61
slave trade ['sleɪv treɪd] Sklavenhandel **T2,** 33
trade unionist [ˌtreɪd 'ju:njənɪst] Gewerkschaftler/-in ⟨**T2,** 34⟩
trailblazer ['treɪlˌbleɪzə] Vorreiter/-in, Wegbereiter/-in **T4,** 81
train yard ['treɪn jɑ:d] Güterbahnhof ⟨**T1,** 12⟩
tram [træm] Straßenbahn **T4,** 86
to **transport** [træn'spɔ:t] transportieren, überführen, bringen ⟨**T2,** 33⟩; **T3,** 70
transportation *(AE)* [ˌtrænspɔ:'teɪʃn] Transport **T3,** 70
*to get **trapped** [get 'træpt] eingeschlossen/gefangen werden **T3,** 63
industrial-scale **trawler** [ɪnˌdʌstriəlskeɪl 'trɔ:lə] Fischereiboot für den industriellen Fischfang ⟨**T3,** 68⟩
treatment ['tri:tmənt] Behandlung, Versorgung **T2,** 34; **T4,** 80
chemo treatment ['ki:məʊ ˌtri:tmənt] Chemotherapie ⟨**T4,** 85⟩
to **tremble** ['trembl] zittern, beben **T2,** 37
to **trespass** ['trespəs] unbefugt betreten, eindringen, überschreiten **T1,** 14
trial [traɪəl] Gerichtsverfahren, -verhandlung **T4,** 84
trial run [ˌtraɪəl 'rʌn] Probefahrt ⟨**T1,** 21⟩
*to be **tricked** [bi 'trɪkt] ausgetrickst/ hereingelegt werden **T3,** 69
to **trip** [trɪp] stolpern **T1,** 12
to trip over [trɪp‿'əʊvə] stolpern über **T4,** 82
to **triple** ['trɪpl] (sich) verdreifachen **T3,** 59
troubled ['trʌbld] mit Problemen belastet, aufgewühlt **T1,** 15; ⟨**T2,** 34⟩
truly ['tru:li] wirklich, wahrhaftig ⟨**T2,** 33⟩
trust [trʌst] Vertrauen **T1,** 16
to face the **truth** [ˌfeɪs ðə 'tru:θ] sich der Wahrheit stellen **T1,** 19
tucked right under [ˌtʌkt raɪt‿'ʌndə] versteckt unter ⟨**T1,** 10⟩
to **tumble** ['tʌmbl] stürzen, (hin)fallen, taumeln **T1,** 12
tune [tju:n] Melodie **T4,** 87
turkey ['tɜ:ki] Truthahn, Pute **T3,** 62
to **turn into** ['tɜ:n‿ɪntə] umwandeln in, umformulieren **T3,** 71
to turn off [tɜ:n‿'ɒf] abbiegen von **T3,** 63
to turn up [tɜ:n‿'ʌp] kommen, erscheinen **T3,** 61
voter **turnout** ['vəʊtə ˌtɜ:naʊt] Wahlbeteiligung ⟨**T4,** 84⟩
twice [twaɪs] zweimal, doppelt **T3,** 71
to **twitch** [twɪtʃ] zucken ⟨**T4,** 82⟩

U

umbrella [ʌm'brelə] Regenschirm **T1,** 17
*to be **unaware of sth** [ˌbi‿ʌnə'weə] sich einer Sache nicht bewusst sein **T3,** 60
under mysterious conditions [ˌʌndə mɪˌstɪəriəs kən'dɪʃnz] unter mysteriösen Umständen ⟨**T4,** 89⟩
underground ['ʌndəgraʊnd] unterirdisch **T3,** 63
understandable [ˌʌndə'stændəbl] verständlich **T3,** 67
*to **undo** [ʌn'du:] aufmachen, öffnen; aufknöpfen **T1,** 21
to **unhook** [ʌn'hʊk] losmachen, abhängen; sich befreien **T1,** 13
trade **unionist** [ˌtreɪd 'ju:njənɪst] Gewerkschaftler/-in ⟨**T2,** 34⟩
carbon **unit** [ˌkɑ:bn 'ju:nɪt] Kohlenstoffeinheit **T3,** 73
unit of measurement ['ju:nɪt‿əv ˌmeʒəmənt] Maß-, Größeneinheit **T3,** 72
unjust [ʌn'dʒʌst] ungerecht ⟨**T4,** 80⟩
unlikely [ʌn'laɪkli] unwahrscheinlich **T3,** 68; **T4,** 82
unmoved [ʌn'mu:vd] unbewegt, ungerührt **T2,** 37
unpopular [ʌn'pɒpjələ] unbeliebt, unpopulär **T4,** 88
near-**unpronounceable** [ˌnɪərʌnprə'naʊnsəbl] fast unaussprechbar ⟨**T3,** 68⟩
unshaven [ʌn'ʃeɪvn] unrasiert ⟨**T2,** 37⟩
up ahead [ˌʌp‿ə'hed] vor **T1,** 12
upon [ə'pɒn] auf ⟨**T4,** 87⟩
to tip sth **upside down** [ˌtɪp ʌpsaɪd 'daʊn] etw. umkippen **T1,** 18
to spiral **upward** [ˌspaɪərl 'ʌpwəd] spiralförmig aufsteigen ⟨**T3,** 62⟩
to **urge sb to do sth** [ɜ:dʒ] jmdn. zu etw. antreiben **T2,** 34
urgent ['ɜ:dʒnt] dringend ⟨**T1,** 18⟩; **T3,** 68
urine ['jʊərɪn] Urin, Harn ⟨**T2,** 38⟩
use [ju:s] Nutzen, Verwendung, Gebrauch **T1,** 10
to **usher sb out** [ˌʌʃər‿'aʊt] jmdn. hinausbegleiten ⟨**T2,** 40⟩

V

college **vacation** ['kɒlɪdʒ vəˌkeɪʃn] Semesterferien **T3,** 62
vague [veɪg] vage, unbestimmt ⟨**T4,** 82⟩
valid ['vælɪd] schlüssig, gültig, stichhaltig **T1,** 29
value ['vælju:] Wert **T3,** 70
verbal ['vɜ:bl] verbal, mündlich ⟨**T2,** 34⟩
verse [vɜ:s] Vers; Strophe **T3,** 58
to **vibrate** [vaɪ'breɪt] vibrieren, zittern ⟨**T3,** 66⟩
victim ['vɪktɪm] Opfer **T2,** 41
to **view** [vju:] ansehen, anschauen ⟨**T4,** 80⟩
viewpoint ['vju:pɔɪnt] Standpunkt **T3,** 58
conflicting viewpoints *(pl.)* [kənˌflɪktɪŋ 'vju:pɔɪnts] widersprüchliche Standpunkte **T2,** 38
vinegar ['vɪnɪgə] Essig **T2,** 49
non-**violent** [ˌnɒn'vaɪəlnt] friedlich, gewaltfrei **T4,** 81
visual ['vɪʒuəl] visuell, optisch ⟨**T3,** 76⟩; ⟨**T4,** 88⟩
to **voice one's opinion** [ˌvɔɪs wʌnz‿ə'pɪnjən] die eigene Meinung äußern **T4,** 84
volume ['vɒlju:m] Volumen; Lautstärke; Band *(Buch)* **T3,** 72
volunteer work [ˌvɒləntɪə 'wɜ:k] ehrenamtliche Arbeit **T4,** 80
vote [vəʊt] Stimme, Stimmrecht; Wahl ⟨**T3,** 66⟩; Abstimmung, Wahl(recht) **T4,** 83
dummy vote ['dʌmi vəʊt] ungültige Stimme **T4,** 83
to take a vote on [ˌteɪk‿ə 'vəʊt] abstimmen über ⟨**T3,** 61⟩
right to **vote (= suffrage)** [ˌraɪt tə 'vəʊt; 'sʌfrɪdʒ] Stimmrecht, Wahlrecht **T4,** 80
to vote on sth [vəʊt] über etw. abstimmen **T3,** 71
voter ['vəʊtə] Wähler/-in **T4,** 83
voter turnout ['vəʊtə ˌtɜ:naʊt] Wahlbeteiligung ⟨**T4,** 84⟩
vulgar ['vʌlgə] vulgär **T4,** 84
vulnerable ['vʌlnrəbl] verletzlich, verwundbar; gefährdet, anfällig **T1,** 12

W

wage [weɪdʒ] Lohn **T2,** 34; **T3,** 74
station **wagon** *(AE)* ['steɪʃn ˌwægən] Kombi ⟨**T1,** 20⟩
waistband ['weɪstbænd] Hosenbund ⟨**T1,** 21⟩
I can't **wait** [aɪ ˌkɑ:nt 'weɪt] ich kann es kaum erwarten ⟨**T2,** 41⟩

gallery **walk** ['gæləri ˌwɔːk] Museumsrundgang, Vernissage ⟨**T4,** 95⟩
guerrilla **war** [gəˌrɪlə 'wɔː] Guerrillakrieg, Kleinkrieg ⟨**T2,** 36⟩
warehouse ['weəhaʊs] Lager(halle), Depot ⟨**T1,** 10⟩
global **warming** [ˌgləʊbl 'wɔːmɪŋ] globale Erwärmung **T3,** 58
wastage ['weɪstɪdʒ] Verbrauch; Verschwendung **T3,** 71
waste [weɪst] Müll, Abfall; Verschwendung **T3,** 58; unnötige Verschwendung; vergebene Liebesmühe ⟨**T4,** 82⟩
wasteful ['weɪstfl] verschwenderisch **T3,** 74
fresh **water** ['freʃ ˌwɔːtə] Süßwasser **T3,** 59
water cannon ['wɔːtə ˌkænən] Wasserwerfer **T3,** 66
weed [wiːd] Unkraut **T1,** 13
weekend box ['wiːkend bɒks] Wochenendschachtel ⟨**T4,** 87⟩
*to **weep** [wiːp] weinen, schluchzen **T3,** 60
to **weigh** [weɪ] (gegeneinander) abwägen **T1,** 14
to weigh up [weɪ‿'ʌp] abwägen **T3,** 68
*to put all one's **weight into sth** [ˌpʊt‿ɔːl wʌnz weɪt 'ɪntə] sein ganzes Gewicht einsetzen ⟨**T1,** 13⟩
Welcome to consumer throwaway living. [ˌwelkəm tʊ kənˌsjuːmə 'θrəʊəweɪ ˌlɪvɪŋ] Willkommen in der Wegwerfgesellschaft. **T3,** 60
well [wel] Brunnen, Quelle ⟨**T3,** 64⟩
well-head ['welhed] Bohrloch ⟨**T3,** 64⟩
… as **well as** … [əz 'wel‿əz] sowohl … als auch … **T3,** 71
well-done [ˌwel'dʌn] gut durch(gebraten) **T2,** 49
well-established [ˌwelɪ'stæblɪʃt] bekannt, etabliert ⟨**T2,** 34⟩
well-suited to [wel'suːtɪd] geeignet für, passend für **T1,** 26
whale [weɪl] Wal **T3,** 60
What's the big deal? [ˌwɒts ðə bɪg 'diːl] Was ist das Problem?, Was ist so wichtig (daran)? **T4,** 83
What's wrong? [wɒts 'rɒŋ] Was ist los?, Was stimmt nicht? **T2,** 36
whatever [wɒt'evə] was auch immer, egal was **T3,** 63
But whatever. [bʌt wɒt'evə] Aber egal. ⟨**T1,** 11⟩
wheat [wiːt] Weizen **T3,** 71
whenever [wen'evə] wann immer; immer, wenn; so oft **T3,** 70
whereas [weə'ræz] wohingegen, während **T1,** 28; ⟨**T3,** 73⟩

a **while** [ə 'waɪl] eine Weile **T1,** 11
all the while [ˌɔːl ðə 'waɪl] die ganze Zeit über **T1,** 13; ⟨**T3,** 62⟩
while [waɪl] obwohl **T1,** 16
while we are about it [ˌwaɪl wi‿ɑːr‿ə'baʊt‿ɪt] wo wir schon dabei sind ⟨**T2,** 41⟩
whisky ['wɪski] Whisky ⟨**T2,** 38⟩
in a **whisper** [ɪn‿ə‿'wɪspə] leise, flüsternd ⟨**T4,** 84⟩
to **whisper** ['wɪspə] flüstern **T3,** 61; **T4,** 82
white lie [ˌwaɪt 'laɪ] Notlüge ⟨**T4,** 86⟩
to **whiz past** [wɪz 'pɑːst] vorbeisausen, vorbeiflitzen ⟨**T1,** 23⟩
on the **whole** [ˌɒn ðə 'həʊl] im Großen und Ganzen **T2,** 39
wicked ['wɪkɪd] böse, schlimm ⟨**T2,** 39⟩
wide [waɪd] weit, breit, groß, ausgedehnt ⟨**T2,** 44⟩
widespread ['waɪdspred] weit verbreitet ⟨**T2,** 35⟩
widow ['wɪdəʊ] Witwe ⟨**T4,** 85⟩
wildlife ['waɪldlaɪf] Tierwelt (in freier Wildbahn) **T3,** 60
*to be **willing to do sth** [biː 'wɪlɪŋ] gewillt/bereit sein, etw. zu tun **T1,** 16
*to **win sb over** [wɪn‿'əʊvə] jmdn. für sich gewinnen, jmdn. überzeugen **T4,** 88
to **wince** [wɪns] (zusammen)zucken ⟨**T2,** 39⟩
*to **wind up** [waɪnd‿'ʌp] aufwickeln; ausholen ⟨**T1,** 12⟩
windfarm ['wɪndfɑːm] Windpark **T3,** 59
shop **window** [ˌʃɒp 'wɪndəʊ] Schaufenster **T4,** 87
windshield *(AE)* ['wɪndʃiːld] Windschutzscheibe ⟨**T1,** 21⟩; **T3,** 64
wine [waɪn] Wein **T3,** 71
wing mirror ['wɪŋ mɪrə] Außenspiegel ⟨**T2,** 40⟩
to **wipe up** [waɪp‿'ʌp] aufwischen **T1,** 19
with regard to [ˌwɪð rɪ'gɑːd tə] im Hinblick auf ⟨**T4,** 88⟩
wondrous ['wʌndrəs] wundersam, erstaunlich **T3,** 62
four-letter **word** [ˌfɔːletə 'wɜːd] Schimpfwort, unanständiges Wort ⟨**T1,** 29⟩
word was going around [ˌwɜːd wəz gəɪŋ ə'raʊnd] es sprach sich herum ⟨**T3,** 65⟩
the complete **works** [kəmˌpliːt 'wɜːks] die gesammelten Werke ⟨**T2,** 36⟩
volunteer work [ˌvɒləntɪə 'wɜːk] ehrenamtliche Arbeit **T4,** 80
world health situation [ˌwɜːld ˌhelθ sɪtju'eɪʃn] Gesundheitszustand der Weltbevölkerung ⟨**T4,** 81⟩
worldwide ['wɜːldwaɪd] weltweit **T3,** 71

worthwhile [ˌwɜːθ'waɪl] lohnend, wertvoll ⟨**T4,** 83⟩
to **wrap sth around sth/sb** [ræp] etw. um etw./jmdn. schlingen/wickeln ⟨**T1,** 22⟩
wrapper ['ræpə] Verpackung; Hülle **T3,** 60
to **wreck** [rek] zerstören; abwracken **T1,** 16
wrist [rɪst] Handgelenk **T3,** 75
writer ['raɪtə] Autor/-in, Verfasser/-in, Schriftsteller/-in **T3,** 68
What's **wrong?** [wɒts 'rɒŋ] Was ist los?, Was stimmt nicht? **T2,** 36

X

to **X-ray** ['eksreɪ] röntgen **T3,** 75

Y

yard [jɑːd] Yard *(Längenmaß: 91,44 cm)* **T3,** 62
train yard ['treɪn jɑːd] Güterbahnhof ⟨**T1,** 12⟩
yet [jet] dennoch, jedoch ⟨**T2,** 39⟩
not (…) yet [nɒt 'jet] noch nicht **T3,** 64
to **yield** [jiːld] Vorfahrt gewähren; nachgeben ⟨**T1,** 20⟩
Yorkshire pudding [ˌjɔːkʃə 'pʊdɪŋ] Yorkshirepudding *(gebackener Teig aus Eiern, Milch und Mehl, der in der englischen Küche als Beilage zu Steaks, Roastbeef und anderen Fleischgerichten serviert wird)* **T2,** 49
You're part of my entity. [ˌpɑːt‿əv maɪ‿'entɪti] Du bist ein Teil von mir. ⟨**T1,** 17⟩
young *(pl.)* [jʌŋ] Nachkommen, Junge **T3,** 60
Youth Service ['juːθ ˌsɜːvɪs] Jugendhilfe **T2,** 46

Z

zoologist [zu'ɒlədʒɪst] Zoologe/Zoologin ⟨**T4,** 89⟩
zoology [zu'ɒlədʒi] Zoologie, Tierkunde ⟨**T4,** 91⟩

Boys' names

Adam ['ædəm] **T3,** 60
Alex ['ælɪks] **T1,** 10

Ali ['ɑ:li] **T2,** 38
Andrew ['ændru:] **T2,** 47
Anwar ['ænwɑ:] **T2,** 36
Christopher ['krɪstəfə] **T3,** 70
Eric ['erɪk] **T3,** 65
Guy [gaɪ] **T4,** 85
Jacob ['dʒeɪkəb] **T4,** 82
Karim [kə'ri:m] **T2,** 36
Parvez [pɑ:'vez] **T2,** 38
Ray [reɪ] **T3,** 62
Ricki ['rɪki] **T2,** 46
Sam [sæm] **T1,** 28
Shaahid ['ʃɑ:hɪd] **T2,** 46
Simon ['saɪmən] **T3,** 61
Singh [sɪŋ] **T2,** 33
Tia ['ti:ə] **T1,** 24
Tommy ['tɒmi] **T1,** 10
Tony ['təʊni] **T1,** 27
Ty [taɪ] **T3,** 62

Girls' names

Abbie ['æbi] **T3,** 62
Alicia [ə'lɪʃə] **T1,** 18
Bettina [bet'i:nə] **T2,** 38
Erin ['ɪərɪn] **T4,** 90
Jamila [dʒə'mɪlə] **T2,** 36
Jeeta ['dʒi:tə] **T2,** 36
Jen [dʒen] **T4,** 85
Josie ['dʒəʊzi] **T4,** 82
Kendra ['kendrə] **T4,** 85
Mel [mel] **T3,** 65
Sharon ['ʃærən] **T1,** 27
Stefanie ['stefni] **T4,** 93
Viviane ['vɪviən] **T4,** 90

Surnames

Alibrandi [ˌæli'brændi] **T4,** 82
Bizier ['bɪzieɪ] **T4,** 85
Cooper ['ku:pə] **T3,** 62
Coote [ku:t] **T4,** 82
Elliot ['eliət] **T2,** 46
Fotopoulos [fə'tɒpələs] **T3,** 75
Glerum ['glɪərəm] **T4,** 85
Hacker ['hækə] **T3,** 65
Hawkins ['hɔ:kɪnz] **T3,** 62
Lindo ['lɪndəʊ] **T2,** 47
Littlefield ['lɪtlfi:ld] **T4,** 85
O'Dea [ə'deɪ] **T4,** 90
Strutz [strʌts] **T4,** 85
Vaughan [vɔ:n] **T4,** 90
Weber ['webə] **T3,** 70
West [west] **T4,** 90

Place names

Atlanta [ət'læntə] **T4,** 81
Bombay [ˌbɒm'beɪ] *(heutiges Mumbai)* **T2,** 36
Brick Lane ['brɪk leɪn] **T2,** 44
Brixton ['brɪkstn] **T2,** 35
Daytona Beach [deɪˌtəʊnə 'bi:tʃ] **T4,** 85
Denver ['denvə] **T3,** 63
Dudley ['dʌdli] **T2,** 41
East End [ˌi:st 'end] **T2,** 44
Essex Road [ˌesɪks 'rəʊd] **T1,** 18
Flagler ['flæglə] **T4,** 85
Hastings ['heɪstɪŋz] **T1,** 28
Kamilo [kə'mɪləʊ] **T3,** 60
Kennebec-Waterville [ˌkenəbek 'wɔ:təvɪl] **T4,** 85
Luton ['lu:tn] **T2,** 33
Memphis ['memfɪs] **T4,** 81
Modbury ['mɒdbri] **T3,** 60
Naples ['neɪplz] **T3,** 73
New York [ˌnju: 'jɔ:k] **T3,** 63
Notting Hill [ˌnɒtɪŋ 'hɪl] **T2,** 35
Peterborough ['pi:təbrə] **T2,** 46
Portland ['pɔ:tlənd] **T1,** 10; **T4,** 85
Sheridan ['ʃerɪdn] **T3,** 62
Slough [slaʊ] **T2,** 33
Timbuktu [ˌtɪmbʌk'tu:] **T2,** 43
Turin [tjʊə'rɪn] **T3,** 68
West End [ˌwest 'end] **T4,** 87

Geographical names

Barbados [bɑ:'beɪdɒs] **T2,** 34
Brazil [brə'zɪl] **T4,** 91
British Empire [ˌbrɪtɪʃ 'empaɪə] **T2,** 34
California [ˌkælɪ'fɔ:niə] **T1,** 10
East Coast [ˌi:st 'kəʊst] **T1,** 10
Florida ['flɒrɪdə] **T4,** 85
Hawaii [hə'waɪi:] **T3,** 60; **T4,** 88
Illinois [ˌɪlɪ'nɔɪ] **T4,** 88
Ireland ['aɪələnd] **T4,** 81
Jamaica [dʒə'meɪkə] **T2,** 34
Kansas ['kænsəz] **T4,** 88
Kenya ['kenjə] **T4,** 88
Maine [meɪn] **T4,** 85
Midway ['mɪdweɪ] **T3,** 60
the Netherlands [ðə 'neðələndz] **T3,** 71
New Zealand [ˌnju: 'zi:lənd] **T3,** 68
North Pacific [ˌnɔ:θ pə'sɪfɪk] **T3,** 60
Oregon ['ɒrɪgən] **T1,** 10
Powder River Basin [ˌpaʊdə 'rɪvə ˌbeɪsn] **T3,** 62
Punjab [ˌpʌn'dʒɑ:b] **T2,** 38
Rwanda [ru'ændə] **T4,** 89
South Devon [ˌsaʊθ 'devn] **T3,** 60
St Lucia [snt 'lu:ʃə] **T2,** 34
Trinidad ['trɪnɪdæd] **T2,** 34
Volusia [və'lu:ʒə] **T4,** 85

Other names

Amnesty International [ˌæmnəsti ɪntə'næʃnl] **T4,** 94
An inconvenient truth [ən ˌɪnkənvi:niənt 'tru:θ] **T3,** 68
Bhaji on the beach [ˌbɑ:dʒi‿ən ðə 'bi:tʃ] **T2,** 41
Bradford Mela [ˌbrædfəd 'mela] **T2,** 51
Brown and Wilson Car Rentals [ˌbraʊn‿ənd wɪlsn 'kɑ: ˌrentlz] **T4,** 93
Carnegie Mellon University [ˌkɑ:negi ˌmelən ju:nɪ'vɜ:səti] **T3,** 70
Cinemambiente [ˌtʃineməmbɪ'ente] **T3,** 68
Civil disobedience [ˌsɪvl dɪsə'bi:diəns] **T4,** 80
Columbia [kə'lʌmbiə] **T4,** 88
Cook High [kʊk 'haɪ] **T4,** 82
Diwali [dɪ'wɑ:li] **T2,** 51
Do They Know It's Christmas [ˌdu: ðeɪ nəʊ ɪts 'krɪsməs] **T4,** 81
Down to earth [ˌdaʊn tʊ 'ɜ:θ] **T3,** 69
Dracula ['drækjələ] **T3,** 65
Eastenders [ˌi:st'endəz] **T2,** 41
Eastside Bridge ['i:stsaɪd ˌbrɪdʒ] **T1,** 10
Finding Nemo [ˌfaɪndɪŋ 'ni:məʊ] **T3,** 68
GCS Construction Inc. [ˌdʒi:si:'es kənˌstrʌkʃn ɪŋ'kɔ:preɪtɪd] **T4,** 85
Gorillas in the mist [gəˌrɪləz‿ɪn ðə 'mɪst] **T4,** 89
Go West [gəʊ 'west] **T4,** 87
Grow your own [ˌgrəʊ jʊər‿'əʊn] **T2,** 41
Happy feet [ˌhæpi 'fi:t] **T3,** 68
Harvard ['hɑ:vəd] **T4,** 88
Holby City [ˌhəʊlbi 'sɪti] **T2,** 41
Ipsos MORI *(Market & Opinion Research International)* [ˌɪpsəs 'mɒri] **T2,** 33
Koyaanisqatsi [kəˌɪɑ:nɪs'kætsi] **T3,** 68
Life in the Woods [ˌlaɪf‿ɪn ðə 'wʊdz] **T4,** 80
Live 8 [laɪv‿'eɪt] **T4,** 81
Live Aid [laɪv‿'eɪd] **T4,** 81
Logan's run [ˌləʊgənz 'rʌn] **T3,** 68
Maine Medical Center [ˌmeɪn 'medɪkl ˌsentə] **T4,** 85
Martin Place ['mɑ:tɪn pleɪs] **T4,** 84
McDonald's [mək'dɒnldz] **T1,** 18; **T3,** 65
Microsoft ['maɪkrəsɒft] **T4,** 81
My beautiful laundrette [maɪ ˌbju:tɪfl lɔ:ndr'et] **T2,** 41
National Geographic [ˌnæʃnl dʒi:ə'græfɪk] **T4,** 89
Natural World [ˌnætʃrl 'wɜ:ld] **T3,** 60

Nobel Peace Prize [ˌnəʊbel ˈpiːs ˌpraɪz] **T4,** 81
Notting Hill Carnival [ˌnɒtɪŋ hɪl ˈkɑːnɪvl] **T2,** 46
Paranoid Park [ˈpærnɔɪd ˌpɑːk] **T1,** 10
Peace Corps [ˈpiːs ˌkɔː] **T4,** 94
Phantom of the Opera [ˌfæntəm‿əv ði ˈɒprə] **T4,** 87
Silkwood [ˈsɪlkwʊd] **T3,** 68
Stetson University [ˌstetsn juːnɪˈvɜːsəti] **T4,** 85
St. Patrick's Day [sn ˈpætrɪks ˌdeɪ] **T4,** 92
Strand [strænd] **T4,** 87
Suburbia [səˈbɜːbiə] **T4,** 87
Thanksgiving [ˌθæŋksˈgɪvɪŋ] **T3,** 65
The Divide [ðə dɪˈvaɪd] **T3,** 62
The emerald forest [ˌði emrld ˈfɒrɪst] **T3,** 68
The Horse Whisperer [ðə ˈhɔːs ˌwɪsprə] **T3,** 62
The nuclear comeback [ðə ˌnjuːkliə ˈkʌmbæk] **T3,** 68
This is England [ˌðɪs‿ɪz‿ˈɪŋglənd] **T2,** 41
UN (United Nations) [juːˈen] **T3,** 71
United Way [juːˌnaɪtɪd ˈweɪ] **T4,** 85
University of Montana [ˌjuːnɪvɜːsəti‿əv mɒnˈtænə] **T3,** 65
University of Twente [juːnɪˌvɜːsəti‿əv ˈtventə] **T3,** 71
Walden [ˈwɔːldn] **T4,** 80
Wall-E [ˈwɔːliː] **T3,** 68
West End Girls [ˌwest‿end ˈgɜːlz] **T4,** 87
Winslow High School [ˌwɪnzləʊ ˈhaɪ skuːl] **T4,** 85
World Health Organization (= WHO) [ˌwɜːld helθ ɔːgnaɪˈzeɪʃn] **T4,** 81
World Trade Organization (WTO) [ˌwɜːld treɪd ɔːgnaɪˈzeɪʃn] **T3,** 65

Famous names

Alexander Fleming [ˌælɪgzɑːndə ˈflemɪŋ] **T4,** 80
Al Gore [æl ˈgɔː] **T3,** 68
Barack Hussein Obama [bəˌrɑːk hʊˌseɪn əˈbɑːmə] **T4,** 88
Benjamin Zephaniah [ˌbendʒəmɪn zefəˈnaɪə] **T2,** 42
Bill Gates [bɪl ˈgeɪts] **T4,** 81
Bob Geldof [ˌbɒb ˈgeldɒf] **T4,** 81
Charles Moore [ˌtʃɑːlz ˈmɔː] **T3,** 60
Chris Lowe [ˌkrɪs ˈləʊ] **T4,** 87
Conan Doyle [ˌkəʊnən ˈdɔɪl] **T2,** 36
Damian Lord [ˌdeɪmiən ˈlɔːd] **T1,** 25
Dev Patel [ˌdev paˈtel] **T2,** 51
Dian Fossey [daɪˌæn ˈfɒsi] **T4,** 89
Emmeline Pankhurst [ˌemɪliːn ˈpæŋkhɜːst] **T4,** 80
Erin Brockovich [ˌɪərɪn ˈbrɒkəvɪtʃ] **T3,** 68
Gandhi [ˈgændi] **T4,** 81
Genesis [ˈdʒenəsɪs] **T3,** 69
Hanif Kureishi [həˌniːf kʊˈreʃi] **T2,** 36
Henry David Thoreau [ˌhenri ˌdeɪvɪd θɔːˈrəʊ] **T4,** 80
Jared Fitch [ˌdʒærəd ˈfɪtʃ] **T1,** 10
Justin Pemberton [ˌdʒʌstɪn ˈpəmbətn] **T3,** 68
Lenny Henry [ˌleni ˈhenri] **T2,** 41
Lewis Hamilton [ˌluːɪs ˈhæmltən] **T2,** 51
Luciano Pavarotti [luːˌtʃɑːnɒ pævəˈrɒti] **T4,** 87
Luis Villazon [ˌluːɪs vɪləˈzɒn] **T3,** 73
Madhur Jaffrey [ˌmadhʊr ˈdʒafri] **T2,** 47
Martin Luther King Jr. [ˌmɑːtɪn luːθə kɪŋ ˈdʒuːniə] **T4,** 81; **T3,** 65
Melinda Gates [məˌlɪndə ˈgeɪts] **T4,** 81
Neil Tennant [ˌniːl ˈtenənt] **T4,** 87
Nicholas Evans [ˌnɪkləs ˈevnz] **T3,** 62
Peter Gabriel [ˌpiːtə ˈgeɪbriəl] **T3,** 69
Pet Shop Boys [ˈpet ʃɒp ˌbɔɪz] **T4,** 87
Rebecca Hosking [rɪˌbekə ˈhɒskɪŋ] **T3,** 61
Sage Van Wing [ˌseɪdʒ væn ˈwɪŋ] **T3,** 70
Sigourney Weaver [sɪˌgɔːni ˈwiːvə] **T4,** 89
Steve Earle [ˌstiːv ˈɜːl] **T3,** 64
Zadie Smith [ˌzeɪdi ˈsmɪθ] **T2,** 51
Zia Haider Rahman [ˌziːə haɪdə rahˈmɑːn] **T2,** 44

Solutions to reference grammar exercises

G1, page 133

Exercise 1:

1. … loves … • 2. … is … • 3. … plays … • 4. … believes …, … is thinking of … • 5. … has had …, … was … • 6. … knows …, … make … • 7. … doesn't often read …, … is reading … • 8. … wants … • 9. … were having …, … said …, … sounded …

Exercise 2:

1. … realize … • 2. … sounds … • 3. … feel … • 4. … are … • 5. … have had … • 6. … love … • 7. … is getting … • 8. … complains … • 9. … is always criticizing … • 10. … look … • 11. … am … • 12. … is seeing … • 13. … do … suppose … • 14. … am even thinking … • 15. … do you think …

Exercise 3:

1. Who does it belong to? • 2. Some people watch TV while they are having supper. • 3. I'm thinking of telling her. • 4. You're always making excuses. • 5. How much do they cost? • 6. I think your new hairstyle looks very nice. • 7. She's always complaining. • 8. At the moment you're being really unfair.

G2 a), page 135

Exercise 1:

Trish: … I never see you anywhere.
Zach: Well, I'm very busy at the moment. I'm doing a lot of revising for French, and on Saturdays I often help my parents in the shop. And I'm having a hard time putting down a terrific book!
Trish: You're joking. You normally don't read any books. You're pulling my leg, Zach.
Zach: … I forget what the book's called, but anyway, the author says that the world we know only looks like a real world. … Whether you believe it or not, Trish. At this very moment, while we're talking to each other, these machines are watching each and every of our movements. And we ourselves are gradually turning into machines, too. …
Trish: You mean *1984*.
Zach: …
Trish: Your book sounds pretty weird, Zach. I think you've been playing too many computer games.

Exercise 2:

1. Is she having a good time? • 2. Who does this dictionary belong to? • 3. Why are you looking at me like that? • 4. Who looks after him? • 5. Is anyone watching TV or can I switch it off? • 6. Is it improving? • 7. Why are you taking an umbrella, Mum? Is it raining? • 8. Does Linda go to the same school as you, Mike? • 9. How often a week do you play tennis, Lisa? • 10. How long does it take you to get to school, Sam?

G2 b), page 137

Exercise 1:

1. She has known him since Christmas. • 2. The train is late again. We've been waiting for over half an hour now. • 3. They've been playing for two hours and still haven't had enough. • 4. I've been looking forward to my trip to Australia for a long time. • 5. The pub has belonged to the MacDonalds since the 17th century. / The MacDonalds have owned the pub since the 17th century. • 6. My father has been working for the same firm for twenty years. • 7. Mike has had his new bike since his birthday. • 8. Please drive carefully. It's been snowing all night.

Exercise 2:

1. … invaded… • 2. … did Henry VIII have? • 3. … did the Industrial Revolution begin? • 4. …was called … • 5. … has Britain been … • 6. … has the United States been independent of … • 7. … became … • 8. … did the American Civil War last? • 9. … was the transcontinental railroad opened? • 10. … has the present British monarch been …

G2 c), page 140

Exercise 1:

1. She's going to win easily. • 2. If the weather is so bad tomorrow we won't not have the picnic in the garden. • 3. … She's going to get badly sunburnt very badly. • 4. … It's going to rain soon. • 5. … I'm going to do a trekking tour in Alaska. • 6. … I'll help you carry them. • 7. … She'll probably be back by six. • 8. … I'll lend you mine. •
9. As soon as I've got the results, I'll let you know. •

Exercise 2:

Trish: I wonder what the weather will be like next week. What are you wearing / are you going to wear on the plane tomorrow?

Zach: I think I'll just put on a pair of jeans and a T-shirt.
Trish: Did I tell you? I'm afraid my parents won't be able to take us to the airport.
Zach: *correct*
Trish: When does the bus leave?
Zach: *correct* … and gets to the airport at 11.30.
Trish: *correct*
Zach: I'll get up at 7 / I'm going to get up at 7.
Trish: Just think – by this time next week we'll have been in San Francisco for six days!
Zach: Yep, and we'll have seen all the sights and have travelled by cable car.
Trish: And we'll be lying on a fantastic Californian beach, enjoying the sun.

Exercise 3:
1. "Who are we playing against at the weekend, Tom?" • 2. "We're playing against United – the most important game / match of the season." • 3. "When does the game / match start?" • 4. "It starts at 3.30 pm. And we're meeting at two o'clock at the station." • 5. "I hope (that) Mike'll play." • 6. "I'm sure (that) he'll play." • 7. "If we lose, we'll never get into the Premier League." • 8. "Yes, right. – Say, are you going to wear your new football boots on Saturday?" • 9. "Of course, and I'm going to score at least two goals." • 10. "I tell you, Sam, at quarter past five we'll be sitting in our club house celebrating our victory."

G3, page 142
Exercise 1a):
Adjectives: beautiful, easy. *Adverbs*: definitely, especially, frankly, hardly, gradually, immediately, lately, luckily, most, never, obviously, particularly. *Adjectives and adverbs:* early, fast, hard, late, long, worse.
Exercise 1b):
I saw immediately … • 2. Luckily, … • 3. It is particularly … • 4. Frankly, … • 5. It is definitely … • 6. … lately. • 7. … gradually getting worse. • 8. Obviously, …

Exercise 2:
1. … late in the afternoon. • 2. The plane flew very fast … • 3. It's easy … • 4. That's the most beautiful … • 5. She never … • 6. … played worse than Tracy. • 7. … is the most attractive …

Exercise 3:
1. A new study on teenage driving was published in Britain in 2008. • 2. Apparently, if teenage drivers travel with a group of friends, this can be extremely dangerous and they are likelier / more likely to have an accident than when they travel alone. • 3. British insurance companies want to introduce drastic restrictions on young drivers immediately. • 4. Drivers under 20 will not be allowed to carry more than one teenage passenger in their car for the first six months after they have passed their driving test. • 5. Young passengers often distract young drivers and encourage them to drive in a riskier / more risky way. • 6. Several states in the USA have already limited the number of passengers a teenage driver can carry in the first six or twelve months. • 7. In those states fatal crashes actually fell by 37 per cent after the strict limits were introduced. • 8. The insurance companies said the limit would drastically reduce the cost of insurance because the number of multi–million pound claims would fall significantly.

G4 b), page 147
Exercise 1:
2. Do you want me to get the car out of the garage? • 3. I'd like you to meet Randy. • 4. I'm wondering who to invite to the party. • 5. Do you want me to go left or right at the crossing? • 6. The Millers are always the first to arrive. • 7. Michael was the only one not to bring anything to drink.

Exercise 2:
1. We are the first to do / to go on this tour this week. • 2. The fresh snow makes / is making it impossible for us to take the usual route. • 3. It is forcing / forces us to take / It is making / makes us take the longer route. • 4. But I expect us to get to the summit by 12 o'clock. • 5. I want you to help each other and to work / to cooperate as a team. • 6. I don't want anyone to overtake me on the glacier. • 7. I don't want to lose any of you on the mountain or on the glacier. • 8. Good night then. I want you all to be fit tomorrow and to have lots of fun.

G4 d), page 148
Exercise 1:
1. Lots of pupils are keen on drinking … • 2. They do so because they have difficulty in concentrating. • 3. Others are worried about doing … • 4. Drug experts say that pupils should avoid drinking … or taking …

• 5. Studies say that pupils who get used to drinking … • 6. They may even be in danger of becoming addicted … • 7. Teachers have complained about pupils becoming … • 8. Most schools have a drugs education programme which warns pupils against taking … • 9. But drug experts suggest checking the use of legal drugs, too.

Exercise 2:
1. … enjoys travelling. • 2. … suggested spending … • 3. She plans to go to Australia and work there … • 4. … finished working there and have succeeded in making enough money, we will see … • 5. … to talk … have stopped seeing … • 6. … stand being away … • 7. … mean not seeing … • 8. … idea of staying … • 9. … mean to go … • 10. … to hearing … • 11. … forget to give … • 12. … remember to write to me and tell me …

G5, page 149
Exercise 1:
1. … rumbling … • 2. … approaching … • 3. … hidden … • 4. … the terrifying scene, but we were fascinated … • 5. … screeching … • 6. … lying on its roof, badly damaged. • 7. … broken … burning. • 8. … driving … • 9. … injured … interviewing … shocked … • 10. … surprising … following …

Exercise 2:
touch, get, carrying, jump, sitting, talking, laughing, approaching, take

G6, page 151
Exercise 1a):
1. … can / will be able to … • 2. … haven't been able to … • 3. … can't … • 4. … can / could … • 5. … could / was able to … • 6. … he'll be able to …
Exercise 1b):
1. … mustn't … • 2. … was allowed to … • 3. May / Can / Will we be allowed to … • 4. … mustn't … • 5. … might … • 6. … mustn't …

Exercise 2:
1. Must Tracy and I / Do Tracy and I have to … • 2. … must clear / have to clear… • 3. … had to make … • 4. … mustn't drink … • 5. … were / must have been terribly … • 6. … needn't bring … • 7. … needn't have bought… • 8. … must / will have to be collected … • 9. … mustn't tell … • 10. … don't have to / needn't warn … • 11. … needn't have …

G7, page 152
Exercise 1:
Mr Bloggs said he wanted us to finish the project. • 2. The careers officer asked me if I enjoyed working in a team. •
3. Ms Turnbull complained that my essay was not very good. • 4. Mr Turner announced that there would be a group of Chinese students visiting our school for a few days. • 5. The secretary told us to collect our school identity cards from the secretary's / her office. • 6. Ms McGregor reminded us not to forget to bring the money for the trip to Stratford on Wednesday. • 7. On Thursday the dinner lady told me (that) there were no more chips and she suggested (that) I had some salad instead. • 8. During the fire drill on Tuesday a fireman told us to keep all the doors and windows shut if there was a fire. • 9. Mr Turner explained that we were no longer allowed to take books home from the library because so many books had got lost recently. • 10. … Mike wondered how you were and he added that he missed you a lot.

Exercise 2:
1. … (that) she was in bed with flu. • 2. … didn't speak any Spanish. • 3. … didn't have a driving licence. • 4. … had bought a red Ferrari. • 5. … was in Canada. • 6. … were a vegetarian. • 7. … had dumped him. • 8. … it would be wet and windy all day.

G8 a), page 155
Exercise 1:
1. A cricket ball is a ball you (can) play cricket with. • 2. A coffee cup is a cup you (can) drink coffee from. • 3. A dictionary is a book you (can) look up (the meaning of) words in. • 4. An ambulance is a vehicle you (can) take (injured / sick) people to hospital in. • 5. A garage is a place you (can) put your car in. • 6. A tennis net is a net you (can) hit a ball over. • 7. A primary school is a school very young children go to. • 8. A snack bar is a place you (can) eat snacks in. • 9. A tent is something you (can) sleep in when you go camping. • 10. A youth hostel is a place / building young people (can) stay in (cheaply) for a few nights.

G8 b), page 158
Exercise 1:
1. We'd have missed the train if we hadn't got(ten) up so early. • 2. If I were you, I wouldn't stay in the sun so long. • 3. *correct* • 4. If I hadn't gone to bed so late last night, I'd go to the beach with you now. • 5. I'd go to

the disco with you if I didn't have a temperature. • 6. *correct* • 7. If only I hadn't played beach volleyball, I wouldn't have hurt my foot. • 8. *correct* • 9. It would be much nicer on the beach if people turned their radios down. • 10. If there hadn't been that awful traffic jam on the motorway, we'd have caught our plane home.

Exercise 2:

1. Jane would have got(ten) the job if she spoke French. / If Jane spoke French, she would have got(ten) the job. • 2. If Sarah wasn't really selfish all the time, people would like her more / better. / People would like Sarah more / better if she wasn't really selfish all the time. • 3. If I were / was hungry, I'd have a big meal tonight. / I'd have a big meal tonight if I were / was hungry. • 4. If Tracy hadn't forgotten to call Pete, he would have come to the meeting. / Pete would have come to the meeting if Tracy hadn't forgotten to call him. • 5. If we had his e-mail address, we could contact him. / We could contact him if we had his e-mail address. • 6. If it hadn't been raining all day, we could have had the barbie on the beach. / We could have had the barbie on the beach if it hadn't been raining all day. • 7. If the bus hadn't been late, I would have been on time. / I would have been on time if the bus hadn't been late. • 8. If it wasn't so hot today, I would play tennis. / I would play tennis today if it wasn't so hot.

G8 c), page 159

Exercise 1:

1G, 2E, 3B, 4F, 5D, 6H, 7C, 8A

G8 d), page 161

Exercise 1a):

1. In spite of working hard, many immigrants didn't get rich quickly. • 2. Some rich people forced poor labourers to work for them for a number of years for paying for their ocean passage. • 3. Before leaving their homes, emigrants sold everything they possessed. • 4. Apart from not having any jobs in their home countries, they were unfree as well. • 5. A few emigrants left their home country quickly without telling anyone where they were going.

Exercise 1b):

1. Moving past the Indian village, they noticed that the place was deserted. • 2. In the evening everybody was busy, collecting firewood, making fires and cooking meals. • 3. Having never been in such a dangerous situation (before), the trapper didn't know how to react. • 4. Surrounded by hundreds of Indians, the wagon train was unable to move on. • 5. Looking at their map, the settlers decided to ride back in the direction they had come.

G9, page 163

Exercise 1:

1. … is being repaired … • 2. … has been stolen. • 3. … will be shown … • 4. … had to be cancelled … • 5. … was built … • 6. … are followed around … • 7. … had been broken into. • 8. Have the dustbins been emptied yet? • 9. … was taken … • 10. … were just being fed.

Exercise 2:

1. The country has been battered by violent storms. • 2. In Gloucestershire a workman was buried by tons of mud. • 3. He was declared dead at the scene by the police, but 4. the body couldn't be recovered (by them) … • 5. … floods were caused by heavy rain … • 6. Hundreds of homes were put at risk by the worst floods since the 1960s. • 7. "… People had to be evacuated from their homes." • 8. Caravan sites all over the country were badly hit by rising river levels. • 9. Two women had to be rescued (by the emergency services) … 10. … it was swept away by the swollen river. • 11. Almost 100 flood warnings were issued by the Environment Agency. • 12. "… water isn't being absorbed any longer." • 13. For today heavy showers are forecast … • 14. And the rain is expected to continue …

Cartoon captions from Topic 3

Cartoon no. 1: "I like to recreate their natural environment."
Cartoon no. 2: "I know what – let's stay in and get some fresh air."
Cartoon no. 3: "Yes, this seems quite a clear bit, have a nice day."
Cartoon no. 4: "I've never worried much about global warming until now."
Cartoon no. 5: "Isn't it nice to see children walking to school?"
Cartoon no. 6: "We have to plant a forest every time we go out."

Bild- und Textquellenverzeichnis

Song- und Textquellen:

Vorsatz vorne: Maps from: Perthes World Atlas, p. 57, ISBN 978-3-623-00100-5, Gotha 2006, 2nd printing revised 2008; **S.10–14** From PARANOID PARK by Blake Nelson, © 2006 by Blake Nelson. Used by permission of Viking Children's Books, A Division of Penguin Young Readers Group, A Member of Penguin Group (USA) Inc., 345 Hudson Street, New York, NY 10014. All rights reserved.; **S.16** by K.T. Logan, www.ehow.com; **S.17** 2082 Music Publ. / EMI April Music Inc. / Songs of Peer Ltd. / Sony/ATV Music Publ. Ltd. Neue Welt Musikverlag GmbH, Hamburg EMI Music Publishing Germany GmbH & Co. KG, Hamburg Peermusic (Germany) GmbH, Hamburg Sony/ATV Music Publishing (Germany) GmbH, Berlin; **S.18–19** © Reprinted by permission of United Agents on behalf of: Nick Hornby; **S.20–23** © 2004 by Sarah Dessen; **S.23** © Reprinted with the permission of Touchstone, a Division of Simon & Schuster, Inc., from GIRL by Blake Nelson. Copyright © 1994 by Blake Nelson.; **S.28** © Reprinted by permission of United Agents on behalf of: Nick Hornby; **S.31** Goethe Institut, München, www.goethe.de; **S.33.1** © Independence Educational Publishers; **S.33.2** © Telegraph Media Group, Christopher Hope, 2007; **S.34-35** BBC London, 2005; **S.36–40** © by Hanif Kureishi, Faber and Faber Ltd., London; **S.41** © www.media-conference.co.uk. On behalf of Lenny Henry; **S.42–43** 'Dis Poetry and 'No Problem' by Benjamin Zephaniah from City Psalms and Propa Propaganda published by Bloodaxe Books. (Copyright © Benjamin Zephaniah) is reproduced by permission of United Agents (www.unitedagents.co.uk) on behalf of Benjamin Zephaniah.; **S.44** © The Sunday Times, 2006; **S. 45** © Welt Online; **S.52–57** © SHE DOESN'T SPEAK by Marita van der Vyver aus "IN THE RAPIDS – NEW SOUTH AFRICAN STORIES", compiled by Linda Rode & Jakes Gerwel, pp. 16–23; **S.58** "Give and Take" by Roger McGough from Good Enough to Eat (© Roger McGough (2002)) is reproduced by permission of PFD (www.pfd.co.uk) on behalf of Roger McGough.; **S.59** © Friends of the Earth; www.foe.co.uk; **S.60–61** © Rebecca Hosking, The Mail on Sunday, 2007; **S.62–67** © AP Watt Ltd on behalf of Nicholas Evans.; **S.68** © Leo Hickman, The Guardian, 2008; **S.69** © Pixar Music/Wonderland Music Company Inc, Musikverlag Intersong GmbH & Co. KG, Hamburg; **S.70** © Erika Engelhaupt, Science News, 2008; **S.70–71** © Amol Rajan, The Independent, 2008; **S.73** © BBC Focus Magazine; **S.79** © 2009 Media Awareness Network, www.media-awareness.ca, reproduced with permission; **S.82–84** © Looking for Alibrandi by Melina Marchetta, Puffin Books, Published by the Penguin Group (Australia). Reproduced with permission by Penguin Group (Australia); **S.85** Originally appeared in the April 15, 2007, issue of USA WEEKEND Magazine. Reprinted with permission.; **S.87** © Cage Music Ltd. Sony/ATV Music Publishing (Germany) GmbH, Berlin; **S.97–101** © Arnold Wesker, Oxford University Press

Bildquellennachweis

UM1.1 Avenue Images GmbH RF (Image Source), Hamburg; **UM4.1** Getty Images (Stone), München; **8.1** tabato/Image Source (RF), Köln; **8.2** Corbis RF (masterfile), Düsseldorf; **9.1** Alamy Images (Mediacolors), Abingdon, Oxon; **9.2** iStockphoto (Alexander Hafemann), Calgary, Alberta; **10.1** From PARANOID PARK by Blake Nelson, © 2006 by Blake Nelson. Used by permission of Viking Children's Books, A Division of Penguin Young Readers Group, A Member of Penguin Group (USA) Inc., 345 Hudson Street, New York, NY 10014. All rights reserved; **10.2** FOCUS (Stephen Voss/WpN), Hamburg; **11.1** Cinetext GmbH, Frankfurt; **11.2** Corbis (Gabe Palmer), Düsseldorf; **12.1** Cinetext GmbH, Frankfurt; **13.1** Cinetext GmbH, Frankfurt; **13.2** Verlag Beltz & Gelberg (Beth Rosenberg), Weinheim; **15.1** InterTopics GmbH (Supplied by Capital Pictures), Hamburg; **15.2** Corbis (Bettmann), Düsseldorf; **15.3** Cinetext GmbH (Sammlung Richter), Frankfurt; **15.4** The Walt Disney Company (Germany) GmbH, München; **15.5** AKG (album), Berlin; **15.6** dfd Deutscher Fotodienst GmbH, Berlin; **16.1** Avenue Images GmbH RF (Image Source), Hamburg; **17.1; 17.2** Getty Images (Frank Micelotta), München; **17.3** Imago Stock & People, Berlin; **18.1** Corbis (Mika/zefa), Düsseldorf; **18.2** Imago Stock & People, Berlin; **19.1** Klett-Archiv, Stuttgart; **20.1** Corbis (Birgid Allig/zefa), Düsseldorf; **20.2** Alamy Images (David R. Frazier Photolibrary, Inc.), Abingdon, Oxon; **22.1** shutterstock (Robert Ranson), New York, NY; **23.1** www.cartoonstock.com (Betsy Streeter), Bath; **24.1** Corbis (Jutta Klee), Düsseldorf; **25.1** Alamy Images RF (Blend Images), Abingdon, Oxon; **26.1** iStockphoto (Phillip Jones), Calgary, Alberta; **27.1** www.cartoonstock.com (Mike Baldwin), Bath; **27.2** Robert Harding Picture Library Ltd. (Robert Harding), London; **27.3** Avenue Images GmbH RF (image100), Hamburg; **27.4** iStockphoto (RF/René Mansi), Calgary, Alberta; **29.1** Avenue Images GmbH RF (Banana Stock), Hamburg; **30.1** imago sportfotodienst, Berlin; **31.1** Fotolia LLC (Philippe Devanne), New York; **32.1** Alamy Images (Jeff Morgan education), Abingdon, Oxon; **32.2; 32.4** Alamy Images (Janine Wiedel Photolibrary), Abingdon, Oxon; **32.3** iStockphoto (Funkystein), Calgary, Alberta; **33.1** Alamy Images (Photofusion Picture Library), Abingdon, Oxon; **33.2** Thomas & Thomas, Hamburg; **33.3** McLachlan Associates, Leicestershire; **34.1** Corbis (Hulton-Deutsch Collection), Düsseldorf; **34.2** Alamy Images RF (terry harris just greece photo library), Abingdon, Oxon; **35.1** Ullstein Bild GmbH (Still Pictures), Berlin; **36.1** BBC Information and archives, London; **36.2** Corbis (Sygma/McPherson), Düsseldorf; **37.1; 37.2; 37.3** BBC Motion Gallery; **37.4** Corbis (Bettmann), Düsseldorf; **38.1** BBC Motion Gallery; **39.1** dfd Deutscher Fotodienst GmbH, Berlin; **41.1** Picture-Alliance (Martin Rickett/PA), Frankfurt; **41.2** Picture-Alliance (Photoshot), Frankfurt; **41.3** Cinetext GmbH, Frankfurt; **41.4** Cinetext GmbH (Allstar), Frankfurt; **41.5** dfd Deutscher Fotodienst GmbH, Berlin; **41.6** Channel 4, Belfast; **41.7** Warp Films, Sheffield; **41.8** First Look Studios, Inc., Century City; **42.1** Corbis (Eleanor Bentall), Düsseldorf; **42.2** Bloodaxe Books, Northumberland NE48 1RP; **42.3** iStockphoto (Peeter Viisimaa), Calgary, Alberta; **43.1** Getty Images (Karl Walter), München;

44.1 Alamy Images (P. Wolmuth), Abingdon, Oxon; **44.2** Imago Stock & People, Berlin; **44.3** Alamy Images (Jon Arnold), Abingdon, Oxon; **46.1** Imago Stock & People, Berlin; **47.1** Alamy Images (ImageState), Abingdon, Oxon; **47.2** Getty Images (Donald Maclellan), München; **48.1** www.cartoonstock.com (Singleton, Adam), Bath; **48.2** www.cartoonstock.com (Streeter, Betsy), Bath; **48.3** www.cartoonstock.com (Lynch, Mark), Bath; **49.1** shutterstock (a9photo), New York, NY; **49.2** Getty Images RF (Photodisc), München; **49.3** CSIPL, New Delhi; **51.1** Alamy Images (ArkReligion.com), Abingdon, Oxon; **51.2** Corbis (Steve Crisp/ Reuters), Düsseldorf; **51.3** Corbis (MC PHERSON COLIN/CORBIS SYGMA), Düsseldorf; **51.4** Ullstein Bild GmbH (imagestate), Berlin; **51.5** Alamy Images (Bernie Pearson), Abingdon, Oxon; **51.6** Corbis (Frank Trapper), Düsseldorf; **52.1** Dr. Hans and Rosemarie Breuer, Stellenbosch 7600; **53.1** iStockphoto (Steven Allan), Calgary, Alberta; **53.2** shutterstock (urosr), New York, NY; **53.3** Ullstein Bild GmbH (Rudi Sebastian), Berlin; **54.1** iStockphoto (Hansjoerg Richter), Calgary, Alberta; **55.1** laif (Christian Heeb), Köln; **55.2** Alamy Images RF (Stock Photos SA), Abingdon, Oxon; **58.1** iStockphoto (Dan Bannister), Calgary, Alberta; **58.2** Fotosearch Stock Photography (Digital Vision), Waukesha, WI; **58.3** Mauritius Images (Stock Image), Mittenwald; **58.4** laif (Nick Hannes/Reporters), Köln; **59.1** Alamy Images (David Hoffman Photo Library), Abingdon, Oxon; **59.2** iStockphoto (Dorota Michalec), Calgary, Alberta; **59.3** Corbis (Herbert Kehrer), Düsseldorf; **59.4** www.cartoonstock.com (Morgan, Ron), Bath; **60.1** Corbis (Frans Lanting), Düsseldorf; **60.2** Getty Images RF (Photo Disc), München; **61.1** iStockphoto (Silke Dietze), Calgary, Alberta; **62.1** Corbis (Colin McPherson), Düsseldorf; **62.2** iStockphoto (Ken Canning), Calgary, Alberta; **63.1** iStockphoto (Ken Canning), Calgary, Alberta; **63.2** iStockphoto (Eric Foltz), Calgary, Alberta; **64.1** iStockphoto (Sascha Burkard), Calgary, Alberta; **65.1** Corbis (Karie Hamilton/ Sygma), Düsseldorf; **66.1** Corbis (Karie Hamilton/Sygma), Düsseldorf; **66.2** Imago Stock & People, Berlin; **67.1** Imago Stock & People, Berlin; **68.1** Action Press GmbH (EVERETT COLLECTION), Hamburg; **68.2** AKG (album), Berlin; **68.3** Ullstein Bild GmbH (united archives), Berlin; **68.4** Cinetext GmbH, Frankfurt; **69.1** Cinetext GmbH (Disney/Pixar/ct-Archiv), Frankfurt; **69.2** Corbis (Tim Mosenfelder), Düsseldorf; **73.1** culture-images (MPI/Hans Dieter Seufert), Köln; **73.2** Getty Images (Christopher Furlong), München; **73.3** Alamy Images (Antony Nettle), Abingdon, Oxon; **73.4** Fotolia LLC (Panos), New York; **73.5** Okapia (Robert Maier), Frankfurt; **74.1** www.cartoonstock.com (Hagen), Bath; **75.1** MEV Verlag GmbH, Augsburg; **75.2** Corbis (Stephen Welstead), Düsseldorf; **76.1; 76.2** Klett-Archiv, Stuttgart; **77.1; 77.2; 77.3** Punch Limited, London; **77.4** Private Eye, London; **77.5** www.cartoonstock.com (Grizelda), Bath; **77.6** www. cartoonstock.com (Slane, Chris), Bath; **78.1** Getty Images (Christopher Furlong), München; **80.1** Ullstein Bild GmbH (Granger Collection), Berlin; **80.2** Getty Images (Topical Press Agency), München; **80.3** Ullstein Bild GmbH (TopFoto), Berlin; **81.1** Getty Images (Michael Ochs Archives), München; **81.2** Imago Stock & People, Berlin; **81.3** Getty Images (Jeff Christensen), München; **82.1** Fotolia LLC (Sunnydays), New York; **82.2** Ullstein Bild GmbH (imagebroker.net), Berlin; **82.3** Klett-Archiv, Stuttgart; **83.1** Alamy Images, Abingdon, Oxon; **84.1** www.cartoonstock. com (Bacall, Aaron), Bath; **85.1; 85.2** USA Weekend Magazine (Originally appeared in the April 15, 2007, issue of USA WEEKEND Magazine. Reprinted with permission.), McLean; **86.1** Picture-Alliance, Frankfurt; **87.1** Ullstein Bild GmbH (Still Pictures), Berlin; **87.2** Getty Images (Dave Hogan), München; **87.3** Punch Limited, London; **88.1** Ullstein Bild GmbH (Popow), Berlin; **88.2** Imago Stock & People, Berlin; **89.1** Cinetext GmbH, Frankfurt; **89.2** National Geographic Society (Robert I.M. Campbell), Washington, D.C.; **90.1; 90.2** Avenue Images GmbH RF (Image Source/RF), Hamburg; **90.3** Alamy Images (Picture Partners), Abingdon, Oxon; **92.1** www.cartoonstock.com (Grosz, Chris), Bath; **92.2** www.cartoonstock.com (Royston -Robertson), Bath; **93.1** www.cartoonstock.com (Noel Ford), Bath; **93.2** www. cartoonstock.com (Naf), Bath; **94.1** Peace Corps, Washington, D.C.; **94.2** amnesty international/walker Werbeagentur; **95.1** Ullstein Bild GmbH (ddp Nachrichtenagentur), Berlin; **96.1** Alamy Images (H. Mark Weidman Photography), Abingdon, Oxon; **97.1** Getty Images (Christopher Jackson), München; **98.1** Ullstein Bild GmbH (ecopix), Berlin; **100.1** iStockphoto (Sean Randall), Calgary, Alberta; **101.1** Alamy Images (Steven Dusk), Abingdon, Oxon; **101.2** Fotolia LLC (Jari Aherma), New York; **102.1** Mauritius Images, Mittenwald; **102.2** Ullstein Bild GmbH (Schroth), Berlin; **105.1** Mauritius Images (age fotostock), Mittenwald; **107.1; 107.3** Avenue Images GmbH RF (StockDisc), Hamburg; **107.4** Fotosearch Stock Photography (PhotoDisc), Waukesha, WI; **107.5; 107.6** Fotosearch Stock Photography, Waukesha, WI; **107.5** Fotosearch Stock Photography (Big Cheese RF), Waukesha, WI; **107.7** creativ collection Verlag GmbH, Freiburg; **108.1** Corbis (Bob Rowan, Progressive Image/), Düsseldorf; **109.1** Alamy Images RF (Stock Photos SA), Abingdon, Oxon; **110.1; 110.2** Image 100 (RF), Berlin; **111.1; 111.2** Corbis (Bettmann), Düsseldorf; **111.3** Klett-Archiv, Stuttgart; **112.1** The Library of Congress, Washington, D.C.; **113.1** Corbis, Düsseldorf; **113.2** www.cartoonstock.com (Harley Schwadron), Bath; **116.1** Punch Limited, London; **117.1** Fotosearch Stock Photography (Stockbyte), Waukesha, WI; **118.1** shutterstock (Jozsef Szasz-Fabian), New York, NY; **118.2** iStockphoto (alvarez), Calgary, Alberta; **120.1** Picture-Alliance (EPA), Frankfurt; **121.1** Fotosearch Stock Photography (RF - IT Stock Free), Waukesha, WI; **122.1** Fotosearch Stock Photography (Design Pics), Waukesha, WI; **122.2** www.cartoonstock.com (Brown, David), Bath; **124.1** Imago Stock & People (Horst Rudel), Berlin; **125.1** www. cartoonstock.com (Le Lievre, Glen), Bath; **126.1; 126.2** Getty Images RF (PhotoDisc), München; **127.1** www.cartoonstock.com (Dan Reynolds), Bath; **128.1** The Cartoon Bank, THE NEW YORKER Magazine, Yonkers, NY; **130.1** www.cartoonstock.com (Hardin, Patrick), Bath; **131.1** iStockphoto (RF/Amanda Rohde), Calgary, Alberta; **131.2** www.cartoonstock.com (Bryant, Adey), Bath; **134.1** Ullstein Bild GmbH (CHROMORANGE/P. Raider), Berlin; **135.1** www.cartoonstock.com (Baldwin, Mike), Bath; **135.2; 135.3** Cinetext GmbH, Frankfurt; **136.1** iStockphoto (Elena Elisseeva), Calgary, Alberta; **138.1** The Cartoon Bank, THE NEW YORKER Magazine (J.M Mulligan), Yonkers, NY; **139.1** AKG (Erich Lessing), Berlin; **140.1** The Cartoon Bank, THE NEW YORKER Magazine (George Booth), Yonkers, NY; **142.1** Getty Images, München; **143.1; 143.2** Ullstein Bild GmbH (United Archives), Berlin; **144.1** Getty Images, München; **145.1** Corbis (George Hall), Düsseldorf; **147.1** iStockphoto (RF/Simon Krzi), Calgary, Alberta; **149.1** shutterstock (Dmitriy Shironosov), New York, NY; **150.1** www.cartoonstock.com (Hagen, Ralph), Bath; **151.1** Alamy Images (Goss Images), Abingdon, Oxon; **152.1** www.

cartoonstock.com (Goddard, Clive), Bath; **153.1** iStockphoto (webphotographeer), Calgary, Alberta; **155.1** Corbis (Alan Look), Düsseldorf; **155.2** Corbis (Car Culture), Düsseldorf; **157.1; 157.2** dfd Deutscher Fotodienst GmbH, Berlin; **158.1** www.cartoonstock.com (Shirvanian, Vahan), Bath; **159.1** BPK, Berlin; **159.2** AKG, Berlin; **160.1** Klett-Archiv (Wolfgang Schaar, Grafing), Stuttgart; **160.2** Corbis (Bettmann), Düsseldorf; **160.3** AKG, Berlin; **161.1** Bridgeman Art Library Ltd. (Private Coll.), Berlin; **161.2** Corbis (Bettmann), Düsseldorf; **163.1** Alamy Images (North Wind Picture Archives), Abingdon, Oxon; **163.2** Interfoto, München; **164.1** Alamy Images (North Wind Picture Archives), Abingdon, Oxon; **165.1** Tee and Charles Addams Foundation, Wainscott, New York

Nicht in allen Fällen war es uns möglich, den Rechteinhaber der Abbildungen ausfindig zu machen. Berechtigte Ansprüche werden selbstverständlich im Rahmen der üblichen Vereinbarungen abgegolten.